MEDIA, FEMINISM, CULTURAL STUDIES

The Sacred Cinema of Andrei Tarkovsky
by Jeremy Mark Robinson

Liv Tyler
by Thomas A. Christie

The Cinema of Hayao Miyazaki
Jeremy Mark Robinson

Stepping Forward: Essays, Lectures and Interviews
by Wolfgang Iser

Wild Zones: Pornography, Art and Feminism
by Kelly Ives

'Cosmo Woman': The World of Women's Magazines
by Oliver Whitehorne

The Cinema of Richard Linklater
by Thomas A. Christie

Andrea Dworkin
by Jeremy Mark Robinson

Cixous, Irigaray, Kristeva: The Jouissance of French Feminism
by Kelly Ives

*The Erotic Object: Sexuality in Sculpture
From Prehistory to the Present Day*
by Susan Quinnell

Women in Pop Music
by Helen Challis

Sex in Art: Pornography and Pleasure in Painting and Sculpture
by Cassidy Hughes

Erotic Art
by Cassidy Hughes

Jean-Luc Godard: The Passion of Cinema / Le Passion de Cinéma
by Jeremy Mark Robinson

Genius and Loving It! Mel Brooks
by Thomas Christie

The Comic Art of Mel Brooks
by Maurice Yacowar

Marvelous Names
by P. Adams Sitney

The Art of Katsuhiro Otomo
by Jeremy Mark Robinson

Akira: The Movie and the Manga
by Jeremy Mark Robinson

The Art of Masamune Shirow (3 vols)
by Jeremy Mark Robinson

Detonation Britain: Nuclear War in the UK
by Jeremy Mark Robinson

Julia Kristeva: Art, Love, Melancholy, Philosophy, Semiotics
by Kelly Ives

Luce Irigaray: Lips, Kissing, and the Politics of Sexual Difference
by Kelly Ives

Helene Cixous I Love You: The Jouissance of Writing
by Kelly Ives

FORTHCOMING BOOKS

Legend of the Overfiend
Death Note
Naruto
Bleach
Vampire Knight
Mushishi
One Piece
Nausicaä of the Valley of the Wind
The Twilight Saga
Harry Potter

TSUI HARK

THE DRAGON MASTER OF CHINESE CINEMA

TSUI HARK

THE DRAGON MASTER OF CHINESE CINEMA

VOLUME 1: TO 2000

Jeremy Mark Robinson

CRESCENT MOON

Crescent Moon Publishing
P.O. Box 1312
Maidstone, Kent
ME14 5XU, Great Britain
www.crmoon.com

First published 2025.
© Jeremy Mark Robinson 2025.

Set in Helvetica 9 on 12pt.
Designed by Radiance Graphics.

The right of Jeremy Mark Robinson to be identified as the author of this book has been asserted generally in accordance with sections 77 and 78 of the Copyright, Designs and Patents Act 1988.

All rights reserved. No part of this book may be reprinted or reproduced, stored in a retrieval system, or transmitted, in any form or by any means, electronic, mechanical, photocopying, recording or otherwise, without permission from the publisher.

British Library Cataloguing in Publication data available for this title.

I.S.B.N.-13 9781861718778
I.S.B.N.-13 9781861711823

CONTENTS

Acknowledgements ❖ 9
Picture Credits ❖ 9
Abbreviations ❖ 9

**PART ONE
TSUI HARK
BIOGRAPHY**

1   Tsui Hark: Biography ❖ 16
2   Tsui Hark: Aspects of His Cinema ❖ 36

**PART TWO
TSUI HARK
MOVIES AS DIRECTOR**

1   *The Butterfly Murders* ❖ 69
2   *We're Going To Eat You* ❖ 75
3   *Dangerous Encounters – 1st Kind* ❖ 80
4   *All the Wrong Clues* ❖ 90
5   *Zu: Warriors From the Magic Mountain* ❖ 95
6   *Aces Go Places 3* ❖ 110
7   *Shanghai Blues* ❖ 114
8   *Peking Opera Blues* ❖ 122
9   *The Master* ❖ 132
10 *A Better Tomorrow 3* ❖ 142
11 *The Raid* ❖ 160

12	*Once Upon a Time in China* ❖	166
13	*Once Upon a Time in China 2* ❖	186
14	*Once Upon a Time in China 3* ❖	197
15	*Once Upon a Time in China 4* ❖	206
16	*Once Upon a Time in China 5* ❖	219
17	*Once Upon a Time in China and America* ❖	226
18	*Twin Dragons* ❖	238
19	*Green Snake* ❖	242
20	*The Lovers* ❖	254
21	*Love In the Time of Twilight* ❖	265
22	*The Blade* ❖	273
23	*Double Team* ❖	288
24	*Knock Off* ❖	299
25	*Time and Tide* ❖	313

Filmography ❖ 327

Recommended Books and Websites ❖ 331

Bibliography ❖ 332

ACKNOWLEDGEMENTS

To the authors and publishers quoted.
To the copyright holders of the illustrations.

ABBREVIATIONS

LM   *The Cinema of Tsui Hark* by Lisa Morton

PICTURE CREDITS

Film Workshop. Golden Harvest. Shaw Brothers. Paragon. Cinema City. China Entertainment. Paka Hill. Eastern Production. Win's Entertainment. Star East. Jing Productions. Media Asia. Beijing Polyabana Publishing. United Filmmakers Organization. China Film Co-Production. Big Pictures. China Juli Entertainment Media. Distribution Workshop. Different Digital Design. Huxia Film Distribution. New Classics Pictures.

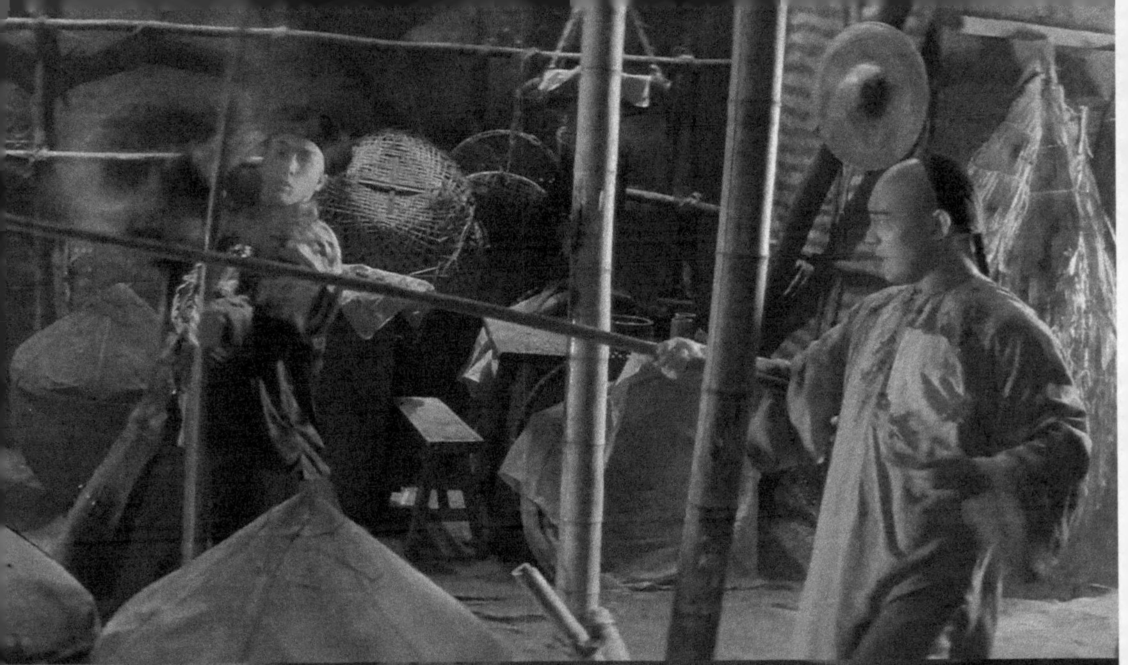

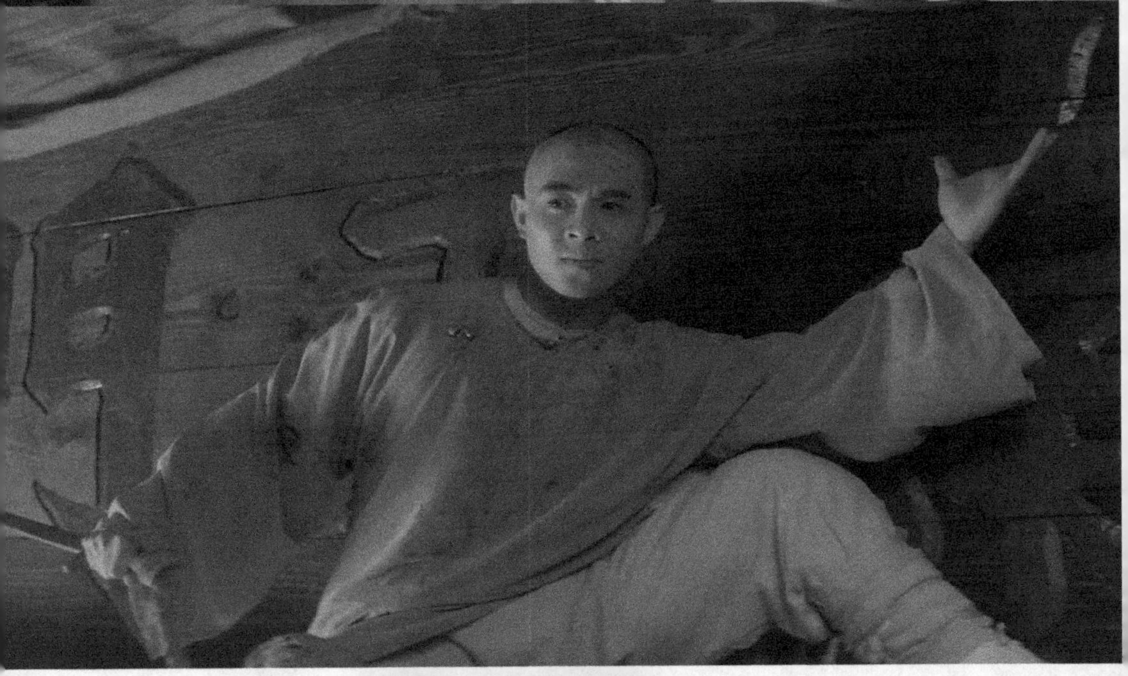

AMASIA
A FILM BY TSUI HARK
ONCE UPON A TIME IN CHINA II
2
FSK
16
JET-LI

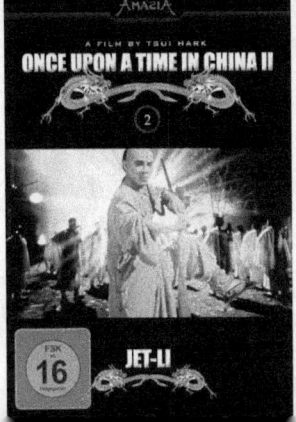

PART ONE
TSUI HARK
BIOGRAPHY

1

TSUI HARK: BIOGRAPHY

Tsui Hark is the dragon master of Chinese cinema (Stephen Teo calls Tsui a 'lion dancer among film directors' [173]). Yes – a master, a lion dancer, a *sifu*, a wizard, a dragon.

Tsui Hark is a one-man film industry – as a glance as his list of credits will show, along with setting up his own film company in 1983, Film Workshop.

Tsui Hark directs movies like a force of nature. The *energy* coming off the screen is stupendous! He is a fearless filmmaker, willing to try *anything* to get a good shot. And I do mean *anything*! That feeling of fearlessness, and wildness, coupled with imagination and technical brilliance, makes Tsui an incredibly *formidable* filmmaker. There are very few filmmakers on the scene today with those qualities in such abundance.

When you come back to a Tsui Hark picture after looking at other movies for a while, you realize, wow, this guy is *so* passionate about cinema, *so* willing to try anything, to experiment, to push the boundaries of what cinema can do, of what cinema can *be*. I've never felt, for example, that Tsui is a 'director for hire', unengaged with the material, or that he is merely punching through the shots as if he's on a factory floor.

No, this man is *on fire*.

BIOGRAPHY

Tsui Hark was born on January 2, 1951 (or February 15; some sources say 1950), in French Cochin China (Saigon, Vietnam). His name was originally Tsui Man-kong (he has also been known as Mark Yu). In Cantonese, his name is Chui Hak; in Mandarin, it's Xu Ke (Xu2 Ke4). He had sixteen siblings (from three marriages). His father was a pharmacist. Tsui changed his name from 'Tsui Man-kong' to 'Tsui Hark' because he thought it was too soft, and for his 'King Kong' nickname (1997, 136). It's pronounced 'Choy Hawk'. Tsui grew up in Saigon until the family moved to Hong Kong in 1966 (Tsui said he migrated around the age of 13, which makes it 1964; Lisa Morton says he was 14).[1]

    Tsui Hark is a truly international filmmaker, as well as being a thoroughly Chinese/ Vietnamese one. After going to Hong Kong, he studied filmmaking in the U.S.A., at Southern Methodist University, Dallas in 1969 (for a year) before transferring to the University of Texas in Austin (Austin is a minor filmmaking centre in North America, with its own film culture, where filmmakers such as Richard Linklater are based). He also travelled around the U.S.A.

    Tsui Hark graduated in 1975 (he studied for 2 years in Austin, where he was known as 'King Kong'). Tsui later worked in New York City: his first jobs were in television, not cinema: he gravitated from TV to film, as so many filmmakers have done (and as his fellow Hong Kong New Wave filmmakers did). His first jobs in Gotham were as a reporter for a Chinese TV cable station; he was a Chinese newspaper editor; worked with a community theatre group (New Art Drama Group); and helped to make a documentary about Chinatown (as a DP) called *From Spikes To Spindles* (Christine Choy, 1976). Tsui moved back to Hong Kong in 1976 (when he was 25).

    Tsui Hark's film career got off to a roaring start with three outstanding pictures. Tsui's first theatrical movie as a director was *The Butterfly Murders* (1979), which combined martial arts, horror, sci-fi, comedy and romance. This was followed swiftly by *We're Going To Eat You* (1980) and *Dangerous Encounter of the 1st Kind* (1980) – both released in 1980.[2]

    Directors often work in contrasts – if they've just done a comedy, they might fancy a drama next. Tsui Hark wanted to do something silly after his first three movies, which were 'very serious and very depressing' (LM, 47). Hence *All the Wrong Clues,* which was his first commercial hit (in 1981). And since then, Tsui had rarely let a year pass without releasing a movie as a director or producer (sometimes two! Sometimes three!). By 2014, Tsui had directed around 43 feature films.

    As a producer, Tsui Hark has been responsible for masterpieces including: the *A Better Tomorrow* series, the *Chinese Ghost Story* series, the *Swordsman* series, *New Dragon Gate Inn* and *The Killer,* plus a host of hugely enjoyable films, such as: *Once Upon a Time in China 4, Once Upon*

---

[1] Some accounts have Tsui coming to Hong Kong at the age of thirteen; others at fifteen (Tsui's year of birth is usually given as 1950 or 1951). It was in 1966 that Tsui's family moved to Canton.
[2] After *We're Going To Eat You,* Tsui Hark became 'very disappointed in myself', and considered giving up filmmaking.

a Time In China 6, Vampire Hunters, The Climbers and Black Mask.

Tsui Hark is much more than a film director. Many directors do the job and go home afterwards. That's it. Some offer to produce other people's projects. Some form their own companies to develop and produce items they might direct themselves, or they might bring in colleagues they know. But only a few opt to take on numerous producing jobs, to the point where their career as a producer is as significant as their directing work. Tsui thus is not only a film director, *and* a film producer, he is also a movie mogul. (To do that amount of work, you have to *really* be committed).

In the press interviews for Detective Dee and the Mystery of the Phantom Flame, Tsui Hark was described by the cast and crew as brilliant, stern, tough, sweet, a free spirit, a teacher, boundlessly imaginative, and someone who lives in a different world from the rest of us.

Like many film directors, Tsui Hark has also filmed TV commercials (tho' not as many as some directors). They include China Motion (1998), for a telecommunications company on the Mainland (which was likened to the 1984 Apple ad); and Singapore National Day (1998).

Change and transformation are key elements in survival in the Hong Kong film industry, Tsui Hark asserted: if you don't change rapidly, you won't survive (LM, 22).

> For me, being commercial is very basic because you need the box office record in order to keep the investor surviving in this industry. But then, you need to be different. You need to be outstanding in terms of film. (2011)

Over the course of his film career, Tsui Hark has worked with practically every big star[3] in the Chinese film industry, as well as every action choreographer,[4] every DP and every major player in film production. (The Hong Kong film industry is small – everybody knows everybody else).

Tsui Hark's energy is legendary. Does he ever sleep? Can he survive on two or three hours sleep a night when he's shooting? (according to rumour). It does seem like that (it seems as if the last time that Tsui slept was in 1978). Tsui is one of those filmmakers who doesn't sit down on set, and is running at a high level of intensity as he's filming.

For instance, in more recent times, Tsui Hark has directed an enormous film production each year! Detective Dee and the Mystery of the Phantom Flame (2010), The Flying Swords of Dragon Gate (2011), Young Detective Dee: Rise of the Sea Dragon (2013) and Taking Tiger Mountain (2014). Plus directing other movies, such as Catching Monkey 3-D.

---

3 As a producer, Tsui Hark has been influential on the careers of Brigitte Lin, John Woo, Chow Yun-fat, Jet Li, Tony Ching Siu-tung, and many others. Jenny Kwok Wah-Lau noted that 'in Hong Kong, most people realize that it is Tsui Hark, the *producer* of *A Better Tomorrow*, who almost single-handedly revised and modernized the action genre and thus directly or indirectly launched the Hollywood careers of John Woo and superstars Chow Yun-Fat (through the same film) and Jet Li (through *Once Upon a Time In China*, which Tsui directed).' (in J. Geiger, 739).

4 Tsui Hark has worked with practically every celebrated action choreographer in the Hong Kong film business: Sammo Hung, Jackie Chan, Yuen Bun, Yuen Woo-ping, Tony Ching Siu-tung, Yuen Wah, Lau Kar-leung, Xiong Xin-xin, etc.

There are times in the writing of this book (starting 2013-14), that I couldn't believe just how much Tsui Hark has achieved. Even compared to other workaholic film directors and producers, Tsui stands out. He really is a one-off. (Sometimes I wonder if 'Tsui Hark' is really a conglomerate of writers, producers, directors and visual effects mavens which uses the person we know and love, Tsui Hark, as their spokesman).

Tsui Hark's films have earned numerous awards. 1992 was one of Tsui's best years for awards – 21 nominations at the Hong Kong Film Awards – for *Once Upon a Time In China 2*, *New Dragon Gate Inn*, *The Swordsman 2* and *King of Chess*.

It's usually the same movies from Tsui Hark that feature in top ten lists – *Zu: Warriors From the Magic Mountain*, *Once Upon a Time In China*, *A Better Tomorrow*, *The Killer*, and occasionally the early, angry films: *We're Going To Eat You* and *Dangerous Encounters of the First Kind*. Tsui Hark has 7 films in the Top 100 Hong Kong Films in *Time Out*.

Some observers reckoned that Tsui Hark's film career stalled somewhat in the late 1990s and early 2000s, and that his movies didn't seem to find an audience during that time. Tsui said, yes, he had been trying different things; but he had also been doing the same thing he always did – make movies. It's all relative, tho', and box office success doesn't always match up with critical praise, or what a filmmaker regards as his best work. We all know filmmakers who produced much better movies than the ones that made the most $$$$$. However, commercial success *is* important if you want to produce movies on an ambitious scale (which Tsui often does).

A filmmaker of Tsui Hark's astounding abilities might be expected to go to Hollywood, as some of his Chinese contemporaries have done (notably John Woo, Tony Ching Siu-tung, Jet Li and Yuen Woo-ping). Tsui could've worked in Europe or Hollywood for all of his career following the big success of *Aces Go Places*. But Tsui's career in the U.S.A. has been patchy and somewhat disappointing. For example, instead of being hired by a film studio to helm a historical epic or a contemporary fantasy blockbuster (*Memoirs of a Geisha*, *X-Men*, *The Avengers* or *Pirates of the Caribbean*, say – Tsui would be perfect for *Pirates!*),[5] Tsui was hired to direct two Jean-Claude van Damme actioners. While John Woo directed *Mission: Impossible* and *Face-Off*, and Ringo Lam Ling-tung and Ronnie Yu made *Maximum Risk* and *Replicant* (Lam) and *51st State* and *Freddy vs. Jason* (Yu), high budget action movies, Tsui helmed a couple of van Damme movies which nobody has seen (altho' Woo also directed a Muscles From Brussels picture, *Hard Target*, 1993, as did Ringo Lam – *Maximum Risk*. Everyone in Hong Kong, it seemed, worked with van Damme at one time or another).[6]

Altho' the three Hollywood pictures helmed by Tsui Hark – *Knockoff*, *Double Team* and *Time and Tide* – were fascinating (and *Time and Tide* was as good an action thriller as has ever been made), the first two were still

---

[5] And he delivered his own version in the *Detective Dee* series.
[6] The deal seemed to be: you can make an American production, but only if van Damme is the star.

below the potential and talents of a director like Tsui. (All three were pointedly *not* filmed in the United States of America, however, but in Europa and Asia).

The anti-American politics in some of Tsui Hark's movies may have contributed towards his lack of success in the U.S.A (LM, 14), even tho' his movies are steeped in Hollywood/ Western cinema.

Following his uneven spree in Tinseltown, Tsui Hark has remained devoted to *Chinese* subjects – nearly *all* of his movies as director and producer have had Chinese settings, Chinese stories, Chinese themes and Chinese characters.

❃

Tsui Hark has gained a reputation for arguing with his collaborators, for taking over from other directors, or for directing when he should be producing. Or for being 'difficult'. Tsui doesn't understand it himself, but there are too many stories for there to be nothing in it! (Yet when actors meet him, expecting a difficult or irritable guy, they find someone very different).

When Tsui Hark is involved in a production, whether as producer, director, writer or backer, you know it's going to be interpreted as 'a Tsui Hark movie' (the same thing happens with filmmakers such as Steven Spielberg or George Lucas – they are such big, influential names in the movie business). Tsui is like that – he's the gorilla in the room that nobody talks about.

But one look at Tsui Hark's filmography, and you see an *enormous* amount of work, containing quite a few classics, plenty of ambitious works, and also several landmark movies in Chinese film history. Any history of recent cinema will have to include an entry on Tsui.

Tsui Hark is not a martial artist, and doesn't practise martial arts. He is not, as are Steven Spielberg, John Milius, Masamune Shirow and Mamoru Oshii, a gun nut.[7] For him, martial arts and guns are part of creating a fantasy.

Stephen Teo likens Tsui Hark's role in Hong Kong cinema to the Taoist priest in *A Chinese Ghost Story*: 'although he's not the hero, the Doaist plays the role of a *deus ex machina* in putting things right and making sure that the natural order is not disturbed' (1997, 228).

That Tsui Hark is a workaholic goes without saying. Tsui could've retired ages ago, or found a much easier way of making a buck than producing movies. Everybody who works with Tsui attests to his boundless energy. On the set, Tsui seems to wear everyone out with his relentless determination to get what he's after.[8] Tsui may come over in interviews as a slim and affable Asian guy who's happy to discuss any topic, but on the set[9] he must be a tough task-master at times.

When it comes to work, Tsui Hark's philosophy is simple: *if you see an*

---
[7] Tsui Hark doesn't know much about guns, or martial arts, and relies on other people for that. Instead, Tsui says that he's a fantasist, he imagines things that're the opposite of his real life.
[8] According to rumours, actors would bring their toothbrushes and pyjamas to the studio, because sometimes filming wended on for 48 or 72 hours.
[9] According to onlookers, the mood on a Tsui Hark set is pretty serious; not much goofing around, but getting on with the job.

opportunity, take it! It sums up Tsui's incredible drive and ambition: this is a filmmaker with a truly extraordinary level of energy.

Hong Kong filmmakers are not known for their integrity: they have to survive, so, as Tsui Hark noted, 'they will do anything' (LM, 27). So it's the worst, because the filmmakers don't have integrity, but it's also the best because they are always looking for the next thing, for change.

Tsui Hark is happy to be interviewed and there are many interviews available of Tsui. Among the pieces on video and television about Tsui (apart from the usual 'making of' pieces on home releases), I would recommend *Action et Vérité* (2006), about the production of *The Blade*, a short but illuminating interview on *The Butterfly Murders*, *The Incredibly Strange Film Show* (1988-89), and *Yang ± Yin*, a documentary on gender in Chinese cinema directed by Stanley Kwan (1997).

Among Western movies, Tsui Hark has cited Orson Welles (*Citizen Kane*), Francis Coppola, John Ford, Roman Polanski (*Macbeth*), and Frederick Wiseman. The Marx Brothers have certainly influenced Tsui's comical style – not the speedy quips of Groucho, but the surreal bickering, and the silent comedy of Harpo.

You can see Tsui Hark's influence in many places: in movies like *The Stormriders* (Andrew Lau Wai-keung, 1999), *Initial D, He's a Woman, She's a Man, Ashes of Time*, and in filmmakers such as Wong Kar-wai, John Woo, Daniel Lee, Tony Ching, Peter Chan, Andrew Lau, Ang Lee, and Wong Jing. And the many Hong Kong movies which have emulated the Tsui Hark approach are easy to spot.

The *Once Upon a Time In China* series, as Jeff Yang put it, 'single-handedly revived the *kung fu* genre,[10] re-energized the Hong Kong film industry, and launched Mainland *wushu* master Jet Li's career into superstardom throughout Asia, and eventually, the world' (2003, 97). Tsui Hark called Jet Li a 'very special person'.

To make so many movies, as producer and director, means that Tsui Hark must *really* ♥ movies and filmmaking. Hooked on it, perhaps. Obsessive, even. Tsui is simply a natural filmmaker, like Jean-Luc Godard, Ingmar Bergman and Akira Kurosawa, filmmakers who seem to be live and breathe cinema. Tsui seems happiest when he's deep into production on a wild adventure in the archaic *jiangzhu*, or exploring a little-known corner of Chinese history.

Some have dubbed Tsui Hark the 'Asian Steven Spielberg', while others have noted that Spielberg should be so lucky.[11] Because Tsui goes beyond Spielberg in some respects. But they share numerous affinities: they are film buffs, they enshrine cinema of the past, they remake and update old classics,[12] they have taken on a wide variety of genres, they prefer storytelling with music and images above all, they are workaholics, they work very fast on set, they make 'movie-movies', they are both

---

[10] Certainly *Once Upon a Time In China* was a key movie in reviving the *kung fu* and martial arts genre – to the level of an artform.
[11] Tsui has remarked: 'I don't know – it's unfair to him, I think. It's unfair to me too: he's so rich' (1997, 136).
[12] Altho' Tsui Hark has gone back and remade the movies he enjoyed as a kid, he also knows that sometimes those movies one enshrined turn out to be silly and disappointing (LM, 23).

moguls with their own companies, they have worked as film producers extensively, they adore visual effects and the artificiality of cinema, and they are master showmen.

Tsui Hark is also a movie and television generation filmmaker, like the 'movie brats' of the 'New Hollywood' era, such as Steven Spielberg, Brian de Palma, George Lucas and Jonathan Kaplan. There's no doubt that, like his N. American counterparts, Tsui is also remaking and updating many of the movies and TV shows he enjoyed as a youth. There is certainly a strong baby boomer aspect to Tsui's cinema, and a postmodern reworking of earlier forms and genres.

Stephen Teo calls Tsui Hark 'Hong Kong cinema's one genuine prodigy', a filmmaker who's 'primitive, even brutish', whose movies are too fast and too cluttered for some and remain indigestible. Teo reckons that the super-fast Tsui doesn't really have a counterpart in the West.

Stephen Teo:

> Tsui Hark has what Hong Kong critics call a "devil's talent" (*gui cai*), a talent so broad and brilliant that it does not seem human. He is one of the prime movers in the industry and an original New Wave director who pushes his commercial instincts to the limit. (1998, 157)

Lisa Morton summed up Tsui Hark in her 2001 study:

> Tsui Hark is unique in world cinema, a prolific filmmaker (Tsui has directed, written, produced and/ or acted in more than 60 feature films since 1979) who is also a master stylist; a political auteur and a populist; an artist with an obsessive private vision who is also commercially successful; and a filmmaker who seems to revel in deconstructing genres even while celebrating their tropes. (6)

Jeff Yang described Tsui Hark as 'one of the most reliable box office breadwinners of the eighties', a conceiver of new trends, a developer of new technologies and new cinematic techniques, a filmmaker who 'has generally beaten a path for the rest of the industry to follow' (2003, 95).

THE FILM CREDITS OF TSUI HARK

MOVIES AS DIRECTOR

The Butterfly Murders, 1979
We're Going To Eat You, 1980
Dangerous Encounters of the First Kind, 1980
All the Wrong Clues, 1981
Zu: Warriors From the Magic Mountain, 1983

Search For the Gods, 1983
Aces Go Places 3, 1984
Shanghai Blues, 1984
Working Class, 1985
Peking Opera Blues, 1986
Spirit Chaser Aisha, 1986
The Master, 1989
A Better Tomorrow 3, 1989
The Swordsman, 1990
Once Upon a Time in China, 1991
The Banquet, 1991
The Raid, 1991
Once Upon a Time in China 2, 1992
Twin Dragons, 1992
Once Upon a Time in China 3, 1993
Green Snake, 1993
Once Upon a Time in China 5, 1994
The Lovers, 1994
The Chinese Feast, 1995
Love In the Time of Twilight, 1995
The Blade, 1995
Tristar, 1996
Double Team, 1997
Knock Off, 1998
Time and Tide, 2000
The Legend of Zu, 2001
Black Mask 2: City of Masks, 2002
In the Blue, 2005
Seven Swords, 2005
Triangle, 2007
Missing, 2008
All About Women, 2008
Detective Dee and the Mystery of the Phantom Flame, 2010
The Flying Swords of Dragon Gate, 2011
Young Detective Dee: Rise of the Sea Dragon, 2013
Catching Monkey 3-D, 2013
The Taking of Tiger Mountain, 2014
Journey To the West: Conquering the Demons, 2017
Detective Dee and the Four Heavenly Kings, 2018
The Battle At Lake Changjin, 2021
The Battle At Lake Changjin: Water Gate Bridge, 2022
The Legend of the Condor Heroes: The Great Hero, 2025

MOVIES AS PRODUCER

All the Wrong Spies, 1983
A Better Tomorrow, 1986
The Laser Man, 1986
A Chinese Ghost Story, 1987
A Better Tomorrow 2, 1987
The Big Heat, 1988
Gunmen, 1988
Diary of a Big Man, 1988
The King of Chess, 1988/ 1992
The Master, 1989
A Better Tomorrow 3, 1989
The Killer, 1989
Just Heroes, 1989
The Terracotta Warrior, 1989
The Swordsman, 1990
A Chinese Ghost Story 2, 1990
A Chinese Ghost Story 3, 1991
Once Upon a Time in China, 1991
New Dragon Gate Inn, 1992
The Swordsman 2, 1992
The Wicked City, 1992
Once Upon a Time in China 2, 1992
Once Upon a Time in China 3, 1993
Green Snake, 1993
The Swordsman 3: The East Is Red, 1993
Once Upon a Time in China 4, 1993
Once Upon a Time in China 5, 1994
The Lovers, 1994
Burning Paradise, 1994
The Chinese Feast, 1995
The Blade, 1995
Shanghai Grand, 1996
A Chinese Ghost Story: The Tsui Hark Animation, 1997
Once Upon a Time in China and America, 1997
Time and Tide, 2000
The Legend of Zu, 2001
Old Master Q, 2001
Tsui Hark's Vampire Hunters, 2002
Black Mask 2: City of Masks, 2002
Xanda, 2004
Seven Swords, 2005
The Warrior, 2006
Triangle, 2007
Missing, 2008
All About Women, 2008

Detective Dee and the Mystery of the Phantom Flame, 2010
The Flying Swords of Dragon Gate, 2011
Young Detective Dee: Rise of the Sea Dragon, 2013
Christmas Rose, 2013
The Taking of Tiger Mountain, 2014
Sword Master, 2016
The Thousand Faces of Dunjia, 2017
Journey To the West: Conquering the Demons, 2017
Detective Dee and the Four Heavenly Kings, 2018
The Climbers, 2019
The Battle At Lake Changjin, 2021
The Battle At Lake Changjin 2, 2022

By any standards, that list of film credits is completely remarkable! And it's a selective list, which doesn't include everything that Tsui has done.[13] You have to add writing credits to that list, and entries in anthology films, plus several TV series, as well as plenty of acting and cameos. And design work, editing and visual effects.

Up to 2013, Tsui Hark had writing credits on 36-42 movies,[14] story credits for 10 films, director credits for 43-45 movies, producer credits for 58-62 productions, and actor credits for 26 films.

Tsui Hark has writing credits on most of the movies he's directed, and he has producer credits on most of them, too. Which means that Tsui can properly be regarded as an *auteur*. The key production credit in many respects, in relation to the cinema of Tsui (and most cinema), is *producer*, more even than director or writer. (But Tsui is also more than a producer, director and writer, he is also a movie mogul with his own production company and visual effects company).

Among the movies directed by Tsui Hark, the following are masterpieces: *Once Upon a Time In China 1*, *Once Upon a Time In China 2*, *Once Upon a Time In China 3*, *Seven Swords*, *Detective Dee and the Mystery of the Phantom Flame*, *Young Detective Dee*, *Zu: Warriors From the Magic Mountain*, *The Flying Swords of Dragon Gate*, *The Taking of Tiger Mountain*, *Shanghai Blues*, *Peking Opera Blues* and *The Swordsman*. Many other movies directed by Tsui are fantastically enjoyable cinema: *Green Snake, The Blade, The Master, Detective Dee and the Four Heavenly Kings, The Legend of Zu* and *Time and Tide*. Only one or two movies with Tsui at the helm are disappointing: *Triangle* (co-directed with To and Lam), and *All About Women*.

One striking aspect of Tsui Hark's output is that fully half or more of his movies as director and producer have been historical pictures, a much greater ratio than most other filmmakers. Tsui is a specialist in costume films, and most of his masterpieces have also been historical movies. Notice, too, that in the more recent part of his career, the 2000s and

---
13 *The Legend of Famen Temple* (*Fa Men Si Mi Ma*), another historical fantasy, was rumoured in 2016-2017, based on a novel by Huang Shang Jin-yu, and starring Kenny Lin, Chen Kun, Zitao Huang and Xun Shou.
14 44 films to 2016, at Internet Movie Database.

2010s, Tsui has been focussing on history – going back to the mid-20th century in the war pictures (*Tiger Mountain, Lake Changjin*) or Ancient China (*Detective Dee*). The last feature films set in the contemporary era was in 2008 (*All About Women* and *Missing*).

So for my book on Tsui Hark, which I started in 2013, I decided to work my way through as much of Tsui's work I could obtain (some of it is difficult to source). And it's taken a *long* time! Not only to see all of Tsui's films as a director, but also his films as a producer. (The movies in a series have been grouped together – the *Once Upon a Time In China* series, etc).

The production roles are important, because we know that Tsui Hark is a very hands-on producer. The role of a producer varies widely, from someone way back in a project's history who oversaw one of the numerous script rewrites to a producer who oversees every aspect of the production.

Well, we know that Tsui Hark has performed second unit direction on some movies he's produced, and also co-directed some of them. And when Tsui insists that he *didn't* direct some of the movies (such as those directed by Tony Ching Siu-tung), his influence as writer or co-writer and of course as producer can felt everywhere in those movies.

TSUI HARK AS FILM PRODUCER

The movies that were produced by Tsui Hark can be regarded as part of his *œuvre* to a greater degree than many films which other directors have acted as a producer on – because Tsui is a hands-on producer.

But what is a film producer? Critics don't really know, yet the Western/ Hollywood film industry is a producer-led, producer-based business, and in the Hong Kong industry, too, producers lead the way. Among the many functions a good film producer does is: (1) buying and developing material; (2) hiring writers; (3) putting together deals; (4) approaching investors, and finding backing/ money/ resources; (5) hiring directors and other personnel; (6) over-seeing the all-important pre-production, which includes 100s of elements; (7) casting; (8) over-seeing shooting; (9) over-seeing post-production (again, this involves 100s of ingredients); (10) music, selecting composers; and (11) publicity, marketing, advertizing.

Tsui Hark has performed all of those tasks many times, and there's no doubt that as a film producer he is right in there, selecting and developing projects, and shepherding them to pre-production (that's when a movie is really made). If he's sometimes a dictator, well, he replies, the creative process needs that.[15]

Among Tsui Hark's numerous production credits, apart from acting as the producer on the movies he's directed, are (Tsui also has writing credits on most of these movies):

---

[15] Is he a dictator? Yes, he admits, 'But the creative process needs that'.

• *All the Wrong Spies* (Teddy Robin, 1983), a sequel to *All the Wrong Clues* (dir. by Tsui Hark). Written by Raymond Wong Pak-min, it starred George Lam, Teddy Robin, Paul Chun Pui, Brigitte Lin, Shing Fui-on, Joe Junior, Tsui Hark and Anders Nelsson. Tsui and his wife Nansun Shi Nansheng are credited as production designers.

• The two *A Better Tomorrow* movies[16] (1986 and 1987).

• *The Laser Man* (1986), was executive produced by Tsui Hark and Sophie Lo, written, directed and co-produced by Peter Wang, and starred Marc Hiyashi, Peter Wang, Tony Leung and Sally Yeh.

• *Gunmen* (Kirk Wong, 1988),[17] starring Tony Leung, Adam Cheng, Elvis Tsui, Waise Lee and Carrie Ng.

• *The Big Heat* (Johnny To Kei-fung & Andrew Kam, 1988), written by Gordon Chan, starring Waise Lee, Philip Kwok, Paul Chu-kong, Stuart Ong Sai Kit, Michael Chow Man Kin, Ken Boyle and Joey Wong. Tsui Hark appears in some credits as the co-director in this very troubled production.

• *Diary of a Big Man* (1988) was produced by Tsui Hark, directed by Chor Yuen, and starred Chow Yun-fat, Joey Wong, Sally Yeh, Waise Lee and Kent Cheng.

• *A Chinese Ghost Story* (Tony Ching Siu-tung, 1987), starring Leslie Cheung, Joey Wong and Wu Ma.

• *A Chinese Ghost Story 2* (Tony Ching Siu-tung, 1990) starring Leslie Cheung, Joey Wong, Michelle Reiss, Jacky Cheung and Waise Lee.

• *A Chinese Ghost Story 3* (Tony Ching Siu-tung, 1991), starring Tony Leung Chiu-wai, Joey Wong, Jacky Cheung and Nina Le Chi.

• *I Love Maria* (a.k.a. *Roboforce*, 1988), was a Hong Kong version of *RoboCop* (1987), co-produced by Tsui Hark with John Sham, directed by David Chung Chi-man,[18] starring Sally Yeh, Tsui Hark, John Sham and Tony Leung.

• *The Killer* (John Woo, 1989), starring Chow Yun-fat, Danny Lee, Shing Fui-on and Sally Yeh.

• *Deception* (a.k.a. *Web of Deception*, David Chiang, 1989), starring Brigitte Lin, Joey Wong and Pauline Wong.

• *The Terracotta Warrior* (Tony Ching Siu-tung, 1989), starring Zhang Yimou, Gong Li and Yu Rongguang.

• *Just Heroes* (a.k.a. *Tragic Heroes*, 1989) was a benefit movie for the Hong Kong directors' union. It starred a host of names, including David Chiang, Danny Lee, Chen Kuan-tai, Stephen Chow, Lo Lieh, Ti Lung, Cally Kwong, Wu Ma, Shing Fui-on, James Wong Jim, Bill Tung, Zhao Lei and Tien Niu.

• *Spy Games* (David Wu Tai-wai, 1990) was a spy movie spoof directed by Wu, who's edited many of Tsui's movies. It was written by Ng Man-fai, Philip Cheng, Lam Kee-to and Lau Tai-mok, and starred Joey Wong, Kenny Bee, Noriko Izumoto, Waise Lee and Shut Yam.

• *The Raid* (Tony Ching Siu-tung and Tsui Hark, 1991) was a 1930s

---

16 The *Better Tomorrow* movies inevitably inspired cash-ins – such as *Return To Better Tomorrow* (Wong Jing, 1994).
17 Critics have discerned the influence of Tsui Hark in *Gunmen* (which he produced), in the romantic atmosphere, and in the action.
18 Tony Ching Siu-tung was 2nd unit director.

adventure comedy co-written by Tsui Hark and Yuen Kai-chi, and starring Jacky Cheung, Dean Shek, Tony Leung, Paul Chu, Fennie Yuen and Joyce Godenzi.

• *The Swordsman* (King Hu *et al*, 1990), starring Sam Hui, Cecilia Yip, Yuen Wah, Jacky Cheung and Cheung Man.

• *The Swordsman 2* (Tony Ching Siu-tung, 1991), starring Jet Li, Brigitte Lin, Rosamund Kwan, Michelle Reiss and Fennie Yuen.

• *The Swordsman 3: The East Is Red* (Tony Ching Siu-tung & Raymond Lee, 1993), starring Brigitte Lin, Yu Rongguang, Joey Wong and Eddie Ko.

• *Dragon Inn* (a.k.a. *New Dragon Gate Inn*, Raymond Lee, 1992), starring Tony Leung, Brigitte Lin, Maggie Cheung and Donnie Yen.

• *The Wicked City* (*Yiu Sau Do Si*, dir. Peter Mak Tai-kit, 1992), a live-action version of the Japanese *animé* (1987), staring Leon Lai Ming, Jacky Cheung Hak-yow, Michelle Reiss and Tatsuya Nakadai.

• *Iron Monkey* (Yuen Woo-ping, 1993), co-written by Tsui Hark with Tang Pik-yin and Lau Tai-mok, and starring Donnie Yen, Yu Rongguang and Jean Wong.

• *The Magic Crane* (Benny Chan, 1993), co-written by Tsui Hark (with Jobic Chui Daat-Choh), and starring Anita Mui, Tony Leung Chiu-wai, Rosamund Kwan and Damian Lau.

• *Burning Paradise*, a.k.a. *Red Lotus Temple* (Ringo Lam Ling-tung, 1994), starring Willie Chi, Wong Kam-long and Carman Lee.

• *Once Upon a Time In China 4* (Yuen Bun, 1993), co-written by Tsui and Tang Pik-yin, was released only four months after the third *Once Upon a Time In China* movie, and starred Vincent Zhao, Jean Wong, Xiong Xin-xin, Max Mok and Lau Shun.

• *Shanghai Grand* (Poon Man-kit, 1996), was a period gangster tale co-written by Sandy Shaw, Matthew Chow Hoi-kwong and Poon Man-kit. It starred Andy Lau Tak-wah, Leslie Cheung and Lau Shun.

• *Black Mask* (Daniel Lee Yan-kong, 1996) was a wild superhero adventure co-written by Koan Hui-on, Teddy Chan Tak-sum and Joe Ma Wai-ho, and starring Jet Li, Karen Mok, Lau Ching-wan, Francoise Yip, Moses Chan and Anthony Wong.

• *Once Upon a Time in China and America* (Sammo Hung Kam-bo, 1997), was co-written by Roy Szeto Cheuk-hon, Shut Mei-yee, Sharon Hui Sa-long, Philip Kwok and So Man-Sing, and starred Jet Li, Rosamund Kwan, Xiong Xin-xin, Chan Kwok Pong, Richard Ng and Jeff Wolfe.

• *Old Master Q* (2001) was co-written by Tsui Hark with Roy Szeto Cheuk-hon, Herman Yau and Man Choi-lee, exec-prod. by Charles Heung and Tsui Hark, and dir. by Herman Yau.

• *Tsui Hark's Vampire Hunters* (2002) was produced and written by Tsui Hark, and dir. by Wellson Chin Sing-wai.

• *Xanda* (*Sanda*, 2004) was wr. by Kai-Cheung Chung, Derick Lau, Ask Lee, Xiao-Long Lin and Tsui Hark, exec-prod. by Satoru Iseki, Nansun Shi Nan-sheng and Le Qun Song, prod. by Tsui Hark, and directed by Marco Mak Chi-sin.

• *The Warrior* (literal title: *Wong Fei-hung: Brave Into the World*, 2006) was a Wong Fei-hung movie as an animation, directed by Tiger Fu Yin and Chen Yue-Hu and produced by Yang Yong.

• *Sword Master* (Derek Yee, 2016) was a 3-D *wuxia pian* produced by Tsui Hark and co-written by Tsui with Derek Yee and Chun Tin-nam.

Another aspect is immediately obvious: there were years when Tsui Hark was directing not one but two movies! And in some years, even more! In 1995: *The Chinese Feast, Love in the Time of Twilight* and *The Blade*! (In the North American film industry, it's typical for a film director to direct every three years).

TSUI HARK AS WRITER

Among Tsui Hark's writing for cinema credits are: *Di yu wu men, Dangerous Encounters of the First Kind, All the Wrong Clues, A Better Tomorrow 2*,[19] *Tit gaap mou dik maa lei aa, The Master, A Better Tomorrow 3: Love and Death in Saigon, A Chinese Ghost Story, A Chinese Ghost Story 3, Once Upon a Time in China, The Banquet, Twin Dragons, The Swordsman, Once Upon a Time in China 2, New Dragon Gate Inn, Once Upon a Time in China 3, The Swordsman 3: The East Is Red, Once Upon a Time in China 4, Iron Monkey, Ching Se, Yiu sau dou si, The Magic Crane, Once Upon a Time in China 5, The Chinese Feast, Love In the Time of Twilight, The Lovers, The Blade, Da san yuan, Black Mask*, the animated *Chinese Ghost Story, Time and Tide, Old Master Q, The Legend of Zu, Black Mask 2: City of Masks, The Era of Vampires, Xanda, Seven Swords, Missing, All About Women, Flying Swords of Dragon Gate, Young Detective Dee: Rise of the Sea Dragon, Sword Master, Detective Dee and the Four Heavenly Kings, The Thousand Faces of Dunjia* and the two *Battle of Lake Changjin* movies.

Tsui Hark has also worked uncredited as a writer, sometimes helping out pictures that are in trouble. For ex, Tsui contributed (along with Gordon Chan) to *Dr Wai* (Tony Ching Siu-tung, 1996), a Jet Li actioner.

Lisa Morton noted that Tsui Hark has only made one proper sci-fi movie – *I Love Maria* (a.k.a. *Roboforce*). Actually, the two *Black Mask* movies are science fiction. But Tsui has acknowledged that he hasn't done much in sci-fi – he prefers Ancient Chinese fantasy and mythology.

However, Tsui Hark has certainly directed movies which portray savage realms that come across like post-apocalyptic worlds: the brutish martial arts world (*jiangzhu*) of *The Blade*[20] and *Seven Swords* come to mind.

---

[19] *A Better Tomorrow 2* (1987) was written and directed by John Woo, produced by Tsui Hark, with action direction by Tony Ching Siu-tung, and starred Chow Yun-fat, Dean Shek, Ti Lung, Leslie Cheung and Emily Chu.
[20] Paul Fonoroff reckoned that 'if movies were judged on visuals alone, *The Blade* would certainly rank as one of the decade's most stunning motion pictures' (527).

THE HONG KONG NEW WAVE

Like other filmmakers of the Chinese New Wave cinema, Tsui Hark is a film school graduate: Ann Hui and Yim Ho studied in London; Tsui in Austin, Texas; and Ringo Lam Ling-tung in Toronto (York University). They studied in the West, or in Western-style institutions in Hong Kong. They could speak English with critics, which no doubt helped, because they'd spent time in the West. And they were familiar with the art film traditions of Europe and the U.S.A.

Following film school, they went to work in television. (Hui, Ho and Tsui were part of the first wave of the New Wave, along with Allan Fong, Patrick Tam, Kirk Wong, and Tony Ching Siu-tung); the second wave included Stanley Kwan, Alex Law, Clara Law, Jacob Cheung, Wong Kar-wai, Cheung Yuen-ting, and Eddie Fong.[21]

The Hong Kong New Wave did not have a unified style or an approach: it took on aspects of youth: 'school, sex, drugs and other travails of growing up in a materialistic society, misunderstood by parents and adults in authority', according to Stephen Teo (1997, 156).

Tsui Hark said that the Hong Kong New Wave wasn't really a *nouvelle vague*, like the French New Wave, and didn't have a philosophy behind it. For some critics, the New Wave of 1979 ended with the crude commercialism of comedies such as *All the Wrong Clues* (1981), directed by Tsui.

It was no surprise that many of the first films of the Hong Kong New Wave were thrillers or crime stories (including Tsui Hark's films) – because they are a staple of Hong Kong cinema, and of cinemas the world over, because they tend to be cheap to make, because the genre was versatile, and because a huge proportion of source material was in the crime or thriller genre.

For Stephen Teo, the two strands of the Hong Kong New Wave cinema – realism and genre conventions – developed towards the latter: the New Wavers started out tackling realism but leant towards genre filmmaking (1997, 149). The forms and conventions of genre were updated for modern audiences in the 1980s. (The first official, Hong Kong New Wave film was *The Extras* (1978), but the unofficial film that launched it, according to Cheuk Pak-tong, was *Jumping Ash* (1976). In 1979, some of the first New Wave films included *The Secrets* (dir. Ann Hui), *The Butterfly Murders* (dir. Tsui Hark), *The System* (dir. Peter Yung) and *Cops and Robbers* (dir. Alex Cheung)).

At the height of the 1990s New Wave, actors and crew were commonly rushing from one movie set to another. Andy Lau Tak-wah slept in his car while filming a movie a month in 1991, and according to rumour making four movies in four locations at the same time. (Chinese filmmakers became geniuses at stretching footage of actors who could only give them a day or so, by using doubles, re-arranging scripts, focussing on reaction shots, etc).

---

21 According to Jenny Kwok Wah-Lau, 30-40 directors made their debut films in 1979-80 (in J. Jeiger, 740).

You'll see the same actors and directors in the New Wave of Hong Kong and Chinese cinema, continuing up to the present day. The actors include: Jet Li, Jackie Chan, Brigitte Lin, Tony Leung, Leslie Cheung, Michelle Yeoh, Zhao Wei, Donnie Yen, Maggie Cheung, Jacky Cheung, Zhang Ziyi, Yuen Biao, Chow Yun-fat, Josephine Siao, Stephen Chow, Gong Li, Rosamund Kwan, Zhao Wenzhou, Kent Cheng, and Xiong Xin-xin.

And directors such as Tsui Hark, Ronny Yu, Ringo Lam Ling-tung, King Hu, Sammo Hung Kam-bo, Zhang Yimou, Ann Hui, Wong Jing, Yuen Woo-ping, Wong Kar-wai, Peter Chan, Stanley Tong, Tony Ching Siu-tung and John Woo.

TSUI HARK AND TELEVISION

Television nurtured the New Wave filmmakers in Hong Kong – becoming something like a Shaolin Temple for *cinéastes*, as critic Law Kar put it. They worked at stations such as C.T.V. (Commercial Television), R.T.H.K. (Radio Television Hong Kong) and T.V.B.[22] (Hong Kong Television Broadcast, Ltd.). Selina Chow, a TV executive, was instrumental in hiring the 'New Wave' filmmakers in television (LM, 221). They were also a film school generation: the New Wave directors studied at film schools abroad partly because they didn't really exist in Asia (the Chinese State film school, Beijing Film Academy, didn't re-open until 1978). Tsui Hark:

> I went to film school simply because I like to express my feelings on certain issues through film, which was a pretty popular medium during the 1960s. We spent a lot of time in movie theaters. At that time I was already thinking how to make Chinese cinema more interesting.

Tsui Hark first worked in television in the late 1970s; his first TV shows were *Golden Dagger Romance* (1978), made for C.T.V., adapted from a novel by Gu Long (during Tsui's 6 months there) and *Aries, Scorpio, Aquarius* (T.V.B., 1978). Tsui was also one of five directors (Ringo Lam Ling-tung was another) of *The Family* (1978, at T.V.B.), a 104-episode soap opera ('people die, get rich, get divorced', as Tsui summed it up [1997, 133]). Tsui came back to television several times – for the *Wong Fei-hung* and *Seven Swordsmen* TV series, for example.

For Stephen Teo, Tsui Hark's cinema is a vivid embodiment of the maturation of the New Wave, and the postmodernism of commercial cinema:

> Using Tsui as a yardstick, the postmodern phenomena grew from a ragbag of causes and effects: new wave æsthetics mixed with Cinema City-style slapstick, anxiety over 1997 and the China

---

22 T.V.B. was the television arm of Shaws.

syndrome, the assertion of Hong Kong's own identity as different from China, and a new sexual awakening arising from an increasing awareness of women's human rights and the decriminalisation of homosexuality. (1997, 246)

CINEMA CITY

Tsui Hark was part of the group of filmmakers at Cinema City (from 1981). A new studio, Cinema City wasn't independent – it was owned by Golden Princess. It had been founded by Raymond Wong Pak-min, Karl Maka (b. 1944) and Dean Shek in 1979 (as the Fun Dao Film Company). The so-called 'Gang of Seven' at Cinema City were Tsui, Maka, Wong, Shek, Teddy Robin Kwan, Eric Tsang and Tsui's wife Nansun Shi Nan-sheng. As Tsui recalled, they would consider everything, go thru scripts at length and discuss them.

All the Wrong Clues... For the Right Solution (1981) was Tsui Hark's first Cinema City production: it was produced by Karl Maka and Dean Shek, written by Roy Szeto Cheuk-hon (a regular collaborator with Tsui) and Raymond Wong Pak-min, and starred George Lam, Teddy Robin Kwan, Maka and Wong Tso-sze (for some critics, this movie announced the end of the Hong Kong New Wave).

Aces Go Places 3 (a.k.a. *Mad Mission 3*, 1984) was another installment in the successful *Aces Go Places* franchise from Cinema City (the earlier films were released in 1982 and 1983. The movies were the top films of each year (the first *Aces Go Places* grossed HK $26 million[23] when ticket prices were HK $15 (= U.S. $1.95).) It was produced and written by Raymond Wong Pak-min, and starred Sam Hui, Karl Maka and Sylvia Chang. According to Stephen Teo, 'Tsui's own dynamic style of filmmaking initiated a level of structural experimentation which was to be highly influential' (153).

The 'Cinema City style' emphasized comedy above all, stunts, visual effects, big budgets, and movies constructed by a creative team. For a period in the 1980s, Cinema City cornered the market for theatrical comedies. About 17% of films were comedies between 1985 and 1997 in Hong Kong.

---

[23] There are typically 7.75 Hong Kong dollars to the U.S.A. dollar. (So when a movie makes HK $30 million in theatrical release in Hong Kong, that equals US $3.87 million).

FILM WORKSHOP

In 1984 Tsui Hark founded Film Workshop with his wife, Nansun Shi Nan-sheng (he had decided to create a company during post-production of *Zu: Warriors From the Magic Mountain*; it was partly because Cinema City were only interested in making comedies). Film Workshop is based in Kowloon Bay.

Terence Chang[24] worked as general manager at Film Workshop in the 1980s (at Nansun Shi Nan-sheng's invitation). Following Tsui Hark's dispute with John Woo over *The Killer* and *A Better Tomorrow 3*,[25] Chang left with Woo. Chang described his time at Film Workshop thus:

> The first year was really exciting. The company was new, vibrant, and a lot of great films came from that time. Tsui Hark was very idealistic. He wanted to round up the best directors in Hong Kong and put them under one roof. He wanted to create an environment where all the directors, under his leadership, could be given the opportunity and nourishment to make artistic, yet commercial pictures.

The productions of Film Workshop include: *Shanghai Blues* (1984), *The Master* (1989), *King of Chess* (1992), *The Swordsman 2* (1992), *Wicked City* (1992), *New Dragon Gate Inn* (1992), *Once Upon a Time in China 2* (1992), *The East Is Red* (1993), *The Magic Crane* (1993), *Iron Monkey* (1993), *Once Upon a Time in China 3* (1993), *Once Upon a Time in China 4* (1993), *Green Snake* (1993), *A Chinese Ghost Story: The Tsui Hark Animation* (1997), *Knockoff* (1998), *Time and Tide* (2000), *The Era of Vampires* (2002), *Xanda* (2004), *Seven Swords* (2005), *Triangle* (2007), *All About Women* (2008) and the *Detective Dee* movies.

Tsui Hark has worked with Golden Harvest for much of his career; they have enjoyed many successes. However, they have also fallen out – over the release of *Zu: Warriors From the Magic Mountain*, for instance. And in the late 1990s, Golden Harvest sued Tsui for over-runs on 8 films (and Tsui's lawyers responded with a counter-suit for revenue from the *Once Upon a Time In China* pictures).

---

24 John Woo's regular producer, Terence Chang (b. 1949), had studied in New York and Oregon before working at Golden Harvest and in TV before joining Film Workshop. Chang also worked at D. & B.
25 He rushed his own sequel to *A Better Tomorrow* into theatres, for instance (which he had co-produced), to beat John Woo's sequel (altho' Woo doesn't like doing sequels).

SOME GREAT MOMENTS IN TSUI HARK'S WORK

- Avoiding the cannibals in *We're Going To Eat You*
- The finale of *Zu*
- Meeting under the bridge in *Shanghai Blues*
- Backstage in *Peking Opera Blues*
- Chow Yun-fat versus the tank in *A Better Tomorrow 3*
- Maggie Cheung in *New Dragon Gate Inn*
- The first act of *Once Upon a Time In China*
- The ladders duel in *Once Upon a Time In China*
- Leslie Cheung in the haunted inn in *A Chinese Ghost Story*
- Wu Ma's Taoist dance in *A Chinese Ghost Story*
- Jet Li versus Donnie Yen in *Once Upon a Time In China 2*
- The Lion Dance competition in *Once Upon a Time In China 3*
- Jet Li in a clinch with Brigitte Lin in *The Swordsman 2*
- The watery finale of *Green Snake*
- The musical/ romantic montage in *The Lovers*
- The final duel in *The Blade*
- The motorcycle chase in *Black Mask*
- The market chase in *Knock-Off*
- The apartment fire-fight in *Time and Tide*
- The arrival of the warriors in *Seven Swords*
- Jet Li vs. Gordon Liu in *Flying Swords of Dragon Gate*
- Andy Lau and Jinger in *Detective Dee*
- The sea monster in *Young Detective Dee*
- The snow tiger scene in *The Taking of Tiger Mountain*
- The Battle of the Buddhas in *Journey To the West*
- The monster battle in *Detective Dee 3*

Tsui Hark on the sets of the Detective Dee films.

2

TSUI HARK: ASPECTS OF HIS CINEMA

FAST FILMS.
This man is *fast*!
Not only does Tsui Hark produce and direct more movies than five filmmakers put together, his movies zip along at a cracking pace. 'Tsui's films move with such breakneck speed that one is hard put to find a Western equivalent,' noted Stephen Teo (153). He can't slow down.[1]

Tsui Hark should offer a competition to movie fans: a $10,000 prize to anyone who can come up with a camera angle [2] he hasn't used in a movie.

One of the great pleasures of Tsui Hark's cinema is the length of his movies. So many filmmakers are tempted into out-staying their welcome, into lingering over scenes, often because they actually don't have much of a story to tell, or their stories simply aren't that compelling in the end.

The typical Tsui Hark movie comes in at 80-90 minutes, a perfect and satisfying length for a picture (filmmakers such as Jean-Luc Godard, Woody Allen and Ingmar Bergman also thankfully keep to that sort of running time). Why carry on into 110, 120 or 140 minutes, when you've said everything you wanna say, done everything you wanna do, and told the story you wanna tell?

A master showman, the two most entertaining segments of a Tsui Hark movie tend to be the opening act and the final act.[3] The first acts tend to be incredibly busy, as the filmmakers cram in everything they can think of – not only to set-up the rest of the movie, but to evoke a huge world (and to dare the audience to be bored). The first acts seem to acknowledge that the audience, if it's watching this movie in a theatre, has just walked in off the streets of Hong Kong which, as we know, can be crazy, busy and loud.

And the final acts are among the greatest finales in movies of recent

---

[1] Grady Hendrix noted in 2013: 'All of his collaborators over the years feel that his movies would be better if he focused on fully expressing one idea rather than several, but Tsui doesn't have the time. He's saving China from extinction and if he has a thousand ideas in the three months when he's making a movie, then that movie will contain a thousand ideas.'
[2] Tho' Tsui Hark is fond of high angle shots, but he doesn't film them himself – he has a fear of heights.
[3] George Lucas often spoke of the importance of a good beginning and ending.

times. Make the opening and the ending special, they say, and the cinema of Tsui Hark certainly does that. At least half of the final act is filled with action, usually comprising several action sequences which run together. And Tsui Hark's movies also know that their audiences are busy people, and they haven't got time to hang about after the plots have been resolved. Thus, the *dénouements* are mercilessly (and quite correctly) short.

SCRIPTS AND ACTS.

As to the issue of who originates the idea for the movies he produces and directs, Tsui Hark is a little ambiguous: he says that most of the ideas come from him first, then he starts to gather the people together to produce the movie (which is what a film producer does). But just who writes the script, and who is originating most of the ideas is a bit vague (LM, 27). However, rewriting scripts is pretty much mandatory: you 'rewrite it and rewrite it and rewrite it' (ibid.). Finding a script that's ready to shoot without requiring rewriting hasn't happened yet for Tsui.[4] Of his relationship with writers, Tsui remarked: 'My common experience is to fight with [writers] all the time. As a result some people think I'm very demanding'.

In 2011, Tsui Hark said (in *Twitch*):

The best thing actually to do is write according to what you feel. If you feel your heart would take you to the point where you would want to express something to do with the story or the film. Sometimes it's not the story; sometimes it's the way you tell the story. Sometimes it's the attitude you have with the story. The attitude is something you build and you accumulate for a long time for no reason and no logic, it's there. When you write that way, you might want to make it that way.

For Jean-Luc Godard, having a good script and a good subject were not the same thing. Having a *subject*, 'a meaning, a belief in something' was more important than having a good script or story. 'A pretty woman is not a subject', Godard asserted (1998, 177). North American cinema tended to have 'no subject, only a story'. For Godard, it's a 'good script when you know the subject and try to [explore] it' (ibid.). And a beginning, middle and an end, as Godard famously observed once (to Claude Lelouch in 1965), 'but not necessarily in that order'.

In her excellent study of Tsui Hark's cinema, Lisa Morton asserts that Tsui doesn't use conventional structures (of acts, or three-act models) for his movies. Actually, yes, he does. Right down the line. In fact, not only Tsui's movies, but almost all Hong Kong movies employ conventional narrative structures. (However, the way that Tsui tells stories is quirky, and it's that which makes his pictures look as if they avoid narrative conventions).

Instead of the three-act model, a better way of thinking of acts in film scripts, however, is to see them as 25-30 minutes narrative units

---

[4] As to storyboarding, Tsui Hark said that he uses animatics now, and used to storyboard a lot for a while, until it became restricting.

(following Kristin Thompson in *Storytelling In the New Hollywood*). Thus, a two-hour movie will have *four*, not *three* acts. However, in Hong Kong, the industry usually releases films of 85-90 minutes, so that, yes, they are three-act movies. (And thus, for the action movies of Hong Kong, the *second act* is the big challenge – because any decent action movie can deliver a couple of great action scenes in the first act, and a Big Finale for the third act. But coming up with something in the middle which keeps the movie (and the audience) afloat is trickier).

For Tsui Hark, it's not necessarily the era or other elements that attracts him to a project, it's the characters (LM, 24). This is certainly true of movies such as the *Swordsman* series, the *Detective Dee* films, and of course the *Wong Fei-hung* series.

Grady Hendrix noted in 2013:

> Tsui's characters are neither here nor there, subject to sudden, traumatic changes in status and identity. Demons become human, men become women, swordsmen become monks, criminals become heroes, and heroes become villains. Shape-shifting aliens become bangable pinball machines, robots turn into sexy sirens, human bodies are pulled apart, hung from hooks, deflated, de-faced, skinned alive, castrated, amputated, and exploded. Twins and endlessly replicating time travelers proliferate exponentially.

Tsui Hark has taken up Chinese folktales and fables and classic stories many times as sources for his films, with movies such as *Zu: Warriors From the Magic Mountain, Seven Swords, Green Snake, A Chinese Ghost Story, The Swordsman, Detective Dee* and the *Once Upon a Time In China* series. In fact, Tsui is extremely fond of exploiting ancient and mediæval fables and tales (and not simply, as with the Walt Disney corporation, because they are well out of copyright!). The ancient and Middle Ages tales offer Tsui a framework that are well-known and familiar to audiences, which're also loose enough for him to do whatever he likes with them.

These folk, mythic and historical stories don't only appear in Tsui Hark's movies – they are the subject of many versions, and every famous Chinese tale will have not one but several television series produced from it. For example, the butterfly lovers theme has been remade many times, including on TV; the *Detective Dee* movies are not Tsui's invention – there are C.C.T.V. series (in the early 2000s), and many writers (such as Robert Van Gulik) have explored Judge Dee as a character; the mythic martial arts movies of Tsui's like *Zu* and *Green Snake* are regular topics on Chinese TV; and of course Wong Fei-hung is a central figure in literally 100s of movies and TV shows.

TSUI HARK THE MEDDLER.

Tsui Hark has been known to muscle in other film directors' projects (which seems to be more common in Hong Kong cinema than in the West).5 Tsui admits that when he produces movies, 'I get too involved in the project, and there is not enough room for some directors to breathe'.

David Chung claimed that Tsui Hark 'took things over completely' during *I Love Maria* (a.k.a. *Roboforce*, 1988), which Tsui was producing and Chung was directing; Peter Wang complained that Tsui 'interfered' with his movie *The Laser Man* (1986); John Woo maintained that Tsui 'wrested away control of the sequel to my greatest masterpiece [*A Better Tomorrow*], and when I left to make the movie I wanted to make, rushed his version out just to make sure that it was a flop'. Rumours of Tsui's influence have also been suggested for *A Chinese Ghost Story* and *The Swordsman*.

However, there are a number of assumptions about this tendency of Tsui Hark's to hijack movies that he wasn't directing and their directors. One is that Tsui has the time to do that. Another is that he even *wants* to. Another crucial point is the assumption that the film directors that Tsui co-opts are weedy people with no defences. Many film directors are actually tough cookies who're over-seeing a large group of creative people. (Another factor is that the roles of director, producer and manager can be more vaguely demarcated than in the Western film industry, which's thoroughly unionized).

But there's no doubt that Tsui Hark is a force of nature, an immensely talented, ambitious and driven personality with seemingly boundless energy who's dedicated a substantial part of his life to movies and television. And apart from directors such as Wong Jing, few talents in Hong Kong cinema or Chinese cinema have been so productive. (Also, the accusations that Tsui has stepped into a director's territory have occurred too many times for there not to be some truth in it).

TSUI HARK THE ACTOR.

As an actor, Tsui Hark has done brief cameos, longer cameos, and full roles. As well as cameos in his own movies, Tsui has worked for other directors (such as *Yes, Madam!,* Corey Yuen Kwai, 1985, and *Final Victory,* Patrick Tam, 1987). His finest turn was as 'Big Bo' in *Final Victory*, according to Stephen Teo (1997, 157).

Tsui Hark also appears in *It Takes Two* (1982), *The Winter of 1905* (1982), *Twinkle Twinkle Little Star* (1983), *All the Wrong Spies* (1983), *Run, Tiger, Run* (1985), *Kung Hei Fat Choy* (1985), *Happy Ghost 3* (1986), *I Love Maria* (1988), and *The Big Heat* (1988).

Here's a fuller list: Tsui Hark has appeared in the following movies:

• *It Takes Two* (Karl Maka, 1982), with Tsui as a priest who poses as a gangster.

• The first two *Aces Go Places* movies: *Aces Go Places* (Eric Tsang, 1982), as a ballet stage manager, and *Aces Go Places 2* (Eric Tsang,

---

5 This has also occurred with Jackie Chan – during *Crime Story*, for instance, where Chan apparently took over from Kirk Wong.

1983), with Tsui as a madman.
 • *All the Wrong Spies* (Teddy Robin Kwan, 1983), a spy spoof sequel to *All the Wrong Clues* (which Tsui helmed), with Tsui as 'Hiroshima Tora'.
 • *Run, Tiger, Run* (John Woo, 1985), a reworking of *The Prince and the Pauper*, which was made in Taiwan and had Tsui as a grandfather figure.
 • *Yes, Madam* (Corey Yuen Kwai, 1985), known as the break-out movie for Michelle Yeoh, featured Tsui as one of three con men (John Sham and Mang Hoi were the others);
 • *Happy Ghost 3* (1986) was part of Cinema City's comedy franchise; Tsui was the 'Godfather' who matches up spirits with their homes.
 • *Final Victory* (Patrick Tam, 1987), playing a nasty gangster ('Big Bo') in a white suit.

TSUI HARK AND CHINA.

Tsui Hark is heavily invested in the theme of nationality, and China, and Chinese nationality, and Chinese identity, and Chinese history. It is a central theme in his cinema. Even in the fantasy martial arts movies, issues such as Chinese history are also being explored. It's not only the *Once Upon a Time In China* series that tackles the question of China's relationship with the rest of the world. Some of Tsui's movies are *very* Chinese, and *very* dense with Chinese tradition – so that Western audiences confess to confusion. 'Tsui has always been the most traditionally Chinese of Hong Kong directors' (Lisa Morton, 98).

In fact, one aspect of Tsui Hark's cinema, both as producer and director, is that it is entirely grounded in Chinese characters, Chinese stories, and Chinese issues. Nearly all of Tsui's films feature Chinese characters as the main characters, for instance. Thus, it might not be a coincidence that the two movies regarded as disappointments, the two 'American' films, *Knockoff* and *Double Team*, had a white European as the main protagonist.

Tsui Hark has tended to focus on making films in China – in Hong Kong and the New Territories, mainly, but also in Mainland China and Taiwan (his first movie, *The Butterfly Murders*, was filmed in Taiwan, and he was filming on the Mainland from early in his career). Why? Because Tsui is concerned with Chinese history and culture: most of his films feature Chinese characters in the main roles, for instance. Not Americans in China, not Europeans in China, but Chinese in China (or Chinese abroad).

Of course, an international filmmaker such as Tsui Hark has also filmed in locations such as South France, Italy, Paris and Los Angeles. And for film festivals and awards and the career that goes with being a film director, Tsui is everywhere.

Tsui Hark has raided Ancient Chinese legends several times – *The Four Great Tales of China*, for instance, are *The Tale of the White Snake* (used in *Green Snake*), *The Story of a Tragic Love* (adapted in *The Lovers*), *The Cowherd and the Weaving Maid* and *Seeking Her Husband At the Great Wall*. Tsui remarked he wanted to make movies with Hollywood's production values but with a Chinese sensibility.

Tsui Hark said he has always wanted to make a movie featuring the Monkey King,[6] a famous mythological figure in Chinese culture. In the end, it was Jet Li who appeared as the Monkey King instead, in *Forbidden Kingdom* (2008). But there have been many appearances of the Monkey King in recent movies and television shows – the *Journey To the West* story has been told many times in the Chinese media. Indeed, one of Tsui's biggest hits economically as a director was the *Journey To the West* sequel of 2017, which finally featured the Monkey King.

Altho' we think of Tsui Hark as a supremely Chinese filmmaker, he was in fact born in Saigon in Vietnam, and only moved to Hong Kong when he was thirteen or fourteen (so he is really a Vietnamese/ Chinese filmmaker). Tsui has become devoted to notions of Chineseness and the history of China in his cinema. Stephen Teo relates Tsui's deep fascination with Chinese history and culture to his background as a Vietnamese/ Chinese citizen, to being an overseas Chinese, not born on the Mainland or in Hong Kong.

Tsui Hark has been criticized for his nationalistic politics, and the denunciations of foreign cultures in his movies. But you can probably find issues of nationalism in most major film directors, and certainly most film cultures around the world use nationalism of some kind in most of their movies. In the West, we almost can't see it, because it's everywhere. But if you watch a lot of Asian movies then come back to a North American movie, it's striking just how strong the nationalism is. (However, some nations neighbouring China have an ambiguous attitude towards the country, and they certainly don't admire it as passionately as Tsui does).

And after a while, you get sick to hell of watching North American movies which crow about the U.S.A.'s dumb family values, its vacuous but all-pervasive capitalism, and, most disturbing of all, North America's war-mongering, its insistence on maintaining, at colossal expense ($798 billion a year in 2021), the military-industrial machine, its pro-military politics, and its insistence on the right to bear weapons: this is what I call 'Amerika Über Alles'.

That Tsui Hark is keenly interested in Chinese history and modern politics is easy to spot: it forms the background of some of his most celebrated works, from *Once Upon a Time In China* to *Seven Swords*. But Tsui doesn't employ historical events to stage spectacle cinema (in the manner of David Lean or Steven Spielberg); there is more to it than that (not least is Tsui's unabashed nationalism, his devotion to the idea of China). Tsui says: 'China has such deep cultural resources – it's just that we haven't utilised them yet'.

Stephen Teo, one of the better critics on Chinese cinema, pointed out that Tsui Hark's movies employ some of the icons and clichés of Chinese culture (such as acupuncture, martial arts, Peking Opera) in order to help make the movies appealing to outsiders. Yes – but as Tsui himself has noted, in the New Wave of Hong Kong cinema, the filmmakers were producing movies for the *local market*, *not* for the global market (that came

---

6 And a monkey-man does appear in *Iron Monkey*.

later). But there's no doubt that Tsui in the movies he directs likes to evoke traditional, Chinese culture and practices – but you could see that as a way of presenting the clichés and icons back to the home audience (just as every American Western flick contains numerous iconic elements which sell the cowboy and frontier lifestyle back to the American audience).

Stephen Teo also talks of 'cultural nationalism', more an emotional desire among Chinese people living abroad for Chinese culture. Chinese nationalism, Teo asserts, is found everywhere in Chinese cinema, from *kung fu* flicks to New Wave films, from Mandarin historical epics to Cantonese melodramas (1997, 110-1). In the *kung fu* movies of the 1970s, Teo identified an abstract nationalism in which *kung fu* heroes were using traditions (often from Shaolin) to fight foreign Manchus to restore the Chinese race (1997, 113).

As more of the Hong Kong film industry angled its products at Mainland China, Tsui Hark was conscious of the limitations that it put upon filmmakers: 'In the last 10 years Hong Kong movies have been gradually moving to the market in China', Tsui said in *Hyphen* magazine in 2011. 'And in that market, there is some degree of restriction on the subjects of the films we can make. We are very much constrained by the kind of rules and taboos of the censorship bureau'.

IDENTITY.

French philosopher Julia Kristeva (b. 1941) has developed a fascinating conception notion of the 'outsider'. Being exiled from Bulgaria helped Kristeva see both her own country and her adopted country (France) more clearly. Her experience of displacement was an ingredient in her idea of the 'cosmopolitan' individual, the 'intellectual dissident'. As Kristeva knows, strangeness or otherness (being a foreigner) is fundamental to being human: as Kristeva put it, *étrangers à nous-mêmes* (we are strangers to ourselves). In *Strangers To Ourselves* Kristeva describes the foreigner as the 'cold orphan', motherless, a 'devotee of solitude', a 'fanatic of absence', alone even in a crowd, arrogant, rejected, yet oddly happy (1991, 4-5). The stranger is always in motion, doesn't belong anywhere, to 'any time, any love' (ib., 7).

Julia Kristeva's notion of strangeness or otherness relates directly to the poet Arthur Rimbaud's 'Je est un autre ('I is an other')', Rimbaud's sense of exile and otherness. Living with a foreigner, then, in Kristeva's view, means not just accepting them but being them:

> Rimbaud's *Je est un autre* was not only the acknowledgement of the
> psychotic ghost that haunts poetry. The word foreshadowed the exile,
> the possibility or necessity to be foreign and to live in a foreign
> country, thus heralding the art of living of a modern era, the cosmo-
> politanism of those who have been flayed. (1991, 13)

This throws light on Tsui Hark's cultural identity as an overseas

Chinese man, always dreaming of China, the homeland.

TSUI HARK'S COLLABORATORS.

Tsui Hark has worked with pretty much everybody in the Hong Kong film industry (and more recently on the Mainland). This is a partial list: the following actors have been important in the development of Tsui Hark's career:[7] Sylvia Chang, Brigitte Lin, Jet Li, Eric Tsang,[8] Leslie Cheung, Karl Maka, Chow Yun-fat, Jacky Cheung, Maggie Cheung, Waise Lee, Lau Shun, Sammo Hung Kam-bo, Rosamund Kwan, Anita Mui, Tony Leung Ka-fai, Joey Wang, Teddy Robin,[9] John Sham, Sally Yeh, Raymond Wong Pak-min, and Vincent Zhao.

Other regular actors in Tsui Hark's cinema include: Kenny Bee, Yuen Biao, Cheriie Cheung, David Chiang, Paul Chun, Paul Chu, Norman Chu, Kent Cheng, Adam Cheng, Andy Lau, Lau Ching-wan, Lau Siu-ming, Carman Lee, Loletta Lee, Leon Lai, Sam Hui, Dean Shek, George Lam, Michelle Reiss, Max (Benny) Mok, Carrie Ng, Tony Leung Chiu-wai, Wu Ma, Anthony Wong, Kenneth Tsang, Elvis Tsui, Donnie Yen, Ti Lung, Fennie Yuen, Charlie Yeung, Yan Yee-kwan, Nicky Wu, Jean Wong, Yu Rong-guang, Anita Yuen, Kenny Lin, Zhou Xun, Stephen Chow and Yuen Wah.

Producers Raymond Chow, Nansun Shi Nan-sheng, Leonard Ho, Terence Chang, Karl Maka, Chen Kuo-fu, Huang Jianxin and Ng See-yuen. (Tsui clearly learned plenty from producers such as Chow and Ho, and rapidly became a major player himself – founding Film Workshop five years or so after directing his first feature film). Writers such as Roy Szeto Chak-hon, Charcoal Cheung Tan, Ng Man-fai, Koan Hui, and Sharon Hui Sa-long.

An important collaborator with Tsui Hark was writer Sze-To Cheuk-Hon (a.k.a. Roy Szeto or Szeto Chak-Hon, b. 1954), the author of *All the Wrong Clues, Dangerous Encounter, Zu: Warriors From the Magic Mountain, Shanghai Blues* and *Once Upon a Time In China and America.* Szeto also wrote the *Lucky Stars* movies, the *Mr Vampire* movies, *The Emperor and the White Snake,* and Jackie Chan movies such as *Armor of God* and *Dragons Forever.*

Composers James Wong Jim, Joseph Koo, Lowell Lo, Mark Lui Chang-dak, David Wu, Romeo Diaz, William Hu, Teddy Robin Kwan, Kenji Kawai, and Woo Wai-laap. (This stable of composers is not to be under-estimated: music is a very big deal in Tsui's cinema).

Composer James Wong Jim has delivered more pieces of music (and songs) for Tsui Hark than anyone else; the incredible Wong, one of those composers who can turn his hand to anything (*very* useful to have on any production), has also appeared as an actor many times. Joseph Koo is another oft-used composer (beginning with *The Butterfly Murders* and the *Better Tomorrow* films).

---

[7] The same actors crop up in movies of the 1980s and 1990s which Tsui Hark either directed, produced, co-wrote or acted in: Sally Yeh, Sylvia Chang, John Sham, Joey Wong, Eric Tsang, Teddy Robin, Karl Maka, Chow Yun-fat, Tony Leung, Leslie Cheung, Kenny Bee, Jet Li, Carrie Ng, Waise Lee, Brigitte Lin, Sammo Hung, etc.
[8] Eric Tsang is another Tsui collaborator – a Cinema City honcho, a director/ writer/ producer with numerous credits, he has worked many times with Tsui.
[9] Teddy Robin Kwan is one of the key figures in Hong Kong cinema of this period – he provided the score for *Black Mask*, directed the *All the Wrong Clues* sequel, and acted in *Working Class, All the Wrong Clues, Twin Dragons* and *It Takes Two.*

For some of the foreign prints of the movies of Tsui Hark (and John Woo), Western rock music was added – Peter Gabriel, the Alan Parsons Project, Jeff Beck, etc (presumably by distributors or companies or producers who thought that rock/ pop music would appeal to Western audiences). But it isn't a good fit – either cinematically or culturally. Altho' we can enjoy the pop music on its own, the original scores would be much preferred, for numerous reasons.

Editors Marco Mak Chi-sin, Gam Ma, Angie Lam On-yee, Poon Hung, Peter Cheung and David Wu Tai-wai (also composer). The significance of editors hardly needs to be mentioned in connection with the films directed, produced and written by Tsui.

DPs such as Arthur Wong (who's probably worked with Tsui Hark more than any DP), David Chung, Peter Pau (*Crouching Tiger, Hidden Dragon*), Lau Moon-tong (Tom Lau),[10] Hermann Yau Lai-to, Andrew Lau Wai-keung (not the singer/ actor – later a director of very Tsui-ian movies like *The Stormriders*), Poon Hang-sang, and Wong Wing-hang. Johnny Choi Sung-fai became Tsui's regular DP from *Seven Swords* onwards.

For such a visually sophisticated and inventive director as Tsui Hark, the on-set relationship with the cinematographer is absolutely vital.

Sometimes five or more DPs are credited on some productions. Why? Because Tsui Hark goes thru DPs like no one else – some only last a day before they're fired. Keeping up with Tsui is very challenging. As Arthur Wong explained:

> Tsui is very creative, but he changes his mind every minute. So sometimes, even though you've done a lot and a lot of preparation, suddenly he comes up with an idea and changes everything! And, he won't even give you enough time! That's the problem! He keeps pushing you, pushing you, pushing, squeezing you, and hurrying you. (D. Vivier)

Production designers William Cheung,[11] Bill Lui and Ma Poon-chiu. (Tsui has done production design himself, as has his ex-wife, Nansun Shi Nan-sheng).

And action directors Tony Ching Siu-tung, Yuen Woo-ping, Yuen Bun, Xiong Xin-xin, Cheung Yiu-sing, Wong Shu Tong, Ma Yuk-shing, Stephen Tung and Corey Yuen Kwai.

Action directors such as Yuen Bun, Yuen Woo-ping, Tony Ching Siu-tung and Xiong Xin-xin are vital in the cinema of Tsui Hark: they are the people, with their tough, hard-working stunt teams, who co-ordinate the action sequences (often appearing in them, too, as actors). Bun, for instance, has credits on a large number of Tsui movies.

MORE ON TSUI HARK'S COLLABORATORS.
NG SEE-YUEN.

A key influence on Tsui Hark's career, and in the *Once Upon a Time In*

---

[10] DP for *The Magic Crane, Once Upon a Time In China 5, The Swordsman 2* and *3, A Chinese Ghost Story 1* and *3*, etc.
[11] Cheung has credits on many of Tsui Hark's movies, and most of Wong Kar-wai's films.

China movies, was the producer, Ng See-yuen (known as 'N.G.'), who had backed Tsui Hark's first movie, *The Butterfly Murders* (Ng also co-produced *New Dragon Gate Inn* with Tsui, plus *We're Going To Eat You, Twin Dragons* and others). Ng (b. 1944, Shanghai) was a major force in Cantonese cinema, starting out (like so many others) at Shaw Brothers (in 1967), and forming his own production company, Seasonal Films, in 1975 (some say 1973). N.G. was one of the first to recognize the importance of Bruce Lee, and tried to convince Run Run Shaw to sign Lee to Shaws.

N.G. has directing credits, writing credits, acting credits and producer credits. He is an industry advisor on many boards and festivals. N.G. is also the founder of Ultimate Movie Experience International Cineplex, a chain of cinemas in China (including an IMAX theatre in Beijing).

Ng See-yuen's movies included the *Secret Rituals* films, *Anti-Corruption* (1975), *Bruce Lee: The Man, the Myth, The Invincible Armour* (1977), *Dance of the Drunk Mantis* and *Drunken Master 2*. N.G. saw the potential of Jackie Chan, and put him in the two important early Chan movies *Snake In Eagle's Shadow* and *Drunken Master* (both 1978, and both directed by Yuen Woo-ping), which made Chan a superstar. ('It was a partnership that was as good as any I've had in my life', Chan said: 'in every way that mattered, this was the first *real* Jackie Chan picture').

Ng See-yuen also introduced Jean-Claude van Damme to the world (in *No Retreat, No Surrender*) – van Damme would later star in two of Tsui Hark's movies, *Knockoff* and *Double Team*. Other credits of N.G.'s include: *Game of Death II, Ninja in the Dragon's Den, The Unwritten Law, The King of the Kickboxers, Superfights, The Soong Sisters, Legendary Assassin, Bloodmoon, Evening of Roses, Kung Fu Wing Chun,* and *The Grandmaster*.

MARCO MAK CHI-SIN.

Marco Mak Chi-sin (b. Nov 6, 1951) is Tsui Hark's regular editor (along with David Wu Tai-wai and Angie Lam On-yee). He has edited not only a high proportion of Tsui's movies as director but also Tsui's producer movies (such as the *Swordsman* and *Chinese Ghost Story* series, plus *The Magic Crane, The Era of Vampires* and *Iron Monkey*). Other credits include *The Stormriders,* the *Conmen* films, and *The Duel* (and several for Wong Jing). Mak is thus a vital collaborator in the world of Tsui's cinema, which puts such a high premium on editing. (Mak has been editing since 1977, and has also directed fifteen movies, including *Xanda, Dancing Lion, Set To Kill, The Wall* and *Haunted Office*).

David Wu Tai-wai (b. 1952) is another of many unsung contributors to the Tsui Hark empire – a regular editor and composer, Wu has directed as well as appeared in Tsui's movies. Wu also edited most of the celebrated John Woo movies. As Bey Logan pointed out, Wu is a key influence on the editing of action cinema, not only in Hong Kong (purely for his work with Woo – add Tsui and Ronny Yu, and you have a very formidable editor of action movies). Wu said he didn't have to talk with Tsui or Woo – they were in sync, and knew what they were doing.

Angie Lam On-yee (b. 1965) is another superstar cutter in Hong Kong. She is particularly brilliant with cutting action sequences. Her C.V. includes *Hero, House of Flying Daggers, Tai-Chi Master, Fong Sai-yuk 2, The Bodyguard From Beijing, C.J. 7, Kung Fu Hustle, The Warlords,* and numerous movies for Tony Ching, John Woo and Tsui Hark (beginning with *Once Upon a Time In China 2* in 1992).

What must it be like being Tsui Hark's editor?! Does the director visit the editing suite and ask of Angie Lam, Marco Mak or David Wu, 'can we make it go even faster?'!

Sometimes it seems as if editors Mak, Lam and Wu are like the crazy cannibals in *We're Going To Eat You*: when Mak, Lam and Wu get going on the celluloid pouring through the cutting rooms each and every day during production, they are chop-chop-chopping like mad axemen who haven't been fed for days. *Slash!* – there goes a gag they liked for about the first 22 times they saw it; *chop!* – there goes a bit where Jet Li turns to grin at Rosamund Kwan (we don't need that, it's covered elsewhere); and *wheee!* – there goes an entire action sequence which took the stunt team weeks to film. Why was it cut out?

Because it's not fast enough!

JET LI.

Jet Li was born on April 26, 1963 in Hebel, China. (In Cantonese, Li's name is Lei Lin Git; in Mandarin, it's Li Lanjie). Li is short (5' 6"), but can take on anyone in movies. Li won the first national *wushu* competition in China since the Cultural Revolution (aged 9); he was the Chinese Men's All-round National Wushu Champion at the age of twelve. (*Wushu* is a form of martial arts as performance, combining Peking Opera, gymnastics, and colourful costumes, developed during the Cultural Revolution). Li moved to San Francisco with a Chinese actress (Huang Qiuyan) in 1988; they married (1987-90) and had two daughters. In the U.S.A., Li received his Green Card. Li later married actress Nina Li Chi (they have two daughters).

Jet Li appeared in several martial arts movies[12] right after the first *Once Upon a Time In China* film, including *Tai Chi Master, New Legend of Shaolin* (about Hung Gar), the *Fong Say-yuk* films, *Last Hero In China*, and *Kung Fu Cult Master* (a.k.a. *Evil Cult*).

Tsui Hark didn't want Jet Li to play villains, and always cast him as the hero. Tsui wasn't convinced by Hollywood's use of Li as a villain (in movies such as *Lethal Weapon 4*); it didn't work, and Li didn't look right, Tsui said. Tsui wanted Li to play the hero, the character who tries to do the right thing. 'When he stars in my movies, he must be a heroic figure'.

One should also note here Tsui Hark's genius with casting. Rarely commented upon by critics (tho' discussed endlessly by fans), casting is enormously important in a movie. And it's not an easy job. Tsui certainly has a knack for finding new talent, for getting the right people for the roles (he has also created roles specially for certain actors), and also for filling in the secondary roles and the character roles with suitable people.

---

[12] Jet Li didn't make much money from his Shaolin pictures (he was paid a State subsidy).

BRIGITTE LIN.

Brigitte Lin is... Brigitte Lin. Lin was born in Sanchong, Taiwan on Nov 3, 1954.[13] (she is Lam Ching Hsia in Cantonese, and Lin Qinhxia in Mandarin; she is also known as Venus Lin). Lin was in many Taiwanese films (beginning in 1973) before appearing in Hong Kong films such as *Zu, All the Wrong Spies, Police Story, Peking Opera Blues*, the *Bride With White Hair* films, the *Royal Tramp* films, *New Dragon Gate Inn,* Wong Kar-wai movies such as *Chungking Express* and *Ashes of Time,* and the *Swordsman* series.

Brigitte Lin is one of the most remarkable of all recent Asian stars. She 'must certainly be one of the most fearless performers in the world' (Lisa Morton, 101). Lin, tho' straight, is known for playing lesbian and crossdressing women in films such as *All the Wrong Spies* (a lesbian disguising herself as a guy), *Fantasy Mission Force* (she shoots the clothes off a tied-up woman), *The Swordsman 3* (she's a lesbian transsexual superhero), *New Dragon Gate Inn* (steals another woman's clothes for herself), *Peking Opera Blues* (she wears men's military uniforms), *Boys Are Easy* (she's a lesbian cop), *Ashes of Time* (she plays both a brother and a sister), *Eagle Shooting Heroes* (she's a butch princess), and *Fire Dragon* (she's a masked male warrior).

Brigitte Lin's crossdressing or transgender character in the *Swordsman* movies (as Dongfang Bubai = Asia the Invincible) draws on the Peking Opera tradition (where actors can be both warriors and princesses. Indeed, the Tsui Hark movie *Peking Opera Blues* explores issues of gender[14] at length).

Brigitte Lin, according to Bey Logan, was one of the few bankable female stars in Asia: 'basically, all the ageless Ms Lin has to do is wave her arms and smile enigmatically and local audiences will pay to watch' (166).

Tsui Hark has tried to entice Brigitte Lin back to acting – for the remake of *Zu: Warriors From the Magic Mountain* in 2001, for instance, and to play the Empress Wu in *Detective Dee and the Mystery of the Phantom Flame*. Lin retired from acting in 1994, when she married businessman Michael Ying and had children.

❂

OTHER ACTORS.

Lau Shun is one of Tsui Hark's favourite character actors, and he's appeared in probably more Tsui movies than anyone else. Lau can do anything – from bumbling, comical servants to imperious government officials to insane sorcerers and deities. (Tsui had originally brought Lau in to advise on Peking Opera culture in *Peking Opera Blues*).

Charlie Yeung Choi-nei (b. 1974) is one of Tsui Hark's favourite actresses: following her winning turn in *The Lovers*, she appeared in *Love In the Time of Twilight, Catching Monkey 3-D* and was the lead in *Seven Swords* (among others, such as *Ashes of Time, Fallen Angels* and *Dr Wai*).

---
13 Some sources say 1957.
14 Peking Opera had a huge impact on the young Tsui Hark – including the play with gender.

Yeung is the classic Tsui Hark Girl – small and slightly-built, tomboyish yet feminine, soft but also tough, and with classical, Chinese features. Yeung retired in 1997, at the height of her fame, but returned to movies in 2004 (with *New Police Story*, and she appeared in *Seven Swords* in 2005).

Xiong Xin-xin (b. 1965), has numerous credits as a stunt co-ordinator and actor. He's one of those faces that you see in many Chinese movies of the 1990s and 2000s, including many of Tsui Hark's films. Xiong has been Jet Li's stunt double since 1986 (on *Shaolin Temple 3*).

❊

One should note again that actors – and crew too – are attracted to great filmmakers like Tsui Hark (or Ken Russell or Orson Welles or Akira Kurosawa) because they get to do things that few others ask them to do. The canvas, the world, the stories that the great film directors move in are huge.

Jean-Luc Godard said that it was natural for him to say to his actors and crew: 'give me more. Let's do what has not been done'.[15] One gets the impression that it's the same with Tsui Hark.

Altho' Tsui Hark has a reputation of being a little demanding on set at times, I would imagine that many actors and crew are happy to work with him. For the simple reason that they know that their work will be seen by millions of people. Which's what it's all about. They also know that Tsui is one of the great, celebrated talents in Asian cinema, and that working on a Tsui movie raises their own profile considerably.

Another reason that actors and crew want to work with Tsui Hark is that he is a powerful presence in the Chinese film business – his movies will get released, a lot of people will see them, they won't be re-cut by studios or backers (or censored – usually), the marketing and promotion will be good, they will be reviewed, and they will have an after-life on TV, cable, DVD, etc.[16]

CASTING POP STARS.

In casting many performers from the world of pop music, Tsui Hark said he and his production teams did that partly because they were seeking acting styles that were different from the stylizations of the old Shaw Brothers movies (which they grew up on), and different from the stylizations of television acting. And, besides, it didn't hurt that pop icons already had a built-in audience and fan base (include teens). Also, pop stars were used to performing and expressing themselves: as Tsui explained:

> I like to use singers in my films because they are already experienced in communicating their feelings to an audience.[17]

Cantopop stars include Alan Tam, Andy Lau, Karen Mok, Aaron Kwok,

---

[15] Quoted in A. Sarris, 1968.
[16] All actors, East or West, have been in or know about projects that were sat on for years, or never got released, or were distributed poorly, or were hacked about by distributors or studios.
[17] Quoted in B. Logan, 181.

Jacky Cheung, Leslie Cheung, Anita Mui, Ekin Cheng and Leon Lai (most of whom have appeared in Tsui Hark's movies).

The 'Four Golden Kings' – singers Leslie Cheung, Andy Lau, Jackie Cheung and Leon Lai – were hugely popular in the 1980s and 1990s. And, as Bey Logan noted, and as we know well, the 'Four Golden Kings' have appeared in numerous Hong Kong movies. In the West, Logan reckoned that it would be like the Osmonds and the Jackson Five uniting for a remake of *The Wild Bunch* (179).

In Asian cinema, casting pop stars has worked so many times. There isn't the stigma attached to using pop musicians as there is in the West (even so, Western cinema has cast from the world of pop and rock numerous times, with some incredible results: Prince in *Purple Rain,* Mick Jagger in *Performance*, Kris Kristofferson in *Pat Garrett and Billy the Kid* and *Heaven's Gate,* and David Bowie in *The Man Who Fell To Earth*).

COMICS.

Tsui Hark is a big fan of Japanese *manga* and *animé*[18] (who isn't?!), and also Asian types of comicbooks, such as *manhwa* (Korean *manga*), and *manwua* (Chinese *manga*).[19] As his wife Nansun Shi puts it, comics are 'Tsui's one big vice' (LM, 224). 'I wanted to be a comic artist', Tsui remembered of his youth (LM, 19).[20] He reads lots of *manga* and other comics: 'because those things are very interesting to me' (ibid.). Tsui draws a lot, including when he's shooting, and he also paints. For Tsui, drawing is a great way of expressing visual ideas.

Manga have moved into many Asian territories, such as Taiwan, Hong Kong, Thailand and South Korea (Thailand is a major market for Japanese *manga*, and all of the main Japanese boys' and some girls' magazines are published there). And Korea has developed an animation industry increasingly in the past few decades (so it's now the third largest producer of animation after Japan and the U.S.A.).

Conversely, one of the biggest markets for Chinese action movies, and Hong Kong action cinema in particular, is Japan. You only have to look at any *manga* or *animé* to see the influence of Chinese action movies (and in particular anything starring Jackie Chan).

And the influence of comicbook style and visuals on the cinema of Tsui Hark is obvious everywhere. Tsui has deployed the comics approach many, many times – even the epic sweep of the history of China evoked in the *Once Upon a Time In China* series is cartoony. And comics pacing and storytelling – which, in Japanese *manga*, is *incredibly* fast, and yet has time for 'pillow moments' and interludes, for character-based scenes (the real impact of Japanese *manga* is in the areas of characters and storytelling). By contrast, Tsui finds N. American comics over-rich (their colours) and too slow (LM, 19).

And Tsui Hark has had a go at making artwork for comics – such as

---
18 'I like Miyazaki a lot' (LM, 31).
19 One reason that *manga* proved popular in Korea, Taiwan and Hong Kong was because the reading system was the same: from right-to-left and from top to bottom. Which meant that publishers didn't need to flip and re-format the pages.
20 He drew a lot as a kid partly because he was inspired by animated films (LM, 31).

Ma Wing-shong's *Red Snow* (1999). Using Photoshop software, Tsui has created images for comicbooks (he says it takes 4 hours to produce an image). Tsui appreciates how cheap drawing is for trying out ideas:

> with drawing you can just start over and do it again. You put it down and look at it and you see the right reaction without really costing a lot of money or causing a lot of commotion because of something going wrong. (LM, 19)

There are numerous *manga* that one could cite in connection with Tsui Hark's cinema: samurai epics are obvious choices (*Lone Wolf and Cub, Vagabond, Yongbi, Lady Snowblood, Blade of the Immortal*), historical stories (*Buddha, Hero Tales)*, fantasy and horror comics (*Akira, Ogre Slayer, Urotsukidoji, Hellsing, Mushishi*), alien babes and goofy guys and harem stories (*Urusei Yatsura, Love Hina, Oh! My Goddess*), gangster/ thriller adventures (*Lupin III, Gunsmith Cats*), hi-tech cyber yarns (*Ghost In the Shell, Appleseed*), and of course the giant franchises of *manga* like *One Piece, Bleach* and *Naruto*.

Indeed, some *manga* come across as Tsui Hark movies: deadly female assassins in *Lady Snowblood* and *Ghost In the Shell*; wispy, wistful other-worldly women and goddesses in *Oh! My Goddess*; epic re-interpretations of ancient history in Osamu Tezuka's incredible *Buddha;* action-adventure in *Lupin III*; and ninja hurtling thru the treetops in *Basilisk* and *Naruto*.

The first animated movie that Tsui Hark saw was *Bambi* (1942) – and it's the same for many filmmakers: many saw a Disney movie as their first movie of any kind (Steven Spielberg, Woody Allen, Hayao Miyazaki, etc). Tsui recalled that his mom wouldn't let him see *Snow White and the Seven Dwarfs* (1937) because there was kissing (!), and because the heroine wore a low-cut dress. But *Bambi* – all animals – was OK. When Tsui later saw *Snow White*, he called it 'my most favorite movie', with a level of artistry and intricacy that's almost impossible to reproduce today.

VISUAL EFFECTS AND TECHNIQUE.

Tsui Hark is a filmmaker who foregrounds the tricks and visual effects of cinema, often in a self-conscious, stagey manner. Western filmmakers who also take this approach include: Orson Welles, Jean Cocteau, Walerian Borowczyk, Sergei Paradjanov, Tim Burton, Vincente Minnelli, Terry Gilliam, Powell & Pressburger, Ken Russell, and Francis Coppola.

Visual effects are one of Tsui Hark's chief concerns in cinema: from *Zu: Warriors From the Magic Mountain* onwards,[21] Tsui has attempted to develop a sophisticated and technically accomplished visual effects resource in China. This has involved nurturing visual effects teams and technical back-up and the infra-structure to make it all possible from scratch. Critics find this aspect of Tsui's cinema very difficult to analyze.

It's the same with crucial elements such as editing and cinemato-

---

[21] As well as the optical and comping visual effects, there is animation, stopmotion, miniatures, and special make-up.

graphy. Critics have no idea how movies are edited, and how vital the process is. Film critics will mention that Tsui Hark's movies are ✂✂✂ rapidly, but that's as far as they go. They have little knowledge of the editorial process.

Tsui Hark says that special effects are there to help the story – but they're not the *raison d'être* of the film, nor the reason why the film is good or bad.

WOMEN AND FEMINISM.

Unlike many of his contemporaries, the films directed/ produced/ written by Tsui Hark offer many great roles for women. Not only are there juicy dramatic roles, but plenty of comical ones, too. Tsui's movies celebrate *active* women, proactive women, busy women, women who drive the plot with their desires, their hopes and dreams.[22] While ancient, mediæval and modern Chinese society might be patriarchal through and through, Tsui fills his films with strong and resourceful women, who are three-dimensional characters. Tsui remarked:

I think I'm trying to do something where the women are less predictable and a stronger character.

The turning-point for Tsui Hark in terms of the roles of women in his cinema was 1984:

So, I think 1984 was a very critical moment when I decided to write about women and simply ignore the men's characters for one project that was called *Shanghai Blues*. I know so many friends that were actresses like Brigitte Lin and they felt very frustrated for having no scripts written about women. That's why after all these experiences with these people; I decided to start making movies with these people being the priority character of the story.

The crossdressing and gender-bending in Tsui Hark's cinema focusses on women – women dressing up as men. No one can fail to notice that the women tend to be tomboyish (the Tsui Hark Girl is short, slim and a tomboy), hinting at the homoeroticism of the romances with men, as well as father complex women (in common with most women in adventure and fantasy fiction). Another recurring motif is a gorgeous woman who turns out to be either an ugly woman underneath, or a guy.[23]

In the historical pictures, the Tsui Hark Girl is typically a proud warrior, a tomboy great at fighting assailants (and with a few moves of her own). She's stubborn, even difficult, but has a soft, feminine side underneath (which she only reveals reluctantly, and only to the hero). Sometimes the Tsui Hark Girl is a punky, aggressive personality, with suitable accessories like tattoos and jewellery. Another Tsui-ian female type is the Kook. She's batty, scatter-brained, clumsy and adorable. She dresses

---

22 A woman who defies tradition is 'something that's very dramatic' for Tsui Hark (LM, 21).
23 Maybe Tsui had a terrible experience with a woman who was actually a man or transvestite, because this scenario pops up so many times in his cinema!

funny, and wears big, Eighties glasses (i.e., she's a female version of Tsui himself).

Far fewer critics tackle the issues of feminism and the role of women in Tsui Hark's cinema.[24] It's not one of Tsui's primary themes, for sure (altho' some critics claim it is),[25] but in the subplots of his pictures (and not only in the romantic subplots), issues revolving around women are explored. 'Tsui Hark's women triumph by remaining or becoming feminine', reckoned Lisa Morton (LM, 13). On the one hand, there is certainly a proto-feminism at work in Tsui's cinema, tho' I'm sure many feminists could find plenty of material to back up their argument that women are portrayed in negative, demeaning and exploitative lights in Tsui's movies (the lesbian lovers in *Time and Tide,* for instance).

The cinema of Tsui Hark features strong, independent women, yes, but some Hong Kong movies have gone further in depicting wild women who can wield guns and kick ass – the *Naked Killer* movies, for instance, or the films of Wong Jing.

SEQUELS AND FRANCHISES.

Many of Tsui Hark's movies as producer and director have been remakes and sequels. But Tsui does something very different with the existing material every time: there is never a feeling that Tsui is rehashing a story, or warming up a corpse. (Compared to Western sequels and remakes, those of Tsui are in a wholly different realm). Tsui has even remade earlier movies he's directed (*Zu: Warriors From the Magic Mountain* and *Flying Swords of Dragon Gate*), as have filmmakers like Alfred Hitchcock and Tim Burton.

Among the franchises and series that Tsui Hark has contributed to as producer and director are: *Black Mask, Once Upon a Time In China, The Swordsman, Detective Dee, Aces Go Places, All the Wrong Clues, A Better Tomorrow* and *A Chinese Ghost Story*. Very significantly, Tsui has been the originator of many of those movie franchises and series, including *Once Upon a Time In China, The Swordsman, Detective Dee* and *A Chinese Ghost Story*.

As with most filmmakers, the majority of the movies directed/ produced by Tsui Hark are adaptations of existing material. Among the movies and stories that Tsui has originated himself are *The Master, Detective Dee, Shanghai Blues, Peking Opera Blues* and *Dangerous Encounters of the First Kind*. (Tsui is not a filmmaker who works predominantly from scripts which are completely original ideas, like Ingmar Bergman and Woody Allen).

REMAKES AND UPDATES.

A very important element of Tsui Hark's cinema is updating and remaking previous movies. Tsui is clearly enamoured of cinema from previous generations, and intent on updating it for a contemporary

---

24 'He may also be the world's greatest feminist director', reckoned Lisa Morton (6).
25 For Lisa Morton, 'the single most defining theme in the œuvre of Tsui Hark, beginning with his very first film', is the deconstruction of male and female roles (LM, 68).

audience. Even though Tsui has occasionally insisted that he is not remaking old movies, because it's disrespectful (*pace Flying Swords* of 2011), some of his most well-known and celebrate movies are remakes and updates: *The Blade* reworks *The One-Armed Swordsman,* the *Once Upon a Time In China* series delivers the familiar *Wong Fei-hung* legend to new audiences, *A Better Tomorrow* is a remake of *True Colors of a Hero, The Taking of Tiger Mountain* is a remake of the famous 1970 production, and *Flying Swords of Dragon Gate* updates both the King Hu-helmed movie of 1967 and Tsui's own *New Dragon Gate Inn* of 1992.

Maggie Lee Man-yuk calls Tsui Hark 'the king of remakes, or, rather, reinvention, drawing on diverse sources and blending genres, tones, and technique with the most imaginative abandon' (2021).

'Not only has he produced or directed films in nearly every conceivable category, he's consistently recreated, resurrected and revitalized dying or stagnant genres', noted Lisa Morton (10). In discussing why he keeps reviving old genres and movies, Tsui Hark said:

> I feel that much of it has to do with my childhood memories, my childhood impressions and my childhood preferences. When I look back at those movies, because of their dated approaches… it's impossible to share these special feelings with the audience today. That's why we're shooting those [old] stories with a contemporary approach.

The adherence to previous genres, forms and movies in Tsui Hark's cinema isn't mere recycling or mindless exploitation (tho' it is that, too). There is more to it than that. At one level, yes, business-wise, it makes sense for all the obvious reasons to update stories and movies that're familiar to audiences (which Hong Kong cinema has always done). But Tsui is doing much more than that. I think he is a true visionary filmmaker, going beyond what many forms of commercial cinema do.

In thriving film cultures, like France, Japan, Korea or the U.S.A., it is completely expected and normal to remake movies and stories all the time. *New actors in old stories* is one of the definitions of the Hollywood movie machine in the glory days of the 1930s thru 1960s, but the phrase still sums up a large proportion of the output of any flourishing filmmaking centre. Often, the remakes and updates are simply old stories dressed up in new clothes, with some new gimmicks to help sell them (such as 3-D,[26] or visual effects, or a postmodern spin on an old chestnut).

But the remakes and updates of Tsui Hark are in a different class, coming from a different place, and operating in a different arena. While Tsui clearly has an *incredibly* keen eye for commercialism and showmanship (you could hire Tsui to over-see any of the big spectacles in the modern era like the Oscars, the Golden Globes, or the opening of the

---

[26] Tsui Hark was interested in 3-D filmmaking immediately it became a possibility again in the 2000s. It would help cinema to compete with TV, the internet and all the other forms of entertainment that audiences could enjoy: 'I think also because movies are sharing audiences' time with TV and the Internet, even with a bigger screen, movies still have to be different from other mediums. Thus when the possibility for 3D came up, it was right away an attraction to me as a filmmaker'.

Olympic Games, whatever, and you'd be guaranteed a real treat), he is also doing much more as a filmmaker.

Hong Kong audiences are used to movies from Canton being different. They know, said Tsui Hark, that a Hong Kong movie won't be normal, will experiment, might not even be understandable or easy, but it will be different (LM, 28).

TSUI HARK'S FLOPS.

Among the movies of Tsui Hark regularly derided by fans and critics are: *The Magic Crane, Twin Dragons, The Master,* both *Black Masks,* with *Double Team* receiving the fiercest venom. *Green Snake* and *Knockoff* divide admirers. (Some also add *Once Upon a Time in China 4*).

I don't agree: *all* of the above movies have their enjoyable aspects, and even *The Master* and *Double Team* aren't as woeful as fans and critics make out. But I care little for *Triangle, Missing* and *All About Women* (movies of 2007 and 2008). And, you'd have to admit, that some of Tsui's choices in the latter part of his career have been a little wayward: *Black Mask 2, Double Team, Triangle, All About Women, Missing* and maybe even *The Legend of Zu* (and yet *Black Mask 2, Double Team* and *The Legend of Zu* contain plenty of entertaining sequences, and some outstanding ones). Of all his attempts at remakes and updates, *The Legend of Zu* was probably a mis-use of his energy and resources. But Tsui roared back to masterpiece form with *Seven Swords,* with the *Detective Dee* movies, and with *Flying Swords of Dragon Gate.*

EDITING.

Tsui Hark's cinema seems to come from someone who never sleeps, who is never bored, who finds every aspect of living in the contemporary world fascinating, and who can operate at a higher level of energy and fever than the rest of us. Lazy, work-shy, boring and restrained are not characteristics you can hurl at Tsui! His stamina and energy are legendary.

Tsui Hark's movies are being edited as he shoots: Tsui likes to see what he's got as he films it. With digital editing workflows, Tsui and his editors can put together scenes quickly (using temporary visual effects, timing and colour grading). Versions of the film, before it's complete, can be sent to producers, distributors, visual effects houses, etc.

Baiyang Yu, Tsui Hark's editorial consultant, commented:

> We had a very good workflow going for several pictures using Final Cut Pro 7. Tsui likes to see things assembled while we shoot, and typically that involves a lot of temporary visual effects compositing, color grading, and retiming. But that meant a lot of time waiting for things to render, and Tsui doesn't like to wait.

And like many filmmakers (such as Stanley Kubrick, George Lucas and Francis Coppola), Tsui Hark likes to work on his productions right up to the very last moment. As Tsui's editor Baiyang Yu noted:

> On *Flying Swords of Dragon Gate* we went through 15 versions and ultimately had to stop when the distributor reminded us the film was about to be released. It's going to be the same for the [*Detective Dee*] prequel. Our editing will not be complete until the last possible moment. We're changing everything all the time.

Like many Chinese action movies, the movies directed and produced by Tsui Hark often employ slow motion, and also step-motion. Indeed, step-motion (a.k.a. step-printed film) occurs just as much as slow motion. True slow motion is of course filmed on the set, with the camera running at higher speeds (48 frames per second or 96 f.p.s. being typical speeds). But step-motion is created after the fact, in the editing room and by optically treating the celluloid in the processing lab (where you can also select different kinds of step-motion). Sometimes Chinese action movies play whole beats of an action scene in step-motion, but with heightened sound effects (and usually a big music cue).

POST-PRODUCTION.
As noted above, the editor of *Flying Swords of Dragon Gate*, Baiyang Yu, said that the movie went thru fifteen different versions in the editing room before they decided on the final cut. Tsui Hark is a film director who, like many filmmakers, works right up to the premiere or general release date, fine-tuning, altering, cutting, re-cutting, rewriting and re-dubbing the movie.27 So, well, yes, a Tsui Hark movie isn't really 'finished' – rather, the movie is released in the state it reached before the final, absolutely final, definitely-this-time-is-the-real-true-final date.

If they had their way, filmmakers would probably keep tinkering with their movie for days and weeks, which would drag on to months and then years. Orson Welles, Martin Scorsese, Michael Cimino and Francis Coppola, among numerous other filmmakers, liked to spend a *long* time in post-production. The trouble with that is, backers, financiers, producers and film studios start crowing for the movie that *they*, *not* the filmmakers, paid for. Yes: commercial filmmakers *don't* pay for the movies they direct and produce and write! It's the financiers, the investors, and the film studios that actually fork out the dough. Consequently, they want a return for their investment, which can only occur when the darn movie is released!

Furthermore, post-production isn't cheap! If it's just Orson Welles and an editorial assistant and one of the Movieolas that Welles carted around Europe, fine, yes, that's not too expensive. And by that time (1950s thru 1970s), Welles was operating outside of the film studio system, and working on very low budget productions.

But in the commercial film business, post-production can be costly, and can involve quite a few people (if it's a visual effects blockbuster show

---

27 Tsui Hark described post-production as a 'very sensitive, emotional stage', when you are polishing and shaping, and you are very emotionally attached to the movie (LM, 30).

in the West, we're talking sometimes hundreds of people). For a filmmaker with an established reputation and proven track record, like Tsui Hark, it's much easier to exert the power to exploit resources and man-power on a production.

A minor but significant factor in the post-production of movies from the 1990s to today is digital technology: movies are now often cut using Avid or similar systems (Tsui has employed Final Cut Pro, Apple's editing software). For a director like Tsui, this means that multiple versions of scenes and sequences can be created and organized: Tsui is the kind of director who likes to edit scenes and whole movies in a number of ways. You could still do that with celluloid and Movieolas, of course (filmmakers such as Jean-Luc Godard and Steven Spielberg like to edit using real celluloid), but digital editing systems allow for multiple versions to be saved and viewed and compared very quickly. Also, optical effects can be applied instantly, such as fades, wipes, dissolves, slow motion, speed ramping, etc (in the celluloid days, optical effects had to be sent to the film labs, so you had to wait to see them).

CHANG CHEH AND KING HU.

Two Chinese film directors loom large over Tsui Hark's output: Chang Cheh (Zhang Zhe) and King Hu, the directors who pioneered *wuxia* films. They both hailed from Northern China, spoke Mandarin, and employed the Northern styles of the Peking Opera.

Tsui Hark has re-made movies by both directors (as well as working with King Hu on *The Swordsman*), and has clearly been heavily influenced by them. But then, it's impossible for a Chinese filmmaker working in action cinema *not* to be influenced by Chang Che and King Hu – between they directed many of the classics of *kung fu* and martial arts cinema. (Also, many of the performers and crew in Tsui's movies will have worked with both directors).

King Hu (1931-1997), born in Beijing, was the director of classics such as his 'Inn Trilogy' – *Come Drink With Me* (1965), *Dragon Gate Inn* (1967) and *The Fate of Lee Khan* (1973) – and his 'Buddhist Trilogy': the epic (and, for a martial arts movie, very long) *A Touch of Zen* (1970), *Raining In the Mountain* (1979) and *Legend of the Mountain* (1979). Hu worked at Shaw Brothers.

A Touch of Zen is the movie which's King Hu's crowning achievement for many, and which was a big hit at Cannes. *A Touch of Zen* was based on the same material used for the *Chinese Ghost Story* movies: *Liaozhai Zhiyi* by Pu Songling.

For King Hu, *kung fu* was choreographed like dance: 'I've always taken the action part of my films as dancing rather than fighting', Hu said (many others, including Jackie Chan, have thought the same). For him, the tradition of the Peking Opera was crucial in developing a way of staging action in cinema. For critics, the choreography in Hu's films was movement for movement's sake, rather than exploring themes or ideas or stories: altho' Hu's movies touched on Zen Buddhism, Confucianism, chivalry, history, nationalism and the supernatural, Sek Kei remarked, they were really interested in 'a free and unfettered state'.[28]

As well as influencing how martial arts was depicted in Hong Kong cinema, Hu also emphasized roles for women in his movies (which further endears him to Tsui Hark).

Chang Cheh (b.1923, Zhejiang Province, d. 2002) developed a team of collaborators which included Lau Kar-Leung as action director (along with Tang Jia), Bao Xueii, Wu Ma and John Woo. Chang wrote many of his own scripts (often with Ni Kuang). Chang's directing career was based around *wuxia* movies, and then the *kung fu* genre (they were produced at Shaw Brothers).[29] Chang's famous works include *The One-Armed Swordsman* (1967, updated in 1970), *The Golden Swallow, The Chinese Boxer, The Water Margin, Man of Iron, The Brave Archer* and *The Assassin*. (At one time, Chang produced 70 movies in 5 years at Shaws).

The Blade is a swordplay action movie, a re-make of *The One-Armed Swordsman* (*Dubi Dao,* Chang Cheh, 1967). The Shaw Brothers' *The One-Armed Swordsman* was the first Hong Kong movie to gross U.S. $1 million in Hong Kong. *The One-Armed Swordsman* starred Jimmy Wang Yu in 'a muscular, angst-ridden epic of blood-thirsty masculinity that ushered in an entirely new sensibility for martial arts cinema', according to Jeff Yang (50).

TSUI HARK AND JOHN WOO.

One would've expected Tsui Hark to have been the filmmaker who made it biggest in North America[30] (he 'out-Spielbergs Spielberg', quipped Roy Hoban in the *Village Voice*), but John Woo seems to have made the move into the North American film industry more successfully than Tsui. Both are Chinese filmmakers with a keen sense of what works commercially, both possess a strong style, both like making genre pictures (and remaking old movies), and both deliver movies to the key market of young males. (Timing has played a part, as has the kind of movies that Woo creates – blood and guts amongst guys and cool gangsters in thriller formats, the sort of films which critics exalt, and which are perhaps easier to sell to audiences than some of Tsui's movies). As to Tsui's influence on Woo, critics such as Tony Williams have noted that Woo's films prior to *A Better Tomorrow* are undistinguished (2002, 153).

Critics trot out plenty of guff about the theme of male friendship or brotherhood in the movies directed by John Woo, but there's just as much in the cinema of Tsui Hark. Really? Sure – to cite some titles: *Lake Changjin, Knockoff, Double Team, Time and Tide, Once Upon a Time In China, Blade, Aces Go Places, Seven Swords, The Master, The Flying Swords of Dragon Gate,* and *Black Mask.* Men fighting alongside each other, men looking after each other, men competing with each other – Tsui's cinema is full of those themes (as well as the proto-feminism).

---

28 S. Kei: "Xingzhe de Guiji", *Film Biweekly*, 13, 1979.
29 They ranged from 'cookie-cutter dreck to creatively innovative masterpieces', as Rovin and Tracy put it (245).
30 Deals such as a co-production with Francis Coppola came to nothing.

Altho' John Woo's form of slow motion, balletic action is utterly compelling, it is *waaay* too slow for Tsui Hark! Tsui's metabolism in cinema runs very, very hot! While Tsui is all for stretching out big dramatic or action-fuelled moments (and much longer than in Western movies), he would never go as far as Woo and editor David Wu Tai-wai in using multiple film speeds to create lengthy, post-Eisensteinian montages of fluttering doves, spattering blood and guttering guns.

TSUI HARK AND AKIRA KUROSAWA.

That Tsui Hark is a huge admirer of the cinema of Akira Kurosawa is obvious (but who isn't?!): the whole look of Tsui's *jiangzhu* and historical pictures derives from Kurosawa's movies (from the meticulously researched costumes and props, to the use of real locations and three-dimensional sets, to the enormous emphasis on environmental elements such as wind, rain, fire and snow). Ever since he saw *Yojimbo* (1961) as a teenager, Kurosawa has been a favourite for Tsui.

For Tsui Hark, Akira Kurosawa managed to produce movies that transcended their cultural origins in Japan. Kurosawa's films are universal, Tsui said, going way beyond the limitations of language and culture (yet you can also argue that Kurosawa's movies remained *very* Japanese).

Tsui Hark has produced his own version of *The Seven Samurai* in *Seven Swords,* and of samurai classics such as *Yojimbo* and *Sanjuro* in *The Blade* and *New Dragon Gate Inn.* The way that Akira Kurosawa filmed royalty, pageants and palaces, the way that he included a huge panorama of human life, from peasants up to kings, the way that he never loses sight of the individual in the epic stories, all have been absorbed by Tsui.

Akira Kurosawa's was a grand cinema that magically crossed international borders, to become one of the great bodies of work in the second half of the 20th century. Kurosawa's cinema is also very big on action, which of course has impressed so many filmmakers as well as Tsui Hark.

Akira Kurosawa's influence has been immense on world cinema. Paul Verhoeven said he put on *Rashomon* or *The Seven Samurai* from time to time to remind himself that films could be art. Terry Gilliam spoke highly of *Rashomon.* Bernardo Bertolucci said Kurosawa (with Federico Fellini) was one of the reasons he wanted to become a film director. And John Woo said he watched the last reel of *The Seven Samurai* before making his films, for inspiration on action. The influence of Kurosawa on Woo is clear to see (a movie such as *Bullet In the Head* is distinctly Kurosawan).

There are Akira Kurosawa moments in Paul Verhoeven (the battles with bugs in *Starship Troopers*); Francis Coppola (the extravagant machine gun death of Sonny Corleone in *The Godfather* recalls Macbeth's demise by arrows in *The Throne of Blood*, or the mythical soldiers in *Apocalypse Now*); George Lucas raided Kurosawa's mediæval *samurai* for the Jedi knights in his *Star Wars* saga; the *samurai* warriors also popped up in *Brazil* (Terry Gilliam); the elaborate gun battles in John Woo's Hong Kong action cinema, and the warrior ethic also appears in John Milius's films; and Bernardo Bertolucci made his own version of a Kurosawa epic in *The Last Emperor*. Other filmmakers who've cited Kurosawa as a key influence include Hayao Miyazaki, Wes Craven and Katsuhiro Otomo.

Akira Kurosawa was one of Ingmar Bergman's favourites. Bergman said he had studied *Rashomon* dozens of times (one can detect the influence of Kurosawa on films helmed by the Swedish genius such as *The Virgin Spring* and *The Seventh Seal*). Bergman said he regretted being so heavily influenced by Kurosawa. 'I want to say now that *The Virgin Spring* was a misadventure, a wretched imitation of Kurosawa. It was a period in which I surrendered so completely to the Japanese film that I almost became a bit of a samurai myself' (*Bergman On Bergman*, 120). That seems unnecessarily harsh.

GENRES.

A large proportion of Tsui Hark's movies are action movies. Comedy is key ingredient, as is violence, along with themes such as China, Chinese culture, nationalism, women, feminism, and food.[31] Doing the right thing and how to live in the world, are key moral concerns.

A huge proportion of the movies directed and produced by Tsui Hark have been historical movies: *Detective Dee and the Mystery of the Phantom Flame, The Blade, Green Snake, The Lovers, Peking Opera Blues, Shanghai Blues, New Dragon Gate Inn, Flying Swords of Dragon Gate, The Swordsman, Zu: Warriors of the Magic Mountain, Seven Swords* and the *Once Upon a Time In China* series. (The movies set in the present day tend to be thrillers and action movies). So Tsui and his film teams have spent years and years exploring the past, from the latter part of the 19th century (in the *Wong Fei-hung* series), to the mediæval period of *The Lovers,* and the ancient world of the *Detective Dee* series.

The *jiangzhu*[32] (= martial arts world) and the *wulin* (= martial forest) is where Tsui Hark gravitates towards in history – the wandering world of a China that never really existed (depicted in *The Blade, New Dragon Gate Inn, Flying Swords of Dragon Gate, The Swordsman, Zu: Warriors of the Magic Mountain, Seven Swords, The Butterfly Murders, A Chinese Ghost Story* and *The Lovers*). Indeed, among filmmakers of his generation, no one else has spent so much time imaginatively in the *jiangzhu* as Tsui.

Tsui Hark said he's had a special affinity with *wuxia pian* since childhood: around a quarter of his output as director is martial arts/ *wuxia pian*, and many more as producer.

Wuxia means swordsman/ martial fighter/ knight-errant (*wu* = military or armed; *xia* = hero, chivalrous. Known as *Mo hap* in Cantonese). Thus, *wuxia* movies were swordplay pictures, and they tended to be filmed in Mandarin. *Kung fu*, meaning fist fighting, and were usually made in Cantonese (with the *Wong Fei-hung* movies as the typical product).

---

[31] Food? Oh yes – it's a motif in movies such as *We're Going To Eat You, Once Upon a Time In China* (eating Western food), *New Dragon Gate Inn, Iron Monkey* and *The Chinese Feast.*

[32] 'In *The Blade*, the *jiangzhu* exists in various manifestations that are no longer so abstract. It is country, community, locality; it is the person's character; it is the hero who knows how to develop his talent and achieve victory through the human dimension of speed rather than the superhuman one of flight', commented Stephen Teo (1998, 156).

Wuxia movies were regarded as more historical and 'authentic' than *kung fu* movies; their trademarks included fantasy, the supernatural, performers flying, and visual effects. *Kung fu* movies (from Canton) tended to be more 'realistic', emphasizing training and the body.

A significant proportion of Tsui Hark's movies are not only action movies, they are martial arts movies: *The Blade*, the *Detective Dee* series, *Green Snake, Flying Swords of Dragon Gate, The Butterfly Murders, Zu, Seven Swords* and the *Once Upon a Time In China* series. Most of the martial arts movies directed and produced by Tsui are set in the past.

Stephen Teo:

> Tsui Hark's world is inclusive, blending the outrageous with the normal, the paranormal (as in his horror films) with the natural world (as in *The Blade*, with its contortions of mud, sand, and wind), and the supernatural (the notion of flight), with the mundane (the notion of speed). (1998, 154)

ROMANCE.
Love. Hearts and flowers. Romance...

Altho' it's the action movies, the historical movies, the thrillers, and the visual effects extravaganzas that Tsui Hark is usually known for (all masculine genres), and celebrated by film critics (most of whom are men), his cinema is filled with love and romance. Jean-Luc Godard wondered if love between a man and a woman was actually *the* chief subject of cinema; it's true of Godard's cinema, certainly (where romantic and erotic relationships are everywhere), and also true of Tsui's cinema. (Tsui comes from a very large family, which probably influenced the depiction of families in his cinema).

There is just as much romance, love and emotion in Tsui Hark's cinema as action, spectacle, history and visual effects. Some of Tsui's finest achievements have revolved around relationships and families: *Shanghai Blues, The Lovers, Green Snake, A Chinese Ghost Story*, etc. The fantasy and adventure movies, for instance, like *Green Snake* and *A Chinese Ghost Story*, are primarily love stories, and it's the love between a man and a woman that is at the core of the stories (and is what powers the stories along). 'I think we filmmakers often find ourselves trying to fill up the missing something of the audience's emotions and psychological needs', Tsui said.

Love crops up even in the titles of Tsui Hark's movies – *Love In the Time of Twilight, The Lovers, Love and Death In Saigon*, etc. Is Tsui, for all his pioneering achievements, his technical brilliance and action-heavy filmmaking, really a softie? Yes. Even in the harsh world of the *jiangzhu* of *Seven Swords* or *New Dragon Gate Inn*, love and romance are absolutely central (*romantic* is a key term in Tsui Land. Tsui thinks that 'women are more romantic than men'; 'romantic is the most key word in everything' [LM, 22]). Is he romantic? Tsui replied that you'd have to ask his wife.

'Romantic' – the word is uppermost in Tsui Hark's conception of cinema and entertainment – alongside 'emotion'. Cinema, Tsui asserts, must be emotional, there must be an emotional investment from the audience:

> I am looking for ways to make my audience feel. If your audience doesn't have a strong feeling from your story, you fail as a storyteller.

COMEDY.

Too few critical appraisals of the cinema of Tsui Hark emphasize the importance of *comedy* his work. But comedy is everywhere in Tsui's movies: *Peking Opera Blues* is a backstage comedy, as is *Shanghai Blues*; *Aces Go Places* and *All the Wrong Clues* are Cinema City comedies; black comedy is integral to *We're Going To Eat You* and *The Butterfly Murders*; horror comedy appears in the *Chinese Ghost Story* and *Swordsman* movies; the romances contain humour (*The Lovers*, *Green Snake*, *Love In the Time of Twilight*); and comedy is found throughout the *Once Upon a Time In China* series. And Tsui Hark added humour to films he produced, such as *A Better Tomorrow* and *Iron Monkey*.

Tsui Hark is particularly fond of gags using crowds – where mobs act as one. Like the crowd gathered outside the nightclub in *Shanghai Blues* which tilts its head to follow the moving sign of a fan covering the breasts on a billboard of a showgirl; like the villagers who cower in fear behind Leslie Cheung in *A Chinese Ghost Story*; like the guys who hide behind each other when the Chief is ranting in *We're Going To Eat You*.

AVAILABILITY

A *major* problem with approaching the cinema of Tsui Hark (and all Chinese cinema) is availability. You will smack up against the issue of availability as soon as you try to see anything other than the movies released in the Western world. Most of Tsui's films (and TV work) was produced for a Chinese market: the markets of Hong Kong and Mainland China are absolutely crucial. (Hence, Tsui's films are usually released with a Cantonese and a Mandarin soundtrack, which's the norm in Chinese cinema). This doesn't mean, tho', that the movies travel outside of China, either in their original form or in dubbed versions.

The language issue – Cantonese, Mandarin, English, whatever – is a minor one compared to general availability (subtitling is yet another issue). It's true that some of the key works directed and produced by Tsui Hark are easy to obtain in the West – the *Once Upon a Time In China* series, for instance, *Zu: Warriors From the Magic Mountain, Detective Dee and the Mystery of the Phantom Flame,* and of course those produced by or in conjunction with North American distributors (such as Columbia/ TriStar/

Sony), like *Double Team* and *Knock Off*. But many important movies are not easily available in the West: *The Butterfly Murders, Peking Opera Blues, Shanghai Blues* and *Dangerous Encounters of the First Kind* (gems of China cinema like *Peking Opera Blues* should be available in supermarket racks like Disney cartoons). It doesn't get better with more recent works, either: *All About Women, In the Blue, The Warrior, Young Detective Dee: Rise of the Sea Dragon* and others of the 2000s and 2010s are hard to source in the West.

Consequently, the following movies, directed by Tsui Hark, have not been explored fully in this study: *Search For the Gods* (1983), *Working Class* (1985), *Spirit Chaser Aisha* (1986), *The Banquet* (1991), *The Chinese Feast* (1995), *Tristar* (1996), *In The Blue* (2005), and *Catching Monkey 3-D* (2013).

The issue of availability affects many celebrated filmmakers – you simply can't find many of their key works. The issue of quality is another consideration: many movies are only available in substandard prints, with bad soundtracks, or in butchered versions (some Hong Kong movies look like they were copied from beat-up release prints that have been kicking around Central for years, then re-copied onto video and back again). Despite new distribution systems like the internet, or streaming, or DVD and Bluray (or older ones like video, or broadcasting on television), it's amazing how many jewels of cinematic art remain in limbo, or are lost, or can only be bought in scrappy versions from dodgy, one-eyed Buddhist monks in the scuzzy end of town for extortionate prices.

Another issue is that the international and Western versions of Hong Kong and Chinese movies sometimes change the following: the music; the dialogue; the scripts (scripts are rewritten during dubbing); add new sound mixes; and whole scenes are dropped.

Thus often the Western/ international cuts of Asian movies are *not* in the form the filmmakers preferred. Tsui Hark has complained many times that distributors have altered his movies for releases overseas.

The practice of dubbing the sound on afterwards in Chinese movies also extends to the stars: it was many years before Chinese movie audiences heard the real voices of Jackie Chan and Jet Li, for instance. Another consequence of dubbing is that the same group of actors tend to be heard in every movie.

For research online, the Hong Kong Movie Database and Hong Kong Cinemagic are excellent (they have photos of the cast and crew, for instance – very helpful when Chinese movies are filled with unusual names (and many alternative names and spellings) in both Mandarin and Cantonese). Love Hong Kong Film has useful reviews.

CRITICAL APPROACHES TO THE CINEMA OF TSUI HARK

The critical reception/ interpretations of Tsui Hark's movies tend to use some of the following approaches:

NATIONALISM AND IDENTITY.
Chinese identity and nationalism – the 'Chineseness' in Tsui Hark's cinema.

What it means to be Chinese, what Chinese history and society is, how Chinese culture relates to the rest of the world – these're some of Tsui Hark's primary concerns, at the thematic level. Chinese identity is a theme that crops up many times in Tsui's movies – in particular how contemporary Chinese identity relates to recent Chinese history.

POLITICAL ALLEGORY.
Politics – ideology – movies as political allegories/ statements.

There are many articles discussing Tsui Hark's cinema as political allegories which explore (1) China's place in the new world order, (2) Hong Kong's political situation *vis-à-vis* Mainland China, (3) Hong Kong as a colony, and, inevitably, (4) Hong Kong during the 1997 hand-over.

Critics often draw attention to the allegorical/ analogical/ metaphorical aspects of Tsui Hark's cinema, how he includes political commentary or side-swipes at authorities, then they castigate the films for not doing more. They forget that movies are *primarily* commercial entertainment – if you want allegory/ metaphor/ political diatribes, look elsewhere. Or, if you've got the guts, make your *own* movie which features hyper-intelligent political satire, pro-socialist/ left-wing propaganda, philosophical essays and metaphysical arguments, while still being highly entertaining, state of the art technically, and cheap to produce.

'Tsui Hark is skillful in channelling the general anxiety of the people in Hong Kong into his films and in manipulating the audiences' responses', noted Leung Ping-kwan (in "Urban Cinema and the Cultural Identity of Hong Kong").[33]

Tsui Hark has not shied away from tackling ideological and political issues head-on: his series about Wong Fei-hung, for instance, *Once Upon a Time In China*, is explicitly political. And the series that sort of follows up *Once Upon a Time In China*, the *Detective Dee* films, also deliver political messages.

For Leung Ping-kwan, Tsui Hark's cinema is explicitly political:

> Among Hong Kong directors, Tsui Hark is the one most obsessed with and skilful in making films into political allegories. In films he produced or directed, in his retelling of old tales as well as in his play with mixed genres, he always weaves in indirect political commentaries as well as references to contemporary issues. (In P. Fu, 242)

A good deal of the political and ideological content of the *Once Upon a*

---
[33] In P. Fu, 242-3.

Time In China movies boils down to simple dramatic oppositions:
   West = guns (bad) ··· East = martial arts (good)
   West = technology (bad) ··· East = tradition (good)
   West = modern medicine (bad) ··· East = Chinese medicine (good)
   West = exploitation (bad) ··· East = mercantile capitalism (good)
   West = individualism (bad) ··· East = communities (good)
(And you'll find these oppositions throughout Hong Kong cinema).

The *Once Upon a Time In China* series pits the Chinese values of the family, neighbours, communities, tradition and righteousness against Western egotism, selfishness, cynicism, money, science, and negative imperialism.

ACTION, IMAGES, SPECTACLE.

'The imagery is one of the aspects I like about movies. It's like creating a virtual world with a lot of imagery, creating an illusion as well as the storytelling.'

That Tsui Hark's cinema is obsessed with creating spectacular and vivid movies everybody agrees. That Tsui is an image-obsessed filmmaker, a guy who can create extraordinary visuals with apparent ease, is central to his cinema (he has one of the most remarkable eyes for an image in film history). But this is an element of his cinema that critics find challenging to discuss, apart from making obvious statements about the beauty and power of Tsui's imagery.

As to action and choreography, Western critics are hopeless. They don't have the background knowledge of how movies are made. Many of them have probably never been on a soundstage.

And yet altho' issues like political allegory and Chinese identity are important in Tsui Hark's cinema, they are *not* the whole story! In the *Once Upon a Time In China* movies, for example, two minutes might be spent in a scene discussing China's role in the modern era (between Wong Fei-hung and a visiting dignitary, for instance), but seven minutes will be spent on a giant fight scene! And that fight scene will consume *far* more attention from the filmmakers than a little bit of dialogue about China and 20th century politics! (three days to shoot the fight scene, and half-an-hour to shoot the political discussion. Or as Jackie Chan put it, half a day for the talky bit, and four months for the action scene!).

But what will film critics talk about? – the two minutes of blether about Chinese politics! And what do audiences love? – the seven minute action sequence, where Jet Li rolls down the back of Iron Robe, or spins round a pillar twelve feet in the air, or whups the bad guys with an umbrella or a rolled-up shirt!

MORE ON ACTION.

Is Tsui Hark the finest director of action in recent cinema? Anywhere in the world? Even despite fierce competition? You could make a case that, *yes*, he is – even amongst the heavyweights of North America movies like Steven Spielberg, James Cameron, Michael Bay, Gore

Verbinski, Stephen Sommers, Michael Mann and Oliver Stone, or the token Brits (Ridley Scott), or one or two Europeans (Wolfgang Petersen, Renny Harlin, Roland Emmerich, Luc Besson, etc). Plus the stalwarts of the Hong Kong/ Chinese industry, such as John Woo, Tony Ching Siu-tung, Yuen Woo-ping, Johnny To Kei-fung, Ringo Lam Ling-tung and Jackie Chan.

You could cut together two or three full-length documentaries about martial arts and action cinema from Tsui Hark's movies alone. Or just one movie: *Knockoff* or *Time and Tide,* among the more recent contemporary thrillers, or the *Once Upon a Time In China* series, naturally.

And of course, Tsui Hark has worked with some of the great action stars – Sammo Hung Kam-bo, Jackie Chan, Jet Li, Yuen Biao, Michelle Yeoh, Jean-Claude van Damme – and some of the great action choreographers: Yuen Woo-ping, Tony Ching Siu-tung, Jackie Chan, Sammo Hung, Yuen Bun, Yuen Wah and Xiong Xin-xin.

> Action is not just by itself; action always comes with a story, it also comes with a style, it comes with extra information about what the director wants to show to the audience. These sorts of things are always with me. (2011)

MORE ON STYLE.

Tsui Hark is very much of the Akira Kurosawa School of Filmmaking – that is, plenty of natural, elemental material on screen – rain, fire, smoke,[34] wind, torchlight, candlelight, and more fire and more rain.[35] It means filming outdoors in sometimes tough conditions. It means leading the production team up mountains and across rivers. And for the actors it means quite a bit of hardship.

To achieve those Kurosawan effects requires stamina, determination, and, perhaps above all, patience (plus the resources of a fully-equipped studio with its technical staff. You can't stage this kind of production on a shoestring budget). This is perfectionist filmmaking, getting every detail right, composing scenes and frames teeming with incident and gesture.

Tsui Hark has a suitcase full of motifs and symbols which he uses – including tigers, butterflies, rain, water, the sea, funfairs, mothers and babies, goldfish and fish in tanks.

(So many of the motifs of the later historical films directed by Zhang Yimou – *Hero, House of Flying Daggers,* etc – can be found in classics of the Hong Kong New Wave cinema such as *The Terracotta Warrior,* the *Swordsman* series, the *Once Upon a Time In China* series, etc. The floating leaves, the dripping water, the rainfall, the billowing hangings of white and red cloth, the slow motion, etc.)

---

[34] Smoke in Hong Kong cinema is not a pretty effect that drifts in the background of a scene to enhance the lighting – it is used as a setting in itself, a real, physical presence in the scenes. Sometimes smoke provides the whole environment of a scene (and, yes, sometimes that billowing smoke is used to hide things).

[35] On a Hong Kong film set, electric fans are always near the camera – clothes must flap and billow.

STORYTELLING – STORIES AND CHARACTERS.

And yet, amazing as it may seem, one of the chief motivations for many filmmakers is simply storytelling. *Movies are stories.* That's all. Just stories. And *filmmakers are storytellers.* So all of the above elements and issues – the political rants, the anxiety over identity in a global marketplace, the critiques of capitalism and Communism, the exploration of women's issues or visual effects, etcetera – are all *secondary* to the *primary* concern. Which is: to *tell a story*.

Yes: that's what filmmakers do.

They tell stories.

Stories which involve characters and things happening and drama and conflicts and battles and goals and motivations and all the rest. That's one of the things that audiences crave: stories • characters • things happening.

This is the level in Tsui Hark's cinema (or any cinema) that's easiest to discuss, and doesn't require too much expertise. Everybody knows what stories they enjoy (even – *gulp!* – film critics!).

But when I say a movie is 'just a story', that doesn't under-value stories! Or filmmakers as storytellers! We love these stories, we want to hear and see these stories, we construct whole cultures and identities around these stories. (However, too many books about Hong Kong cinema focus solely on the stories and the characters, forgetting everything else. And Hong Kong movies are *supremely* and properly, fully *cinematic*. Ignoring the filmic aspects of the movies misses too much).

FURTHER THEORETICAL APPROACHES.

For those readers/ students who appreciate suggestions for theoretical approaches to subjects, here are some more:

• The relation of identity to art, to being an artist/ filmmaker.

• Approaching the issue of cultural and national identity using postmodern theory is an obvious angle for looking at Tsui Hark's cinema, and Hong Kong cinema.

• Forms of identity: psychological, social, cultural, national, historical, ethnic: for example, one could explore the relation of the Asian/ Chinese cultural identity of Tsui Hark's cinema to the issue of working as a filmmaker.

On the set of Flying Swords of Dragon Gate (above).

PART TWO

TSUI HARK

MOVIES AS DIRECTOR

1

THE BUTTERFLY MURDERS

Dip Bin

The Butterfly Murders (1979) was one of the first works that made audiences and critics sit up and take notice of Tsui Hark. *The Butterfly Murders* wasn't the first thing that our man directed (at 28/ 29 years-old), but it is usually taken as the First Significant Work helmed by Tsui.

The Butterfly Murders (*Die Bian* in Mandarin = *Butterfly Transformation*), starred Lau Siu-ming,[1] Michelle Chan (Yim), Wong Shee-tong, Cheong Kwok-chu, Mai Suet, Tsui Siu-keung and Eddie Ko Hung (he had appeared in *Golden Dagger Romance*, directed by Tsui Hark at C.T.V). It was written by Lam Chi-ming and Lam Fan (Fan Lin). Fun Chin Yu was DP. Editing by Wong Chi Hung and David Wu Wai-tai. Costumes by Kung Chuan-Kai. Action choreography by Tino Wong Cheung, Danny Chow Yun Kin, and Wong Shu Tong (and he played Tien Fung). The music was by Joseph Koo (the first of many collaborations with Tsui), Frankie Chan Fan-Kei and Jimmy Lo Kwok-Jim. Released: July 20, 1979. 88 mins.

The Butterfly Murders was produced by Ng See Yuen (known as 'N.G.'), for Seasonal Film Corporation (and co-produced by See-Kin Ng and Quan Zhang); Ng became one of the key collaborators in the cinema and television work of Tsui Hark. (The movie came about because Ng was moving into film production, with Jackie Chan's early movies, and wanted to make some more. He offered Tsui the chance to direct, and was open about the subject matter. And Tsui, as we know, will take an opportunity when it presents itself. He said he wasn't planning to make his debut in cinema like this, but there was this offer, so he took it).

Tsui Hark said that shooting *The Butterfly Murders* was not a happy experience: 'a nightmare for me': 'every day was a disaster. Some days we'd be in the air, everybody hanging on wires, and it's too dark, we don't have enough lights, and there's no crane' (LM, 37). Shooting the butterflies was tough – Tsui said they would stay in the air for 30 seconds at a time. Then they'd have to pick them all up off the ground and re-set.

---
1 The witch in *A Chinese Ghost Story*.

And filming in a volcanic region was difficult. Inevitably, Tsui later found flaws in the film, and didn't regard it as finished (but then, Tsui thinks that none of his films are 'finished'!).

The 1979 movie was made in Taiwan[2] (Tsui's first visit there), with a largely inexperienced crew. It was produced partly in ignorance and innocence, Tsui recalled – they didn't really know what they were doing. But it's not a 'low budget' production: Tsui reckoned they spent about HK $3 million (US $385,000), and he was worried that it was too much.

The Butterfly Murders is the first expression of several elements in Tsui Hark's cinema which became signature items: the elevation of female charas; nature; rapid cutting; genre updates;reworking genres (and mashing genres together); technology; and Chinese tradition (Lisa Morton, 34). And, of course, fantasy: from the beginning of his movie career, Tsui was diving wholesale into fantasy. (To the point where he says that even today he is making the same sort of material). It's notable that Tsui's first two movies have little connection to 'real life' – both *The Butterfly Murders* and *We're Going To Eat You* are very fantastical, with killer insects and crazed cannibals.

The Butterfly Murders is a monster movie in part – a horror movie in which the killer beasts this time are butterflies. In this respect, it recalls movies in the West such as *The Birds* (1963) or *Pirahna* (1978). Killer snakes, killer sharks, killer ants – even killer bees. It's a genre movie (like many other debuts of film directors). Monster movies of this ilk have been a staple of world cinema since at least the 1950s. Some directors have made them part of their regular output – Joe Dante, John Carpenter, Brian de Palma, Wes Craven, Sam Raimi, David Cronenberg, Dario Argento, George Romero, Tobe Hooper, and Abel Ferrera and of course Roger Corman (there is a *lot* of Cormanesque filmmaking in Tsui's early films, as he acknowledges).

Thus, one can place Tsui Hark's 1979 movie (and his next film, *We're Going To Eat You*) in the cycle of horror movies in the West which began with the 'slasher', 'stalk 'n' slash' and 'video nasties' (also called 'stalker', 'slice 'n' dice' films, 'body count' films, and 'teenie-kill') of the late 1970s and early 1980s. These included: the *Friday the 13th* films (1980 onwards), the *Nightmare On Elm Street*/ Freddy Kruger series (1984 onwards), the *Hallowe'en* series (1978 onwards), the *Psycho* sequels, the *Amityville Horror* films (1979 onwards), *The Exorcist* sequels (1977 onwards), *Final Exam* (1981), *My Bloody Valentine* (1981), *Deadly Blessing* (1981), *New Year's Evil* (1981), *The Burning* (1981), *Happy Birthday To Me* (1981), *Night School* (1981), *The Slumber Party Massacre* (1982), *Visiting Hours* (1982), *Driller Killer* (1979), *The Toolbox Murders* (1979), *Terror Train* (1980), *Prom Night* (1980), *Hell Night* (1981), *Graduation Day* (1981), *The Evil Dead* (1983), the *Hellraiser* films (1985 onwards), the *Lawnmower Man* series (1992 onwards), the *Candyman* films (1992 onwards), and the seminal slasher, *The Texas Chainsaw Massacre* (1974).

Economics played a large part in the revival of the horror flick in the

---

2 King Hu had filmed *A Touch of Zen* and *Dragon Gate Inn* in Taiwan.

late 1970s in the West: as soon as studios, executives and distributors saw that gorefests could be lucrative, they started to make their own, re-made earlier films, or got into endless rounds of sequels, copies and spin-offs. Splatter movies could be made cheaply: they did not require A-list stars; they could use young and largely unknown (i.e., cheap) casts; they did not require expensive sets or costumes; they could be set in pre-existing (contemporary) locations; and they did not need extensive script work or rewrites. (Most of them follow the simple formula of a girl and a monster, or a group of kids and a monster).

The Butterfly Murders, however, is much classier than your average monster/ slasher/ body count movie, tho' it uses pretty much all of the attributes of the formula, from the characters and the situations to the music and the camerawork. *The Butterfly Murders* is, in short, Tsui Hark's interpretation of a genre pic, but set within a distinctly Chinese, historical and political context,[3] and given the Hong Kong cinematic treatment (which includes some *kung fu* action, some swordplay, some Asian eccentricity and oddness, and evocations of Chinese customs and folklore). Tsui would revive this formula in movies such as the Chinese films, in *Zu: Warriors From the Magic Mountain,* in *Vampire Hunters*, in the *Detective Dee* movies, and in parts of the *Once Upon a Time In China* series.

For those interested in the later career of Tsui Hark, there are elements in *The Butterfly Murders* which would pop up in subsequent movies: the evocation of Ancient Chinese superstitions and customs, the setting in the early modern period[4] of China, the glorious, rapidfire action scenes (with many filmed at night), the spunky, female kick-ass character, the re-invention of genres (horror, mystery, historical), and visual effects.

How do you make butterflies scary? Ah, cute, li'l butterflies, so pretty, so delicate, so transient! In the *Butterfly Lovers* legend, which was the basis of Tsui Hark's 1994 love story, butterflies were employed in their usual symbolic guise as embodiments of all that is fleeting and oh-so mortal. The same aspects of symbolism are used in *The Butterfly Murders*, of course, but now the butterflies are cast as a ferocious critters, bloodsuckers, pests. They evoke bats in vampire and *Dracula* tales, as well as all of the usual poetic/ symbolic issues – such as: nature-gone-wild, retribution from the gods/ God/ fate, plagues/ disease/ contamination, etc, which have been found in horror flicks like *Jaws, Dracula, The Exorcist et al.* You can wheel in whatever allusions or interpretations you like for the butterflies – ideological, political, cultural, social, psychological – and, while fun, it doesn't make a lot of difference.

So, how do you make butterflies frightening? Oh, using the same means that filmmakers have used for ages: rapid cutting (absolutely essential – never linger!), weirdo sound effects (here, a kind of scraping/ droning effect), creepo music (vital), atmospheric lighting, and, most

---
[3] Chinese tradition is evoked throughout *The Butterfly Murders* – the butterflies, of course, plus birds, dragons, temples, feasts and embroidered silk.
[4] Thus, Tsui's first movie as director is a period piece.

important of all, actors *reacting* horrifically to the horror.

Yes, that's the single most effective ingredient in the genres of horror/ thrills/ suspense: have your actors going nuts. Because, let's face it, butterflies aren't the scariest of critters. Giant, slathering aliens, yes, stampeding T-rexes and velociprators, yes, insane, serial killer mutants wielding axes, yes. So the filmmakers have used real butterflies, chucked in front of the camera (and blown by fans), dead ones or models taped to the set, and that old stand-by of amateur filmmakers, animals floating on strings.

Butterflies have their limits as fearsome opponents, and when the writers have exhausted the possibilities of fluttery butter-bugs attacking yet another hapless victim (amidst plentiful flailing of arms and screaming – *errr*, how about covering up your face, neck and hands with thick clothing? How about giving everyone a cloak or netting?), they introduce a masked, mysterious, ninja-style baddie in a black costume. Which leads to some of the finest action scenes in *The Butterfly Murders* – an outstanding smackdown in a small room, a lengthy duel with wires between Green Shadow and the villain outdoors (a scene where Michelle Chan really shines), and a rooftop bust-up between Fong Sai-yuk and the black knight.

What makes *The Butterfly Murders* work is a combination of elements: the script, above all, which takes the topic seriously; the actors playing it straight; the technical aspects (such as the gorgeous, widescreen cinematography and lighting); and the attention spent on texture and atmosphere (*The Butterfly Murders* has atmosphere to spare – from the outset of his film career, this was one of Tsui Hark's major considerations. When he walks onto a set, he's got to have smoke, intricate lighting, flickering light, and art direction which layers sets with masses of detail. DP Fun Chin Yu and his team contribute enormously to the textural look of *The Butterfly Murders* – especially in the cavern scenes, where there is a *lot* of creeping about with candles, horror movie-style).

❂

This being a Tsui Hark outing, *The Butterfly Murders* features a prominent role for an actress: it's the gift of a role to Michelle Chan, playing the hero's sidekick, Green Shadow. *The Butterfly Murders* is among the earliest of Tsui Hark's many evocations of superheroes, or characters who act like superheroes, or who have superhero powers: Wong Fei-hung, Black Mask, Asia the Invincible, etc. The lovely Chan is an appealing sidekick,[5] with a sly charm that undercuts the solemn approach of the hero (take the scene where Green Shadow is introduced: she is leaping about the trees on wires, ninja-style, while Fong Sai-yuk just stands there; she is all motion, he is all stasis).

It's true that *The Butterfly Murders* is not only played completely straight, it is somewhat lacking in humour.[6] But then, maybe that's due to audience expectations – in North American movies of this type (especially ones from the 1980s onwards), quips and jokes are common (however,

---
5 Tho' she's given a glam make-up job more suited to a daytime soap opera.
6 Michelle Chan, tho', plays Green Shadow with a flirtatious tone at times.

Lau Siu-ming does play Fong Sai-yuk as a rather strait-laced and unemotive character). But Tsui Hark said he liked the staginess of the actors standing there and declaiming.

In *The Butterfly Murders*, our heroes end up at the home of Lord Shum, which's being attacked by the killer butterflies. The building acts as the haunted house or Dracula's castle for much of the piece (physically containing horror is another fundamental ploy – horror in wide-open spaces, under big skies, is harder to evoke than the traditional dimly-lit, shadowy cave/ castle/ tunnel/ tomb).

In this early pic, Tsui Hark displays his penchant for staging action scenes at night – and, well, any scenes at night (for all the obvious reasons). However, on this production, cinematographer Fun Chin Yu and his team are really struggling to light[7] the outdoor night scenes, which demand massive amounts of light (for the Green Shadow versus the black warrior sequence, for instance, where the villain is in black against a black sky, and they are moving across huge areas of the exterior set).

The first act of *The Butterfly Murders* is rather slow narratively, in terms of Tsui Hark's later movies, as the set-up is introduced, plus the customary exposition, the characters, and several flashbacks depicting the butterfly attacks.

The Butterfly Murders is marred by a ridiculously long exposition scene towards the end of act two. It has a character speaking in monologue for what seems to be 20 pages of script while everybody esle stands around and listens. Sure, the filmmakers keep the guy moving a little, and change the camera angles, but it is still an amazingly lengthy scene – especially for a filmmaker like Tsui Hark, who's renowned for rapid movement.[8] Thankfully, the end of this boring scene is announced by the arrival of the warrior-in-black. (*Boring?* A 'boring' scene in a Tsui Hark-directed movie?! Yes, but Tsui has far less scenes of this kind than 99% of filmmakers. Even the 'greats', even Alfred Hitchcock, that supreme master of suspense and advocate of cinema as visual storytelling, have talky scenes which deflate tension and interest).

The finale of *The Butterfly Murders* is of course a Giant Fight – or, rather, one fight after another, as the black knight takes on Fong Sai-yuk, then the Green Shadow, and then many others (there's also a guy wielding fire/ explosives). All of this plays within the tight confines of the tunnels underneath Shum Castle. And of course the building is collapsing around their ears. No need to reprise the killer butterflies – instead, a killer bird will do! (Yes, and it's a bird fitted with explosives! Hong Kong action filmmakers like nothing better'n blowing stuff up, and there're plenty of scenes in *The Butterfly Murders* of Stuff Blowing Up!).

Lisa Morton summed up *The Butterfly Murders* thus: 'it practically burns with the excitement of a gifted young filmmaker who loves movies and wants to pay homage to an art form he simultaneously challenges on

---

7 Ngai Cheng-Biu oversaw the lighting.
8 Novice directors often make this mistake. But at 29, Tsui Hark wasn't really a novice anymore. He had already directed TV shows.

several levels' (LM, 34). *The Butterfly Murders* was 'pure fantasy with a touch of parody, meant as a tribute both to the martial arts genre and Hollywood' (Stephen Teo).[9]

SIDE-NOTE ON FONG SAI-YUK: *The Butterfly Murders* features legendary hero Fong Sai-yuk, tho' it's not known as a *Fong Sai-yuk* movie. The *Fong Sai-yuk* cycle of movies ran from 1938 to 1972 (the first *Fong Sai-yuk* movie was in 1928: *Fong Sai Yuk's Battle In the Boxing Ring*). The black-and-white *Fong Sai-yuk* movies (just under 30 of them) starred Shi Yanzai as the Southern Chinese *kung fu* hero. Other actors who played Fong Sai-yuk (mainly on telly from the 1970s onwards) included Wong Yu, Alexander Fu Sheng and Leslie Cheung.

The two *Fong Sai-yuk* movies[10] of the early 1990s were clearly created in the wake of the *Once Upon a Time In China* series: you can see how film producers, studios and distributors in Hong Kong would've noted just how much the *Once Upon a Time In China* movies were making at the box office, and set their writers to work on the challenge of coming up with something similar. Then they put together an impressive package of star Jet Li (Wong Fei-hung himself!), top flight director Corey Yuen (Yuen Kwai in Cantonese), a strong supporting cast, and the now-familiar, magical mix of elements of the *Once Upon a Time In China* movies: action + spectacle + romance + comedy + Chinese tradition/ history + politics.

Fong Sai-yuk (Corey Yuen Kwai, 1993) is yet another masterpiece of Hong Kong cinema, a perfect blend of action, comedy, drama, romance and spectacle. *Fong Sai-yuk* is a feel-good, high entertainment outing that unrolls at a thousand miles an hour in gorgeous colour and blink-and-you-miss-it movement. It has a beautifully written script (by Lam Chi-ming and Lam Fan), a cleverly worked out plot, and some tender, romantic scenes (as well as tragic beats) in amongst the action. It boasts an outstanding cast headed up one of the great duos of recent Asian cinema – Jet Li and Josephine Siao. So that *Fong Sai-yuk* isn't only an updating of another mythical Chinese hero and *kung fu* genius (like the *Once Upon a Time In China* movies, to which it refers a few times), it is also a mother-and-son comedy – but a mom and son who act more like bickering but affectionate siblings (and a movie with a powerful subplot about families, filial devotion, and loyalty to a cause which opposes an oppressive political regime).

Fong Sai-yuk may have been tough to shoot, as the filmmakers attest, but they manage to hide all the hardship behind scenes of joyously dynamic action and charmingly intimate comedy between seasoned veterans and try-anything newcomers.

---

9 In P. Fu, 2002, 105.
10 In the West *Fong Sai-yuk* was re-titled *The Legend* (a useless, generic title).

2

WE'RE GOING TO EAT YOU

Dei Yuk Mo Moon

We're Going To Eat You (*Diyu Wu Men* in Mandarin = *Hell No Door*, a.k.a. *No Door To Hell*, *Hell Has No Gates*, *Kung Fu Cannibals*, 1980) was produced by Ng See Yuen and Kuen Cheung for Seasonal Film Corporation, and written by Roy Szeto Cheuk-hon and Tsui Hark. Action dir. by Corey Yuen Kwai and Chin Yuet Sang. Music by Frankie Chan Fan-kei. Editing by Hung Poon. Hung-Chuen Lau and Law Wan-Shing were the DPs. Art dir. by Yuen-Tai Ting. Costumes by Shui-Lin Lo. Make-up by Ko Siu-Ping. Sound fx editing by Kuo-Hua Wu. Yu Ting was Cantonese dubbing editor. Released Apl 2, 1980. 86 mins.

We're Going To Eat You starred Norman Chu Shiu-keung (as Agent 999), Eddie Ko-hung[11] (as the Chief), Melvin Wong (as Rolex), Siu Gam (as the giant), Fung Fung (the priest), Hon Gwok Choi (as the Wanderer With the Dark Glasses), Michelle Mai Suet (a.k.a. Yim, as Eileen, a.k.a. Ah Lin), Tam Tin Nam and Baan Yun Sang.

We're Going To Eat You was the second film directed by the 29 year-old Tsui Hark, and the second film he helmed to be released in 1980 (the other was *Dangerous Encounter of the 1st Kind* in Dec, 1980). So Tsui was certainly saying 'yes' to offers of work, and was happy to work like mad.

All three movies – *The Butterfly Murders*, *We're Going To Eat You* and *Dangerous Encounter – 1st Kind* – express anger and uncertainty, and they explore the shadowy sides of humanity. The amount of aggression and violence, plus of course blood and gore, is striking. Self-loathing, too, and a very ambiguous attitude towards authority and even society (which is expressed as blunt political satire). Stokes & Hoover dub *Dangerous Encounters – 1st Kind* 'an unrelentingly violent urban realist, anti-colonial rant' (36). These are the movies that 'mark him down clearly as an opinionated, thoughtful and downright political filmmaker', as Lisa Morton put it (LM, 15).

---

11 Eddie Ko had appeared in *Golden Dagger Romance*, helmed by Tsui. He pops up in *The Swordsman 3*.

Each of the three early Tsui Hark movies exhibit powerful horror ingredients – perhaps reflecting the era (1979-80), when the horror genre enjoyed the height of its popularity in the West, and stalker/ slasher movies seemed to be everywhere (and horror movies were making plenty of $$$$, entering the top 25 movies of the years from 1978 onwards).

So when Hong Kong producers looked round and saw that North American and European horror movies were making so much money, and were obviously easier and cheaper to make than many other genres, they joined the gold rush (or blood rush). (Do the math: *Hallowe'en* (1978) cost $320,000 but made $47 million domestic and $75m worldwide; which put *Hallowe'en* at no. 6 in 1978, in the company of the top-grossing flicks in the U.S.A. like *Superman, Grease* and *Jaws 2* – and *Superman* cost $55 million!).

Filmed partially in the New Territories (the forested shorelines and vine-infested woodlands are very familiar in Hong Kong movies), *We're Going To Eat You* displays many of Tsui Hark's cinematic flourishes: self-consciously flamboyant camerawork, kinetically-staged fights, rapid cutting, goofy humour, and re-hashing of well-worn film genres (*kung fu*, horror, comedy, etc).

The influences on *We're Going To Eat You* are easy to spot: Roger Corman cheapies[12] (*We're Going To Eat You* had 'a lot of Roger Corman elements' in it, Tsui Hark said); 1970s flicks like *The Texas Chainsaw Massacre* (and many other N. American horrors, including of course the George Romero zombie flicks); Spaghetti Westerns; and the Italian movies of directors like Mario Bava and Dario Argento (*We're Going To Eat You* takes much of its soundtrack from *Suspiria* (1976), a technical *tour-de-force*, one of Argento's operatic flicks, with music by Argento and Goblin. Why? Because there wasn't the budget for a composer, or to licence music for *We're Going To Eat You*).

(Side-note: Dario Argento is a favourite director with filmmakers – he's a 'filmmaker's filmmaker': innovative, bold, anarchic, wicked, and possessing bags of flamboyant style in the baroque, Italian manner. Argento's cinema, like Tsui's, revels in the sheer joy of telling stories with the biggest train set a boy ever had.[13] Argento, too, is a master of updating genre pictures like Tsui, dressing up old chestnuts in shiny, new clothing. And Argento, like Tsui, has been very influential – his influence is all over North American horror cinema, for instance).

We're Going To Eat You is the first movie displaying a very important ingredient in Tsui Hark's cinema: comedy. The humour is introduced immediately in *We're Going To Eat You*: altho' the opening scene, depicting the hunt and capture and butchery of the first two victims of the cannibals, is played fairly straight, it also contains comedic elements,[14] which signal, clearly, that the filmmakers aren't taking this completely

---

12 Corman would probably have used the title *Kung Fu Cannibals*.
13 And Argento, like Tsui, doesn't care if the elaborate lighting is coloured blue and red and looks too obviously theatrical.
14 *We're Going To Eat You* opens with a shot of a guy pissing.

seriously.15

The tone of *We're Going To Eat You* is perfectly judged – it's very black humour, and crude, too, and tasteless, but it's funny. The actors play it just right, staying just this side of going too broad.

And *We're Going To Eat You* is also a *kung fu* actioner, tho' slanted towards *kung fu* comedy – sections of *We're Going To Eat You* might be cut into Jackie Chan's *kung fu* comedies of the period and fit perfectly (such as *Drunken Master* and *Snake In the Eagle's Shadow*).

Tsui Hark said he had been asked by the film producer (Ng See Yuen) to make a *kung fu* actioner. Somehow, though, the production ended up as a political satire: 'I was thinking we were actually shooting a martial arts action movie, but it ended up as a political satire' (LM, 40).

As a political satire, *We're Going To Eat You* is delightfully blunt – this is satire like a meat cleaver smashing into muscle and bone. *We're Going To Eat You* is Tsui Hark's *Battle of Algiers* (Gillo Pontecorvo, 1965), his *Weekend* (Jean-Luc Godard, 1967), his *Salò* (Pier Paolo Pasolini, 1975), his *kung fu* comedy as horror movie as political assault, where everybody is running around wearing a silly mask16 (made of human skin),17 screaming incoherently as they wave knives and cleavers, hooks and pitch forks, spears and nets, trying to bring down any humans to use as fresh meat. (Why have one screaming madman, *à la Texas Chainsaw Massacre*, when you have whole hordes of them?!). All of the inhabitants of the island of cannibals are depicted as dopey – all they care about is food. Not just any food – *meat*! (Yet Tsui would revisit this territory of mad outlaws in his epic tale of post-World War Two China in *The Taking of Tiger Mountain*).

As with other movies that take up cannibalism as a motif – *Weekend*, *Salò*, *Blow Out* (Marco Ferreri, 1974), *Delicatessen* (Jeunet & Caro, 1990), *The Cook, The Thief, His Wife and Her Lover* (Peter Greenaway, 1989), *Consuming Passions* (Giles Foster, 1988), *The Silence of the Lambs* (Jonathan Demme, 1991), and zombie flicks – political satire seems almost mandatory. Meat-people-exploitation-authority-control-survival and all of the other obvious issues are mashed together in one big, ideological pie. In *We're Going To Eat You*, the targets, as critics are quick to point out, include the People's Republic of China, Chinese Communism (and Communism in general). But they are extended, as in other cannibal yarns, to advanced capitalist societies. (We are all cannibals is an oft-heard view, and it's also expressed in *We're Going To Eat You*).

We're Going To Eat You is also a shamelessly schoolboyish movie, with a mental age of eleven, and where humanity is reduced to the state of Stone Age guys waving knives and bellowing like idiots as they chase after their lunch. The action features numerous dumb gags involving severed limbs, eviscerated organs, slashings and impalements (the cartoony action reflects Tsui Hark's love of comicbooks).

You *can* talk about the political satire elements of *We're Going To Eat*

---

15 Another Tsui-ian motif is the giant dressed in traditional, Chinese costume – with the threat of male rape being played for laughs, as s/he corners victims and seduces them.
16 Masks of course hide the stunt guys and actors, so they can be continually replaced.
17 A nod to *The Texas Chainsaw Massacre*, perhaps.

You, but, really, come on, folks, if you wanted to deliver a truly serious critical appraisal of Communism, or Communism in the People's Republic of China, or political systems, or capitalist societies, would you do it in a movie filled with comical *kung fu* action and Stone Age men wielding meat cleavers?

Maybe you would! But nobody would take you seriously. You might be better off making a documentary, a painting, a stage play, etc., forms which might be taken straight by audiences. Truth is, using cannibalism as political satire in this sort of comic/ horror/ *kung fu* mishmash is a non-starter at the conceptual stage. Cannibalism is deployed as too broad a motif in *We're Going To Eat You* (as it is in many other movies which use it).

❖

The first act of *We're Going To Eat You* rocks along at the pace we've come to expect from Tsui Hark and his teams: it contains a whole bunch of action scenes: two victims being chased (one's killed, the other's diced up on the slab); Agent 999 being strung up from trees and fighting a masked madman; the 'Wanderer With the Dark Glasses' (as the credits have him, played by Hon Gwok Choi) encountering a crossdressing giant (Siu Gam) and barely escaping, yelling, 'rape!'; Agent 999 fighting off a mass of islanders in the office; and act one climaxes with an insane one-man-versus-hordes action sequence.

The script of *We're Going To Eat You* is at its weakest in that traditional weak spot, act two (here, it's the second half of act two). Because once the set-up has been evoked, once the characters and their goals are in place, and the obstacles that mount up for Agent 999, at the end of act one, the movie demands, like all genre movies do, further obstacles, complications, and developments. This is where really good screenwriters and filmmakers show what they're made of, and where lesser writers and filmmakers come unstuck. In *We're Going To Eat You*, there is simply a little too much creeping thru dark rooms or running about at night down brick-lined corridors, and even the fights, impressive as they are, become repetitive (the Wanderer has his own adventures, for example – hunted down, captured, put in prison, escaping, encountering a blind man (Siu-Ming To), etc. And, like the Wanderer, Agent 999 has an unwelcome tryst with the giant/ess).

One of the complicating elements in act two of *We're Going To Eat You* is the introduction of the only significant female character, Eileen/ Ah Lin (Michelle Mai Suet a.k.a. Yim). But the scenes between Eileen and Agent 999 go nowhere in particular (later, Eileen becomes the princess to be rescued, as Agent 999 acts the knight in shining armour).

We're Going To Eat You ends exactly as you'd expect it to: the cannibals eat the heroes, including poor Eileen, and then they dance naked round a colossal bonfire. No – of course there's a giant *kung fu* fight between the heroic Agent 999 and the villainous Chief[18] (one of those hero-vs.-villain smackdowns that run on far longer than they would do in a

---

[18] There's a gag where the Chief is reading *King Oedipus* and weeping, saying it's not easy being the leader.

Western movie, with literally 100s of moves). The Chief has no chance of triumphing (he's nobbled by falling on his own spear), and in another raw steak-sized slice of black humour, his corpse is torn apart by the perpetually hungry cannibals.

For the other charas, there are massed battles featuring roller skates and Chinese fireworks – oh man, you had to be there! It's completely dumb, as the mad horde of man-eaters is scared away by the heroes lighting fire crackers and chucking them on the floor like it's Chinese New Year or another Lion Dance Festival, gleefully destroying every iota of suspense. As our heroes flee on a raft, there's a final fight, and a final gory gag, with Eileen gouging out her victim's heart (and seeming to offer it to Agent 999 as the kind of gift a cannibal'd give. That's a call-back to the early scene depicting the Chief and Eileen – what does she ask of her lover? A heart – no, *two* hearts – and she's not talking metaphorically! She means two real human hearts!). It's typical of the wicked Tsui Hark that the very last shots of *We're Going To Eat You* should be a woman cutting out a still-beating heart and presenting it lovingly to the viewer.

(Side-note: there's a Wong Fei-hung reference in the chaotic *melée*, and the famous Wong music – 'Under General's Orders' – starts up; it's the first appearance of a Wong-related gag in Tsui Hark's career, in what later became his signature work.

In fact, towards the end of *We're Going To Eat You*, the sound editors give up on using the bought music seriously, and there are several music-related gags (including the music suddenly starting and stopping).)

3

DANGEROUS ENCOUNTER – 1ST KIND

Dai Yat Lui Ying Ngai Him

At that time I was quite angry, and I tried to do something anarchistic. When you don't care what you put on the screen, a heavy burden is lifted from your shoulder, and you start to make film like a student. And that becomes effective in some way.

Tsui Hark (1997, 134)

PRODUCTION.
Dangerous Encounter – 1st Kind (1980, Mandarin: *Diyi Leixing Weixian = First Kind of Danger,* a.k.a. *Dangerous Encounter of the First Kind, Don't Play With Fire* and *Playing With Fire*) was co-written by Tsui Hark and regular collaborator Roy Szeto Cheuk-hon, produced by Thomas Wing-Fat Fung (for Fotocine Film Production Limited), with David Chung Chi-Man as DP, action directed by Tony Ching Siu-tung, and directed by Tsui. Edited by Cheung Kan Chow and Wai Wu Tsi. Art dir. by Tony Au Ting-Ping. Make-up by Man Chuen Chow. Hair by Tak-Hing Yeung. Music by Siu-Lam Tang and Leun Yu. Some of the music was from *Dawn of the Dead* (1979), composed by Goblin and Dario Argento.[19] It starred Lin Zhenqi, Lo Lieh, Tse Bo Law, Lung Tin Sang, Au Siu Keung, Ray Lui, Bruce Barron, and Richard Da Silva. Released Dec 4, 1980. 92 mins.

    Dangerous Encounter – 1st Kind is a stunning piece of work. It's an angry, black comedy[20] featuring a disturbed, young woman, Wan Chu, ak.a. Pearl (Lin Zhenqi/ Lin Ching)[21] who blackmails three losers in their

---

[19] One of the versions of *Dangerous Encounter – 1st Kind* has an electronic soundtrack (of the usual moody synthesizers), augmented by slices of Pink Floyd (from 'Echoes'), the Alan Parsons Project and Jean Michel Jarre (from *Oxygene*).
[20] 'Tsui Hark's darkest film (it's *anybody's* darkest film)' (Lisa Morton, 44).
[21] Lin Zhenqi was an actress at Shaw Brothers Studio (from 1974-1982); she retired from movies not long after *Dangerous Encounter – 1st Kind*. Born in 1955, she is too old to be a teenager, but the movie gets away with it.

late teens, Paul (Albert Au), Ah Lung (Tin Sang Lung) and Ah Ko (Paul Che), into a series of hijinks and juvenile delinquency which rapidly escalate into mayhem (Wan Chu happens to be the younger sister of a cop, Tan, played by Lo Lieh).

There are thus five charas in *Dangerous Encounters – 1st Kind*:
- Wan Chu – the anti-heroine
- Ah Ko – the three accomplices
- Ah Lung   "   "
- Paul   "   "
- Tan – a cop, the anti-heroine's brother

The performances of the central quartet of kids in *Dangerous Encounter* are stellar – this movie completely convinces at the level of performance (and the casting is dead-on, too). So much depends on the characterization of Wan Chu, and Lin Zhenqi nails it. She gets the tone, the subtlety, the anger perfectly. And she has attitude to spare. You buy it that she is a very dangerous character, despite being a slim-built, short girl (if she survives, and grows up, she'll be running the fiercest Triad syndicate in all Asia).

Dangerous Encounter – 1st Kind benefits from some lively location shooting in contemporary Hong Kong (there are few studio sets for this low budget picture).[22] And Tsui Hark's eye for an arresting image, for moving the camera, and for using every trick that cinema offers, is very much in evidence in this his third feature movie.

Dangerous Encounter – 1st Kind is also an action movie – there are many scenes which are dramatized and choreographed in an action-based manner, using the body moving dynamically in space (way above the requirements of the narrative). One of Tsui Hark's regular collaborators, Tony Ching Siu-tung, was one of the action directors (they had already worked in television by this time; this was their first feature film together). In a Western movie, the juvenile delinquency of Wan Chu might involve a lot more talk then a bit of action at the end of a scene; in *Dangerous Encounter – 1st Kind,* the actors (like the camera), are moving all the time.

THE SCRIPT.

Dangerous Encounter – 1st Kind is an original concept in the Tsui Hark canon – it's not an adaptation of an ancient folktale (*The Lovers*), a remake of famous martial arts epics (*The Blade* or *Dragon Gate Inn*), or an update of a national hero's story (*Once Upon a Time In China*).

The script is, once again, classical in construction. For instance, the act one closer is dead on time: it occurs at 26 minutes and has the narrative hook of Wan Chu announcing to the boys: 'there are lots of funny things to do'. (The narrative hook perfectly sets up act two of *Dangerous Encounter – 1st Kind,* that there are lots of funny things to do).

Dangerous Encounter – 1st Kind demonstrates for all to see that the combo of Roy Szeto Cheuk-hon and Tsui Hark *as writers* is very powerful: *Dangerous Encounter – 1st Kind* explodes largely because the *script* is so

---

22 The budget for *Dangerous Encounter – 1st Kind* was likely fairly small; there are no stars, for instance, and the four main characters are all young actors (i.e., dead cheap).

solid, so inventive. First, the *concept* is granite-hard: if you start with something so good, you are most of the way there.[23] Second, the narrative develops the concept with total confidence (it includes the necessary dramatic elements of, for instance, escalating violence, complicating events, unexpected twists and all the rest of the list to tick off in the screenwriters' manual). Third, it performs all of the functions of a great script – it thrills, teases, amuses and startles.

From the outset, with *The Butterfly Murders*, Tsui Hark enters the world of cinema as a master showman – and by the time of the outrageously black material in both *We're Going To Eat You* and *Dangerous Encounter – 1st Kind,* his talent is almost scary it's so good. (As Stephen Teo noted, Tsui certainly has the 'devil's talent'!).

Dangerous Encounter – 1st Kind is a black comedy, but there are some moments of genuine sadism and dissidence. It's a movie made by a totally confident group of filmmakers (Tsui Hark was 30 at the time); these guys *really* know what they're doing! There's no flab or fat in *Dangerous Encounter – 1st Kind,* no meandering, no wandering off the point (and not even much milking moments for every ounce of dramatic juice). Instead, *Dangerous Encounter – 1st Kind* is too busy telling its compelling story (it's almost anti-bombastic filmmaking, avoiding the bathos and sentiment that scuppers all too many movies). And, once again, it's the *rapid pacing* that helps to prevent *Dangerous Encounter – 1st Kind* from out-staying its welcome.

'Bluntly put, *Dangerous Encounter* is probably the most nihilistic film ever made', reckoned Lisa Morton, with only *Dawn of the Dead* being comparable in terms of 'sheer, numbing, anarchic violence', making *Dangerous Encounter* 'among the most compelling 90-minutes of film in all of cinema' (LM, 41).

AN INCENDIARY MOVIE – LITERALLY!

Bombs, terrorism, rebellion, anger, anti-sociality, and anti-authoritarianism, *Dangerous Encounter – 1st Kind* sticks its finger up at a host of moral figures (including parents and adults). *Dangerous Encounter – 1st Kind* coalesces a bunch of social tensions, including the younger vs. older generation, the individual vs. the mass, femininity against masculinity, Hong Kong vs. the People's Republic of China, teens vs. authority, etc. (The rebellious, anti-social fury in *Dangerous Encounter – 1st Kind* is reminiscent of the 1960s movies of Jean-Luc Godard, when Jean-Pierre Léaud, Anne Wiazemsky, Anna Karina, Jean-Paul Belmondo and many others would get up to similar pranks, usually with a passionate Maoist, Marxist, anti-capitalist agenda).

Other movies which come to mind with a similarly bleak outlook include the zombie movies of George Romero, and *A Short Film About Killing* (Krzysztof Kieslowski, 1988). Plus some of Ingmar Bergman's angrier films (such as *Persona*, 1967). And perhaps *A Clockwork Orange* (1971).

---

[23] That's the biggest challenge of a movie – coming up with that initial, white-hot idea.

Stephen Teo called *Dangerous Encounter – 1st Kind* 'a film made with extreme prejudice, it did not whitewash its nastiness or its vision of a miasmic social reality' (1997, 164). It was a film which placed 'youth within a society that despises youth, building up a relentless momentum of emotion in the process' (ib., 148). Lisa Morton described *Dangerous Encounter* thus: 'the bleak, nihilistic, ultraviolent and finally wrenchingly tragic film was a fireball captured on silver nitrate, one of the most incendiary films ever made' (11). Chuck Stephens called *Dangerous Encounter – 1st Kind* 'Tsui's greatest, weirdest film, a true psychotronic wonder' (F. Dannen, 409).

Dangerous Encounter – 1st Kind ran into censorship problems (including in its home territory of Hong Kong),[24] after it had been screened at the Berlin Film Festival. A re-cut version appeared in 1981 (it was thus Tsui's fourth theatrical release). Tsui and the team went back and re-edited *Dangerous Encounter – 1st Kind,* and also re-shot the plot about the foreign gun-runners, to make the piece more palatable (and also lessening the depiction of the three youths as bomb makers and teenage terrorists; new scenes involving the Hong Kong cops were included, taking the emphasis away from the kids; that Tsui was born in Vietnam and the Yanks are Vietnam War veterans is part of the political subtext of *Dangerous Encounter – 1st Kind*).

Dangerous Encounter – 1st Kind was a flop at the box office (like Tsui's other two movies as director of the time). However, *Dangerous Encounter – 1st Kind,* like *The Butterfly Murders* and *We're Going To Eat You*, showed that Tsui Hark was just getting started!

ANGER.

Like other early Tsui Hark movies, *Dangerous Encounter – 1st Kind* is much less known in the Western world than later outings such as *Once Upon a Time In China* or *New Dragon Gate Inn* (being a flop at the box office didn't help). But it's worth seeking out for its vivid, abrasive, aggressive and highly cinematic qualities, its evocation of the scuzzier, grittier sides of Hong Kong, its portrait of youngsters seeking a place and an identity in the hard and heartless Big City and the tough, contemporary, Asian world, its dramatization of the tensions between the younger and the older generations, and of course its unsuppressed social and political anger.

I was so angry, angry with myself, angry with everybody in the industry. (Tsui Hark, LM, 45)

Like *Rome, Open City* or *The Battle of Algiers*, *Dangerous Encounter – 1st Kind* is a movie with Something To Say (tho' it is not a 'message

---

[24] There was a coda to *Dangerous Encounter – 1st Kind* which evoked the 1967 riots in Hong Kong, which the authorities also didn't like. As Leung Ping-kwan put it, the newsreels 'provide the audience with the political and social contexts for a better understanding of the anger and anxieties expressed in the film and the raw yet daring efforts of the director to define the urban space of Hong Kong'. ("Urban Cinema and the Cultural Identity of Hong Kong", in P. Fu, 239).

movie', and it doesn't preach to its audience like too many Western movies branded as 'political' do).

Dangerous Encounter – 1st Kind may be 'realistic', but that is only a product of the surface element of filming on location in contemporary Hong Kong with characters that appear to be 'contemporary'. In fact, *Dangerous Encounter – 1st Kind* is very heightened, improbable and fantastical cinema.

'NO MICE WERE HARMED IN THE MAKING OF THIS MOVIE.'
Maybe – but don't bet on it!

This is a film that opens with cute, white mice having pins pushed through them, in amongst a series of gloomy-ugly images – barbed wire, a heavy storm, neighbours being pranked, shabby tenements – while a newcaster relates that day's horror stories of death and destruction (including darkly compelling news stories about schoolboys who drowned in a quarry). *Dangerous Encounter – 1st Kind* announces from the outset that this is a horrible world, and it's horrible at home as well as outside.

WAN CHU.

At the centre of *Dangerous Encounter – 1st Kind* is the young woman Wan Chu,[25] who's full of barely suppressed rage (and a search for identity) which is exhibited in a range of anti-social behaviour. (From the opening minutes, when we see Wan Chu torturing pet mice in her den, she moves on to throwing a cat out of her fourth story window so it's impaled on a barbed wire fence and expires with monster-loud screeches. She is one nasty girl!).

That her brother Tan is a key authority figure, a cop (tho' a cool, charismatic, but not particularly successful one), is a dramatic cliché (but it works). That there are no parental presences in Wan Chu's life is significant (meanwhile, one of the three boys, Ah Lung, doesn't get on well with his folks or his home life at all).

Wan Chu is one of the most vivid portraits of a strong woman in Tsui Hark's cinema (and a gift to actress Lin Zhenqi), and the 1980 movie probably works partly because of the gender reversal. That it's three guys being manipulated by a young woman is a classic Tsui-ian approach to the story (as Tsui put it, a woman throwing a spear is just more interesting than a guy throwing it. Tsui feels very strongly about reversing the arrangement of gender in cinema).[26]

Dangerous Encounter – 1st Kind depicts Wan Chu as effortlessly ahead of the boys every time, from the moment she first meets them after their cinema prank. For ex, inviting them to her digs,[27] she pulls a gun on them. Ah, it's only a plastic toy, one of them replies. Wrong! Wan Chu has

---

[25] Placing Pearl at the centre of this bleak view of life 'flies in the face of all Western film convention' (Lisa Morton, 44).
[26] Hayao Miyazaki feels the same: a woman wielding a weapon is automatically more compelling than a man, he says.
[27] Wan Chu sees the lads nervously performing a prank involving a timed bomb in a crowded cinema, and she knows that she can bring them into her twisted realm. (The movie showing in the cinema is a thunderously loud war movie, cleverly reminding us that it's war everywhere in the real world).

modified it so it can shoot needles, and she pulls the trigger and smashes a glass behind them as they duck. And what Wan Chu wants from the boys – this is great screenwriting – is for them to be her friends. (The lads don't know what Wan Chu is going to do or say next, but none of them were expecting that! Nor that Wan Chu would be dangling a wriggling mouse in front of them, which she's just pierced!).

A girl in a world of boys – surely the issue of love/ romance/ sex is going to raise its ugly-pretty head? It does – *Dangerous Encounter – 1st Kind* needs to get the issue of love and sex out of the way early on, to demonstrate that this movie isn't about girls and boys, and it isn't romantic twaddle! No, it's a ferocious, black comedy: to illustrate this, there's a scene at a basketball court on a sunny day where a cocky kid who fancies his chances ambles up to Wan Chu and slings her a chat-up line, as men have done with women for at least 500,000 years. And what does Wan Chu do? Throws a lighted cig into his shorts. Ouch! (The consequences are played for comedy – Wan Chu isn't smashed in the face, for ex (that comes later); instead, she huffs off, and the boy's buddies pour soda down their friend's shorts).

THE SET-UP.

So the narrative set-up of *Dangerous Encounter – 1st Kind* is disarmingly goofy (and unsettling): the three dweebs[28] have built a homemade bomb which they intend to set off in a crowded cinema. While a movie plays involving a battle of WW2 tanks (and soldiers using bombs),[29] the jape works far better than the youths reckoned. They manage to flee, but Wan Chu spots them, and comes after them, threatening to turn them in unless they join her in a series of crazy pranks.

That might be the set-up and hook for a charming, Hollywood comedy-action-adventure flick – *Home Alone* meets *The Goonies*, say, with fresh-faced moppets getting the better of hopeless crooks and annoying parents. Oh no, not in the hands of Roy Szeto Cheuk-hon and Tsui Hark! They push the premise to the max, announcing just how malicious they're going to go in the first three minutes, with images of the torture of animals accompanied by a catalogue of depressing events on the news.

Soon the three kids are being shown how to *really* be a nutcase in public when Wan Chu explodes a bomb in a restroom on a street, threatens a coachload of Japanese tourists with another homemade bomb, and forces them to strip (dropping them off in the middle of nowhere), and douses the boys in gasoline and tries to set them on fire!

That's it's a skinny female teenager who's manipulating the three boys without them seeming to (be able) do anything to counter her is part of the amusement. At one point, one of them (Ah Lung) can't take it anymore, leaps on top of her and throttles her. She kicks him in the balls, then threatens to jump off a high building (or allow them to push her off).

---

28 The nerdy boys all wear glasses (and so does Wan Chu – possibly taking after the lads – this is the era of very large glasses, which Tsui also sported at the time).
29 There are some wicked jokes here – a girlfriend asks her man, about the movie, 'are those bombs real?' And he replies, 'of course they are, this is a foreign film!'

Whatever the boys come up with, Wan Chu is always ahead of them, always has an answer.

Dangerous Encounter – 1st Kind is entertaining/ compelling partly because you don't quite know what Wan Chu is going to do next (so that the boys, and the police, are always reacting to her actions). As with other movies of mentally unstable characters (such as *One Flew Over the Cuckoo's Nest* and *The Dark Knight*), that gives the 1980 picture an unpredictable element which keeps the narrative fresh. (And not only is Wan Chu unpredictable, she is also lethal).

If you take *Dangerous Encounter – 1st Kind* straight, you'll see a bizarre movie about a nasty, bratty girl who leads a bunch of boys astray in contemporary Hong Kong (she starts off by sticking pins in her pet mice, then gets more'n more vicious). If you clue into the humour (which is everywhere in *Dangerous Encounter – 1st Kind*), you'll see a comedy (albeit pretty dark) in which the filmmakers use the anti-social, anti-authoritarian pranks of Wan Chu and her cohorts to attack a bunch of targets and social issues.

There is an undercurrent of anti-consumerism in *Dangerous Encounter – 1st Kind,* which pokes fun at the shallow lives of the bourgeoisie (including their idiotic consumption of television). Television is a sub-theme in *Dangerous Encounter – 1st Kind* – in many scenes TVs are burbling in the background (one shows *Tom and Jerry*). It's clear that, in the world of *Dangerous Encounter – 1st Kind,* life is so nasty the populace dope themselves up with cretinous entertainment. (Who needs L.S.D., Jean-Luc Godard said in the 1960s, when you've got colour television?).

THE SECOND AND THIRD ACTS.

So the pranks and juvenile delinquency in *Dangerous Encounter – 1st Kind* escalate until the gang of misfits encounters a North American gangster, Bruce (Bruce Baron) working for Chinese Triads. At this point, *Dangerous Encounter – 1st Kind* becomes a somewhat different movie, with more conventional gangster/ thriller ingredients. (Several scenes don't quite fit with the rest of *Dangerous Encounter – 1st Kind,* dramatically or tonally. For example, there's a very ugly scene featuring a nude call-girl or girlfriend (Jenny Liang)[30] who's stabbed and killed by Bruce,[31] for no apparent reason other than he's irked that he lost the important documents being carried for the Triads. Sure, the man's angry and fears for his life, but killing someone else? That's over-the-top).

However, you buy it partly because the filmmakers come up with a truly outrageous scene to bring together the wannabe terrorists plot and the adult gangsters/ thriller plot. It is one of the most out-there scenes in all of Tsui Hark's cinema: Wan Chu sets upon the boys with gasoline and burning rags! This is one *very* difficult girl! She douses them with gas and

---

[30] In the credits, she's a prostitute.
[31] The nudity seems included purely for gratuitous reasons. It doesn't fit because *Dangerous Encounter – 1st Kind* has already shown us that it *won't* be about sex or male-female relations.

chases after them carrying flames (a scene with very Godardian[32] aspects); in the chaos, as the lads strip off so they won't be burnt alive, they run into a hoodlum in a car. Wan Chu makes off with the precious cargo the hood was carrying, thus knitting together the world of organized crime and arms dealing with teenagers pushing at the ethical boundaries of society.

A lot of screen time in *Dangerous Encounter – 1st Kind* is given over to the repercussions of Wan Chu accidentally-on-purpose stealing the hood's booty, which includes Japanese Yen money orders, which the youths try a number of times to cash (seeking the aide of a dodgy DJ in a white suit (by name of Uncle Hark, played by Richard Da Silva) who's stepped right out of 1970s blaxploitation cinema. The scene is another pounding disco setting).

Wan Chu certainly has guts – she goes right up to this guy Uncle Hark and asks him to help her make the deal to cash in the Japanese Yen bank orders. And earlier, she approaches the youth in the basketball court, asking to see his boss. This crook was the one who came on to Wan Chu, only for her to toss a cigarette down his shorts!

As the plot of *Dangerous Encounter – 1st Kind* depicts the kids getting more'n more involved with the criminal underworld, there are inevitable run-ins with Triad gangs (it's not a Hong Kong action or thriller picture unless there are Triads running around with knives. John Woo built his whole career around that).

The big action scene that climaxes the second act of *Dangerous Encounter – 1st Kind* has the kids improbably out-witting and out-running a large group of Triad heavies. The action team (led by Tony Ching) delivers plenty of running, fighting, driving and explosive gags in a basement car lot (these teen terrorists uses bombs and bottles of gasoline as their chief weapon).

Improbable this scene is, but it's also hugely entertaining – Tony Ching Siu-tung has few peers in action direction: this man is a genius at staging action. This is a textbook action sequence of startling gags and escalating mayhem. Now we see why the Triad henchmen are all young guys armed with *knives* – because with a handgun, they'd be able to shoot at the kids, and this sequence is all about the kids somehow trouncing swarms of henchmen.

❂

For the finale of *Dangerous Encounter – 1st Kind,* the violence builds to greater levels: a bodyguard is killed from one of the bombs the kids explode (at the car of a money-changer); Wan Chu is menaced and attacked by Triad heavies on the street outside her home, until she's rescued by her brother, the cop Tan (who then beats up his sister repeatedly in a nasty sequence, to punish her);[33] chained to the window by Tan, Wan Chu is set upon by some thugs who enter her apartment at night; finally, during a struggle outside, Wan Chu falls and is impaled on the same

---

32 *Dangerous Encounter – 1st Kind* is reminiscent of many 1960s movies by Jean-Luc Godard, including *Bande à Parte, Pierrot le Fou, La Chinoise* and *Weekend.*
33 As they tussle, the photograph of their dead father topples and the glass smashes.

spikes that took the life of the cat she hurled out of the window in the opening reel (while Tan is also at the scene, but entering the building from the rear, so he's too late to save his sister).

Each of these scenes is a *tour-de-force* of action cinema, containing numerous memorable details – like the sight of Wan Chu flailing wildly with a knife in the midst of a bunch of henchmen in the street, and then being menaced by Uncle Hark, who sets fire to her hair.

The death of Wan Chu is an incredible scene of suspense and threat – to keep her out of mischief, Wan Chu has been tied by her brother to the window bars (by a plastic tie). Extreme, but it puts the anti-heroine in a position of high vulnerability, when the *gweilo* hoods smash their way into the apartment.

The filmmaking here, and in the rest of *Dangerous Encounter – 1st Kind,* is absolutely rock-solid – there's a clean, efficient methodology to Tsui Hark's direction. Altho' it's showy, Tsui's staging and filming of scenes is direct and to the point. Bringing Tan back home right at this point is wholly conventional, but the punchiness of the orchestration of mayhem carries it all through. How, for ex, the neighbours are brought into the action sequence at the edges (the lady next door who fumes loudly, and the guy downstairs is blasé). How Wan Chu makes one final bid for freedom, only to end up impaled on the fence outside.

With the death of Wan Chu, *Dangerous Encounter – 1st Kind* shifts its centre of gravity, but it has to tie up the fates of the three lads, and of the thriller/ Triads subplot.[34] Thus, policeman Tan is hot on the case, determined to track down and bring to justice the killers of his sister Wan Chu (tho' his irritated superiors (Inspector Lui played by Ray Lui) order him to take some leave. There are several scenes where Tan explodes with frustration, including pouncing on some white guys in the street – who turn out to be Mormons).

The three youths have fled to the New Territories: *Dangerous Encounter – 1st Kind* stages its action climax in a large, rural cemetery in the foothills of the New Territories.[35] Cop Tan closes in on the bickering boys, mistaking them for his sister's murderers; when the N. American hoods turn up, the filmmakers mount an elaborate running fire-fight and cat-and-mouse chase.

The ending of *Dangerous Encounter – 1st Kind* has the quality of the nihilistic Westerns helmed by Sam Peckinpah, where everybody dies (and in a pathetic, hopeless manner). The action is brilliantly choreographed by Tony Ching Siu-tung (a low budget is no limit if you have a terrific imagination and a great stunt team who're willing to try anything).

This is one of the great action sequences in all of Tsui Hark's cinema – and he's delivered quite a few! What makes it soar is partly that the heroes/ anti-heroes are three kids, who, despite their big talk and posturing, are still three nerdy cowards from Hong Kong. Another

---

[34] There's a hilarious scene where Paul freaks out at the sight of a white guy at the bar – a foreigner! A white devil! (But even tho' Paul is playing up, over-reacting and running away, it's also a recurring gag in Hong Kong cinema – look out, there's a white man!).
[35] Filmed during the day, probably for budgetary reasons, but it really should be a night sequence.

significant ingredient is the desperation of the boys, as their lives seem to fall apart (they have tried drinking Dettol, in a sort of half-hearted suicide pact, which of course backfires). And the lads are pitted against serious hoods, fully armed. (That the teens accidentally shoot each other enhances the pathos. Ah Lung is shot to pieces in his hiding spot).

Guns, knives, pieces of wood, stones – the filmmakers throw everything into the mix, and it all pays off. This is Hong Kong action cinema in its rough-and-ready approach, where there's dust and grime and blood and sweat, and characters land hard on the ground. Look, for instance, at the details in the visuals: long shots of the cemetery with barbed wire snaking thru the sky; the kids dodging bullets behind the gravestones.

At the end, somehow having survived, Ko loses it, cackling and laughing as he fires a machine gun at the thousands of already-dead people in the graveyard. It's an ending of chaos and despair, and the sound of gunfire continues over a short montage of b/w photographs of riots in Hong Kong in 1967 (adding an overtly political/ historical veneer to the narrative, which hardly needs it – we can see that it's war everywhere in this movie).36

This is a one-of-a-kind movie, and really worth seeking out.

---

36 Besides, the photos replay the motif of the war movie in the theatre scene.

4

ALL THE WRONG CLUES
Gui Ma Zhi Duo Xing

All the Wrong Clues... For the Right Solution (*Gui Ma Zhi Duo Xing*, 1981) is not 'A Tsui Hark Film', not an *auteur* film, not a movie where the director is king, or has 'something to say': it is, thru and thru, a Cinema City comedy, a movie for mass consumption – in short, it's a Hong Kong comedy. (And it was part of a series).

All the Wrong Clues was Tsui Hark's first production for Cinema City, and it featured all the Cinema City regulars: Raymond Wong Pak-min, Roy Szeto Cheuk-hon, Eric Tsang, Karl Maka, Teddy Robin Kwan and Dean Shek. *All the Wrong Clues* was produced by Maka and Shek, written by Szeto and Wong (Tsui, Maka and Tsang have story credits), with music by Teddy Robin,[37] prod. des. by William Chang Suk-Ping, costumes by Yiu Hiu, make-up by Chan Kok-Hong, editing by Tony Chow Kwok-Chung, the DP was Bill Wong Chung-Piu, action dir. by Tina Lau Tin-Lan and O Sing-Pui. Released 1981.7.23. 90 mins.

All the Wrong Clues starred George Lam, Teddy Robin Kwan, Karl Maka, Kelly Yiu, Eric Tsang, Tang Kei Chan, JoJo Chan Kei Kei, Marilyn Wong Cho Shut, Walter Tso Tat Wah, Fung King Man and Wong Tso-sze. It was another period movie for Tsui Hark – it was set in the 1930s, and drew on the North American gangster movies of the 1930s-40s. It was largely a studio-bound movie, classily designed and staged – one of those movies where the costumes, the make-up, the props, the lighting, and the look pop out, a movie of actors dressed as Al Capone and shiny, classic cars.

Altho' *All the Wrong Clues* is not a Tsui Hark project, or script, or concept, he does make his influence felt on the screenplay: there are several female characters, for instance, where only one (the gangster's moll) is really required (leading to the ultimate reversal of genders in *Peking Opera Blues*, where three women take the lead roles).

All the Wrong Clues includes numerous clichés of Hollywood genre

---

[37] The score for *All the Wrong Clues* – by Teddy Robin Kwan – which's mainly electronica – doesn't always suit the material.

movies – private detectives, *femme fatales* and gangster's molls, classic motors and guns, shoot-outs, etc. It's a movie-movie, a movie about other movies – and, crucially, it's a comedy. Every scene of *All the Wrong Clues* is played for laughs: thus, Tsui Hark's second movie as director (*We're Going To Eat You*) was a horror comedy, and his fourth movie, this one, *All the Wrong Clues*, is a crime comedy (you can see how *All the Wrong Clues* leads directly to the *Blues* films, *Shanghai Blues* and *Peking Opera Blues*, with their Thirties *milieu,* ensemble casts and big city settings).

And it's funny – Tsui Hark is a solid director of comedy: for a start, the timing is great (crucial). Second, the staging is simple – no tricksy, show-off cinematic guff to get in the way of the humour.[38] Third, it has a great cast, who know what they're doing and what their strengths are. And the premise – a couple of useless private detectives going up against tough gangsters – has plenty of potential for comedy.

The middle (second) act of *All the Wrong Clues* is bolstered by a romantic farce that might be seen on stage involving Yoho hiding all of the women in the film from each other (many gags with doors and sudden, unwanted appearances), a break-out from an ice factory[39] while the hero and heroine are roped together (echoes of *The 39 Steps*), and an insane barroom brawl sequence (with everybody diving into the fray, characters popping up inside grand pianos, actors grinning at the camera, super-exaggerated fight moves, actors being bopped over the head by bottles, and culminating in custard pies in the face). For energy and movement, Hong Kong cinema rivals the heyday of silent movie comedy. Humour might be a trickier element to export in cinema, but when the slapstick is as broad as this, it cuts through.

All the Wrong Clues climaxes with a Big Shoot-out, of course, in the time-honoured many of Hong Kong action comedies, and crime movies everywhere. The gags are right out of silent comedy – including every hood holding a gun at everyone else. And despite the 100s of bullets expended, nobody is hurt.

---

38 But *All the Wrong Clues* has high production values for a Hong Kong comedy of the era.
39 According to legend, this scene was shot straight through three days, because the ice was melting – leading to the rumours that if you worked on Tsui Hark movie, you might be stuck in the studio far longer than the usual working day!

The Butterfly Murders (1979).

We're Going To Eat You (1980).

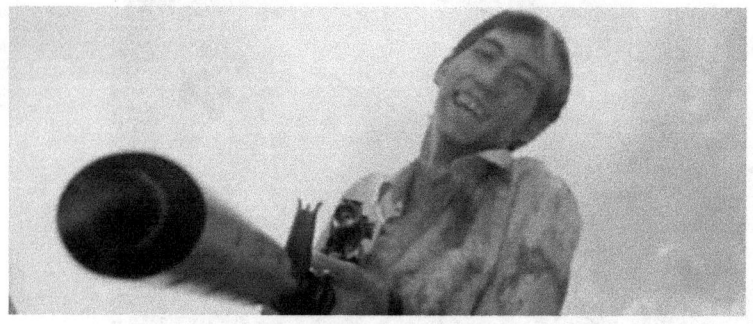

Dangerous Encounter – First Kind (1980).

5

ZU: WARRIORS FROM THE MAGIC MOUNTAIN

Suk Saan San Suk Saan Gim Hap

THE PRODUCTION.
In 1983 Tsui Hark worked for Golden Harvest, one of the famous Chinese film studios, to direct *Zu: Warriors From the Magic Mountain* (Cantonese: *Suk Saan San Suk Saan Gim Hap*; Mandarin: *Xin Shu Shan Jianxia* = *Suk Mountain: New Suk Mountain Sword Heroes*, a.k.a. *Zu: Warriors of the Magic Mountain*, *Zu: Warriors From Magic Mountain* and *Zu: Time Warriors* or *Time Warriors*). It's a completely wild action-adventure movie. *Zu: Warriors From the Magic Mountain* is a blissfully bonkers, fervently energetic, very enjoyable, and technically dazzling swordplay (*wuxia pian*) and fantasy epic.[1] It features a stellar (and huge) cast (one of the finest in all Hong Kong cinema), including Yuen Biao, Brigitte Lin, Sammo Hung Kam-bo, Mang Hoi, Adam Cheng, Judy Ongg, Moon Lee, Corey Yuen Kwai and Feng Ke'an (Tsui also has a cameo in the movie, as a Blue Army soldier – he appeared in quite a few movies around this time. Many of the actors were Tsui regulars). *Zu* is the first, giant masterpiece in the Tsui canon.

The script of *Zu: Warriors From the Magic Mountain* was by Shui Chung-Yuet and Sze-To Cheuk-Hon (Roy Szeto). It was produced by Raymond Chow, Leonard Ho Koon-cheung (planning) and Paragon Films, and distributed by Golden Harvest (Golden Harvest had approach Tsui to make a movie). The budget of *Zu* was in the region of HK $30 million (= US $4.25m) – very high for a Hong Kong picture of the early 1980s. The action directors were Corey Yuen Kwai, Yuen Biao, Fung Hak-On and Mang Hoi (all of whom also appeared in the movie). William Chang designed the movie; Bill Wong Chung-Piu was DP; Kwan Sing-Yau and Tang Siu-Lam composed the music; Peter Cheung Yiu-Chung was editor; make-up by Chan Kok-Hong; Chu Sheng-Shi was costume designer; props by Ma Man-

---
[1] Bey Logan described *Zu: Warriors From the Magic Mountain* as boasting 'an energy and visual style that only a Hong Kong action movie could generate' (106).

Chun; sound by Chow Shao-Lung and Ping Wong;[2] visual effects supervisor was Arnie Wong; lighting by Lam Wong; and the ADs were Yeung Wa and Lam Chi-Yan. The release of *Zu: Warriors From the Magic Mountain* was disappointing, with a Canton gross of only HK $15.88 million. Released Feb 5, 1983.[3] 94/ 98 minutes.

Zu: Warriors From the Magic Mountain was filmed largely in the studio at Golden Harvest – home-from-home for Tsui Hark, and where he has forged most of his finest works. Location shooting took place in the New Territories (inevitably),[4] plus a brief excursion to Taiwan (for the exterior battle scenes).

The version of *Zu* which was cut for overseas was called *Zu: Time Warriors*. It featured a time travel section, leading the audience into the ancient world of China via scenes in modern-day Canada featuring Yuen Biao.

Tsui Hark fell out with Golden Harvest over *Zu*, which was released in a form the director wasn't happy with. Tsui said he offered to film re-shoots for nothing, but, no, Golden Harvest didn't want to put any more money into the production (a very familiar story: once a movie has gone over-schedule and over-budget, backers are very reluctant to spend any more $$$$).[5] Later (in the Nineties), Golden Harvest and Tsui sued each other over revenues and over-runs).

The DVD release of *Zu: Warriors From the Magic Mountain* contains a marvellous commentary from Tsui Hark, in conversation with martial arts movie expert Bey Logan. The commentary gives you many insights into Tsui's working methods, his philosophy of cinema, and what he'd like to fix on *Zu: Warriors From the Magic Mountain*! You can feel Tsui's disappointment with aspects of *Zu: Warriors From the Magic Mountain*.

Tsui Hark has since recalled that making *Zu: Warriors From the Magic Mountain* was tough, that the shooting wended on for months, that they seemed to be re-shooting stuff constantly that didn't work.[6] *Zu: Warriors From the Magic Mountain* is clearly a production that Tsui was never quite happy with, that he found difficult to watch in later years (because he saw all of the mistakes, and all of the things he'd like to change). To the point where he remade his own movie in 2001, with *The Legend of Zu*. Unfortunately, that movie was a 'disaster', Tsui confessed. (A follow-up to *Zu* was announced in 2013: Yuen Woo-ping would direct the $35 million, 3-D production, backed by Bona Film Group, entitled *Zu Warriors: Dawn of Darkness*).

---

2 Special sound fx were by Yau-Tim Chung and Julian Pena.
3 *Zu: Warriors From the Magic Mountain* is a New Year's movie, with many of the attributes of a New Year flick – the emphasis on sheer entertainment, and on comedy.
4 You will recognize many of the locations – such as rocky cliffs and hillside roads (which crop up in the *Swordsman* and *Fong Sai-yuk* movies, among many others).
5 Tsui Hark found the visual effects 'one part of the production where I felt so frustrated' (LM, 53).
6 'The production seemed to last forever. I never really knew when to end it. Every day we were shooting, but then we feel like we were shooting more, and reshooting, and reshooting, and more reshooting'.

THE JOYS OF *ZU*.

The ambition of *Zu: Warriors From the Magic Mountain* is immense: you get the feeling from this movie that the filmmakers were not afraid to try *anything*, to see if it would work. 'In the end we put everything into the movie and it looked kind of fun' (LM, 52). Tsui Hark's movies are often pushing against the boundaries of what is possible. He is a true experimenter in cinema, like Géorges Méliès or Orson Welles: give him a bunch of tools and he will invent a whole bunch more in order to achieve what he has in his head.

No matter what the budget is, or what is available in terms of resources, in a movie such as *Zu: Warriors From the Magic Mountain* you can feel the filmmakers pushing against the boundaries. Thus, even tho' some might regard the visual effects in *Zu: Warriors From the Magic Mountain* as less impressive as those in Hollywood cinema, it doesn't matter – because the filmmakers, and the film itself, are really stretching, and expanding the possibilities.

As a film of exotic locales, *Zu: Warriors From the Magic Mountain* has got the lot (many are common in the swordplay genre): grandiose palaces, ancient, Buddhist temples, lush waterfalls, craggy mountains, rocky valleys, tunnels and caves, forests, beaches, and the sea.

Martial arts and wire-work are all over the place in *Zu: Warriors From the Magic Mountain*,[7] with actors in perpetual motion, battling, sword fighting, leaping, flying, and striking memorable pose after pose. Nothing and no one keeps still for long in *Zu: Warriors From the Magic Mountain*. It's a wire-work movie with no boundaries, and is without doubt one of the two or three greatest wire-work movies.

It's true that for a Western audience sometimes the story could become a little muddled in *Zu: Warriors From the Magic Mountain* (actually, it isn't, really), but stories and characters are only *part* of the whole effect and experience of a Tsui Hark-helmed or produced movie. His films are very much about entertainment, thru and thru – like the concept of 'total cinema' developed by Harry Saltzman and Cubby Broccoli, the producers of the *James Bond* movies. Total cinema – movies as entertainment, as an experience, as a rollercoaster ride. Or to put it another way, when the visuals and stunts and gags are this manic and skilful, you don't care so much about elements like stories and themes and characters (that's expecting something far too literary and intellectual from a movie like this! Not every movie has to be *Persona, Tokyo Story* or *Pather Panchali*!).

Tsui Hark is a master showman, there's no doubt about that. Tsui is the equivalent of any of the great showmen of cinema – recent ones such as Francis Coppola and Steven Spielberg, or past masters like Cecil B. DeMille and D.W. Griffith.

Thomas Weisser enthused about *Zu*:

> This is the epic Oriental fantasy movie filmed with extraordinary visual delights. It fluctuates effortlessly from outrageous to ascetic. Almost

---

[7] Characters fly throughout *Zu* – as Lisa Morton pointed out, in an American movie, there would be a 5-minute explanation of how they do it; in a Tsui Hark movie, they just fly (50).

every scene ambushes the viewer. This is a perfect introduction to the genre. (216)

ACTING.

The performance style in *Zu: Warriors From the Magic Mountain* is remarkable for its invention, its expressivity, its speed and its agility. Actors don't walk across sets, they tumble or spin across them.[8] *Zu: Warriors From the Magic Mountain* is not only *A History of Chinese Legends and Mythology*, not only a fantasy *wuxia* (swordplay) picture *par excellence*, it is also *A History of Peking Opera*. And it's a *History of the Movies*; it's Tsui Hark's *Guide To My Favourite Movies*.

Yuen Biao plays Dik Ming-kei (Ti-Ming Chi), a classical youth of legends and myths, our audience identification figure: naïve, energetic, stubborn, persistent, and rather simple-minded, Biao is charming as Dik, irrepressible and easy to like and watch (as with Biao in many another movie). It's a wonderful role for an actor, because Biao is in most scenes (tho' *Zu: Warriors From the Magic Mountain* doesn't feel like a 'Yuen Biao vehicle', as it might be if someone like Jackie Chan or the Hollywood equivalent played the part. Biao keeps Dik's characterization humble, deferring to the numerous wizards, warriors and creatures).

However, Dik Ming-kei is *not* driving the plot in *Zu: Warriors From the Magic Mountain* – at least, not at first, and not as a hero with a mission, with motives, with a back-story and all the rest. Instead, he is our go-between, our observer figure, thrust into the *jiangzhu* of Chinese legend: we follow Dik, but we're really meeting the other characters, encountering the out-size scenarios, and exploring the high fantasy world.

But at the end of act one of *Zu: Warriors From the Magic Mountain*, Dik Ming-kei is given a mission by the old wizard Chang Mei, a.k.a. Whitebrows/ Long Brows (Sammo Hung Kam-bo): to find the Twin Swords (Purple and Green) on Heaven's Blade Peak so that they can defeat the Evil Sect villains. It's very late for the primary story/ quest to be stated – some 34 minutes into the picture, but it comes in a classic manner – from an authority figure (a wizard) to the film's hero (who, up this point, has been carried along by events rather than driving them, as a hero. However, the movie has retained Dik in the foreground in every scene up to this moment).

Chang Mei ('Longbrows') is a wonderful, cranky, old sorcerer character[9] with magical eyebrows and beards (he's first encountered pinning his eyebrows to Dik Ming-kei's); Sammo Hung Kam-bo is perfect for roles like this – the camera loves Hung, and Hung loves playing up to the camera. Whenever Hung is in a scene, in any movie, he always steals it. (However, once Chang has pinned down the Blood Demon – using his eyebrows to pull it out of the sky like a skull-encrusted kite – he remains there, holding it in check. A pity – it would be great to see Dik travel the story with Chang; instead, Dik is paired up with the warrior Ding Yan).

---

8 The gymnastic tumbles and leaps of Yuen Biao and Mang Hoi, and how they work as a team, are especially impressive (they were both action directions for *Zu*).
9 Of course he's one of the good guys, he yells at Dik – have you ever seen a bad guy dressed in white?!

Story-wise, *Zu: Warriors From the Magic Mountain* does boil down to good guys and bad guys, with the baddies intent on the usual things (chaos, destruction, power), and the heroes are trying to combat all of that negative intent and energy.

Adam Cheng lends the Swordsman Ding Yan (Ting-Yin) an easy-going charm, but he's also stern when necessary (with Dik Ming-kei at first, being reluctant to train him or have him tag along. The bickering between the two is a send-up of the usual *sifu*-and-pupil relationship). Cheng makes it look effortless in playing the brilliant-at-everything hero. And tho' he's not a martial artist (or a gymnast like Yuen Biao or Mang Hoi), Cheng certainly convinces as a magical swordsman (with an impressive arsenal of weaponry including missiles, bolts of energy, and an extraordinary device of multiple swords).

VISUAL EFFECTS.

As a visual effects extravaganza, *Zu: Warriors From the Magic Mountain* is absolutely remarkable, and one of the great visual effects movies in the history of cinema. Further – it is unique in the way that it uses visual effects and special effects.

The fact that Tsui Hark, Shui Chung-Yuet, Roy Szeto Cheuk-hon and the team were trying out many visual effects and practical effects techniques for the first time enhances the feeling of experimentation and openness. Optical effects are not actually new in Hong Kong cinema, Tsui said, *pace Zu* – and he'd even used them in his teenage movies. (They had some people from the U.S.A. helping out with the optical effects: Arnie Wong (visual fx supervisor) and John Scheele, who worked on Disney's *Tron* as animators, Chris Casady (*Star Wars*), Tama Takanashi (*Blade Runner*), Peter Kuran (*Star Trek*) and Robert Blalack[10] (*Star Wars*).)

Miniatures, matte paintings, puppetry, animatronics, stopmotion, optical effects, multiple film speeds, and plenty of animation – *Zu: Warriors From the Magic Mountain* has the lot. Many of the visual effects were created in front of the camera, on set – what're called practical or physical effects (and also special effects – visual effects these days referring to effects created in post-production). Yuen Biao said it was new, though, to be reacting to nothing instead of the usual man in a monster suit.

Special make-up includes the expanding body of Yuen Biao when he's receiving the healing energy from Adam Cheng (reminiscent of the special make-up effects in *An American Werewolf In London*, with animatronic body parts, though it's played for comedy, not horror).

There is thus a lovely handmade feel to *Zu: Warriors From the Magic Mountain*, that you also find in the stopmotion movies of Jan Svankmajer, for instance, or anything made by Géorges Méliès or Orson Welles. A strong sense of *play*, of the filmmakers trying *anything*, to see what could be done. It's one reason why a movie like *Zu: Warriors From the Magic Mountain* is such fun, because the impression of play and experimentation is so appealing. It's as if nobody is going to say, 'no, we can't do that'; the

---
10 Robert Blalack, shared the Oscar for vfx on *Star Wars* alongside John Dykstra, Richard Edlund, Grant McCune and John Stears.

filmmakers're going to try it. On *Citizen Kane*, Orson Welles pointed out that ignorance was bliss – it was his first movie, and he simply didn't know how to do a lot of the technical things. So he and the team would try them (and cinematographer Gregg Toland recalled standing back to let Welles go ahead and try stuff. There was a moment during the shooting of *Citizen Kane* when Welles went and adjusted the lighting, not realizing that for a unionized Hollywood production the director didn't do that (and, as far as unions are concerned, isn't *allowed* to do that). Toland appreciated that level of youthful idealism).

Zu: Warriors From the Magic Mountain is like many of the Hong Kong New Wave movies in simply Trying Out Stuff, to see if it works. The experimentation becomes part of the picture. As Tsui Hark recalls on the priceless DVD audio commentary, yes, he would go back and change many things (with computers, for instance, some of the visual effects could be achieved quicker and slicker. But not necessarily 'better' – because practical, physical effects have a charm of their own. You know that the actors are physically in the same space as the effects).

The emphasis on real, physical effects is certainly one of the reasons that New Wave movies from China, particularly the action and *wuxia* movies, are so appealing. It's all tricky and fakery in cinema, of course (*whatever* the scene is), but there is a magic to seeing (or believing you're seeing) something real, something or someone that was there.

EDITING.

The *invisible* weapon in the arsenal of Chinese action movies – and in all movies – is of course *editing* (*Zu: Warriors From the Magic Mountain* was cut by Peter Cheung Yiu-Chung). In the editing, *Zu: Warriors From the Magic Mountain* employs everything available, including full slo-mo (and under-cranking),[11] step-motion, freeze frames, rapid dissolves, wipes, and flashcuts.

It's the *editing*, more than any other single technical element, that knits all of the effects and trickery together. Look at how brazenly[12] and joyfully *Zu: Warriors From the Magic Mountain* cuts from a model to live-action, from an optical superimposition to a squib exploding, from an animated snake-like cloth to a real piece of cloth puppeteered on the set. No shot in *Zu: Warriors From the Magic Mountain* lingers on screen more than 2 or 3 seconds (it seems that way, tho' the average shot length in *Zu: Warriors From the Magic Mountain* is probably longer). However, rapidly edited movies, in general, tend to age better than slower movies with the same sort of stories and genres.

And *Zu: Warriors From the Magic Mountain* sure doesn't hang around! Indeed, it's one of the fundamental ingredients of the cinema of Tsui Hark that the cutting has an urgency to it – it's not just 'fast' cutting, it's not just shorter shots, it's cutting with a high, nervous energy to it. However,

---
11 *Zu* is full of subtle, rapid lap dissolves, from two parts of the same shot, to enhance the feeling of speed.
12 'Brazenly' – the movie seems to be daring you to shout out 'that's a model!' Yes, because in movies it's all a model, it's all a pretence, it's all dressing up and putting on a show.

the pacing and the storytelling is also very swiftly moving along. They are not the same thing: for instance, many recent Hollywood movies are edited in very short shots, yet the *storytelling* and the *pace* is still s-l-o-w. So that rapid cutting is applied to what are basically *slow* scenes. All you get nowadays is four camera angles of part of a scene where one shot would've sufficed in the past (it's called over-cutting). Hollywood movies of recent times cut from an over-the-shoulder shot to a single to a wide shot to a different wide shot for no other purpose than keeping the cutting rapid (as if a new angle is enough to maintain or create interest. It isn't). Many of those editing decisions have no impact on the storytelling or pace, which's *still* slow. (Thus, accelerating the editing is often a false or fake way of adding excitement/ energy to what are boring scenes, like shaky camerawork).

By contrast, Tsui Hark's movies, including *Zu: Warriors From the Magic Mountain*, hurtle along. Tsui's movies are very much of the express train kind, the roller-coaster sort of movie: you get on the train and go along for the ride. And it's a *fast* ride! An e-ticket ride! (If someone let Tsui design big theme park rides at Universal or Disney, you just know what they'd be like!).

The cutting style in *Zu: Warriors From the Magic Mountain* became Tsui Hark's preferred style – *very rapid*! And not only in the action scenes. Tsui's filmic metabolism simply won't allow him to edit at a snail's pace. He could never make a film as slow as the ones directed by Carl-Theodor Dreyer, Robert Bresson or Michelangelo Antonioni. He'd be bored out of his mind!

STORY AND STRUCTURE.

So the first act of *Zu: Warriors From the Magic Mountain* depicts Dik Ming-kei in the *jiangzhu* as a soldier/ messenger who gets caught up in the fierce conflicts between warring clans (simply coloured red, blue, yellow, etc, a satire on political factions. It's dubbing China and the Soviet Union and Communism as 'red' – childishly simplistic). The storytelling is so fast, *Zu: Warriors From the Magic Mountain* has already depicted (A) Kurosawan[13] horsemen with banners on a beach and in the hills, (B) a comical battle in a forest, (C) Dik teaming up uneasily (and humorously) with Sammo Hung's Red Army soldier, (D) a tussle on a boat,[14] and (E) has sent Dik into the mountains – and this is only the *first half* of the first act! (*Zu* is a three-act movie, with a longer first act (34m) than the usual 25-30 minutes; *Zu* runs 98 mins in the Chinese cut.

The second half of act one of *Zu: Warriors From the Magic Mountain* is a *tour-de-force* of fantasy filmmaking, in which the production chucks in everything, plus several kitchen sinks (which, of course, explode in showers of sparks! – after zooming across the set!). The settings are vivid

---

[13] The way that the commanders of the blue, red and yellow armies (Chung Fat and Dick Wei) yell at each other imperiously seems to be a conscious nod to the mediæval movies of Akira Kurosawa. Meanwhile, the soldiers on horseback, the banners, the elaborate headgear, the beach setting and the regimentation of the troops is a marvellous tribute to Kurosawa's films.

[14] Where Hong Kong film veteran Sai Gwa-Pau plays a hapless onlooker.

and fully Gothic and atmospheric, in the Chinese ghost story manner: eerie, craggy mountains (the Magic Mountains of the title), with deep, rocky canyons (with a giant, yellow moon hanging above), and a Buddhist temple of bells, statues and shadowy spaces (which's the lair of the Evil Sect).

Our heroes are challenged by numerous foes: the leader of the Evil Sect and his henchmen, a spirit in red,[15] demons with glowing eyes, and the sheer hell of traversing inhospitable mountains. Each new set of characters is given a proper and lavish introduction: the Evil Sect, for example, perform intricate acrobatics as if they're on stage at a Peking Opera show).

Part of act one of *Zu: Warriors From the Magic Mountain* comes across as a version of *A Chinese Ghost Story*, with Dik Ming-kei taking refuge from a storm in the mountains in a dark temple. It's comic-horror time, as Dik dodges masked, cloaked assailants with blazing eyes who can fly thru the air and frazzle anything in their path.

Dik Ming-kei teams up with Adam Cheng's Ding Yan, a swordsman of the traditional, Chinese type (Dik begs to be taught martial arts, and for Ding to become his *sifu*. Ding refuses, repeatedly – sometimes calmly, sometimes in exasperation).

Ding Yan delivers a lengthy, righteous speech (to Dik Ming-kei) about the woes of the times (as soon as they meet), about how human life isn't valued, and how things keep going wrong. (Critics might view this as a critique of the Communist regime in the People's Republic of China by the Cantonese filmmakers, but it's a gripe general enough to apply to any era in human history).

The bickering between the heroes is a recurring motif in *Zu: Warriors From the Magic Mountain* – it's established early in the relationship between Dik Ming-kei and the Red Army soldier, and continues between Dik and Ding, and the two new charas, the Buddhist monks Yat Jan (Mang Hoi) and Xiao Yue (Liu Songren). Anyhow, if Hong Kong cinema puts two guys together in an action-adventure setting, arguing and joshing is pretty much mandatory (and in *Zu* the humour and upbeat attitude tells us how we're meant to take the movie – comically. As opposed to, say, a John Woo-directed picture, where the banter between the two male heroes is melancholy, introspective and pained). The movie also makes the usual jokes at the expense of Buddhist monks – no meat, no women, no wine, etc.[16]

In an impressive Buddhist temple set (designed by William Chang), the second half of act 1 is pretty much continuous action, with each of the four heroes having their chance to shine (at this point, Dik Ming-kei is still the apprentice/ novice, preferring to hide behind Ding Yan or Yat Jan). The set of course is multi-level, and includes numerous props for our heroes to bounce off, over, under, beside, inside – bells,[17] beams, ropes, pots,

---

[15] A marvellous creation using a billowing costume/ cloak, which forms and reforms.
[16] There's also a joke about Dik's virginal status, but Ding reminds him that he doesn't need to be pure to battle the forces of evil.
[17] In a brilliant touch, the semi-human henchman hide inside the giant bells, where they are a pair of gleaming eyes, before erupting upwards, to attack Dik.

statues, etc. By the end of the very complex series of fights, the action choreographers have exploited every square inch of the temple set, and everything that the props dept (led by Ma Man-Chun) can build.

The action and choreography, the rhythm, flow and editing, the pacing of the storytelling, and, crucially, the imagination and invention on display, is at a whole other level from a Western action-adventure movie. (The shapeshifting villain in the billowing scarlet costume, for instance, is a delightful example of live puppeteering on set – and very beautiful, too).

Tsui Hark is wary of dubbing movies 'pioneering' or 'new' – for him, it's all been done before (he's right – and it was all done by 1917, by Géorges Méliès, Charlie Chaplin, Cecil B. DeMille and D.W. Griffith). But you can certainly sense that the filmmaking team in *Zu: Warriors From the Magic Mountain* appear to be breaking thru barriers. Hong Kong cinema hadn't seen the combination of action choreography with visual effects at this level before (even tho' *wuxia* films are known for their emphasis on special effects and fantasy).

❂

The second act of *Zu: Warriors From the Magic Mountain* explores some unexpected territory – instead of battles between the heroes and the villains, and the expected long and arduous quest to find the magical swords, the heroes take a detour – to travel to the Ice Queen's palace,[18] in order to heal the monk Xiao Yue (who's been poisoned by the Evil Sect). However, the introduction of the regime at the palace is inevitably (and delightfully) expressed in action terms. The heroes don't simply turn up, say 'hi', and ask for healing for Xiao. No! There are several confrontations – with the characters zooming all over the place. And, in true Tsui Hark style, the denizens of the Ice Queen's palace are a band of women. So our heroes're surrounded by women armed with swords on all sides. And of course, healing is not instantly forthcoming, because the Ice Queen (or Countess) lives on a higher plane from the rest of us. She is played by Brigitte Lin Ching-hsia[19] with her usual cool, implacable beauty, self-possession, and Screen Goddess charisma – and she receives a startling introduction – flying through the palace set and instantly engaging out heroes in combat.

This is the first of the amazing Brigitte Lin's appearances in a Tsui Hark movie – the first of many (including in films he produced), the peak of which was her star turn as Asia the Invincible in *The Swordsman 2* and *3*. One thing's for sure, for an actress, you got to do stuff in a Tsui Hark movie you never did anywhere else!

Ding Yan also becomes infected, in an unexpected twist (just as Xiao Yue is healed). So now Xiao demands that Ding be healed, as he was (unfortunately, the Ice Queen has been exhausted already by healing Xiao).

In amongst the extremely rapidly delivered storytelling, Dik Ming-kei

---

[18] Another playful set by William Chang in the action-adventure mode (out-size statuary and intricate wall carvings).
[19] The costuming for Brigitte Lin was one of those times, which crop up occasionally, where the team couldn't find (or decide on) what would work: 'we'd put on piece of fabric on her, take another piece out – she was standing there for a week!' Tsui recalled (LM, 53).

inadvertently becomes Ding Yan's pupil, and is reluctantly recognized by Ding in his debilitated state (he gives Dik his second sword). When Dik is also poisoned, Ding transfers some his energy to him (and, seemingly, some of his martial arts powers).

So we have two teachers and two students, and two *sifus* who become injured and require special, magical healing, and thus two pupils who have to take up the slack and become leaders/ heroes in themselves.

Now, if we're in a palace of swords*women* in an fantasy adventure outing, there's bound to be some dramatic fireworks in the interplay between the genders. So *Zu: Warriors From the Magic Mountain* sets the Ice Queen against Ding Yan: there's a flirtatious and spectacular encounter between the two superheroes which really forms the love scene in the 1983 movie: they ride on top of stone statues of elephants which walk and fly. It's an intricately choreographed sequence which resembles the dance number between lovers in a Hollywood musical, and stands in for the sex scene which can't be shown. (In the ascetic morality of the legends, even to touch is suggestive: the women in the Ice Queen's fortress bridle at the merest hint of bodily contact. Especially from Buddhist monks, who should know better! Tsui Hark, as expected, milks the asceticism of monks to the max – especially when Xiao Yue reawakens, to find himself surrounded by young women).

Thus, the second erotic flirtation in the second act of *Zu: Warriors From the Magic Mountain* features the two lowly disciples of the teachers, Dik Ming-kei and Yat Jan, and involves nudity. No, not the beautiful, young women disrobing, but the two hapless guys (a typical comic turnabout, and typical also of Tsui Hark's form of comedy: if there's a palace of women, and men enter it, you can bet there will be gender reversals of power). No restrooms in the Ice Queen's palace – well, not for mere pupils: the farcical goofing around ends up with the lads naked and the girls giggling as their leader (the Queen's guard, Chi-wu Shang), teases them by shredding their clothes with her sword.

Ding Yan's infection is an unexpected twist in the narrative of *Zu: Warriors From the Magic Mountain* – putting a major spanner in the works for the heroes. Now Dik Ming-kei, the ever-faithful pupil, carries Ding back to the Magic Mountain, only to find that the Ice Queen isn't well enough to heal Ding after just fixing up Xiao Yue. After Ding runs amok in the Ice Palace, and the Ice Queen freezes everything over with ice, act two ends (the pupils have managed to escape, through an exit into water).

❦

The third act and finale of *Zu: Warriors From the Magic Mountain* (*Zu* is constructed on a three-act model) involves the heroes versus the villains, of course: as usual, the heroes're trying to stop the villains from spreading their evil everywhere. Except, Swordsman Ding Yan has now become infected by the Evil Sect's poison, so in effect he's also a villain. Consequently, it's up to the duo of Dik Ming-kei and Yat Jan (the working class pupils) to save the day – tho' they have support from Chi-wu Shang, and from the goddess Lady Li I-Chi (Judy Ongg/ Weng Qian-Yu). The monk, Xiao Yiu, is elsewhere.

In the last scenes of *Zu: Warriors From the Magic Mountain,* the filmmaking becomes abstract and other-worldly, with the battle taking place in a magical realm of swirling clouds of colour (predominantly reds). Our heroes float in the heavens, duelling Swordsman Ding Yan in his evil guise (using the twin magical swords of heaven and earth from Heaven's Blade Peak. These are given a lightsabre glow, reminiscent of *Star Wars* – tho' *Star Wars* was by no means the first movie to depict magical swords as illuminated).

Chang Mei gets his chance to shine, too – when the Blood Demon erupts from the cocoon of horns, where Chang has been keeping it imprisoned with his magical mirror (for 49 days). Some humour is mined from the spiritual inter-connectedness of the characters, so that Chang Mei and Lady Li I-Chi speak thru Dik and Yat.

The finale of *Zu: Warriors From the Magic Mountain* allows for several return appearances, too – so Brigitte Lin comes back briefly, as the Ice Queen, sacrificing herself to save the world (by nobbling Ding Yan). And Sammo Hung's Red Army soldier pops up again (still fighting in massed battles) – this time tussling with the director himself, Tsui Hark, in a short but typical cameo right at the end of the movie (which ends with a freeze frame of Tsui and Sammo, followed by the credits).

The form of the final confrontations in *Zu: Warriors From the Magic Mountain* – cosmic battles in visionary realms where visual effects are primary – will be revisited in Tsui Hark's career several times: the ending of *Green Snake,* the *Swordsman* films, the *Chinese Ghost Story* movies, the *Detective Dee* movies, and of course the *Zu* remake, *The Legend of Zu.*

THE FRAMING STORY.

The U.S.A. (international) cut of *Zu: Warriors From the Magic Mountain* was called *Zu: Warriors From Mount Shock* (a.k.a. *Zu: Time Warriors).* It featured a framing story set in the present day (a formulaic, over-used device), in which college student Yuen Biao travels back in time.[20] (The Asian guy in a North American context, the time travel, the figures from the past appearing in the present, have been employed many times – it's like a cheapo, Orientalized version of *Back To the Future* or *Peggy Sue Got Married.* Tsui revived the frame concept several times).

The framing story in the U.S. cut (featured on the DVD release) is rather boring: it's flatly directed,[21] with dull scenes and dull characters (and crudely dubbed). The framing story has every feature of being designed specifically to appeal to an international (North American) audience, a sequence to be tacked onto a wacky, Chinese fantasy movie so it'll appeal to a Western audience.

So, yes, Yuen Biao is a college student with a car, apartment, and chums, who discovers a real, young, Asian woman (Moon Lee) who looks like the figure Chi-wu Shang/ Mu Sang (the Ice Queen's guard) in an ancient, Chinese painting that he sees in a museum (the painting,

---
20 It's meant to be the U.S.A., but seems to have been filmed in the New Territories.
21 Some of it doesn't look like it was helmed by the Tsui Hark we know and love.

explained by a curator (Leslie Clarke), offers the simplistic visual link between the past and the present). He spends a (dream-like) night with her (where she, unusually, seduces him); she's gone next morning; driving at night, he crashes (avoiding her in the road), waking up in the *jianghzu* world of *Zu: Warriors From the Magic Mountain*. (There is also a scene where Dik Ming-kei goes to a fortune-teller (Dani Bishop), who talks about his past life).

Dik Ming-kei is also involved in a tussle in a sword training scene with a cocky bruiser (this opens the framing story of *Zu*); he uses his martial arts to best the jock (who later turns up with two friends to enact vengeance. But Dik trounces the guys). Tsui Hark would later revive this clichéd scenario in *The Master*, with the Asian fish-out-of-water in the North American city, getting into fights with local gangs.

Three more (short) scenes are included in the framing story. Two are set in the past: a scene where Dik Ming-kei encounters a guy in a forest, where the Story So Far is explained to him. And a scene where Dik meets the Queen's guard, reminding her that they were once an item (but Chi-wu Shang huffily claims she doesn't know him at all). The device of a bracelet is employed as a further link between the lovers.

Finally, a scene where Dik Ming-kei wakes in hospital, only to find the mysterious Chinese woman once again waiting for him. A happy hug and there's our upbeat ending. Run credits!

The problem with the framing story of *Zu: Warriors From the Magic Mountain* is that it's a dumb film producer's concept: no decent historical, fantasy movie needs to take the poor, fragile audience by the hand and lead them gently into its fantasy world. You do that by simply getting on with telling your story with total confidence. At most, a bit of preamble, a voiceover, a short prologue of exposition, is all that might be required (which the Chinese version has). But even then, film audiences are so sophisticated, so knowing, they've seen so many movies, they don't need to be treated like kids.

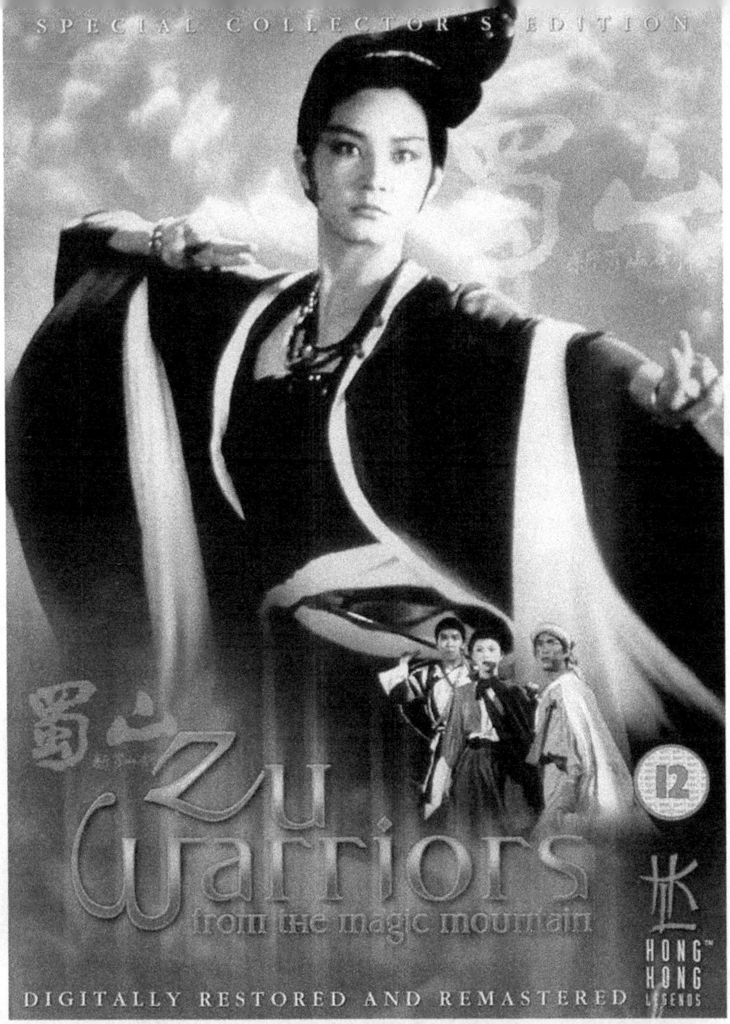

Zu: Warriors From the Magic Mountain (1983) This page and over.

6

ACES GO PLACES 3: OUR MAN IN BOND STREET

Jui Gaai Paak Don: Nui Wong Mat Ling

Aces Go Places 3: Our Man In Bond Street (*Jui Gaai Paak Dong: Nui Wong Mat Ling* in Cantonese = *Best Partners: Her Majesty's Secret Order*, a.k.a. *Mad Mission 3*, 1984) was another entry in the successful *Aces Go Places* franchise from Cinema City. The Cinema City team produced the movie: it was written by Raymond Wong Pak-min and Jason Lam Kee To, and produced by Dean Shek, Karl Maka and Wong. Music by Noel Quinlan, Samuel Hui Koon-Kit, Lynsey de Paul and Tang Siu-Lam, the DPs were Bill Wong and Joe Chan, editing by Tony Chow Kwok-Chung, costumes by Poon An-Ying and Elsa Chan Ki-Ling, action dir. was Corey Yuen Kwai, Oliver Wong Yui-Man, Yiu Yau-Hung, Leung Chi-Hing and Nanshun Shi (Tsui's wife) were production designers. Released Jan 26, 1984. 94 minutes.[1]

    Aces Go Places 3 starred Sam Hui Koon-kit, Karl Maka and Sylvia Chang Ai-chi, and many other familiar faces in their usual roles (the cast included Jean Mersant, Ken Boyle, Wong Sau-man, Yue Chi-ming, Toby Russell,[2] Cyrus Wong, John Sham, Huguettte Funfrock, Tsuneharu Sugiyama and Naomi Otsubo).

    Aces Go Places 3 is typical of Hong Kong comedy: it's gimmicky, it's flashy, it's throwaway, it's very over-the-top, it's crude, it's simplistic and formulaic, it's clichéd – you name it. Indeed, *Aces Go Places 3* exhibits all of the sins that people who don't like comedies complain about – but these are precisely the same things that people who love comedies enjoy!

    Aces Go Places 3: Our Man In Bond Street/ Mad Mission 3 is a film producer's movie, a studio and corporate movie, and a second unit director's movie, but not especially a director's movie (100s of directors

---
[1] The North American dub, released as *Mad Mission 3*, lost about 20 minutes, including a scene with Albert, the maid and the baby, and Ho at the hospital.
[2] Ken Russell's son, who has been involved with Hong Kong movies.

could've filmed it). But, released for (Chinese) New Year's in 1984, it was important in Tsui Hark's career because it was a big hit in Hong Kong (with some HK $29 million – making it the number one movie of 1984, and one of the few times that Tsui has had a top-grossing movie).

The *Aces Go Places* series (of six movies), which began in 1982, was a considerable success for Cinema City. It's a formulaic product, packaged and processed. Sam Hui Koon-kit, a well-known Hong Kong TV and film star, appears as the super-thief and Bond-a-like, King Kong,[3] with Karl Maka as the foolish, hen-pecked detective on his tail, and Sylvia Chang as the inspector's wife. It's a jewellery caper movie (with the target being the Crown Jewels of Great Britain).

The *Aces Go Places* movies are caper movies, spy movie spoofs, comedy-adventures, which combine Hong Kong/ Chinese humour with insane stunts (and gadgets), and Western/ Hollywood send-ups and allusions (to *The Godfather, Mission: Impossible* and of course the Big One, *James Bond*). *Aces Go Places 3* includes references to *Jaws,* and the two earlier *Aces* flicks. There are shades of *Pink Panther* and *Lupin III* in the caper genre influences (and the detective hunting the master thief motif). The incredible *Airplane!* (1980), in which Peter Graves also appears, would be another reference point. The *Aces Go Places* are forerunners of Jackie Chan's adventure comedies (in their use of international locations, for instance), and a very similar tone (except that Chan wouldn't play a criminal like the King Kong character, and the bumbling detective character is not someone Chan would play, either).

Aces Go Places 3: Our Man In Bond Street comes across as a stream-of-consciousness *James Bond* spoof, taking in every stunt and gadget from the United Artists/ Eon franchise which began in 1962 with *Dr No*.[4] So there's Richard Kiel and Harold Sakata, reprising their roles in the *Bond* flicks; there's a Sean Connery-a-like actor in a white tux (played by Connery's brother Neil), and a Queen of England look-a-like (Jean Mersant); and there's Peter Graves from the *Mission: Impossible* TV show (as Tom Collins).

Aces Go Places 3: Our Man In Bond Street relies heavily on model photography (especially in the finale and the flying chase) – another example of the emphasis on visual effects in the films of Tsui Hark. There are model helicopters, men, boats and submarines (a sub in the form of a shark – cue a riff on the famous *Jaws* musical theme). And plenty of process shots and opticals. And Tsui's beloved animation. With so much of the finale occurring on, in and under water, and at night, the challenges for the team at Cinefex Workshop were huge.[5]

❋

If you view *Aces Go Places 3* (or any Hong Kong comedy) in a dub, there are even more barriers between you and the humour. It's a problem that nobody has found a really good solution for: subtitles mean you get

---

[3] Tsui's nickname at film school in Texas.
[4] There's an impressive element of globe-trotting (to Paris, to London), altho' much of the movie is set firmly in the home ground of Hong Kong (and back in the studio, once again).
[5] Kevin Chisnall was special fx supervisor, and Sai-Hung Wong oversaw the miniatures.

the original soundtrack but reading subtitles ruins the timing (so important in comedy), and skews some of the meaning, and turns movie-going into reading. But dubbing misses so much of the original tone and performance.

This is certainly the case with *Aces Go Places 3*, which begs to be viewed in a packed theatre of Chinese-speaking movie-goers. (And, with a gross of HK $29 million, it performed very well for Asian audiences).

Aces Go Places 3 seems light and inconsequential, altho' you can admire the energy and attitude of the piece, which has a punky, anarchic quality. It's a movie that knows it's dumb, and revels in the fact. It's a movie that requires some good will from the audience: if you fight this kind of movie, it's completely pointless. You'd be better off filling out your tax claims. Thus, *Aces Go Places 3* is another type of picture that critics loathe (partly because they watch them in dreary screening rooms on rainy, Monday mornings with only other film critics in the audience. Which is, let's face it, the worst audience for this kind of movie!). And yet, movies like *Aces Go Places 3 need* an audience to work (or to even exist).

It's a movie that tries to out-do itself several times. In the second heist sequence, for instance, you've got thieves addressed as Santa Claus forming an acrobatic pyramid to filch the MacGuffin diamond, zooming thru the ceiling on rocket packs, and riding on motorbikes *en masse* and flying between rooftops (like *The Italian Job*, but cheated with optical effects). Followed by duels with guards riding quad bikes.

And the 1983 flick opens with its version of the *James Bond* teaser sequence, which is typically a hi-octane action scene in some exotic locale involving lots of stunts and goofy humour. In *Aces Go Places 3*, the film opens in Paris with a lengthy sequence on and under the Eiffel Tower (where else?), and next to and in the River Seine. Multiple gags, fights in an elevator, a tussle with a slinky assassin, the teaser apes gleefully numerous movies, before whisking the hero into the jaws of a submarine in the Seine for the exposition scene. In true formulaic script style, *Aces Go Places 3* climaxes its first act with a lavish action sequence, as Kong snaffles the precious diamond from a laser-guarded vault.[6]

❉

Aces Go Places 3 also reminds us that comedy has been an important element in Tsui Hark's cinema. Altho' comedy is routinely neglected by film critics, many of the greatest film directors have made comedies: Ingmar Bergman, Charlie Chaplin, Buster Keaton, Woody Allen, Federico Fellini and Jean Renoir. Indeed, before *Aces Go Places 3,* Tsui had already directed *All the Wrong Clues* (a gangster comedy, which the *Aces Go Places* movies drew on), *We're Going To Eat You* (horror comedy), and humour forms a key element in many of Tsui's finest achievements in cinema: *Zu,: Warriors From the Magic Mountain Peking Opera Blues*, the *Chinese Ghost Story* films, the *Swordsman* movies, and the *Once Upon a Time In China* series.

[6] Note that it's the inspector Albert's wife (Inspector Ho – Sylvia Chang) who kills James Bond at the end of *Aces Go Places 3* (where, in a genre movie of this kind, it would usually be the hero, Sam).

Aces Go Places 3 reminds us too that comedy has been central to Hong Kong cinema for decades, and that many of the great directors of Hong Kong movies have produced comedies: Sammo Hung Kam-bo, John Woo, Ann Hui, Jackie Chan *et al* (tho' directors such as Woo haven't returned to comedy for many years).

7

SHANGHAI BLUES

Soeng Hoi Zi Je

Oh, man, Tsui Hark – he's crazy. Once you go into a studio with him, you never know when you're going to come out. He has so much energy.

Sylvia Chang

Starring Sylvia Chang, Kenny Bee, Sally Yeh, Loletta Lee and Shing Fui On, *Shanghai Blues*[7] (Mandarin: *Shanghai zhi Ye = Shanghai Nights,* 1984) was a fluffy, romantic comedy in the screwball style, filmed in glorious, glowing colours (also in the cast were: Rachel Lee Lai Chun, Tin Ching, Wu Fung, Ding Yue, Patrick Lung Kong and Manfred Wong Man Jun).[8] Altho' Tsui Hark's name dominates discussions of *Shanghai Blues* (as in talk about many (most) of the movies he's involved with), it was in fact not written Tsui, but by Chan Koon-chung, Raymond To Kwok-wai and Roy Szeto Cheuk-hon. It was produced by Tsui; prod. des. was by Hing Yee Ah Yeung; costumes by Poon An-Ying; hair by Wan Yuk-Mui and Lai Wai-Yin; make-up by Jan-Hoi Yam; the DPs were Chang Hui-Kung, Peter Ngor Chi-Kwan, Bill Wong Chung-Piu, David Chung Chi-Man and Lau Hung-Chuen; music by James Wong Jim and Tang Siu-Lam; music editor: Yu Ting; sound fx editor: Sek-Kei Kwong; stunts by Chi-Keung Chiu; editors: Chew Siu-sum and Ng Kam-Wah. Released Oct 11, 1984. 104 mins.

Shanghai Blues was the first in a planned trilogy, in which *Peking Opera Blues* (1986) was the second installment; it remains incomplete. Altho' *All About Women* could be seen as the third film). *Shanghai Blues* was important for Tsui in being the first production from his new film company, Film Workshop (when he broke away from Cinema City; it's

---

[7] It's Tsui Hark's wife, Nansun Shi Nan-sheng, who created the English titles for his movies. Shi came up with *Shanghai Blues* and *Peking Opera Blues,* but there's no blues music in either movie (LM, 70).
[8] New Wave director Allen Fong also appeared in *Shanghai Blues.*

probable that Tsui pitched *Shanghai Blues* to the folks at Cinema City and was rejected);[9] *Shanghai Blues* is also Tsui's favourite among his own films. Easy to see why: *everything works*.

To explain further: *Shanghai Blues* is a favourite because: first, everything soars, all the pieces fit, it's a satisfying whole. Second, it contains so many aspects of cinema that Tsui is fond of. Third, it states issues and themes important to Tsui. Fourth, it makes good the disappointments of *Zu* of the year before. Fifth, it is more personal than fun-but-formulaic Cinema City comedies such as *All the Wrong Clues*. Sixth, it dissipates the anger/ negativity of the first three Tsui-helmed features (*Butterfly Murders, We're Gonna Eat Ya, Dangerous Encounter*): *Shanghai Blues* is blissfully upbeat and optimistic.

And *Shanghai Blues* is a musical! Yes, for his seventh theatrical picture, Tsui Hark staged a musical, one of the most difficult, complex and tricky challenges of all film genres.[10] *Shanghai Blues* opens with a nightclub song,[11] and revisits the nightclub periodically. Not only are there humorous (and tender) songs at frequent intervals, there is also plenty of dancing, and theatrical performances. *Shanghai Blues* is also (like *Peking Opera Blues*), a backstage musical (and a good one, too).[12]

Bordwell and Thompson note of Tsui Hark's form of cinema in *Shanghai Blues* and *Peking Opera Blues*:

> These dazzling, hyperactive mixtures of action, comedy, and sentimental romance borrow openly from the New Hollywood. Tsui's scenes are busy to the point of exhaustion: the camera rushes up to the actors and wide-angle setups multiply rapidly. (650)

For Stephen Teo, *Peking Opera Blues* and *Shanghai Blues* are 'modern examples of the hyphenated musicals of old: combos of comedy, adventure, the woman's film, plus the extra bonus of MTV giving an already eclectic genre a postmodern tinge' (38).[13]

The golden age of Shanghai cinema ended in 1937, with the occupation of Japan. The Japanese took over film production in Shanghai, as well as in Peking and Manchuria. This period has been explored many times in Chinese cinema, and several movies in the 1980s and 1990s went to 1920s-30s Shanghai (including the Tsui Hark-produced *Shanghai Grand*). Tsui had already explored the 1930s in *All the Wrong Clues*.

Indeed, one of the forerunners of Tsui Hark's form of fantasy martial arts cinema was the 1927 picture *Romance of the West Chamber* (a.k.a. *Way Down West*), produced by movie mogul Li Minwei in Shanghai.

---

[9] *Shanghai Blues* certainly draws from the same cinematic pool as *All the Wrong Clues*, Tsui's 1981 Cinema City comedy.
[10] A musical comedy as lavish as *Shanghai Blues* requires a huge amount of resources and a film studio.
[11] The song is cut into a montage, where we also visit characters such as Tung, then working as a clown, and the introduction of Stool.
[12] It captures the social scene backstage, as the performers gather round their make-up tables and talk-talk-talk (as well as the inevitable bitchiness).
[13] Mandarin musicals of the 1950s were a cultural mix of Western/ Hollywood, Shanghai cinema, and Hong Kong style.

The first act of *Shanghai Blues* begins[14] with a song, features a Latin dance which goes very wrong, includes a brass band, and ends (at the usual 30-minute mark), with a sweet violin melody (played by Tung Kwok-man, this fuels another montage, in which Stool beams with joy – almost at the simple experience of being able to hear music). The script, as usual in Tsui's cinema, is constructed along classical lines. Act 2, for instance, opens and closes with music, and climaxes with the farce in Tung's apartment.

Effervescent, bubbly, airy, light as a rainbow – *Shanghai Blues* is all that (it is definitely a movie-movie), but it also delivers plenty of heart and soul underneath the gaudy baubles of its marvellous surfaces and colours (*Shanghai Blues* is a technical *tour-de-force*). The cinematic architecture of the 1984 movie is extravagant (and entrancing), but none of that is allowed to overwhelm the romantic comedy or the characters (the misunderstandings, the disguises and the revelations, the to-ings and the fro-ings of a screwball comedy form).

Shanghai Blues also exhibits a form that Tsui Hark employs many times: slamming genres together, sometimes within the same scene. The musical, the backstage musical, the romantic comedy, and the romantic triangle are some of the most obvious genres; yet there are also elements of the historical drama, and the war-time drama. And yet sistershood/ friendship and the women's film may be even more significant.

The reason that Tsui Hark offered for setting *Shanghai Blues* in the past was that it had been conceived as a contemporary story, or perhaps in the future (in 1997, seen from 1984). But instead he proposed going back to the 1930s/ 40s, an era filled with similar fears (LM, 59).

There are three main characters in *Shanghai Blues* (the dramatic model is friendship between women, plus a romantic triangle):

• Sally Yeh's young, naïve refugee Stool.

• Sylvia Chang's cabaret singer Shu Shu (Shu Pui-lam), a.k.a. Skinny Bags.

• Kenny Bee's musician/ clown/ soldier Tung Kwok-man (he's dubbed Do-Re-Mi).

Needless to say, all three actors are outstanding, and an absolute delight to watch. The casting of Yeh + Chang + Bee is dead-on in *Shanghai Blues*. Meanwhile, the vast retinue of supporting players (and the extras) contribute immensely. There are many scenes of strong ensemble acting (a common ingredient in Tsui Hark's cinema). With *Shanghai Blues*, actors start to be nominated for acting awards for the first time in Tsui's film career. (Side-note: Loletta Lee, who plays Shu Shu's assistant Chicken Fung at the club, is a porn star – she appeared in Category III movies and went on to be nominated at the Hong Kong Film Awards for mainstream films such as *Final Victory*, 1987. Which makes it ironic that her character is shy, clumsy and innocent, and is hit upon by guys).

One of the joys of *Shanghai Blues* is its hectic pace (as befitting a

---

14 Like many Tsui Hark movies, *Shanghai Blues* starts *big* – with busy, expensive, production value scenes. Ever the showman, Tsui likes to open his movies by displaying their high entertainment value.

screwball comedy) – this movie *really* moves! – and yet it is also a character study. *Shanghai Blues* works in large part because we get to know the three main characters very well in the first act. The film spends time with them, sometimes doing nothing more'n joking about in the apartment block (this is definitely partly down to the script by Chan Koon-chung, Raymond To Kwok-wai and Roy Szeto Cheuk-hon. Not all of the movies helmed or produced by Tsui Hark perform this all-important function – they get consumed with the toys and technical gimmickry of cinema, or they focus on plots and events).

Shanghai Blues is a comedy with running gags: a mouse on the loose; arguing over the bed or the couch; stolen money; mistaken identity; and being blind ('I can see the glittering lights of Shanghai!', 'You're blind!', 'I'm guessing!').

Shanghai Blues is not a feminist film – but it does display proto-feminism in its selection of two female leads and one male lead to form the romantic triangle (reversing the usual scenario), and to make the women economically independent (tho' of course they are struggling, as is everybody in this cinematic portrayal of Shanghai after WWII – everyone in Europe and Asia and Africa was suffering).

Thus, we look at Tung Kwok-man from the viewpoint of the women, rather than the usual set-up of two men with a woman between them. The first act instigates several gender reversals: for example, it's Tung who's naked and taking a shower when the two women spy on him (this is the first time we see Tung from the women's point-of-view). And he is the butt of their joshing around.

Indeed, some of the most enjoyable scenes in *Shanghai Blues* are those involving the two female leads, Sylvia Chang and Sally Yeh: Tsui Hark is a very good director of actresses, and brings out the best in them (this is true with all of the actresses who have appeared in Tsui's movies as director). Some of the time, you can see Tsui and the team simply standing back and letting the actresses do their thing (*Shanghai Blues* is generous in giving so much screen time to Chang and Yeh so they can take off).

Indeed, Tsui Hark has acknowledged the influence of Sylvia Chang[15] on his thinking at this time: Chang told Tsui that women could be 'richer subjects, more complex than guys', altho' Tsui at first resisted this argument. Later, he came around to that view, and *Shanghai Blues* expresses it, as does his next film but one, *Peking Opera Blues*. Tsui's subsequent career displays his feminist views clearly.

The struggle to survive is a key theme in *Shanghai Blues* – money is pulled out into the open and waved many times (Stool has some money stolen, which she keeps in a purse tied to her thigh. An important act for Tung Kwok-man has him accosting the thief and getting the purse back; but then he's unable to find her. Money is thus used by the writers to link the two charas). Everybody's focussed on $$$$ – the pedicab drivers ask for payment before anything else (and several times in the first act; we

---
15 Sylvia Chang was herself a director and writer (*Red Violin, Tempting Heart*); Chang also ran the Taiwan arm of Cinema City.

also see in the prologue that inflation is out of control – toilet paper costs thousands!). Meanwhile, the bums under Soochow Bridge are selling their blood for food (to Tung's distress – they are former soldiers).[16] Stool lodges with Shu Shu because she has nowhere else to go (and when she leaves the apartment in a fit of pique, she slinks back to ask for money for food). Shu Shu and Stool bond over a jokey, mistaken suicide scenario (a rather melodramatic way of bringing the two charas together), where they both end up in the river (the river setting chimes with the moment when Shu Shu meets Tung, under the bridge). As with North American films set in the Depression (1930s), poverty is never far away. As Lisa Morton noted, 'Shanghai Blues is probably the best American Depression-era romantic comedy never made in America' (54).

So getting a good job in the Big City is an important minor theme in Shanghai Blues: there's a wonderful sequence in the middle acts of Shanghai Blues which sends up Hong Kong Beauty Pageants (many actresses (including the very finest in China) have entered the Hong Kong film industry thru beauty queen competitions):[17] the delightfully naïve Stool goes there in a mix-up of addresses (hoping to find work at a kindergarten, as a teacher), changing into a bathing suit and inevitably causing mayhem (when she loudly announces that she's naked). And yet the beauty queen contest isn't merely a one-scene skit – it provides plenty more humour later when Madame Yu, the imperious boss of the contest, decides that Stool is the winner, and sends out a $10 million reward to find her.

Like many characters in Hollywood musicals, the people in Shanghai Blues are struggling to better themselves, to work from the street upwards. Tung Kwok-man, for instance, is a composer, desperate to have his songs performed by the stars (his moment of epiphany is hearing one of his songs on the radio). When Tung visits a theatrical agent, Mr Ma, there's a mix-up of musical manuscripts and actor's agents which is pure Marx Brothers.

❂

Taking Shanghai as its setting, Shanghai Blues references a large slice of the history of Chinese cinema: for decades Shanghai was the movie capital of China (b4 WW2). Shanghai Blues is thus another of Tsui Hark's pæans to the movies he grew up watching. Shanghai Blues invokes the glitz and the showbiz of Shanghai in its heyday, as well as the grit and the poverty and the hustling to make a dime and survive.

Shanghai Blues is another of Tsui Hark's Big City movies – not Hong Kong this time, but the city that was the forerunner of Hong Kong in so many ways, Shanghai. A city of hustlers, hookers, thieves, monsters, sailors, nightclubs, scuzzy tenements infested by mice, rickshaws, and bums living on the streets.

One of the impressive aspects about Shanghai Blues is how

---

16 And they don't want his Western music (his trombone – actually, it's a horn) adding to their traditional, Chinese instruments.
17 The beauty contest sequence was used in He's a Woman, She's a Man (Peter Chan, 1994).

successful it is at reproducing the teeming streets of pre-WW2 Shanghai, when it became one of the great cities of the world. *Shanghai Blues* is a studio-based (and back-lot) movie, but it employs plenty of extras to generate the hustle and bustle of a grand metropolis.

With a time scale on either side of WW2 (the 8-minute prologue is set in 1937, with the bulk of the movie set in 1947), the historical background is evoked in broad, neon-drenched brushstrokes. (In the prologue of *Shanghai Blues*, Tung Kwok-man, a wannabe musician working as a clown at the nightclub, decides, along with his fellow clown (his long-suffering uncle, Uncle Twenty, a delightful performance by Tin Ching), to abandon the show (just b4 they're due to go on stage), and enlist in the military forces – the Japanese are invading). Shanghai fell to the Japanese on Aug 13, 1937 (Japanese occupied all of Shanghai except for the foreign concessions of Western powers; that changed in 1941, when Japan entered WW2).

That's merely the socio-political setting, however, because *Shanghai Blues* is first and foremost a musical comedy about love and romance in the Big City (the key scene in the prologue occurs underneath Soochow Bridge, where Tung Kwok-man bumps into Shu Shu as they take cover from Japanese bombers during an air raid. In a moment of fairy tale cheese, they vow to meet again in ten years in the same place). And yet the political and social environment is skillfully and wittily evoked in *Shanghai Blues* – this is very much a movie set in a particular place and time.[18]

And just look at how much information and drama is squeezed into the 1937 prologue of *Shanghai Blues* (it is a masterpiece of editing) – it includes two big set-pieces (the Latin dance and the bombing of Shanghai), plus introducing the two major characters, plus information about their lives, plus the minor charas around them, plus a romantic encounter while Shanghai is under attack. This is *sensational* filmmaking.

✲

Stylistically, *Shanghai Blues* recalls a movie released two years earlier – *One From the Heart* (1982), an expensive, elaborate and troubled Francis Coppola/ American Zeotrope production (which went over-schedule and over-budget, and had a feeble performance on releases in theatres). The neon-bright Las Vegas fakery of *One From the Heart* threatened to swamp its bittersweet, romantic comedy narrative, and despite being a majestic movie, the critics panned it. *Shanghai Blues* has the same saturated, glowing colours as *One From the Heart*, and even scenes set amongst neon signs on rooftoops. (It's also a film where filters're used, a favourite Tsui Hark technique – most obviously with the star-shaped filters in the nightclub). And *Shanghai Blues* has a unified look, despite using five cinematographers (the credited ones – there may be more): Chang Hui-Kung, Peter Ngor Chi-Kwan, Bill Wong Chung-Piu, David Chung Chi-Man and Lau Hung-Chuen.

As Stephen Teo put it:

---

[18] It opens with good times scenes in the French concession.

the beautifully designed and elaborate sets, with bright colour schemes and dazzling movements enhance an intricately choreographed, exquisitely timed, crazy comedy that effortlessly segues into dramatic scenes. (1997, 167)

Shanghai Blues also recalls many romantic/ musical comedies from Hollywood's Golden Age (just as *One From the Heart* did).[19] Meanwhile, *The Umbrellas of Cherbourg* (the celebrated French musical of 1964) is referenced in a light-hearted, rain shower sequence (filmed partially from above, to show off the multi-coloured umbrellas – *Singin' In the Rain* (1952) is an obvious reference). Tsui Hark has a cameo as a 'man with umbrella' (who's drenched by Stool). *Crossroads* (*Shizi Jietou*, 1937) is another reference point in *Shanghai Blues*, along with other movies of Shanghai's heyday in the 1930s.[20] Tsui Hark acknowledged that *Shanghai Blues* was consciously created as an *hommage* to earlier movies in China ('it looks similar to a lot of other movies' [LM, 59]).[21]

❋

Cinematic ambition is everywhere in *Shanghai Blues*, as the 33 year-old Tsui Hark demonstrates his mastery of the musical comedy form. Not least among the ambitious qualities of *Shanghai Blues* is the skilful orchestration of the huge cast of secondary characters, who're flitting in and out of scenes at the speed of light. Many of the secondary charas are types, of course, as befitting the musical comedy genre (the street thief, the lowly bum, the showgirl's bitchy rival, the cool gangster, the hero's war-time buddies), but the actors embody them with an energy and a roundedness that's very appealing (making them much more than mere 'types').

Some of the most enjoyable and slickly staged scenes in *Shanghai Blues* are those involving Shu Shu at the nightclub, where she works as a dancer. This being a comedy, and a backstage musical, the performances often hit the skids (in one skit, Shu Shu, arguing with a rival (whom she calls 'Big Boobs'),[22] falls into a bubble bath in the shape of a giant clam shell, and then has to save face by singing from the stage).

There is a lengthy farce scene[23] (in the vaudeville/ theatrical tradition) in the middle of *Shanghai Blues* where the main characters are hiding in Tung Kwok-man's apartment, as people call at the door)Shu Shu is hiding from Stool while wearing Tung's pyjama top).[24] And a sex scene farce when several characters converge around Stool, the new Beauty Queen and Madame Wu, who runs the contest (Stool gets comically drunk, and there are men undressing in Madame Wu's bedroom and climbing into bed with her – again, Tsui Hark has men disrobing, not women).

---

19 Tung, for instance, is written very much like a Gene Kelly character.
20 S. Teo, 1997, 167.
21 Some scenes end with a freeze frame, which may've inspired John Woo (LM, 57). Woo says his freeze frames derive from François Truffaut (in *The 400 Blows*, the usual classy reference).
22 There's an on-going rivalry with 'Big Boobs' which turns nasty for Skinny Bags when she's threatened by 'Big Boobs'' boyfriend (twice).
23 A reprise of *All the Wrong Clues*.
24 There's an extended version of this sort of scene in the Jackie Chan picture *Project A, Part 2*.

The men in *Shanghai Blues* are often portrayed negatively – as lecherous, money-hungry, or aggressive. Men preying upon women is a recurring motif in *Shanghai Blues*. For instance, a bunch of guys cluster around Stool at the beauty competition party, desperate for a kiss; the old pervs swamp Stool, who's completely out of her depth. Tsui Hark is very fond of loud, crowded scenes which reflect the big city *milieu* of Hong Kong and the movie-cities which stand in for it. Tsui likes nothing better'n cramming the frame with teeming masses of humanity.

❀

A director's movie, assuredly, yet it is the writers (Chan Koon-chung, Raymond To Kwok-wai and Roy Szeto Cheuk-hon), and whoever came up with the concept, that deserves just as much adulation for the all-out success of *Shanghai Blues*. Look at the script – it cleverly delivers the twists and turns of a romantic comedy – and it is genuinely romantic, and genuinely funny (unlike many rom-coms).

But only one woman can get the guy – by rights, it has to be Shu Shu, the woman who vowed to meet Tung Kwok-man in ten years' time at Soochow Bridge during the air-raid in the 1937 prologue. So poor Stool doesn't get her beloved Do Re Mi (however, Shu Shu heroically sacrifices herself, and opts to leave for Hong Kong with an older man, the nightclub manager (Wu Fung) – Shu Shu is the sort of attractive woman who has men hitting on her regularly, as at the nightclub; but she rejects them). But then, at the last moment, Stool remembers how Shu Shu helped her when she was on the streets, and gives up Do Re Mi, sending him off to the railroad station. (Thus, both women act heroically and selflessly. However, the bond between Tung and Shu Shu is much stronger, and is romantic, whereas Tung hasn't reciprocated Stool's affections).

The moment when Tung Kwok-man and Shu Shu realize that they've met each other after ten years is played out on the rooftop of their apartment, during another power cut. It's a sweet moment, the end of the romantic search.

So *Shanghai Blues* closes at the romantic setting of a railroad station (as all routes lead to Hong Kong, and the charas head for Canton from Shanghai – the movie opens and closes with arrivals and departures).[25] It's unashamedly movie-ish and drenched in treacle, a *Casablanca* ending, a *Graduate* ending.

The smart, witty script ties up the plots with a candy-light touch (listen to the music (by James Wong Jim) – once again, it's the miraculous power of music to conjure emotion that lifts the montage editing even higher). Shu Shu and Tung Kwok-man are re-united in a cute scene in the midst of the train carriage (it's staged as another of the crowd scenes that Tsui Hark likes to depict, with the passengers watching the lovers' reunion like it's a sporting match, heads swivelling to and fro, and applauding when the embrace inevitably occurs). A crowd-pleaser, but *Shanghai Blues* couldn't end any other way.

---

[25] No need to comment on the journey the characters intend to make from Mainland China to Hong Kong.

8

PEKING OPERA BLUES

Do Ma Daan

INTRO.

Peking Opera Blues (*Dao Ma Daan* in Mandarin = *Knife Horse Actresses*, 1986) was directed and co-produced by Tsui Hark; Raymond To Kwok-wai wrote the script; Claudie Chung Jan and Tsui were producers for Cinema City/ Film Workshop; David Wu Tai-wai was editor; Hang-Sang Poon and Horace Wong Wing-hang were DPs; prod. des. by Kim-sing Ho, Chi-hing Leung and Vincent Wai; costumes by Bobo Bo-ling Ng and Peggy Cheung Siu-ping; hair by Lee Kin-tai; make-up by Fung Cho-tak; Tony Ching Siu-tung and Stephen Tung Wei were the action choreographers; music by James Wong Jim and David Wu Dai-wan; it was distributed by Golden Princess.[26] Released Sept 6, 1986. 104 minutes.

Peking Opera Blues featured a stellar cast, many of whom were Tsui Hark regulars: Brigitte Lin Ching-hsia, Sally Yeh Tse-man, Cherie Chung, Mark Cheng, Kenneth Tsang, Paul Chun Kong and veteran Wu Ma. Also in the cast were: Kwok Keung Cheung, Feng Ku, Po-Chih Leong, Ha Huang, Yin Szema, Ching Tien, and Dean Shek.

Peking Opera Blues is a 100% Tsui Hark classic movie: there's nothing not to like and enjoy in this slice of pure showbiz. *Peking Opera Blues* is a favourite with Hong Kong cinema fans,[27] regularly placed in fans' top tens: it's a terrific, feel-good movie (and a wonderful Christmas movie, too).

Peking Opera Blues is a historical movie, a nostalgic[28] movie, a backstage comedy, and an action-adventure spy story (with plenty of action – Tony Ching Siu-tung and Stephen Tung Wei were the action directors). *Peking Opera Blues* happily skids between these genres, blending them and subverting them – which's one of the hallmarks of Tsui Hark's cinema (but genre-bending is also a hallmark of Hong Kong cinema

---

26 Tsui Hark said that they had subtitled *Peking Opera Blues* for under $100 and in 2 days.
27 It was nominated for 6 awards at the Hong Kong Film Awards.
28 Several of Tsui Hark's movies benefitted from (and helped to create) the rise in the cinema of nostalgia of the late 1980s (with movies such as *Peking Opera Blues*).

– sometimes Hong Kong movies look as if they are entries in a competition to mix the most genres within a single movie).29

Tsui Hark has a thing for Peking Opera, and reckoned it would be good material for a comedy (LM, 70). The main titles feature Peking Opera performers, costumes and props. (The film's title, like *Shanghai Blues*, emphasizes the links to the great movie centres of Chinese history).

Peking Opera Blues is also a reminder that *comedy* is a big part of Tsui Hark's cinema; this was the mid-1980s, of course, when Tsui had been working for Cinema City (a film studio devoted to comedy), and had been involved with comedies such as *Aces Go Places* and *All the Wrong Clues*. But humour continued to play an important role in Tsui's output, whether it was in the *Once Upon a Time In China* series, or in movies that Tsui produced (such as *A Chinese Ghost Story* or the *Swordsman* series).

The background of *Peking Opera Blues* involves warlords vying for power during the regime of Yuan Shikai (the first President of the Republic), and his ambitions to expand his territory following the 1911 revolution in China. (It's set in Peking in 1913). A loan agreement between Chinese and foreign powers is one of the issues (and the documents of the loan form one of the MacGuffins).

Peking Opera Blues raises issues such as democracy, nationalism, government and politics in a self-conscious manner: *Peking Opera Blues* is not a history lesson, nor a message movie – it's primarily a piece of entertainment; but it is a satire on the Chinese ignorance of democracy, as Tsui Hark put it (and it contains sly digs at regimes such as the British in Hong Kong, and the People's Republic of China).

The celebrated 1993 movie *Farewell My Concubine* seems like a melodramatic sequel to *Peking Opera Blues* – *Farewell My Concubine* similarly focusses on a Peking Opera troupe to explore recent, Chinese history. Tsui Hark has adapted books by the author of *Farewell My Concubine,* Lilian Lee, and Tsui regular Leslie Cheung starred in it.

The stars of a movie like *Peking Opera Blues* include the production designs (Kim-Sing Ho, Chi-Hing Leung and Vincent Wai), the costume designers (Bobo Bo-Ling Ng and Peggy Cheung Siu-Ping), the hair (Lee Kin-Tai) and make-up (Fung Cho-Tak) supervisors, the DPs (Poon Hang-Sang and Horace Wong Wing-Hang), and the props guys (Lee Kuen-Long and Cheung Foo-Wing).

Peking Opera Blues is *fast*, it's light, it's frothy and it's beautifully designed (a riot of colour, especially in the costumes). *Fast* – at the usual Tsui Hark rate of 1,000 miles-an-hour, and very nimble on its feet. There is a light touch to Tsui's comedies: the gags are not laboured over, and there's no pause built into the editing to allow the audience to laugh (but I bet this movie played like gangbusters in Hong Kong theatres).

Peking Opera Blues is another Tsui Hark movie which crams in several movies into 104 minutes, as well as careening around several genres. If only, the nay-sayers complain, Tsui could stick to a *few* issues

---

29 *Project A* (1983) may have influenced the setting of *Peking Opera Blues*, and the female leads might've been inspired by *Golden Queen* (1984), which also starred Brigitte Lin and Sally Yeh.

and *one* genre and *one* stylistic approach. No, that's just not enough for Tsui! He'd be bored sick! Thus, *Peking Opera Blues* veers from bawdy slapstick comedy one minute (where Sheung Hung tries to grab a gun), to serious melodrama (where Tsao Yun cradles her dying father) the next, to full-on action cinema a moment later. For Lisa Morton, it's 'a film that created its own genre (the period-comedy-women's-actioner?)' (LM, 65).

Fast but not superficial, merely flashy, or incoherent: it's fast but always clear and readable: Hal Henson noted of the editing style in *Peking Opera Blues*:

> The action moves almost incomprehensibly fast, and the editing rhythms crackle like machine-gun fire. Not in a long time has a filmmaker made the screen jump with energy and wit and invention the way Hark does here. But though directed for speed, it doesn't have the sort of heedless acceleration that closes out beauty or coherence. (1988)

If you go back and look at (1) the shots in *Peking Opera Blues*, how they are staged, the information they convey, and then (2) look at how the beats are constructed, and then (3) consider how the beats are edited together to make mini-scenes, and then (4) see how those mini-scenes are placed end-to-end to form a whole scene, you will find that the construction, the selection of camera angles, the shot sizes, the lenses, the framing, and all of the other technical/ artistic choices are dead-on, are carefully worked-out, and, crucially, add up to a mesmerizing *flow*. David Wu Dai-wan is of course one of the greatest editors in world cinema.

By contrast, if you look at rapid editing in films which don't work or flow, you can see that cutting quickly (over-cutting) isn't the whole deal: it's about how the shots work in themselves, and together, to form a sequence. Some filmmakers are simply naturals at this construction (which is intuitive and instinctive).

There is plenty to enjoy in *Peking Opera Blues*: the enormous ensemble cast (which features a host of familiar faces in Hong Kong cinema); the sleek, sexy persona of Brigitte Lin Ching-hsia (here crossdressing for one of the first times of many in Chinese cinema); the breathless pace; the fizzy comedy; the dazzling visuals and designs (the production design and cinematography are outstanding); and of course the deftness and ingenuity of the action sequences.

And for those who need it or demand it (i.e., many Western film critics), *Peking Opera Blues* features political themes and subtexts a-plenty. Filmed in Hong Kong, set in Peking in a time of political unrest in the early years of the twentieth century (in 1913), *Peking Opera Blues* has everything a critic could desire in evoking political and ideological discourses.

If you like backstage comedies and backstage musicals (and who doesn't?!), *Peking Opera Blues* doesn't disappoint. *Peking Opera Blues* satisfies like the finest backstage musical comedies (such as, in the

West, *42nd Street* or *Singin' In the Rain*). It's got the bitchy, very camp actors; it's got the exasperated veteran who runs the theatre and is focussed above all on keeping his business thriving; it's got the newbies who have to dress up and venture on stage to avoid detection; it's got performances going wrong; it's got crossdressing and disguises; and it's got the actors and the theatre being swept up in larger, political events.

The *exuberance* of this 1986 Cantonese movie, its panache, its all-out efforts to entertain, completely swamp the viewer. It's impossible not to be carried along by this artfully artificial confection.

A candy confection, admittedly, but one with blood and guts and a real passion for ideological and political issues. There's no doubting Tsao Yun's devotion to the political cause (or Ling Pak-hoi's), and how she will risk her life for it. There's no getting away from the fact that quite a bit of *Peking Opera Blues* is pretty gritty and hard-hitting: the torture scene, where Tsao Yun is whipped, is extremely nasty and intense (and *very long*, too). And when it's a woman being beaten and slathered over (and when that woman is played by Brigitte Lin),[30] the violence inherent in the scene (in the patriarchal system, you might say), is vividly manifested. (It's too much, really, and the movie doesn't need it – or to see this much of it).

Fluffy and romantic and nostalgic *Peking Opera Blues* might be at heart, but it doesn't draw a veil over the costs of political idealism when it's put into practice in the complicated, corrupt real world. The torture scene might come from another movie, and seems way over-the-top for this kind of backstage comedy mixed with a spy melodrama and a Shanghai-esque musical. (And, along the way, the other women also suffer, getting into all sorts of scrapes).

Peking Opera Blues is a pæan to the movies that Tsui Hark grew up with, to the history of Chinese cinema, to an old-fashioned way of making movies, and to aspects of traditional, Chinese culture (such as the Peking Opera performance style). *Peking Opera Blues* is also an *hommage* to the live performances from the Peking Opera schools that Tsui would've seen in Hong Kong (Jackie Chan, Yuen Biao and Sammo Hung Kam-bo were famously part of the China Drama Academy of Peking Opera, which was portrayed in *Painted Faces*, released in 1988).

In *Peking Opera Blues*, Tsui Hark and his team are also exploring the past: around half of Tsui's films as director have been set in the past. In *Peking Opera Blues*, Tsui goes back to 1913, to a crucial period in the formation of modern China. That Tsui is dedicated to investigating Chinese history and culture everybody knows (it's positively a crusade for him): in *Peking Opera Blues*, the political and ideological aspects of this particular historical period are highlighted. It's a similar era to the *Once Upon a Time In China* series (the third *Once Upon a Time In China* movie is very close in its time period to *Peking Opera Blues*).

For some critics (such as Stephen Teo), *Peking Opera Blues* is more style over substance, with Tsui Hark and the team being absorbed by production and costume design, action choreography and movement, and

---

[30] Nobody wants to see Brigitte Lin being whipped and tortured.

the look of the whole thing, rather than with delivering a story with weight and characters with three dimensions.[31]

It's true that *Peking Opera Blues* has affinities with an M.G.M. musical comedy movie like *Singin' In the Rain* or *The Pirate*, but it also wants to dance away into multiple genres and forms, without being shackled by notions of classical structure and characterization. Even so, *Peking Opera Blues* is still telling a story all the time, and the narrative and the editing are firmly fixed to the characters and their goals (and when we look closely at the script we find that, yes, once again, it *is* classical in structure, as nearly all of Tsui's films are). There is a strong foundation to the narrative of *Peking Opera Blues*, despite how colourful and luxurious it is (and Hollywood musicals, too, are actually telling a story, and are classical structurally, no matter how much the filmmakers seem to be engrossed in camera moves or over-the-top costumes).

WOMEN AND GENDER.

A reason that Tsui Hark often gives for the success of his movies is that he was able to cast certain actors at a certain time in their lives. Thus, he made *Peking Opera Blues* partly because he wanted to use the three actresses before they retired and got married: 'for that moment they are very fantastic and silly characters in the movie; probably later they would never have that chance again' (LM, 69).

In focussing on women, Tsui Hark's thinking was simple: 'I said, "Why don't we just make a movie with no guys, just women?"' (LM, 69). Not only would *Peking Opera Blues* be about women, it would be a period piece, and a comedy (there was resistance, Tsui recalled, to rendering important historical events in a comical style).

Gender is foregrounded in *Peking Opera Blues* from the outset: this was a movie in which, as with *Shanghai Blues*, Tsui Hark wanted to explore female protagonists, to see a story from a female/ feminine/ proto-feminist perspective. Hence the three women (Sally Yeh, Brigitte Lin and Cherie Chung) at the heart of *Peking Opera Blues*. Hence the setting of the Peking Opera theatre, where all the roles are played by men (as in many theatre traditions around the world and throughout history). Hence Tsao Yun dressing in a black suit with short hair as a man. Hence Sheung Hung being unable to dive into the dressing room to find the box of jewels. Hence a woman being thrown out of the dressing rooms. The gender issue is employed throughout *Peking Opera Blues* to create situations and to drive the narrative (as if the producers asked screenwriter Raymond To Kwok-wai to foreground gender as much as possible).

Part of the pleasure of *Peking Opera Blues* is simply that writer Raymond To Kwok-wai and the filmmakers have put women in roles usually taken by men (tho' it does take some finagling from To Kwok-wai to orchestrate scenarios where the women can convincingly do what male heroes usually do, and even more fiddling around with the mechanics of the plot to get the three women to work together and be in the same

---
[31] Stephen Teo suggests that the comedies of Frank Tashlin might be a Western equivalent.

scenes together). But all of that hard work at the script meetings pays off (and thru much of the first act), because the most satisfying scenes are definitely those where the three women are adventuring as a trio.

Brigitte Lin is crossdressing in *Peking Opera Blues* and yet her gender is not disguised – this occurs throughout Tsui Hark's cinema. It's gender-bending with identity not obscured: altho' Tsao Yun would be played by a guy in most other movies, her femininity isn't hidden (LM, 68).

Splitting the heroine into three means that the filmmakers can explore several aspects of the key themes: Bai Niu/ Pat Neil (Sally Yeh Tse-man) is the performer, the artist, who wants to go on stage in her father's theatre; Xiang Hong/ Sheung Hung (Cherie Chung) is a woman on the make, with her eye on treasure (money, capitalism); Tsao Yun/ Wan (Brigitte Lin) is the political idealist, striving to do the right thing. You can regard the three women as aspects of China, of Hong Kong, of cinema, of politics in contemporary China, of contemporary youth in Canton, of anything you like.

Seeing each of the three actresses embody these issues and personalities is a treat. There's no doubt that Brigitte Lin Ching-hsia steals the 1986 movie, that she is the heart and the conscience of *Peking Opera Blues*, and that she is the principal character (the narrative is most often following her, and is structured around her). Lin is sensational in *Peking Opera Blues* (is she ever less than sensational?!), and went on to become one of the greatest stars in Asian cinema (including essaying some key roles in the cinema of Tsui Hark, such as her Asia the Invincible in the *Swordsman* series).

Altho' the relationships between the three women Tsao Yun, Sheung Hung and Bai Niu are at the heart of *Peking Opera Blues*, their relations with two young men (Ling Pak-hoi and Tung Man)[32] and two fathers (General Tsao and Boss Wong) are also significant. Much emotional juice, for instance, is squeezed out of Tsao Yun's relationship with her father (she is clearly a father's girl, and a woman with a father complex).[33] There are several touching scenes of tenderness between father and daughter, with Wan weeping, and feeling awful about betraying her father.

Meanwhile, Bai Niu/ Pat Neil exasperates her daddy, Boss Wong, with her ambitions to go on stage. And Sheung Hung gets to seduce Wong (played by the wonderful Wu Ma), in a comical scene which's delivered in a deliberately old-fashioned and stagey manner.

THE STORY, ACT BY ACT.

Much of the first act of *Peking Opera Blues* is set-up – not only is it exposition (as in any narrative-based movie), it is exposition designed to lead to the scenarios we see later. To keep the narrative set-up and exposition light and breezy, two MacGuffins are employed: first, and the easiest to grasp, is the box of jewels which Sheung Hung is desperate to

---

32 However, the romantic subplots of the two women with the two youths are only lightly brushed in to the picture (which isn't that interested in them in the end).
33 At times, Tsao Yun's relationship with her pa threatens to over-shadow that between the three women.

get hold of; a simple treasure hunt plot, then, but one which gets Sheung into all sorts of situations (hiding in a car/ creeping around a mansion/ fainting at the sight of a bloody operation, etc).

The second MacGuffin of *Peking Opera Blues* is the more serious one, the political plot about the warlords, the Republic, the President, China and Peking: the loan documents involving foreign powers. Cleverly, writer Raymond To ties the two MacGuffins together when Sheung cadges a ride with Tsao Yun, and arrives at the general's manse (ending up in the same room as the safe where General Tsao has put the documents).

Act two of *Peking Opera Blues* continues the rapid to-ing and fro-ing of the charas and the 1,000 m.p.h. storytelling focusses on the Peking Opera performances at the theatre. The camera dwells lovingly on the actors in close-up with that stunning make-up (Fung Cho-tak was make-up head, with hair by Lee Kin-tai). Part of the time it seems as if *Peking Opera Blues* is stunned and delighted to have actresses such as Sally Yeh and Cherie Chung in full Peking Opera make-up and costume, and just wants to contemplate them at length in C.U.

And with the star of the Peking Opera show, Fa Kam-shu, leaving (after an ugly scene backstage where the mobster Liu seems intent on adding him to his collection of lovers), *Peking Opera Blues* makes the inevitable decision to put Sally Yeh on stage (to cover for Fa). Which's amazing enough – but then it tops that, by shoving Cherie Chung's Sheung Hung onto the stage, too (much to Bai Niu's father's dismay).

This is cinema at its most self-indulgent and glorious – and it's wholly in tune with Tsui Hark's project of reviving older forms of Chinese entertainment, history and mythology. And the balance of elements is perfect – because the second extraordinary, Peking Opera performance winds up with a massive fire-fight. It's acrobatic, comedic, and insanely fast (there's a great gag of the punters leaping onto the benches as the gunmen shoot it out on the floor, then ducking to the floor when the heavies stand up and fire).

It's scenes like this which encourage critics to rate *Peking Opera Blues* as the perfect Hong Kong (action) movie. It's got the lot.

And at the end of act two, *Peking Opera Blues* has put together the three female stars, Brigitte Lin, Cherie Chung and Sally Yeh, side-by-side (paying off that complicated script-work in act one). In some movies, it's enjoyable to witness the formation of the trio or team, so to speak: *Peking Opera Blues* brings together the women legitimately and coherently.

And there's also the feeling that the filmmakers (and Tsui Hark in particular), are revelling in seeing the three girls together, when Tsao Yun, Sheung Hung and Bai Niu retire to Wan's place (after fleeing from the theatre), dressed in floaty, white, Western dresses (and getting drunk).

The action finale of *Peking Opera Blues* is a staggering *tour-de-force* of a fire-fight and chase across the nighttime rooftops of Peking.[34] Action director Tony Ching Siu-tung employs his customary elaborate and dazzling cable-work, encouraging the stunt team to ever-greater heights

---

[34] The fighters employ the idea of 'crossing the sea' literally, taken from the play *Eight Fairies Cross the Sea*.

of acrobatics and daredevil stunts. 'An absolute masterpiece of Hong Kong action cinema' (Lisa Morton, 67). The finale of *Peking Opera Blues* is a joyous celebration of every trick that cinema can perform, but there's plenty of blood and near-deaths for our heroes, too (you don't really believe that the movie is going to sacrifice any of the three women or the two men, but sometimes it looks as if it might). Tsao Yun, for instance, is riddled with bullets.

CRITICS ON *PEKING OPERA BLUES*.

And the critics loved it.

If there is a 'best' Hong Kong picture, it is probably *Peking Opera Blues*, claimed Andy Klein (he had seen it over 20 times).[35] As Barbara Scharres noted of *Peking Opera Blues*, 'everything works'.[36] 'One of the most astonishing things about *Peking Opera Blues* is that its occasionally extreme tone shifts work so well' (Lisa Morton, 66). 'One of the best female action films' (Jenny Kwok Wah-Lau, 2005, 741). *Time Out* called *Peking Opera Blues* 'a speed-crazed riff on what happens when a spy melodrama meets a backstage comedy: Feydeau with blood at 150 beats per minute'. Howard Hampton wrote of *Peking Opera Blues*:

> Still unsurpassed. Tsui Hark recapitulates nearly the whole history of cinema – from slapstick farce to tragic heroism – in one gleeful, manic burst of inspiration. The last twenty minutes are so exhilarating, it's as though your entire moviegoing life flashed before your eyes.[37]

Ric Meyers on *Peking Opera Blues*: 'a soaring, romantic action-comedy, with loads of eye-popping color, French-farce-flavored set pieces, and high-octane cinematic imagination' (F. Dannen, 375).

---

35 Quoted in F. Dannen, 351.
36 Ib., 401.
37 Ib., 339.

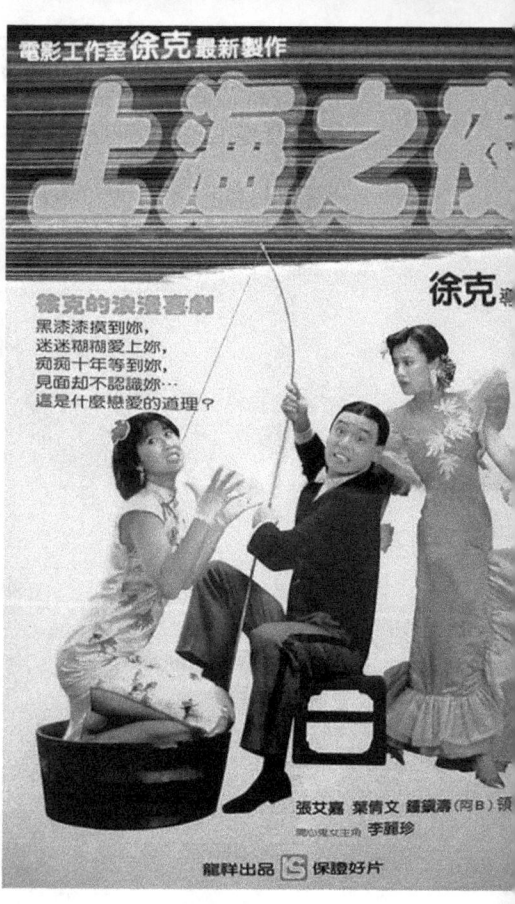

Shanghai Bues (1984).

Peking Opera Blues (1986).

9

THE MASTER

Lung Hang Tin Ha

The Master (1989, *Lung Hang Tin Ha* in Cantonese = *Dragon Travels Land Under Heaven* – and as *Huang Feihong 92 Zhi Lóng Xíng Tiánxià* for its 1992 release), was co-written by Tsui Hark with two other writers – Jason Lam Kei To and Lau Tai Muk (both of whom collaborated with Tsui on other movies he made around the same time, including *The Swordsman*). *The Master* was yet another Golden Harvest production (with a number of Chows, from Raymond Chow on down, involved), Film Workshop/ Vast Art Film Ltd/ Paragon Films. It was produced by Tsui, lit by Chan Jun Git and Paul Edwards, the actions dirs. were Brandy Yuen Jan-yeung and Yuen Wah, with music by Tang Siu Lam, and editing by Gam Ma, Marco Mak Chi-sin, and Peter Cheung (who has edited many of your favourite action movies, including many Jackie Chan flicks). Released: May 26, 1989 (in 1992 in the West). 88/ 92 minutes.

    Jet Li heads up the cast, in his first collaboration with Tsui Hark, with strong support from another Chinese action movie legend, Yuen Wah, playing Uncle[1] Tak (Yuen is of the same Peking Opera school as Sammo Hung and Jackie Chan, one of the 'Seven Little Fortunes', and has appeared in numerous Hong Kong movies, and doubled for Bruce Lee). Also featured in *The Master* are Jerry Trimble[2] as the heavy, Jonny, Anne Rickets as the gymnast Anna who befriends Uncle Tak and Jet, and Crystal Kwok as May, a Chinese banker.

    In 1988, Jet Li moved to the U.S.A., obtaining a Green Card; while there he filmed *The Master* with Tsui Hark. By then, at 26, he'd already appeared in five films, and was married. Li moved back to Hong Kong in 1990, joining Golden Harvest for the first of the *Once Upon a Time In China* movies.

    The North American version of *The Master* was re-edited from the Chinese version (among the scenes altered or dropped included the

---

[1] Elders in China are often called Uncle or Aunt, even when they're not related by blood.
[2] According to Bey Logan, Trimble and Li didn't get along.

gymnasium fight featuring Anna). It was also dubbed into American English.

If *The Master* isn't quite the classic movie it hopes to be (that every movie wants to be!), it's hugely enjoyable – in large part because of the superstar-in-the-making at the heart of the piece, Jet Li. For detractors, *The Master* is a botched and awkward attempt by Tsui Hark and the team at entering the U.S. film market, made bearable only by the presence of Jet Li.[3]

Maybe *The Master* is less successful than some of Tsui Hark's previous films, but remember too that by 1989 Tsui had already directed and produced no less than six masterpieces: *A Better Tomorrow, A Better Tomorrow 2, A Chinese Ghost Story, Peking Opera Blues, Shanghai Blues* and *Zu: Warriors From the Magic Mountain,* and he had helmed several fascinating, disturbing features: *The Butterfly Murders, Dangerous Encounters – First Kind* and *We're Going To Eat You* and two OTT comedies: *All the Wrong Clues* and *Aces Go Places 3.* And also in the same year (1989), he directed his own Vietnam epic, *A Better Tomorrow 3.* That collection of works – created in ten years! – is very impressive. And *The Master* wasn't Tsui's first time in North America, of course – he'd studied in Texas in 1975, and worked in Gotham in the late Seventies in the Chinese media.

Tsui Hark said he spent three months in the U.S.A. making *The Master* (a month for prep and 1 1/2 months for filming). Jet Li was injured during shooting, so Tsui had to avoid filming his hands. Tsui also discovered that there were things that Li didn't want to do, and Li didn't act how Tsui had expected (this was their first of many collaborations).

●

The Master is a contemporary action thriller set in Los Angeles, yet it contains so many attributes of the historical, Chinese *kung fu* picture that you can regard it as a *kung fu* movie in modern dress, or a Wong Fei-hung movie transplanted to the U.S.A. The gangs, the street brawls, the rival *dojos*, the bullies, and of course the martial arts – are all staples of *kung fu* movies (it can be regarded as a remake of the Bruce Lee movie *Way of the Dragon*, which was also a forerunner of Jackie Chan's breakthrough film in the U.S.A., *Rumble In the Bronx*). Meanwhile, the characters of Uncle Tak and Jet are very reminiscent of Wong Fei-hung and his father Wong Kay Ying (Uncle Tak's clinic is even called Po Chi Lum), with the usual teacher-disciple relationship,[4] so that *The Master* comes across as a dry run for *Once Upon a Time In China*, which was produced two years later.

In watching *The Master*, we have to remember that altho' it's set in the U.S.A., its primary audience is *not* N. American, but Chinese: at this time, as director Tsui Hark noted, Hong Kong filmmakers were still making movies largely for the local (Hong Kong) audience. And *The Master* was

---

[3] This is Lisa Morton's view (187). Morton also contends that *The Master* is 'poorly made' (no, it's technically fine), with 'weak and lifeless humour', and is 'so mind-numbingly bad it's almost impossible to believe this could be the same Tsui Hark who delivered *Once Upon a Time In China* and *Peking Opera Blues*' (ibid).
[4] So, the pupil of *sifu* Uncle Tak becomes his own *sifu* when he trains the Mexican dweebs in some amusing staples of the martial arts genre.

only dubbed into American English and released in the New World in '92, following Jet Li's success in movies such as *Once Upon a Time In China*. (So I would reckon that the comedy, for instance, plays much better for a home audience than it does for a Western audience.)

Intriguingly, altho' *The Master* is set in Los Angeles and is made primarily for a Chinese and Hong Kong audience, it *doesn't* include many images one might expect: if this was a Jackie Chan[5] or Stephen Chow movie made ten years later, for instance, one would expect to see montages of the famous sights of Tinseltown: Grauman's Chinese Theater, the Hollywood Sign, C.B.S. Records, Santa Monica Pier, Venice Beach (with all the freaky-deaky people), Rodeo Drive, the glitz of Sunset Boulevard, and of course Beverly Hills (the stars' homes, the swanky cars, the swimming pools, the palm trees, etc).

Instead, *The Master* stays resolutely downtown. Patches of waste ground, scruffy alleys with metal fences, graffiti everywhere, and the dirty sidewalk outside the Po Chi Lum store. There isn't a single image of middle class North America or upper class North America or celebrities or parties or even a single swimming pool (and only one scene with a television!).

Placing Chinese visitors in the Land of the Free, however, adds further layers of politics and culture: the social and cultural differences between China and North America are played up throughout *The Master* (sometimes for comedy – like the Chinese taxi driver, who's become fatally Americanized). Quite a bit of mileage is squeezed out of the language barriers in *The Master* (including between Cantonese and Mandarin, but mainly between English and Chinese). Tsui replayed the cultural differences angle in *Once Upon a Time In China and America*.

For New World audiences, there is the added quirk in *The Master* of seeing a bunch of foreign filmmakers offer their view of contemporary North American life (that thing of visitors coming to your home town and revealing it to you as it really is – because you've been there so long you can't see it anymore).

Inevitably, there are some quaint, naïve aspects to 1989's *The Master,* as the Chinese filmmakers offer some rather simplistic interpretations of what it means to live in contemporary U.S.A. Like the portrayal of the three goofy, Hispanic youths who worship Jet, calling him *sifu* when he bests them; or the inter-gang rivalry (when the Hispanic kids get beaten up by a black mob); or how Po Chi Lum is conveniently situated on a street in downtown L.A. that has a great view of distant skyscrapers.

Yet, the Chinese filmmakers also bring out some of the aspects of living in Los Angeles that some North American movies miss. This is a scuzzy L.A., where the streets're grey and dirty and graffitied; skyscrapers are still being built in the area around Century City (*The Master* certainly benefits from a good deal of location shooting). *The Master* captures the glamour of La-La Land, but being an urban thriller, it focusses on the gritty, tough elements (the filmmakers shoot L.A. as if it's Hong Kong. So they never miss an opportunity for another helicopter shot

---

5 As in *Rush Hour* featuring Jackie Chan.

of the collection of skyscrapers downtown. Everybody films L.A. like that, but actually that group of buildings isn't really representative of L.A. at all – rather, L.A.'s miles and miles of freeways, strip malls, Taco Bells, gas stations, car lots, supermarkets (Vons, Jons, Safeway), 99 Cent stores, and grungey condos).

The Master is also a straightahead action movie, too: there's the big bust-up of Po Chi Lum by the chief villain, Jonny (Jerry Trimble), when he storms in and hurls himself at Uncle Tak (and smashes up the place, too, delivering the all-important scenes of breaking glass, mandatory in any martial arts movie set in the contemporary era). It's a brutal bust-up, with glass flying everywhere, and Uncle Tak being soundly beaten. This creates the initial wrong that has to be righted by the hero, Jet. (No need to draw attention to the stereotyping of Jonny as a tall, blond, blue-eyed American – he is the epitome of the *gwailo,* the 'foreign devil' that crops up in many Chinese action movies (and Japanese *anime*). Remember that this 1989 movie was made first of all for the local Chinese market, so Jonny performs the same function in this story as a vicious Nazi thug in an *Indiana Jones* movie).

❖

If you had to pick a single element that's lacking from the conception, construction and script of *The Master*, it would have to be the characterizations. The story, admittedly, is predictable and not especially compelling (we have seen this story many times b4). No, it's the characters: they simply don't enchant and interest us at a more'n superficial level. Look at the characters in, say, *Shanghai Blues*, another Big City outing: the central trio in *Shanghai Blues* are wonderfully drawn characterizations (and played to the full by Sylvia Chang, Kenny Bee, Sally Yeh). But in *The Master*, *all* of the characters are *under-written*: Jet, as the fresh-faced youth trying to make it in the New World lacks depth, and Uncle Wah is too much of a one-note grouch. Jonny is a one-dimensional character, to the point where he's not really a character but a function of the plot (i.e., the rival/ the heavy/ an obstacle). And in the characterization of May, something more poignant or political could be delivered. But no, May too is under-developed (as is Anna).

All of this means that we don't care for or root for these characters much – beyond the default, movie-ish response of: we hope the bad guys are trounced for being so nasty! We hope that Uncle Wah and Jet prevail, and create a New Life in the New World).

There's a girl-on-girl fight in the gymnastics class between Anna and a rival in *The Master* (tho' it's brief – more significant in that scene are the fan service shots of young, attractive women in leotards performing gymnastics, very 1980s,Tsui Hark does *Footloose*); a car and motorbike chase (when Anna saves Uncle Tak from the hoods); an extended chase on foot, when Jet pursues the Mexican kids who snatched his luggage (the sequence includes many beats, including Jet jumping over hurdles along Wilshire Boulevard, and sliding down an enormous banner in a multi-level parking lot in a Jackie Chan-style stunt); a face-off with an African-

American gang; a challenge in a martial arts school (followed by the heavies trashing the place); another fist-and-kick fight in the Po Chi Lum store, with Anna being cruelly set upon by the thugs;[6] a big action sequence with cars and guns on a rooftop parking lot; and of course the finale of *The Master,* where Uncle Tak takes on hordes of martial artists in their black and red uniforms, with Jet coming to the rescue. *The Master* is like an update of BruceLee's movies, transplanted to L.A.

One man, many assailants – and every beat caught with its own camera angle – it's become such a staple of martial arts movies that we forget that it's a distinct departure from the traditional *kung fu* movie, where participants would perform their actions in static medium and long shots.

In *The Master,* there are a number of examples of the one-guy-versus-a-mob chestnut. Like Jackie Chan and Bruce Lee, Jet Li is one of the great action stars for delivering outstanding versions of what has become an action cliché. Is it the joy of seeing one guy beat a whole bunch of guys? Is it the thrill of watching someone with such physical grace and skill? Is it the satisfaction of seeing a large group of bullies being taught a lesson? Is it wish fulfilment, something we'd all love to be able to do in the school playground?

It's all of that. Even better when it's a little guy (Jet Li and Jackie Chan are both under 5' 8"). The first group action scene in *The Master* occurs in a waste ground filled with graffiti, where the Hispanic kids have their home: the African American mob arrives (in beaten-up, customized cars, of course!), and pins down the hapless Mexicans. Jet Li performs the first of many Wong Fei-hung-style acts, rescuing the kids from under the feet of the thugs. Then he proceeds to rough them up, a single guy in the middle of a ring of men (of course, this being the U.S. of A., in many another movie one of the mob would pull out a handgun and blow Jet away! But guns are *so* boring! And a cheat!). The second nighttime raid on the Po Chi Lum store culminates with a superb duel between the hero and the heavy on top of a police car. Certainly the Chinese filmmakers use cars in a way never seen in North American movies.

❂

The Master isn't the finest script that Tsui Hark has developed for a movie (it was co-written with Jason Lam Kee-to and Lau Tai-muk). Parts of the plot don't make sense. The villains, for instance, seem nasty and antagonistic simply for the sake of it. Jonny and his pals want to close down the *kung fu* schools (a staple motif in the Chinese *kung fu* genre, tho' it's often aligned with other motivations, such as politics, race, culture). They repeatedly pick on Uncle Tak and his herbal medicine store for apparently no other reason than Tak rejected Jonny as his student. The antagonism culminates with the bad guys kidnapping poor Anna, and hoisting her up over the edge of a skyscraper on Wilshire Blvd.

But, jeez, let's not be too tough on *The Master* here! *Loads* of action movies don't bother to explain or explore the villains' motivations and

---

6 There is, once again in a Hong Kong picture, no holding back when it comes to hitting women.

goals. Their function is often just to provide antagonisms, to get the story rolling, to provide obstacles of the heroes (and henchmen to be beaten up). And the action movies that *do* think up motivations and goals often come up with really naff ones.

Better not to bother. Better to have, in *The Master,* Jonny and his pals being simply antsy, angry, crude thugs (and this's why an action movie that *does* deliver complex and layered villains, such as the *Once Upon a Time In China* movies, can be so satisfying. When, on top of incendiary action and attractive stars and romance and comedy you have complicated villains with coherent (if nasty) goals).

An action movie doesn't *have* to be a story with the depth, complexity and super-meaningfulness of a play by Euripides. But occasionally an action movie is created which does have a really satisfying script (such as, in Tsui Hark's cinema, *Once Upon a Time In China* or *Seven Swords*).

But many critics have drawn attention to the racial, ethnic and nationalistic elements in *The Master*: this is, in the top dramatic layer, a Chinaman in North America story, automatically evoking ideological and political oppositions like China vs. the U.S.A., Chinese culture and society vs. N. American culture and society, etc. Add to that the demonization or negative stereotyping of the Yanks – blond, proto-Nazi Jonny being the classic, white foreigner of many a Chinese movie. Jonny is crude, aggressive, and seems to be perpetually angry and about to explode. Other Americans in *The Master* are ruthlessly sent up (such as the police station scene, where everybody is stuffing their gobs with food and getting stomach ache. And Jet performs some of his Wong Fei-hung medical remedies).

Taking the racial/ ethnic angle into account, at the most simplistic level, Jonny and his mob want to destroy the Po Chi Lam clinic for one reason: it is Chinese. It is 'other', foreign, different. The irony that Jonny and co. are using *Asian* martial arts seems to have escaped them.

Put *The Master* into context, however: it was *not* made for a North American audience (like, say, Jackie Chan's internationally-oriented films of the 1990s). *The Master* was produced for the local, home audience – in Hong Kong. So it's a Chinese view of North American society and culture.

Think of it the other way around: Western/ American movies set in China or featuring Chinese culture, like *Big Trouble In Little China*, or the start of the *Indiana Jones and the Temple of Doom*, or the *James Bond* movies that went East: they trot out sometimes offensive stereotypes of Asian culture, society and people.

Movies like *James Bond, Indiana Jones* and other silly action outings are, like *The Master* or other Tsui Hark films of this period (such as *A Better Tomorrow* or *The Big Heat* or *Aces Go Places 3*), popcorn flicks, pure entertainment pictures. They are movies where you don't expect an intellectual, philosophical deconstruction of culture and society. You don't expect *Star Wars, The Terminator* or *Indiana Jones* to analyze the morality and philosophy of ethic and racial stereotypes, using the theories of, say, Jean Lyotard, Fredric Jameson or Gayatri Chakravorty Spivak.

There's a romantic subplot in *The Master,* and it's played primarily for a kind of chaste comedy (which is a recurring motif in movies with Jet Li in the lead role). So there's plenty of horsing around, with Crystal Kwok's May thinking there's more to their relationship than just friendship, and Jet thinking that May is simply a kind friend. Kwok is lovely and sweet, but her role, like Anna's, is kept somewhat vague and unresolved (she is presumably intended to mirror Jet, as a youngster trying to find their place in the world, and later she's the Princess Who Must Be Rescued). At times May's more like a female version of the male buddy, in a buddy movie or cop movie: she's there as someone to talk to for the hero. The writers explore the possibilities of erotic comedy for a while, too (like the scene where May climbs on top of Jet in the driving seat, when a cop pulls them over. May pretends they're newly weds, and kisses Jet; he's bemused, as ever (and taken aback) – this became Jet Li's standard response to any erotic play).

So May doesn't make a move on Jet, and he doesn't make a move on her. But their scenes are a welcome respite from the action scenes: their conversations also highlight one of the themes of *The Master:* China and America, living in China and living in the U.S.A., and what 'home' is, and where one should live.

The character of Jet is very concerned with this idea: the Chinese, he says, are strong and can go anywhere under the sun. But if it doesn't work out, he will go home, to China. This is a recurring issue in the cinema of Tsui Hark: just *where* is home, and what does 'home' mean? (We recall that Tsui himself came to the U.S.A. to study film in Texas, and later worked in Gotham. So, in a way, you could regard *The Master* as a kind of exploration of the notion of 'home' and being Chinese in North America in a story with autobiographical overtones).

When the would-be lovers go to the beach, for instance, instead of the expected Santa Monica Pier scene, we have the nearly-couple walking in the surf and talking about 'home' and China.

The romantic subplot in *The Master* is also classic Tsui Hark in that it's largely one-sided – but from the *woman's* point-of-view. She likes Jet more'n he likes her; Tsui and his writers mined this ploy in relation to Jet Li throughout the *Once Upon a Time In China* series, where Wong Fei-hung is continually bemused by 13th Aunt's attention. Thus, in the farewell scene at the coach depot, May hopes that Jet will warm to her and is angry when he doesn't.

At this point in the romance subplot, May is all for staying in the New World and trying to make it work (she has been having an affair with her bank manager. Until she discovers him fooling around with another woman; and then she immediately walks out – and bumps into Jet, of course, where she encourages Jet to lay into the manager). That May is an Asian already established in the West is important – that she isn't going to give up and return home (she derides the idea to Jet in the Santa Monica scene). But she does meet problems in living in N. America; that the issues attached to May's character are romantic is part of the genre (and the function of her character in relation to the character of Jet), but it's also somewhat chauvinistic. (Meanwhile, Uncle Tak also tells Jet that going back to China is not for him – but Tak also says that nowhere is 'home').

Thus, you can see that altho' the character of May is included in the script of *The Master* to provide the formulaic 'love interest' (and eye candy in the form of Crystal Kwok), it actually also explores some of the major issues in Tsui Hark's work (which also form the ideological backbone of the *Once Upon a Time In China* series, for instance). What seems at first mere film fluff, throwaway romantic interludes in between boysy fight scenes, actually carries some of the deepest concerns of Tsui's cinema.

❂

Jet Li also plays many scenes for comedy in *The Master*: a Chinese guy without any English, he soon learns important phrases like, 'shut up!' He kisses people because May tells him it's what friends do (which she did in the car). It's very funny when Li is allowed to let rip, and do his version of a neurotic, Chinese Woody Allen. Because he's so often seen in serious, dramatic roles, Li's flair for comedy is often under-appreciated (but it is an essential ingredient in the success of the *Once Upon a Time In China* series).

Anna, meanwhile, is under-used in *The Master*: she's introduced in scenes, and you think something's going to happen, but it never quite does (maybe scenes involving her were cut out).[7] Her relationship with Uncle Tak is a quaint father-daughter one (with no hint of sexual relations), but Jet doesn't really understand her at all. (Meanwhile, in some scenes, Anne Rickets plays the role at near-hysterical pitch, and in others she's very roughly manhandled by the Mexican punks). Anna is also the Princess That Has To Be Rescued in the finale of *The Master* (tho' it makes more sense narratively that it be May. However, Jonny's beef seems to be primarily with Uncle Tak, not Jet, so his mob kidnap someone precious to Tak, not Jet).

Anna's role also suffers from something that occurs elsewhere in Tsui Hark's cinema – that of splitting the heroine into two. So as May becomes more prominent in the story (halfway thru act two), Anna is sort of forgotten. The writers (Tsui, Lam and Lau), having created the character of Anna, haven't quite decided what to do with her. (They seem to have wanted an All-American Girl, a straightforward, girl-next-door blonde[8] to counterpoint May's career woman (and Chinese) brunette, but Anna's also a bit of a tomboy, a great athlete, can ride a motorcycle and out-run the bad guys).

❂

The finale of *The Master* is split into two parts: the first is a smackdown in the Po Chi Lam clinic between the heroes and the rivals. This is a replay of fights we've already seen, including the opening one

---

7 The gymnastics scenes were cut from the American print.
8 Anna's kind of 'white trash' – she lives in a trailer (quite possibly a trailer that was used by the filmmakers on location).

where Uncle Tak is beaten. Here, we see Jet's pupils going into action (not entirely successfully), and the expected punch-up btn the hero and the d' Jonny. The conflict shifts outside, at night, onto a car, but it's put on pause by the arrival of the cops.

A side-story in the finale of *The Master* features a bus hijacking: all that the movie needs is to have Jet return so he can fulfil his duties as the main hero (the ruse of forgetting his passport is enough. We've all been there!). But, in typical Hong Kong, action movie style, the bus scene becomes a Big Action Sequence, with a runaway vehicle, a dead driver, screaming passengers, and Jet fighting a dreadlocked assailant armed with a shotgun. (The movie won't portray Jet as a killer, though – not here, nor in the bust-up with Jonny – so the action choreographers, Brandy Yuen and Yuen Wah, engineer an unconvincing gag where the bad guy shoots himself repeatedly with his shotgun. And then, for good measure, impales himself on smashed glass in the window).

Jonny's acts don't make sense, but then, he's angry, stubborn, and also incredibly stupid. For ex, after getting out of jail (using money), he rounds on the manager of his martial arts *dojo* and kills him! Jonny's just complained about escaping from the law, then he commits murder – and for no decent reason. If you want to stay out of trouble with the cops, you don't kill someone! The murder is an artificial means of upping the stakes, and justifying any amount of force the heroes might use.

The second part of the climax of *The Master* is delightfully preposterous: it takes place on the rooftop of a huge skyscraper in downtown Los Angeles, with the backdrop of the city, the smog, the clouds and the distant Hollywood Hills.[9] The bad guys from the *dojo* have strung up poor Anna from a rope and pole, dangling over an enormous drop (it's an early version of the high falls and rope gags which became a staple of Tsui Hark's action cinema).

As critic Bey Logan noted on the excellent audio DVD commentary of *The Master*, it's Shaw Brothers Time, with the uniformed martial artist lined up on the roof and Uncle Tak entering the battleground alone. One guy versus a mob, yet again. Yuen Wah as Tak does a brilliant job of polishing off plenty of assailants, before being beaten to the ground (and he's kicked when he's on the ground – the lowest of the low). Jet Li's Jet arrives in a suitably splendid introductory image[10] (rising from below the camera in a low angle), and takes on all-comers as he fights his way to the ringleader, Jonny.

All thoughts of narrative, theme and character are forgotten as the second section of the finale of *The Master* moves into its second half – the one-on-one confrontation between the big, blond American dude and the small, dark Chinese guy. It's a wonderful mix of kickboxing and *wushu* moves, and it's intercut with the scene of Uncle Tak saving Anna from certain death as she falls from the 'scraper.

---

9 The crew must've schlepped up to the roof of the skyscraper everyday for a week of more to film this sequence.
10 Did he arrive at reception in the foyer and ask where's the giant battle involving 100s of martial arts? Only to be directed to the roof.

To separate the hero vs. heavy smackdown from the rest of the action in *The Master,* the filmmakers have them fall into a utility room, a smaller, compact space, with props that spice up the fight (a power unit, a gas pipe, a wheel that traps Jet's foot, giant, cooling fans and the mandatory broken glass). The lengthy duel is exciting and rough, climaxing with an over-the-top beat: a huge gas explosion followed by the participants landing on an enormous clock face outside the building, hanging onto electrical cables. Well, it's not the first time in movies we've seen this (nor the last!). And we know what's going to happen: the villain's going to fall to his death. He does. Splat! (This gag, like the one of Anna falling, and Uncle Tak swinging out over the side of the building, seems to have been achieved in part for real. Tho' not, we know, filmed by Tsui Hark himself, due to his fear of heights).

The *dénouement* of *The Master* is a happy, jokey, sunny scene of multiple farewells – to Anna, to May, to Uncle Tak, to Jet, to the Latinos sidekicks – as our heroes drive off into the sunset on a Greyhound bus. May takes the initiative in her relationship with Jet, and buys a flight to Hong Kong, only for the passport gag to be revived, with Jet now forced to stay (for the mo') in North America (with Uncle Tak suggesting Canada as a possible place to try their luck; many Hong Kong filmmakers have moved to Canada). Tak re-affirms the upbeat message of *The Master*: Chinese people can go anywhere.

10

A BETTER TOMORROW 3: LOVE AND DEATH IN SAIGON

Ying Hung Bun Sik III

INTRO.
Three great actors (Chow Yun-fat, Anita Mui Yim-fong and Tony Leung Ka-fai) and a genius director (Tsui Hark) – plus the Vietnam War – how can it fail?! Who cares if *A Better Tomorrow 3* was supposedly wrested away (boo! hiss!) from John Woo by Tsui Hark? Who cares if if it wasn't Woo in the director's chair, when you have a director as astonishing as Tsui taking his place? Who cares if the heroic boys-will-be-boys macho posturing of the Wooian crime flick was displaced by Tsui & co. by a boys-plus-girl scenario (especially when that girl is Anita Mui! The sight of Miss Mui blasting away with a machine gun in one hand and a pistol in the other is worth the price of admission alone!).

OK, enough of the fan-boy prattle (but you've got Anita Mui! And Chow Yun-fat! And Tsui Hark! In Vietnam!), let's consider *A Better Tomorrow 3: Love and Death In Saigon*[11] (1989, *Jing Hung Bun Sik III* in Cantonsese, *Ying Xiong Ben Se III* in Mandarin) in the proper film crrritic fashion (i.e., all sober and serious-like): it was directed and produced by Tsui Hark, exec. prod. by Claudie Chung Chun, supervising producers were Margaret Wong, Yun-Chuen Geung and Anthony Lo,[12] and starred Chow Yun-fat, Anita Mui Yim-fong and Tony Leung Ka-fai. Edward Yiu-ming- Lung and Foo Ho-tai wrote the script (Tsui's credited with the story). The throbbing electronic score was by Lowell Lo and David Wu Tai-wai (Anita Mui sang the theme song); Wing Hung-wong, Yun Chun-Wah and Chik Kim-Kit were DPs; Luk Chi-Fung was art dir.; make-up by Ko Siu-Ping; Marco Mak Chi-sin, Tsui and David Wu were the editors; Siu-Lung Ching was sound fx editor; action dirs. were Lau Chi-Ho and Lau Fong-Sai; and Dora Chu Lai-Ha, Rosa Chow Man-Git and Chiu Suk-Wah did the costumes. 145 minutes (in the

---
[11] You can bet that poncy, poxy subtitle – *Love and Death In Saigon* – was added by Western distributors. The Chinese title translates as *Gun-Death-Sad-Bang-Bang-Hong-Kong-Vietnam*. No, actually the sub-title is: *Song of the Setting Sun.*
[12] John Woo has a producer credit.

Tawianese version;[13] 114 mins in the Hong Kong version).[14] Released: Oct 20, 1989.

In the supporting roles were: Shih Kien (Shek Kin), Foo Wang-Tat, Cheng Wai-Lun (as Pat), Maggie Cheung Hoh-Yee (as Ling), Andrew Kam Yeung-Wa (as Jimmy), Ling Nam-yin (as Bong or Bond), Wan Seung-Lam (as a general), and Saburo Tokito (as Sam Ho Cheung-ching a.k.a. Tanaka).

The first two *A Better Tomorrow* movies are discussed in the chapter on Tsui Hark's pictures as a film producer.

There are three main characters in *A Better Tomorrow 3*:

Mark Gor	Chow Yun Fat
Cheung Chi-Mun	Tony Ka Fai Leung
Chow Ying-Kit	Anita Mui Yim-fong

A Better Tomorrow 3 has four acts (with a running time of 114 mins in the Hong Kong cut, and 130/ 145 mins in the Taiwan cuts).

The prequel to *A Better Tomorrow* was apparently John Woo's idea, but it was Tsui Hark who took it up and directed the movie (it was the first time that Tsui had set a film in his homeland, and the first Hong Kong production to be (partially) made in Vietnam[15] since the war). Tsui and Woo went their separate ways during the *Better Tomorrow* sequel when, according to Woo, Tsui deliberately rushed his sequel into production in order to beat Woo's movie to the theatres.

Bullet In the Head was the picture that John Woo directed as *his* version of the third *Better Tomorrow* movie: it had Chinese guys in the Vietnam War, in Saigon, plus elements such as a bomb on the street; black market trades; and the heroes trying to get back to Hong Kong. (See below).

▶

So it's 1974 in Saigon in Vietnam, Tsui Hark's home country (and Tsui's home town – he was born in Saigon): an early scene in *A Better Tomorrow 3* stages a big production number with 100s of extras on the streets of downtown Saigon, with the Vietnamese Army facing a crowd of student demonstrators (this is a massive, logistically challenging sequence – Tsui does David Lean or Steven Spielberg, and puts the budget up on the screen early on). Screenwriters Yiu Ming-leung and Foo Ho-tai literally thrust our heroes into the *melée* by having them hurtling along the street in a motorized rickshaw (after a long airport scene, with the two stars arriving (Chow Yun-fat and Anita Mui) – which, in terms of scriptwriting, isn't the most inspired concept to start a movie (the very first shot is of a jet landing; the second image is of a tank). And nor is the getting-released-from-prison scene soon afterwards (which introduces the third star, Tony Leung Ka-fai, unfortunately hampered by giant, thick-framed glasses)).[16]

But you can't expect a Hong Kong crime and action movie to consist

---
13 There is also a 130-minute Taiwanese version, and a German print running to only 88 minutes.
14 Note the running time: 145 mins, a very long movie by Tsui Hark's standards.
15 *A Better Tomorrow 3: Love and Death In Saigon* was filmed mainly in Thailand.
16 Maybe a reference to Tsui Hark, who used to sport chunky glasses like this.

entirely of truly original narrative ideas, with nary a cliché in sight! In fact, the *Better Tomorrow* series happily trots out every cliché imaginable in the crime genre (such as the reason for the giant action scene which climaxes act one of *A Better Tomorrow 3* – two groups of crooks meeting at night to exchange money which rapidly explodes into double-crossing and violence).

I noted that the airport setting in the opening scene of *A Better Tomorrow 3* is clichéd, but, to be fair, the airport does conjure up notions of borders, travel, immigration and national identity, and a zone of perpetual anxiety and transience (our three heroes are of course classic outsiders, people who don't fit in anywhere, or who are always displaced: when they're in Vietnam, they hanker after Hong Kong; when they're in Canton, they worry about the situation in Vietnam).

The airport scene also includes some characterization: it portrays Mark Gor as a wannabe cool customer who's not as cool, calm as collected as he hopes to be. He swaggers a little, and smirks, but, following, the mild flirtation with Chow Ying-Kit (over lipstick), finds himself being strip-searched by corrupt customs officers who rip him off. Only the nod by Kit, in the corridor, to one of officers, lets Mark off the hook. That Mark is near-naked, vulnerable (and doubled-over from one punch from a truncheon) tells us plenty about his situation (i.e., it usually takes more to crumple a hero). The Mark we know from the previous *A Better Tomorrow* movies wouldn't be pushed around like this, or brought to the floor from one hit.

The airport and customs scene in *A Better Tomorrow 3* also portrays Chow Ying-Kit as a mysterious but powerful figure – how she seems to know everybody, and also has the influence to let Mark Gor walk free. This sequence also demonstrates that the *woman*, not the two men, is going to be the top dog in this movie.

But back to Saigon: *A Better Tomorrow 3* evokes brilliantly the jittery anxiety of a nation teetering on the edge of implosion. The noisy, chaotic demonstration sequence stresses the highly political nature of this 1989 movie. So there's all manner of political and ideological explorations being evoked here, from a look-back to the Vietnam War and the Fall of Saigon, to the furore over the Tiananmen Square massacre (which took place on Sunday, June 4, 1989, right before production started), to Hong Kong as an Imperial colony (Hong Kong has been lorded over by another Western power in the Far East, echoing the U.S.A. in Vietnam), to the Hand-over, and to the People's Republic of China.

So *A Better Tomorrow 3* can be regarded as a crime story smashed into a political story, or a political story which just happens to have a thriller plot weaving thru it. What's for sure is that *A Better Tomorrow 3* is explicitly political, and far more so than the cinema of John Woo (or most Hong Kong cinema). As we know, Tsui foregrounds politics much more than many of his Hong Kong contemporaries – his third film, *Dangerous Encounters — First Kind*, had a bold, loud political theme. And even in his popcorn flicks, Tsui slips in political commentary.

As well as the anti-government demonstrations on the streets of Saigon, *A Better Tomorrow 3* also includes in its first act a key discussion between the three lead characters about China, Hong Kong and Vietnam. 'We're all Chinese' is one concept raised, as is being an 'overseas Chinese' (as Tsui Hark is).

Is *A Better Tomorrow 3* vintage Tsui Hark? Yes. His fiendish third eye once again finds arresting and poetic images everywhere; *A Better Tomorrow 3* has that dream-like quality in its flow of images (edited together by Marco Mak Chi-sin *et al*) that mesmerizes the viewer (any filmmaker who can do that is going to be admired by audiences – and critics). *A Better Tomorrow 3* is also filmed in the full, Tsui Harkian style for texture and atmosphere: from the camera angles and blocking alone you can sense that the filmmakers are fully engaged with the material.

▶

Well, *A Better Tomorrow 3* is also a sequel, as everybody knows, and most critics seem to come down on the side of John Woo, seeing him as the poor sod whose movie concept was hijacked by the domineering and quick-as-lightning Tsui Hark. Thus, naughty, bossy Tsui stole shy, gentle Woo's project away from him.

And thus *A Better Tomorrow 3* does all of the things a sequel does (including all the things a prequel does). For instance, presumably actor Ti Lung opted not to return (maybe he was loyal to John Woo?), so his (notable) absence is covered in familiar sequelizing fashion (with a monologue from Chow Ying-Kit about how Sam Ho Cheung-ching is hiding away in Holland for three years, and, yes, of course they were lovers, and they were going to rule the world, etc etc etc).[17]

However, *A Better Tomorrow 3* is one of the rarer sequels that works fine without knowing about or seeing the earlier installments. Why? Because it throws away most of the material! By telling an 'origins' story, *A Better Tomorrow 3* happily junks most of the elements of the previous *Better Tomorrow* films, but without bothering too much with joining the dots, from the past to the present.

Or, rather, many elements from the previous *Better Tomorrow* movies are acknowledged, but you don't need to know them to get the full impact of this movie (the acknowledgements and connections are relatively minor). For ex, only Chow Yun-fat, among the principal actors, appeared in the earlier outings of *Better Tomorrow*. (There are nods to the charas in the names: Kit and Ho, for ex).

Script-wise, *A Better Tomorrow 3* does have the feeling of a Hong Kong crime yarn parachuted awkwardly into a Vietnam War scenario – planted on top, you might say, so that some of the elements don't mix, as narrative layers are squashed together like pieces of meat shot to ribbons by white-hot bullets.

But the Vietnam War is a bigger backdrop than hyper-capitalist Hong Kong for the crime genre elements – now the political and ideological

---

[17] Actually, that doesn't make total sense – because this is 1974, 13 years before the events in *A Better Tomorrow 2*. But it still explains away Ti Lung's Ho's absence from *A Better Tomorrow 3*.

ramifications are made explicit – partly by placing the army versus the students demonstrations up front, in act one. We know that relations with Mainland China, or the anxiety over the Hand-over, lie behind or underneath many Hong Kong films of the 1980s and 1990s, but a movie set in the Vietnam War is something else. (However, it's also true that some Hong Kong actioners are staged just like wars – epic battles between rival gangs of outlaws).[18]

▶

THE CAST.

Striding thru *A Better Tomorrow 3* with her shock of raven-hued, carefully-teased hair,[19] sunglasses and big, pouty, bright crimson lips[20] is the 26 year-old Anita Mui Yim-fong (1963-2003),[21] playing Chow Ying-Kit, a.k.a. Kit,[22] a scary, formidable and individual operator. For many years in the 1980s and 1990s, before her untimely death, Mui was a distinctive and idiosyncratic star in Hong Kong New Wave cinema, embodying a scorching sexual heat that burns up the screen. (But Mui can also express a gentleness, a wistful melancholy underneath, that makes her characters even more appealing).

And what a welcome addition to the *Better Tomorrow* enterprise Anita Mui Yim-fong is, dispersing some of the stench of testosterone that permeates the cinema of John Woo like a locker room fog. Yes, men will be men, and they will run around like schoolboys firing guns (with none of them sustaining so much as a scratch!), and the proto-fascism is scary as hell (tho' no Western film critic seems to notice it).

But *A Better Tomorrow 3* is most definitely a Tsui Hark project in placing a young woman at the heart of this macho crime series. John Woo simply isn't much interested in kick-ass women, in women with guns, in women driving the plot, or including women anywhere in his operatic evocations of men being men and men loving men and men being loyal to men (except as princesses to be rescued, which's what happened in *The Killer*, released the same year, 1989, and also starring Chow Yun-fat).

But Tsui Hark is! Tsui likes nothing better'n putting a woman (preferably young and attractive – purely for box office reasons, you understand) at the heart of film genres usually deemed the sole province of men (the crime genre, the war genre, the political genre, and the martial arts genre). So Tsui gets his own way: he wanted Michelle Yeoh to play Mark Gor in the first *Better Tomorrow* film: here, he has Anita Mui play the Mark role.

Chow Ying-Kit is the mystery at the heart of *A Better Tomorrow 3*, and what is at stake (the heart, the conscience of the movie).[23] It's as if, once they've met Kit, neither Mark Gor nor Cheung Chi-Mun can live without her

---

[18] Among the useful studies of the Vietnam War in cinema are: J. Smith, 1975; R. Wood, 1986; G. Adair, 1981, 1989; M. Anderegg, 1991; A. Auster, 1988; K. French, *Apocalypse Now*, Bloomsbury, London, 1998; and M. Lanning, 1994.
[19] Linda Lam and Alice did the hair.
[20] Siu-Ping Ko did the make-up.
[21] Tsui regular William Chang was Mui's costume adviser.
[22] The name Kit of course echoes the character that Leslie Cheung played in *A Better Tomorrow* (and Kit here is similarly caught between the two blood brothers).
[23] The very pale make-up given to Anita Mui helps to emphasize her otherness, as if she's a Peking Opera character in a modern story.

(tho' Mun seems much more concerned with Kit, and tho' Mark has spurned her, he is still keen to follow her/ search for her). Mark and Mun embody the platitudes of blues music and pop music from the 1930s to the present day: *I can't live without you, baby!* How many times have we heard (usually middle-aged) men singing this line (or something like it)? So, *duh*, you can't live without her, eh? – but somehow you managed to live just fine for years before you knew her!

Meanwhile, Chow Yun-fat is... Chow Yun-fat! That is, an astonishing Asian star who can suggest multiple layers of psychology and emotion with a single look. Seldom has someone so apparently modest and easygoing heated up the camera lens with such fire. How Chow can go from playing a regular guy, the sort of man you could chat to, to a superstar, within the same scene. In *A Better Tomorrow 3* Chow is once again the super-cool Mark Gor of the *Better Tomorrow* series, tho' playing a much younger Mark, more naïve, more wide-eyed, and not yet morally broken by the criminal system as he was halfway thru *A Better Tomorrow* (where he's reduced to being a dogsbody for the crime syndicate).

So Chow Ying-Kit teaches Mark Gor everything in *A Better Tomorrow 3: Love and Death In Saigon*? Of course, that would rankle with fan-boys and Wooians, for whom John Woo's form of heroic brotherhood is practically a religion (along with Jedi-ism and Tarantinoism). Thus, Kit teaches Mark how to fire a handgun, in the familiar *sifu*-and-pupil scene. That Kit is the wise-guy guru, and not some wrinkly mobster, is a typically Tsui-ian move: 'one of the most subversive elements of *A Better Tomorrow 3: Love and Death In Saigon* is the idea that Kit and Mark can stand as equals, and yet also be romantically entwined', noted Lisa Morton (LM, 169).

❂

ACTION.

In terms of action, *A Better Tomorrow 3* is another extraordinary job of visual effects, practical effects, stunt work, and action choreography. Always with the smoke, the wind machines, the fire effects,[24] the squibs, the bullet hits in the walls, and of course the blood.

The action sequence that tops act one of *A Better Tomorrow 3* (when the dodgy deal with General Bong (Ling Nam-lam) goes haywire) – it takes up half of act one, really – is an enormous fire-fight in the John Wooian manner, with lots of slow motion, slewed camera angles, billowing smoke, jabbering sound effects, and of course those ridiculous two-gun gestures (looks great, tho', shooting with two guns – ever tried it? While diving at the same time? While landing on tarmac? While being utterly exhausted? While being shot at?!).

The scenario of the exchange of a suitcase of money (which's reprised later), is a cliché upon a cliché in Hong Kong cinema (yes, it's at night, yes, smoke billows about, yes, there are plenty of henchmen to

---

[24] The pyrotechnicians were Hon Cheung Lau and Se-Kwan Leung. They certainly earned their fee on this production. Sadly, one of the pyrotechnics experts died during pre-production on *A Better Tomorrow 3*, when his house went up in flames after smoking a cigarette.

waste, etc), but the Vietnam War *milieu* and the warlord character of General Bong gives the sequence a feeling of the Wild West with its outlaws running amok combined with the real Vietnam War (the stunts climax with the *deus ex machina* arrival of a tank and an exploding Jeep).

In the midst of it, Chow Ying-Kit reveals her true colours as a one-woman army: Anita Mui Yim-fong is stunning as a gun-totin' warrior in a swishy white coat, happily shooting an automatic rifle one-handed (with a pistol in the other hand, of course). And she stands her ground, bold as brass, undaunted that General Bong's grunts're coming in thick and fast. There's a great reaction shot of Chow Yun-fat and Tony Leung looking in awe at Anita Mui. This is a woman who, at the end of the sequence, smacks General Bong in the face (in many a Hong Kong picture, she would be immediately punched to the ground).

❂

What fan-boys have disliked about *A Better Tomorrow 3* – that the lads are being over-shadowed by *femme fatale* Anita Mui's Chow Ying-Kit – is exactly what I love about it (Chow Yun-fat recalled that 'the audience don't believe that Mui Yin Fong is Mark Gor's sifu!'). Tsui Hark and co. adding a powerful female figure into the mix is a kind of betrayal of the John Wooian æsthetic, isn't it?, rather like someone in the crime syndicate betraying one of their kind. You just don't do it! And if you do, it's a bullet in the head!

In 1986's *A Better Tomorrow*, it was a trio of blood brothers – the brothers-in-crime Ho and Mark Gor, and the kid brother, Kit (who's a cop, admittedly, but still, in the Wooian moral universe, a man doing men's work). The trio in *A Better Tomorrow 3* completely buggers up that holy male brotherhood by introducing a sexy, fearsome (and single!) woman (and she soon has both guys worshipping her!).

❂

When will the *hommage* to Tsui Hark's birth city come?, you wonder in *A Better Tomorrow 3*. After all, here is Tsui returning to the city of his birth to make a huge movie. Well, it does come – but *after* the climax of act one (the end of the shoot-out).[25] Thus, beginning act two is a lyrical montage sequence (accompanied by a pretty song by Lowell Lo and David Wu Tai-wai), depicting Saigon in its everydayness, its bustling streets, its boats on the river, and the trio of characters in a more lighthearted mood.

So this romantic triangle forms part of the rather saggy two middle acts of *A Better Tomorrow 3*. Instead of bickering over the phenomenally beautiful Chow Ying-Kit, a strong, independent woman in the tough man's world of organized crime, Mark Gor gallantly gives her up[26] and encourages Cheung Chi-Mun to go for it (Mark's motivations are left vague, and Mun is reluctant, because he knows how much Kit means to Mark). So, with Mark surrounding himself by paid-for women at a hostess bar, Kit exits, weeping, leaving Mun to take her home (the actors are

---

[25] And that's right – it would be misleading to open this franxious movie with a poetic montage of everyday Saigon.
[26] We see Mark Gor do this in the scene where Kit arrives at night at their place: he turns away from the kiss, and calls for Cheung Chi-Mun. Then he stands back and watches them embrace. Anita Mui doesn't have a single line in this scene, but she's acting plenty.

terrific, as always, but they are also trying to make the script work when it's rather unconvincing).

Well, if *A Better Tomorrow 3* becomes a little soap opera-ish for ten or so minutes in *A Better Tomorrow 3* (and lacking the hothouse political atmosphere of Saigon to add that extra element of desperation and time running out), it is swiftly curtailed by a return to the crime thriller elements (which, it has to be said, are also rather confusingly delivered). Ignoring the ins and outs of the plotting in the middle acts of *A Better Tomorrow 3*, all we need to know is that Mark Gor and Cheung Chi-Mun are getting out of their depth, and not even Kit can bail them out this time.[27]

That *A Better Tomorrow 3* is a portrait of loneliness comes over strongly – each of three main protagonists (and Uncle Shek) is alone, and rather desperate. No one is happy in this movie, and every attempt at happiness is foiled (a recurring motif of Chinese crime movies – you take a gamble,[28] and in this film you lose). The characters that reach out – like Chow Ying-Kit and Cheung Chi-Mun – find their attempts at connection rejected (Kit wants Mark Gor but he spurns her; Mun wants Kit, but she's not interested – because he's not Mark! Yes, it's a cliché romantic triangle, where A wants B but B doesn't want to know, and C wants A, but only B will do for A! Yet it works. Sort of. Mostly).

❃

The guys return to Hong Kong[29] (leaving Chow Ying-Kit behind), which's what Mark Gor went to Vietnam for in the first place (to bring back his cousin and uncle), and resume their life there. Not so easy to leave, tho', is it? The high anxiety over exit permits, visas and crossing borders, and leaving home,[30] is given a melodramatic twist: first, Cheung Chi-Mun's pa Uncle Shek finds it traumatic saying goodbye to his business and home in Saigon (and to the Vietnamese youth Pat (Cheng Wai-Lun) he's taken in). So strung-out is Uncle Shek, he collapses in the customs office where the officers are taking apart the travellers' luggage. (And at the airport the scenes are again chaotic, full of crowds hoping to flee Saigon).

The customs office sequence is a mirror of the one that opens *A Better Tomorrow 3*, tho' with the stakes noticeably higher: Uncle Shek is near death, and Mark Gor is flailing around a truncheon[31] when one of the officers decides to snaffle his loot (note how that's a reversal of the opening scene, when the naïve Mark Gor was floored by a truncheon). Throughout *A Better Tomorrow 3*, death (in the form of gunshots and/ or violence) is a hair's-breadth away: *A Better Tomorrow 3* is one of those movies played at an intensely neurotic pitch (neurotic and tense even for Tsui Hark!), where things can go wrong *very* quickly (it recalls political thrillers of the 1980s in countries that're falling apart like *Salvador* (1986) and *The Killing Fields* (1984)).

A Better Tomorrow 3 is also one of those pictures where no matter

---

27 Some of the crime thriller scenes are filmed against giant backdrops of Hong Kong, as if this is grand opera.
28 Ho mentions gambling when he orders Mark Gor and Cheung Chi-Mun to leave. If you gamble, you have to be prepared to lose.
29 Introduced with more plane shots, and a brief montage of the busy life of Hong Kong.
30 The anxiety was already evoked in the opening scene in the airport.
31 The truncheons, ridiculously, are kept on display on the wall of the room.

what the characters do, things are going to hell. As if the forces at work are so much larger than them (social, political, ideological), and no matter how they manœuvre, they can't out-run fate. It's a story of a permanent decline, with nobody able to stop the slide into chaos and loneliness (in which case, *A Better Tomorrow 3* has the suggestion of the structure of a classical tragic play, rather like *The Godfather 3* (released a year later, in 1990) which took up *King Lear* as one of its models).

Once again, Chow Ying-Kit steps in to save the day (tho' taking longer to appear this time, and with no fore-warning that she's going to do so, apart from Mark Gor's reassurance that Kit has connections).

❋

The crime genre plot of *A Better Tomorrow 3* kicks back in with the arrival of Ho Cheung-ching back in Hong Kong after several years in the Netherlands, in the third act (of four acts). Ho's introductory scene portrays him in the customary ruthless crime lord manner – by dealing with a traitor. The execution of the guy is inter-cut, *Godfather*-montage style, with Ho's simultaneous assault on our heroes (with a bomb disguised within a flower arrangement). The bomb kills Uncle Shek, which ups the stakes. Ho also receives Chow Ying-Kit warmly (kissing her on the mouth).

From time to time Hong Kong production crews drive up to the hills overlooking Hong Kong to get that spectacular vista of the 'scrapers and the famous harbour: *A Better Tomorrow 3* uses this setting[32] (also found in *A Better Tomorrow 2* and *The Killer*),[33] for the scene[34] where Ho and his boys show Cheung Chi-Mun and Mark Gor what gangsters are really like. Precisely why Ho lets them off the hook (after sending them a delivery of high explosives), isn't quite clear. Instead, they get roughed up and told to clear out of Canton.

The filmmakers don't lose sight of the emotional tensions in *A Better Tomorrow 3*: they include a scene (in act 3) where the heroes pay their respects to the altar of the dead father, Uncle Shek (in Hong Kong), Mark Gor and Chow Ying-Kit finally making love, and many arguments between Mark and Cheung Chi-Mun (over Kit, over going to Vietnam, over going back to Canton), and between Mark and Kit.

THE MULTIPLE ENDINGS.

Tsui Hark thought that *A Better Tomorrow 3* was 'out of control' and 'too long' (1997, 135). He was right: the 1989 movie has about three endings, as the characters hurtle from Hong Kong back to Vietnam (*back* to Vietnam?! *Back* to a country falling apart in war?!). Tho' it's not made quite clear just *why* everybody has to return to Vietnam – oh, we know it's partly due to the money/ crime plot (crime lord Ho Cheung-Ching has ordered the lads to leave Canton, plus Ho wants to get his $$$$ out of Vietnam), and partly because both guys seem to be trailing after Chow Ying-Kit for much of the time, and partly thematic.

---
[32] Partly chosen because it's meant to be the mid-Seventies, which's easier to hide from a distance.
[33] A scene which also featured Mark.
[34] Filmed on a *very* windy day.

The multiple endings of *A Better Tomorrow 3*, plus the completely ridiculous series of action scenes which climax the 1989 movie, undo some of the great work that the film has achieved. *A Better Tomorrow 3* goes *way* off the rails in the final action sequence, which has Cheung Chi-Mun single-handedly taking on some of General Bong's soldiers, only to be joined by Pat and Mark Gor, and harassed by a tank driven by the somehow still-alive Bong!

The ending of *A Better Tomorrow* is one of those bloodbath finales, where seemingly everybody dies. Certainly it delivers the concept of visualizing the crime genre as a war, so that a Hong Kong action movie becomes a Vietnam War movie. (Style-wise, we are in the realm of classic Hong Kong action: slo-mo, filled camera angles, a throbbing electronic score, and a massive amount of practical effects).

Clearly, the filmmakers desperately wanted the image of a man in front of a tank, with the Tiananmen Square massacre having taken place only just before filming began (you can almost hear Tsui Hark yelling on the soundtrack: 'get me a tank! I want Tony Leung being run down by a tank!'). Unfortunately, it takes a little more work than this lame piece of scriptwriting to stage a man vs. tank scenario (two good examples occur in the *Akira manga* by Katsuhiro Otomo, and in Hayao Miyazaki's *animé* classic *Nausicäa of the Valley of the Wind* (1984). Plus, we've already seen that scenario in the climax of act 1).

However, the scene is also pure wish-fulfilment: this is the filmmakers' response to the act of the rulers of the People's Republic of China in Beijing: they have Hong Kongers blowing the hell out of the tank!

The multiple endings of *A Better Tomorrow 3* include: (1) a giant fire-fight in – where else?! – a Buddhist temple! Where, once again, Anita Mui Yim-fong busts caps into a host of henchmen, while our heroes scrabble about looking for the exit. At this point, pretty much everyone in the cast sustains major injuries, is stained with theatrical blood, but somehow manages to keep going (which means: they keep firing guns!).[35] The battle continues outside, with explosions and gags and stunts with the Jeep, as Pat, Mun and Kit seem to be staging their version of Vietnam War within the wider context of the war. It's here that Mun's thrown out of a Jeep, and seems to expire in an explosion.

And then, (2) the big fire-fight in the pay-off of the crime story: Ho Cheung-Ching and Chow Ying-Kit make a striking underworld couple, but Kit, we know, has eyes solely for Ho – if Mark Gor's out-of-bounds (Ho, confidently and subtly played by Shut Yam Saam-long (replacing Ti Lung), is an imposing presence in the final act of *A Better Tomorrow 3*. He needs to be impressive, to act as a counterfoil to Chow Yun-fat dramatically and also romantically). The usual MacGuffin in crime pictures (a suitcase full of money) offers a banal preamble to the real meat of the scene: people firing guns at each other in an enclosed space, diving behind tables, crawling

---

[35] The sound effects team (Siu-Lung Ching was sound fx editor, Jacqueline Brassart was location sound editor, and Chung Keung Lee was dubbing editor for the Cantonese print) add bullet whizzes and hits which eclipse the celebrated sound design of the opening of *Saving Private Ryan* by ten years.

across the floor, and taking multiple hits. It's all in a day's work (or, in this case, probably two weeks' work) for actors in a Hong Kong action movie.

Incendiary and punchy as the action sequence is between Mark, Kit, Ho and his syndicate, and General Bong and his men, it doesn't have the depth of catharsis or the emotional pay-off it tries to evoke. Ho dies, with Kit in his arms, and Kit is mortally wounded (not by Ho or Mark, tho' – but Ho's chief henchman). How anyone can speak let alone move or stand after all of this beggars belief.

The device of the bomb in Chow Ying-Kit's bag which's counting down even before she leaves the hotel, is a powerful dramatic commentary on time running out for everyone here, and it demonstrates how desperate Kit has become, willing to die if she can take Ho and the other corrupt guys with her. You can apply that countdown to the Hand-over seen from 1989, to the People's Republic of China, to any political scenario, or to more metaphysical/ spiritual concerns, including the Big One: D-E-A-T-H.

Finally, (3) the street battle where Cheung Chi-Mun, Mark Gor and Pat are pitted against General Bong in a tank, plus a bunch of soldiers (handily, and ridiculously, there just happen to be guns, ammo and bombs lying around, so our heroes can suit-up and gun-up in true style!). An ambulance, barbed wire, sandbags and a motorcycle are added to the mix.

The sequence can only climax with explosions, right? Right! In a John Wooian gag, Mark Gor straps some explosives in a box to a motorbike, and drives the bundle into the tank. It' a challenging scene, where the practical effects team are throwing in everything they've got: fire, smoke, explosives, squibs, blood, as the filmmakers recreate a slice of the Vietnam War in the middle of Saigon, and play out Tiananmen Square in Hong Kong action movie terms. The gap was reprised many times in *The Battle of Lake Changjin*.

❂

The problem that *A Better Tomorrow 3* faces is a common one in movies: by two-thirds into the running time, it has said everything it wants to say, and it has staged every action sequence and every variation on emotional and psychological issues it can think of. So that the final act is largely repetition, and slight alterations to things we've already seen and heard over the course of the movie so far. (In Western movies made in the 1990s, 2000s and beyond, this meant that a 100 minute picture now ran to 130, 140 or 150 minutes. That's far, *far* too long! Tsui Hark naturally lives in the 90-100 minute range for a movie: to go over two hours requires a *very* good reason in the world of Tsui Hark. *Once Upon a Time In China* justifies it; *A Better Tomorrow 3* doesn't).

So that by the time the audience reaches the final scenes, staged as a mass exodus at a military airfield (to embody the Fall of Saigon and the citizens fleeing the city), it is as exhausted and desperate as the characters are. Just how many times can you see Tony Leung, Chow Yun-fat and poor Anita Mui looking stressed and worn-out and blooded? (Mui has to be lugged around looking nearly dead in the arms of Chow (and

Leung)36 for most of the final reel. Good job she's tiny, and he was brawny!).

By far the strongest scene in terms of performance in act 4 is where Mark Gor explodes over Cheung Chi-Mun's death at Chow Ying-Kit's place: Mark slaps Kit twice (hard), and she collapses and weeps. (However, the filmmakers aren't paying off the story arcs honestly – they have Mun surviving the explosion after falling from the Jeep near the Buddhist temple. Is this a last-minute rewrite? It would leave Mark the only survivor, carrying the dead Kit back to Hong Kong).

A Better Tomorrow 3 is certainly a powerful portrait of a city, a nation, being torn apart by war. The hospital scene brings it all home, when Mark Gor carries in Chow Ying-Kit for aid, only to find the ward full of wounded and bloody citizens (including children), and a doctor without the medical supplies to tend them (*A Better Tomorrow 3* might've benefitted from a few more scenes of this kind, offering the wider political and social perspective of the Vietnam War: instead, the movie tends to be caught up with the trials and the squabbles of the central characters. They are so blinkered, so absorbed in themselves and their ultimately petty desire for money, they don't see the bigger picture. However, Kit does voice those concerns occasionally, when she tells Mark/ Mun that in this situation, all of the other stuff doesn't really matter. Kit voices the common sense view: in a war, it's all about survival).

Throughout the final act of *A Better Tomorrow 3*, the screenwriters (Foo, Tsui and Leung) insert some more philosophical and metaphysical speculations, as the characters muse on their fate. Unfortunately, the ruminations on morality (often coming from Chow Ying-Kit) don't quite have the impact they should have. But there is a strong ethical subtext in *A Better Tomorrow 3* of survival no matter what, of deciding what is precious (no, it's not money), and valuing it. Once again, Tsui Hark inserts one of his primary motifs: time and the passing of time (there are shots of clocks, and Kit's bag contains a bomb which seems to be counting down the lives of everyone).

❋

So *A Better Tomorrow 3* is too long, as Tsui Hark admitted: it doesn't out-stay its welcome, but it would've benefitted from combining at least two of the action sequences in the finale (the Buddhist temple fire-fight and the Ho-Bong vs. Kit-Mark scene, for instance). The 1989 movie has already done everything it intended to do by the time of the second action sequence – and, compared to a David Lean or an Akira Kurosawa epic movie, there isn't enough new material or new conflicts to sustain the story.

But the images of Mark Gor holding Chow Ying-Kit as she dies in his arms, while Anita Mui Yim-fong starts singing on the soundtrack, are definitely moving (Chow Yun-fat can sell sorrow and pain as well as any actor in the history of cinema). The song is suitably wistful and sentimental – precisely the sort of rather slushy song that Hong Kong crime movies

---

36 Tony Leung nearly drops Mui.

use (and Tsui Hark is very fond of such songs). So that the final images of the helicopter flying into the setting sun (of the title) are hugely ironic.

Altho' most film critics seem to crown the first *A Better Tomorrow* as the best of the three pictures, several critics regard *A Better Tomorrow 3* as finer, more emotional, and with a fuller appreciation of female characters. 'Simply the best of the series. It has what John Woo's entries are lacking – honest emotions, and a strong female presence', opined Barry Long (F. Dannen, 363). And Howard Hampton confessed: 'this is the best of the series' (ib., 337).

A Better Tomorrow 3: Love and Death In Saigon is 'simultaneously sprawling and meditative, a politically-minded epic and an examination of gender roles' (Lisa Morton, 169).

BULLET IN THE HEAD

So in *Bullet In the Head* (*Diexie Jietou*, 1990), John Woo, Terence Chang (executive producer) and company delivered *their* version of a prequel to the *Better Tomorrow* movies, while Tsui Hark and co. went off to film his version, *A Better Tomorrow 3*. So it was the production that Tsui Hark directed that retained the all-important title *A Better Tomorrow*, and also the all-important characters. Thus, *Bullet In the Head* comes up with a new trio (making them much younger), and thus it isn't really a *Better Tomorrow* story. Released: Aug 17, 1990. 136 mins.

The two movies share many elements, of course, not least members of the production team: many in *Bullet of the Head*'s cast and crew worked with Tsui Hark over the years (and both filmed in Thailand), and some such as David Wu Tai-wai and James Wong Jim on both films).

Bullet In the Head is one of the finest collaborations between John Woo and Terence Chang, his regular producer. Assoc. producers: Wan Allen, Catherine Lau and Patrick Leung. Music: Sherman Chow, James Wong and Romeo Diaz. DPs: Wing-Hang Wong, Wilson Chan, Ardy Lam, and Chai Kittikum Som. Editors: Woo and David Wu Tai-wai. Costumes: Bruce Yu. Prod. des.: James Leung. *Bullet In the Head* exists (or has existed) in several versions[37] – some edits had scenes cut for length, and some for censorship.

At the heart of *Bullet In the Head* is a brotherhood of three friends, played by Tony Leung Chiu-wai, Jacky Cheung and Waise Lee. A great cast already, then – add to that Simon Yam[38] (who's in Vietnam with the lads, as a former C.I.A. operative), Fennie Yuen Kit-ying, Yolinda Yam, Chung Lin, Kan-Wing Tsang, Hang Shuen So, Tin Hung Yee and Shek Yin

---
37 Including running times of 80, 96, 100, 116, 126 and 136 minutes.
38 Woo wanted Chow Yun-fat for the role (Yam's character has several affinities with the way that Chow plays characters in Woo's films, including the white suit). Chow, however, may have declined because it wasn't a starring role.

Lau (plus 10,000 stuntmen) and you have a top-of-the-line group of performers.[39] The acting in *Bullet In the Head* is very fine – Tony Leung and Jacky Cheung[40] are outstanding.

The three friends were:
Ben (Siu Bun)   Tony Leung Chiu-wai
Frank (Fai Jai)   Jacky Cheung
Paul (Sau Ming)   Waise Lee
And they're joined by Luke/ Ah Lok (Simon Yam).

Bullet In the Head and *A Better Tomorrow 3* share numerous narrative components, all of which are obvious: they start in Canton and go to Vietnam (with the charas continually talking about returning home); they include political protests (and they put the charas into the middle of the chaotic, crowded street scenes just as they arrive in Saigon); the characters embark on small-time crimes, working for (i.e., being exploited by) a boss; Tiananmen Square scenes between people and tanks; the Vietnam War impinges on events in a spectacular fashion; there are massive fire-fights; scenes in restaurants and in bars;[41] and numerous motifs of the gangster/ crime picture.

Despite its genre – the (Vietnam) war movie – *Bullet In the Head* shares many aspects with the regular Hong Kong gangster and crime picture, such as the fire-fights, the nightclub scenes, the betrayals, the MacGuffin of money (here, it's gold), and the internecine warfare between rival outfits.

As well as Vietnam War movies like *The Deer Hunter* and *Apocalypse Now*, critics have found influences on *Bullet* such as *Hamlet*, *Rebel Without a Cause*, *The Treasure of Sierra Madre*, *Taxi Driver*, *The Man Who Would Be King* and *One Flew Over the Cuckoo's Nest*.

Comparing *Bullet In the Head* and *A Better Tomorrow 3* is fascinating. Both are extremely violent, and portray multiple deaths and injuries, both are downbeat and apocalyptic, where it seems as if the world is ending, not only during the Vietnam War. *A Better Tomorrow 3* displays desperation in almost every single scene. But maybe John Woo is a more optimistic soul than Tsui Hark at times – certainly, no one can deny that Woo's Hong Kong films have an optimistic undercurrent, with their imagery of (religious) salvation and redemption (and continual belief in/ adherence to issues of honour, chivalry and integrity). Tsui Hark's films can be (but are not always) more nihilistic (and yet also much funnier); after all, Tsui started out with two very angry films released in 1980: *Dangerous Encounters – First Kind* and *We're Going To Eat You*).

A man in a white suit going into battle – an image from *The Killer* is reprised in *Bullet In the Head*, in the figure of the wonderful Simon Yam. Yam recalled that John Woo likes shots to be big: for a scene in *Bullet In the Head*, where a bomb goes off in the jungle, Yam had his hair singed off his head because the explosion was so big. Yam suffered, but Woo was

---
[39] Director Raymond Lee has a cameo, as does Woo.
[40] Known for his pop idol status (he is one of the 'Four Golden Kings' of Cantopop), and often cast in light-hearted or romantic roles, Jacky Cheung delivers on the drama here (particularly impressive is his physical acting).
[41] The Bolero bar run by Mr Leong.

delighted: 'Good, good, good!' Anything for a good shot! Chow Yun-fat said that Woo loved the sound of gunfire, and didn't wear ear-plugs on set.

Simon Yam recalled that he was making four other films at the same time as *Bullet In the Head*, and that it was nice that John Woo allowed actors time to really nail their scenes, instead of being rushed, in the usual Hong Kong manner.

Music – although James Wong Jim and Romeo Diaz are two of the finest composers in Hong Kong cinema (they worked extensively for Tsui Hark), and have created some outstanding scores, some of the cues in *Bullet In the Head,* also composed by Sherman Chow, seem repetitive and underwhelming (there are plenty of washes of electronica, which you hear everywhere in Hong Kong films of the 1980s and 1990s).

Among the deleted scenes were Leong forcing the heroes to drink urine, and a victim being killed in the protest scenes. There are other deleted scenes, some suggested by photographs, and some from viewers who claimed they saw scenes which were later cut. Many of the deletions were due to violence.

❂

Bullet In the Head orchestrates familiar Wooian issues: honour, friendship, chivalry – and how noble values are corrupted into betrayal and envy. Gold and greed are set against friendship and brotherhood. In a key speech, Ben berates Paul for selling out their friendship for a pile of gold (this is the film's MacGuffin – a crate of gold with 'U.S. Army' stamped on it). And of course, this being a John Woo movie, the argument is staged with two characters training guns on each other! Woo simply can't resist putting guns into every scene, if he can find a way (and he usually does!). On one level, it's exciting drama, on another it's cretinously childish, and on another it's very disturbing.

A gun is always close at hand in a John Woo actioner – in a very creepy way, it's as if a gun can solve any issue, and can even be used for 'healing' (when Ben kills Frank out of mercy). Sometimes you yearn to take the guns out of the picture and let the characters fare without blowing holes in each other. The continual resorting to gunplay makes for exciting drama and cinema in Woo's output, but it's also very oppressive.

The riots on the streets of Hong Kong (in the first scene of *Bullet In the Head)* link up the Vietnam War with unrest in Asia in the former colony, as if everywhere is potentially volatile. It's as if the world has always been at war, as if war is one of the central experiences of the human condition, as if humans can't stop making wars. (Sure – what other species would waste so much time, energy, resources and life itself on wars?).

The women in *Bullet In the Head* are once again in a Woo-directed movie roughly treated: poor Sally (Yolinda Yam), the former Hong Kong singer, becomes a gangster's moll (for Mr Leong), hooked on heroin and used as a prostitute. And Jane (Fennie Yuen) plays the dutiful Wife Back Home (tho' there is a reunion scene at the end between Ben and Jane).

❂

Taking its cue perhaps from movies such as *The Deer Hunter* (1978),

Bullet In the Head spends its first act at home (in Hong Kong), and depicts the trio of friends at work and play (i.e., lots of fighting).[42] Ben gets married but helps out Frank on his wedding night, and kills the guy Ringo (stuntman Tin Hung Yee), who smashed a glass bottle on Frank's head (the bone of contention? Money, of course. And 'face' – looking good in the eyes of the community). Some of the scenes seem very *Deer Hunter*-ish (like the dance that opens the movie, and the wedding sequence, with *West Side Story* as another reference point – the lads even dress a little like the famous rival gangs of Gotham – the Sharks and the Jets – in *West Side Story*).[43] And, as in *The Deer Hunter*, we know for sure that these scenes of bonding, brotherhood and romance will pay off later, when things get nasty (as we know they will!). Yes, it's the classic story of a fall from grace, a descent from innocence into corruption (tho' our heroes weren't pure as the driven snow before – they were already petty criminals).

Getting involved on the edges of the criminal world is expected in a prequel to *A Better Tomorrow* (so the youths are shown doing just that, stepping deeper into outlawdom), but *Bullet In the Head* brings in other elements – principally, the political situation in 1967 of political unrest. There are impressive scenes of political protests which're put down savagely by the authorities. Youths waving the *Red Book* and chanting about Chairman Mao (and about getting the British out of Hong Kong), are powerful statements, situating *Bullet In the Head* within an important historical epoch.

❂

In act two, the heroes have become anti-heroes and minor hoods – now they can take on Mr Leong and his corrupt outfit centred around the Bolero nightclub. This provides one of the finest action bust-ups in John Woo's cinema, where our three tykes gun down pretty much everybody, aided by the suave, cool Ah Lok; they're able to survive the gun battle, save the princess, and escape in a big, white car (Mr Leong is a despicable character – he shoots Sally in the back, as he holds her hostage!). The sequence might be intercut with *A Better Tomorrow* or *The Killer* with no problem.

Act three of *Bullet In the Head* delivers some of John Woo's finest scenes in terms of non-stop mayhem on an epic scale, with several running battles, plus a scorching prisoner-of-war camp sequence (which again seems to draw on *The Deer Hunter*, as well as *Eastern Condors*, 1986, a Sammo Hung-helmed actioner set in Vietnam). Even tho' there were bits apparently cut out (some for censorship reasons), *Bullet In the Head* delivers a horrific portrayal of war-time, including the murder of civilians and children.

In *Bullet In the Head*, the filmmakers stage their version of classics of the Vietnam War movie genre such as *Apocalypse Now* (Yanks in helicopters),[44] *Platoon* (massive and sorrowful fire-fights), and war-is-hell

---

[42] The lead actors are playing teenagers, which they just about get away with doing.
[43] They dance to an instrumental version of Neil Diamond's 'I'm a Believer' – which might be one of John Woo's mantras.
[44] The helicopters in flight are stock footage.

scenes from *The Deer Hunter* (1979). The practical effects crew and the pyrotechnics specialists threaten to swamp the stars in enormous explosions, smoke, fire, and bullet hits.

Many scenes in act three of *Bullet In the Head* are played at the familiar super-hysterical level that not only John Woo but all of Hong Kong cinema is very fond of: why hold back now?! Forget whispering your lines, or giving the subtlest of subtle looks! Forget using those quirky tics you learnt in drama school which worked so well for soap operas! This is *way* bigger than that – this is filmmaking as an extravagant Peking Opera show, but set within the context of war-time, which turns former humans into psychotically violent monsters who cackle as they kill.

❊

The last act of *Bullet In the Head* goes off the rails spectacularly – which seems to be apposite for this over-blown epic war movie. Several narrative beats throw suspension of disbelief out of the window (with loud, smashing glass, of course, and another petrol explosion): poor Frank is mercy-killed by Ben because he's become a mentally deranged victim with a bullet lodged in his head (the sympathetic characterization of Ben is happily jettisoned here).45 Ben brings Frank's skull to a high-power business meeting back in Hong Kong (William Shakespeare? *Hamlet*? Maybe, but this is just preposterous. In a movie about barbarians in the era of Genghis Khan, maybeit would fly). Finally, *Bullet In the Head* rounds off its myriad conflicts with an extended car chase and car duel, filled with the mandatory massive explosions, slow motion, bullet hits, gouts of blood, breaking glass, and of course yet another harbour setting (one of the only places in Hong Kong that the authorities will allow filmmakers to play like kids blowing stuff up).

The grandeur and insanity of the P.O.W. scenes in the Vietnam War sequence in *Bullet In the Head* are frittered away somewhat in too many gangster genre-based bits of business, as if we're back in *A Better Tomorrow* territory (which we thought we'd left far behind in Vietnam and the Fall of Saigon).

For once in a John Woo-directed production, the narrative slips into too many clichés and over-done routines. Or maybe our expectations are high for a film director like Woo – from many another filmmaker, the ending of *Bullet In the Head* would be applauded (and it would happily round off many a regular Hong Kong actioner). But when you've evoked the Vietnam War, and war in general, and Tiananmen Square, to return to Hong Kong with so many stereotypes of the crime/ action genres seems misguided and a let-down (no matter how brilliantly they are filmed).46

❊

Bullet In the Head was described by director John Boorman as 'over two hours of remorseless mayhem, balletic deaths, ingenious killings, delightful detonations, rivers of blood, acrobatic flights'.

The lack of success commercially for *Bullet In the Head* was blamed

---

45 Bey Logan suggests that the movie might end satisfactorily here, instead of leaping into another act involving the bust-up and car joust back in Hong Kong.
46 By stunt co-ordinator Bruce Law and his team.

on the audience not wanting to see such tragic material, and so soon after Tiananmen Square. But *Bullet In the Head* went on to thrill critics. For John Woo, *Bullet In the Head* was an important and personal work, into which he poured much of his thoughts and feelings about the issues he upholds, like friendship and loyalty and chivalry. *Bullet In the Head* remained one of Woo's favourites among his movies, because of how much he invested in it personally.

11

THE RAID

Chok Suk Hi Wang Chin Gwan

The Raid (*Choi Suk Ji Wang Siu Chin Gwan,* 1991) was co-directed by Tsui Hark and Tony Ching Siu-tung. Tsui produced for Film Workshop and Cinema City; Tsui co-wrote with Yuen Kai-chi, from a story by Michael Hui Koon-Man; Tony Ching and Ma Yuk-sing were action dirs.; art dir. by Chung Yee-Fung; make-up by Man Yun-Ling; costumes by Lee Pik-Kwan; hair by Gloria Lam Wai-Lok; sound: Foo Leng Luk Yam Sat; music: James Wong Jim and Romeo Diaz; editor: Marco Mak Chi-sin; DPs: Arthur Wong and Tom Lau Moon-tong.

The Raid starred Jacky Cheung, Dean Shek, Tony Leung, Paul Chu-kong, Fennie Yuen, Chiu Man-yan, Lau Siu-ming, Corey Yuen Kwai, and Joyce Mina-godenzi. Released: Mch 28, 1991. 100 mins.

Uncle Choi by Michael Hui, a comic, was the basis of *The Raid* (it was published in Hong Kong from 1958 to the mid-1970s). In a nod to its origins in comicbookland, the movie deployed treated still photographs and optically altered footage in little snippets, as segues between scenes (and for the main titles).

Genius director Corey Yuen Kwai pops up in a cameo in *The Raid* as the big-nosed gangster, one of his rough-and-ready characterizations (he mainly has scenes with Jacky Cheung, which involve lots of shouting and bickering). And a big scene with Dean Shek, hanging off the cliffs we've seen in 1,000s of Hong Kong movies (which also involves plenty of arguing and yelling).

The lovely Fennie Yuen plays Tina, the main female chara amongst the heroes: she is another Tsui-ian woman – large glasses, short, dark hair, slight and skinny and tomboyish (and also a dab hand with the long spear).

The Raid is an adventure comedy, drawing on earlier Tsui Hark outings such as *Peking Opera Blues* and the *All the Wrong Clues* films, and Hollywood models like the *Indiana Jones* series. It is also reminiscent of

The Terracotta Warrior, which Ching Siu-tung helmed in 1989.

The concept of *The Raid* – an aged Chinese soldier-doctor using healing to do the right thing in the run-up to the Sino-Japanese War in the Thirties – is perfect for Tsui Hark (it's another reworking of a Wong Fei-hung motif, another very Chinese story, and another political context), while the emphasis on comedy and action is Tony Ching Siu-tung's *forte*.

There are numerous Tsui Harkisms in *The Raid* – like the bust-up in the tent in act one, when everybody is suddenly armed, crowding around the heroes, and the heroes're dodging flying axes (it recalls the comical brawls in *We're Going To Eat You*). And visual effects a-plenty, with miniatures. 47

<small>ૐ</small>

In act two *The Raid* stages a bedroom farce, with characters on the bed, someone knocks at the door, a character dives to hide under the bed, and so on. Tsui Hark had delivered this sort of adolescent desire-and-embarrassment scenario in *Shanghai Blues* (and much better, too). Another slice of farce has a love letter being read by several charas, who think it's for them (a classic piece of Tsui-ian humour).

The set-piece that climaxes act two contains several classic Tony Ching Siu-tung moments: ninja brandishing swords leaping off a bi-plane onto railroad tracks at night, for instance. Logistically, these set-pieces are a nightmare, where moving aircraft have to be hung from cranes and cables. But Ching and the crew make them look so easy. However, in this set-piece there aren't enough shots or angles to make it flow satisfyingly, and again the low budget and tight schedule cuts into the production. (Ching and Tsui had already done these sort of stunts in *The Terracotta Warrior* – and twenty years later, in *Time and Tide*, Tsui was staging the same sort of gags with planes).

The finale of *The Raid* plays out exactly as expected: fire-fights, outrageous stunts, the hero and the villain tussling, and everybody gets their moment to shine. In a beat that seems very bad taste, yet is also part of the action-adventure genre, and has been used many times before and since, the heroes are rounded up and thrust into a sealed chamber, where they are gassed. The allusion to the death camps is clear and crude (and also, historically, *The Raid* is set in the 1930s).

Brother Big Nose redeems himself by helping the heroes to escape; guns are fired all over the place; actors are diving for cover every 30 seconds; stuff blows up; and the villain and the vamp expire in a giant explosion.

❂

This time, the critics were right about *The Raid* – somehow, despite all of the elements being present and correct, before and behind the camera, it doesn't quite work. The cast is great, the production personnel are the best in the business, and technical elements are superb... but... the characterization of Uncle Choi doesn't really compel (and the way that Dean Shek plays him, like an older Tsui Hark with a white beard, isn't

---

47 The action beat involving a bi-plane attacking Uncle Choi hanging from a water dam is cribbed from *Indiana Jones and the Last Crusade*, down to the use of a model for the plane.

appealing, either).

Tsui Hark (and Tony Ching Siu-tung) have trod these adventure trails before (and since), and with much more satisfying results (prior to *The Raid*, in *Shanghai Blues* and *Peking Opera Blues* and *All the Wrong Clues*, and afterwards in *Time and Tide* and *Shanghai Grand*). The Chingster and Tsuister should be able to pull this movie off, with this cast and these resources, but it remains still-born.

The Raid is wrestling with its too-low budget as well: it's trying to deliver *Indiana Jones and the Last Crusade* (1989), which cost U.S. $55.4 million, using under 2 or 3 million dollars. There are many scenes which are noticeably cutting corners.

The Master (1989/ 1992).

A Better Tomorrow 3 (1989).

The Raid (1991).

12

ONCE UPON A TIME IN CHINA

Wong Fei-hung

INTRO.

Once Upon a Time In China is called *Wong Fei-hung* in China (*Huang Feihong* in Cantonese) – a better and more accurate title (tho' probably meaningless to a general Western audience, who've never heard of Wong Fei-hung). Western distributors tend to give Chinese movies titles which'll be understood by the target market (the title *Once Upon a Time In China* is misleading, tho', being a movie reference. Also, *Once Upon a Time In China* is far too significant to be reduced to a filmic title, and also to a reference to a 1968 Western called *Once Upon a Time In the West*.[1] However, it was Tsui Hark who decided that *Once Upon a Time In China* would be a good title – it suggested for him 'that actually *Once Upon a Time In China* can be now, can be the future' [LM, 82]).

The first two *Once Upon a Time In China* movies were filmed in Hong Kong; Golden Harvest produced (with Raymond Chow as executive producer); Tsui Hark's Film Workshop was the production company (with Paragon Films); the writers were Kai Chi Yuen, Elsa Tang, Yiu Ming Leung, Dang Bik-min and Tsui; Arthur Wong, Bill Wong, David Chung, Angry Lam, Lam Kwok-Wah, Tung Chuen Chan and Paui Kai Chan were the DPs (6 DPs, but the look is consistent);[2] Mak Chi Sin (Marco Mak) was editor; Lau Kar-wing,[3] Yuen Shun-yee, Yuen Cheung-yan,[4] Chia Yung Liu, and Bruce Law were the action choreographers (with Yuen Woo-ping also helping out uncredited); costumes were by Bruce Yu Ka-on; hair by Siu-Mui Chau and Yuk-Mui Wan; make-up by Ka-Pik Lai, Yun-Ling Man and Min-Hua Pan; sound by Chow Shao-lung, Leung Ka-lun and Kwok Wing-kei; and music by

---
[1] Yes, *Once Upon a Time In the West* is regarded as a classic movie, and its title has been used many times. But it demeans *Once Upon a Time In China* by seeming to ride on the coattails of another movie.
[2] One of the DPs of the *Once Upon a Time In China* series, Park Yoon Kyo, was also a director (*Bloody Smile*), as is Arthur Wong.
[3] Tsui said he and Lau Kar-wing had not gelled in their view of how the action in *Once Upon a Time In China* should be delivered.
[4] Yuen Cheung-yan is one of Yuen Woo-ping's many brothers: he is the guy who loses to Wong Fei-hung's rival, and he's the Taoist Priest in *Tai Chi Master* and *Drunken Tai Chi*.

James Wong Jim and Romeo Diaz (George Lam composed the theme song). Many in the team were regulars in the Tsui Hark Movie Circus.

Jet Li and Rosamund Kwan are the top-billed stars (sharing the billing on-screen); others in the cast included Jacky Cheung (Bucktooth So), Kam-Fai Yuen (Kai), Kent Cheng (Pork Wing), Lau Shun (commander of the Black Flag militia), Yan Yee-kwan (Iron Robe Yim), Wong Chi-yeung (Governor), Wu Ma (Grand-Uncle Cheung), Jian-Guo Chiu (Shaho gang leader), Xin-xin Xiong (member of the Shaho gang), Leung Gam-san (the leader of the opera troupe) and Yuen Biao (Leung Foon). Many in the cast crop up in the later installments. Simon Yam and Shih Kien have cameos. Playing the Westerners (boo! hiss!) were: Jonathan James Isgar (Jackson), Steve Tartalia (Tiger), Mark King (General Wickens, a British general), and Colin George (Jesuit Priest). Released August 15, 1991. 134 minutes.

The film is set in Guangdong.[5] *Once Upon a Time In China* cost U.S. $8.4 million.[6] It has four acts (not three). Three acts is usual for Tsui Hark's films, because they generally come in at 80-90 minutes (each act being 25-30 minutes).

That *Once Upon a Time In China* is a masterpiece, pretty much everybody agrees.[7] For Maggie Lee, the *Once Upon a Time In China* movies are 'thrilling action movies. Here, the highest-caliber martial artists and stunt experts were able to reach the peak of their skills' (2021). It's a labour of love – clear to see in every frame. Like *Zu: Warriors From the Magic Mountain*, *Once Upon a Time In China* is a movie that Tsui Hark was born to make.

In it, Tsui Hark and the production team have not only delivered a marvellous updating and reworking of the Wong Fei-hung legend,[8] they also created a terrific action movie, and a satisfying textured and layered historical drama, which also contains a beguiling mix of other elements (such as romance, comedy, nostalgia and political commentary). Tsui won Best Director for *Once Upon a Time In China* at the Hong Kong Film Awards. *Once Upon a Time In China* was his best movie, Tsui thought – until he looked at it again, and saw all the flaws (1997, 136).

In *Once Upon a Time In China*, Tsui Hark throws in a feast of numerous Chinese traditions and cultural forms which fascinate him: Peking Opera performance, Chinese healing and herbalism (and acupuncture), a Lion Dance, fireworks and martial arts *dojos*.

Once Upon a Time In China is a rich movie in its portrayals of the secondary characters – which's one of the marks of a great movie (in many action movies, minor characters are vaguely conceived, often under-written, and usually depicted along stereotypical lines). You can feel the love the film has for its large cast – it's clear throughout *Once Upon a Time In China*: this is definitely a movie made with love.

---

[5] Wong was born in Guangdong, the son of Wong Kai Ying, one of the 'Ten Tigers of Canton', a herbalist and fighter.
[6] Lisa Morton claims it was $12 million, which seems too much (LM, 216).
[7] 'As pure entertainment, it's a hoot from first frame to last' (Lisa Morton, 216).
[8] Tsui Hark: 'When a film genre's [popularity] goes from its peak to its trough to its peak again, it always has to do with new angles, new approaches and new feelings. That's why our movies are always going through cycles.'

Once Upon a Time In China features literally 100s of minor bits of business placed around the edges of the plot and the main characters. You can tell if filmmakers are engaged with their material if they keep coming up with things for the secondary characters to do, where they explore all sorts of details and corners of the sets, where the entourage around the central charas is so vividly evoked.

Thus, *Once Upon a Time In China* is stuffed with Tsui Harkisms, those bits of action and visual gems which Tsui snuffles out and foregrounds.

For example, the fierce, devoted but angry Porky Lang, one of Wong Fei-hung's followers, but someone who's fury at the 'foreign devils' leads him to explode at many points. Porky is not a one-dimensional character, not just the fat, buffoon sidekick: the scene where he stubbornly kneels outside in the rain because the *sifu* hasn't asked him to come inside (after yet another scene where he lost his temper), is moving. And the scenes where Leung Foon makes friends with Iron Robe Yim (Yan Yee-kwan)[9] forms another subplot in *Once Upon a Time In China* which's touching: how Iron Robe, tho' a martial arts master, doesn't even have enough money for food, so he performs in the street, in the rain (much to the scorn of the prostitutes nearby). And how Foon later steals some soup to take to Iron Robe.

We think of *Once Upon a Time In China* as an all-out action and martial arts extravaganza – which it is! – but it also contains numerous intimate scenes, quiet scenes, scenes of characterization and humour. The budding romance of Peony and Wong, the friendship of Leung Foon and Iron Robe, Bucktooth So impersonating the *sifu* – *Once Upon a Time In China* is full of these small-scale scenes which thicken the characters out, making this far more than your average chop socky flick.

Christianity certainly is a grotesque religion to some observing it from the outside. In the chapel inside the British Embassy, for instance, there's a scene where Wong Fei-hung looks up at the large stained glass window of Christ crucified on the cross. How can people worship a god that suffers so much? Yes, it's question that many people have asked (and compared to the smiling Buddha, the crucified Son of God does seem a gruesome icon).

The laserdisc edition of *Once Upon a Time In China* was problematic: as Tsui Hark recalled, the distributors wanted the movie to be reduced from 120 to 90 minutes. Anybody looking at the amount of story packed into *Once Upon a Time In China* can see that it would a tougher challenge than with many another movie. But Tsui and his editors duly acquiesced, tho' it was frustrating – because the distributors decided to release it as a 120-minute movie anyway, but 'the music and everything was kind of weird', Tsui said (LM, 82). Another release had bad sound when the distributors tried to use a Dolby system.

---

[9] Yan Yee-kwan is one of Tsui's regular actors – appearing in *The Swordsman 2* and *3*, *Iron Monkey*, and *New Dragon Gate Inn*.

THE OPENING SCENE.

The opening prologue of *Once Upon a Time In China* is an important scene which compresses the whole 1991 movie into several minutes. It states many of the key themes (and even uses banners unfurled to make sure the audience gets the messages: 'the people, the land', 'bravery' and 'loyalty'). It also introduces the star, the main character, the period setting, the costumes, and the *very* flamboyant cinematic style that the filmmakers will be employing in the rest of the piece.

It's typical of Tsui Hark that the whole *Once Upon a Time In China* series should open with a model shot – of boats on the ocean (it's a historical movie, but it opens with visual effects).[10] The miniature image is soon intercut with full-size vessels, leading up to the introduction of the star, Jet Li, on a boat, with the commander of the Black Flag militia (played by Tsui regular Lau Shun).

As well as miniatures, *Once Upon a Time In China* makes much use of matte paintings and optical printing to add skies, buildings, etc. You don't think of *Once Upon a Time In China* as a visual effects movie, but actually it is a major vfx picture (for the fire and pyrotechnic effects alone).

The opening shots of ships at sea, tho', announces instantly one of the key themes of the first *Once Upon a Time In China* movie (and of the series as a whole): the arrival of foreign (Western) powers. The boats evoke West meets East; Europe and China; Guangdong as a trading zone; and new, Western technology (guns, boats, firepower) versus older, Asian ways (the gun vs. sword is a recurring motif in Chinese action cinema, as well as Japanese cinema). It wasn't long before the time of *Once Upon a Time In China* that British gun-boats were deployed as superior firepower in the struggle to control trade in China.

The opening scene of *Once Upon a Time In China* has Wong Fei-hung joining the general of the Black Flag Army on board a vessel where a Lion Dance is taking place, led by Hsin Shen (as they do on auspicious occasions. The Lion Dance looks forward to the third *Once Upon a Time In China* movie, and was also a key ingredient in another Wong Fei-hung movie, 1993's *Last Hero In China*. Lion Dances appear in the earlier *Wong Fei-hung* flicks, such as *Dreadnaught*, 1981). It's no surprise that the first scene in *Once Upon a Time In China* is a very traditional, Chinese practice.

The notion that (French?) soldiers on a ship nearby open fire with their rifles when they mistake the fire crackers going off during the Lion Dance for gunfire is over-wrought (and a little unconvincing), but dramatizes one of the central tensions of the *Once Upon a Time In China* series: between foreign powers and the Chinese, between the new, capitalist world then emerging, and the old, traditional, Chinese world (with its Lion Dance customs), between outsiders who come to China to trade, and the Chinese people's ambivalence towards them (the British wanted tea from China; China didn't want anything that the British had to offer; so what did the

---

[10] To show ships on the ocean, I wonder if Tsui Hark saw *Othello* (1952), Orson Welles' version of William Shakespeare which used a scale model of a boat moved by grips offscreen, to suggest a boat on waves.

British government do? It created an opium addiction in China, supplied from India – one of the creepiest things the British rulers have achieved in recent times).

That capitalism and trade is backed up by force, vividly evoked in the opening scene of *Once Upon a Time In China*, is of course a key issue in the late 19th century/ early 20th century period. And it's an issue that remains totally contemporary – it's about the relationship between capitalism and militarism, between the exploitation of capitalism and the individual and the community, which resonates today in issues such as 9/11, or the West's military presence in Afghanistan, or the Western territories' goals of trading into Asia.

These background/ geo-political issues are not why the *Once Upon a Time In China* series is so compelling – who goes to the cinema for a lecture on market forces, global capitalism, and nationalism? But they do give the *Once Upon a Time In China* series a distinctly and overtly political and ideological ambience. There's no doubt that these political issues are uppermost in the *Wong Fei-hung* movies, providing the framework for the stories and the characters, and consciously put there by the filmmakers.

But this is *filmmaking*, this is *storytelling*. If the filmmakers wanted to deliver a lecture, or a PhD thesis, or a Communist or right-wing diatribe, they might've chosen a different arena. The political and ideological elements of the *Once Upon a Time In China* series are only *part* of the mix, yet they have been seized upon by Western critics as one of the main things to discuss about the series. Why? For all the obvious reasons – not least that it's easier for journalists and reviewers to discuss global politics in relation to Chinese filmmaking than *kung fu* or swordplay or action or the characters or the technical aspects of the movies.

However, it is precisely those ingredients – the spectacle, the *kung fu* action, the humour, the romance, the characters and the situations – that draw punters into a theatre (as well as their favourite stars). If an audience wants a lecture or political rant, they can read a newspaper or watch telly (which never miss an opportunity to lecture their audiences). They go to a Chinese action movie for something else!

Some of the gunfire hits the Lion Dance performers, so it's up to Wong Fei-hung to save the day. The opening scene introduces some bravura wirework and nimble rope-straddling footwork from Wong, as he rescues the situation (Wong takes up the lion's head, and dances it up the ropes of the ship). If it's an action movie, you want to see action upfront, right? Yes! And you want to see your star in action too, right? Yes! The scene offers the delight in seeing Jet Li performing aerial stunts.[11] It shows Wong doing the right thing, and the values he embodies (such as upholding traditions, nobility, fighting for Chinese culture, as well as incredible physical agility. Wong is linked to Lion Dances in many *Wong* movies, and he is of course the best Lion Dancer). It pits Wong Fei-hung and his entourage against the foreigners. It shows Wong using martial arts skills

---

11 Tho' Jet Li is of course doubled throughout the *Once Upon a Time In China* series for more dangerous gags.

against Western firepower.

In short, the scene encapsulates numerous narrative themes which'll play out through the *Once Upon a Time In China* series. Wong Fei-hung repeats this sort of scene many times. The patriarch general advises Wong to train up his Black Flag followers, because they are going to need them in these troubled times. This leads directly into the credits sequence, one of the great set-pieces of the *Once Upon a Time In China* series, the training scene on the beach at sunset involving a hundred or so topless trainees in the Black Flag militia, to the sound of the famous Wong Fei-hung music, 'Under the General's Orders' (reworked as 'A Man Should Better Himself' by James Wong Jim, and sung by George Lam (Cantonese version) and Jackie Chan (Mandarin version)).

Every time that Wong Fei-hung does something noble and heroic, the celebrated music starts up (it has a similar function to the *James Bond* theme music, the twangy guitar, which comes in when Bond performs some incredible stunt). The music has been associated with Wong right back to the 1930s and 1940s.

The opening scene is filmed with Tsui Hark's customary lavish cinematic style: elaborate slow motion, very low camera angles, tilted camera, richly saturated colours, meticulously researched costumes,[12] designs and settings, heightened action, and punchy sound effects.

The prologue introduces the extravagant political conflict (here, white Europeans firing on and wounding Chinese locals), which's a staple of the Tsui Hark approach to movie-making. And the prologue also has Wong Fei-hung and the general unfurling banners which state some of the key themes of *Once Upon a Time In China* (and of Tsui Hark's cinema).

THE STYLE.

Action! *Once Upon a Time In China* is a masterpiece of action cinema, as are the other two movies among the first three *Wong Fei-hung* outings. The first act might've been somewhat leisurely with its set-ups and character introductions (yet is still contains plenty of action compared to most movies). But once this 1991 Hong Kong picture gets going, it doesn't stop! One outstanding action sequence follows another: Iron Robe Yim versus an opponent who dares to take him on by firelight;[13] Iron Robe against Wong Fei-hung in the rain at the medical clinic; Wong beating Hung and the Shaho gang in a restaurant, armed with an umbrella; the attack on the clinic at night; the brawl in the Pearl Restaurant; the tussle with the Governor and his soldiers; the street fight with the Shaho gang; the enormously complex theatre sequence...

This is truly remarkable filmmaking. The feeling of freedom, of movement, of colour, of light, of sound, of music, is just phenomenal. The *sensuality* of *Once Upon a Time In China*, and many Chinese action movies, is *so strong*. You might not see any sex on screen in *Once Upon a*

---

[12] Tsui Hark wanted the costume designer to go to England to find the wardrobe for *Once Upon a Time In China*, because he was after authenticity. The costumes for *Project A 2* (1987), a Jackie Chan actioner, were hired from Britain for the same reason.
[13] This was choreographed by Lau Kar-wing.

Time In China (the only kiss is when Aunt Lee chastely kisses Wong's shadow! And even that's enough to make him recoil!), but these movies are steaming with beautiful, erotic imagery, movement and sounds.[14]

Like some horror movies, and like some musicals, with their emphasis on the body, on blood, on dance and movement, the *Once Upon a Time In China* series (and Chinese action movies in general) are hugely *sensual*. They possess the grace and elegance of the finest movie musicals and dance pictures – the choreography alone is fantastically sexy. These movies are *radiant* with bodies, with the body in motion.

And *Once Upon a Time In China* is also a gorgeous movie of *light* – from magic hour photography (the director's favourite time of day, but not the cinematographer's, as it only lasts 10 minutes), through muted, overcast days, to sunsets and dawns, to candlelight, lamplight, firelight and a full-on burning sequence. (Historical movies are dream projects for cinematographers, of course, with their natural light, firelight, candlelight, fireworks, and flaming torches – you'll often find that DPs deliver their most satisfying work on a period picture. And so does everyone else – historical movies raise everyone's game).

The amount of slow motion is striking in *Once Upon a Time In China* – considerably more than in many of Tsui Hark's pix as director. And it's used in places where conventional shots would work just as well.

But *Once Upon a Time In China* didn't please everyone: David West complained in his book on martial arts in movies that the *kung fu* on display in *Once Upon a Time In China* has no relation to Southern Chinese martial arts: 'The film presents a paradox – it is a kung fu movie that contains no kung fu' (182).

THE CHARACTERS.

After the spectacular opening scenes, *Once Upon a Time In China* settles into a much slower, ambling first act. Many characters're introduced, and their relationships: Aunt Lee or Yeo (a.k.a. Cousin Lee, a.k.a. 13th Aunt, a.k.a. Peony),[15] played by the delightful Rosamund Kwan (born on Sept 24, 1962, Kwan is one of the iconic faces of the New Wave of Chinese cinema, but she was never better than playing the 13th Aunt in the *Once Upon a Time In China* series). Kwan's speciality is sweet, cute, rather naïve, young women, the older sister or girl next door figure. She has a lovely chemistry with Jet Li. She is consciously not a fighting female, and doesn't go into battle beside the hero (Kwan has refused to do fight scenes). In *Once Upon a Time In China*, she's more the princess who needs to be rescued by the hero. However, in later installments, such as the American jaunt of 1997, she is given more action to do. And in the Peking Opera theatre sequence, she has a pistol and shoots a guy.

Aunt Lee is a woman enamoured of Western ways, including its technology (such as cameras, both still and movie cameras), and its

---

14 The celibate master or teacher is a common type in traditional, Chinese culture – it's all about conserving *chi* and power.
15 Aunt Lee was created as someone who was separate from the family around Wong Fei-hung, who could comment upon him and his life objectively (LM, 82).

fashions. Wong Fei-hung is asked to look after Lee by an uncle figure (Grand-Uncle Cheung, played by Wu Ma), which begins the romantic subplot in *Wong Fei-hung* (despite her innocence, Peony is more worldly than Wong when it comes to modern ways; the *Once Upon a Time In China* series squeezes much humour from the difference in knowledge between the two potential lovers, with Peony often playing the teacher and Wong the pupil).

For Tsui Hark, Wong Fei-hung was a chauvinist, from a chauvinistic society, who is 'being threatened by a very strong woman who knows lots of things about the world that he doesn't know'.[16] The introduction of Aunt Lee early on thus announces that *this* interpretation of the Wong Fei-hung mythology will be overtly proto-feminist, and it will place a woman at the centre of what is usually, in Wong Fei-hung movies, a patriarchal and masculinist world.

Both Aunt Lee and Bucktooth So have recently returned from North America, a plot point which is brought out as soon as they meet Wong Fei-hung (such as in the Western custom of shaking hands, the Western style of clothes,[17] and of course the camera and tripod). Several of the Chinese characters comment despairingly on Aunt Lee speaking or acting like a foreigner. The cultural/ social differences, however, among the Chinese, are often played for comedy; between Chinese and Western characters, they are treated more seriously.

Then there's Porky Wing (Kent Cheng), another staple figure in the Wong Fei-hung legend, one of many Chinese characters in the *Once Upon a Time In China* series who're really angry at the foreign presence in China (Porky cries 'foreign devil!' at the Jesuit Priest, and rushes at him, before Wong tells him to calm down). Porky's an endearing character, but he was dropped from subsequent outings (re-appearing in film 5). And there's Bucktooth So (Jacky Cheung Hok Yau), a rather foolish sidekick with a comical stutter (and another regular character in the Wong Circus); foolish, but So has been to the U.S.A. with Aunt Lee (and, as he points out to Porky, he can read, too). Ling Wan-Kai (Kam-Fai Yuen) is prominent as one of Wong's aides.

Leung Foon, played by the wonderful Yuen Biao (another key face of the Chinese New Wave cinema), is introduced arriving at Po Chi Lam clinic, hoping to learn from Wong Fei-hung (but meeting Bucktooth So instead: the comical scene plays to Biao's strengths as an eager, naïve, acrobatic personality (similar to his character in *Zu: From the Magic Mountains*); the skit is based on a misunderstanding, with So impersonating Wong). The scene is also constructed to introduce another star in Chinese cinema, Jacky Cheung (playing So behind thick glasses).

Ah Foon is shown helping out at a waterside playhouse.[18] In the first act, Foon is given quite a bit of story, including a run-in with the local gang,

---

16 In L. Stokes, 336.
17 Even tho' Aunt Lee is very feminine, she also dresses in (tomboyish) Western clothes, is feisty and assertive, and in some of the later installments she is given key acts in action scenes.
18 He's up on the roof, fixing it, complaining that he's scared of heights – a trait that comes from Tsui Hark.

the Shaho Triads, coming to the theatre for their protection money (the Triad gang's leader Tong is a mean heavy played by Yau Kon-kwok).

As the characters're introduced, the story of *Once Upon a Time In China* gradually emerges – but in leisurely fashion. Meanwhile, the technical aspects of the movie are breathtaking – from the exquisite production design and art direction by Kenneth Lee Chung-man and Ben Lau Man-hung, to the cinematography (of six DPs).

MULTIPLE LEVELS OF VIOLENCE.

Once Upon a Time In China is a very violent movie. Not the martial arts duels, which seem to exist in a cinematic world of their own – a realm of movement, gesture, dance and choreography – but the violence within the story. *Once Upon a Time In China* features scenes of soldiers firing upon civilians and killing them; a very brutal rape; the Shaho gang unloading guns into a victim at point-blank range, etc. (The *Once Upon a Time In China* series are Category II films = 'not suitable for children' but still for general audiences. They are not Category IIB, the equivalent of 'R' rated films, as films such as *The Blade* were).

And *Once Upon a Time In China* contains many other disturbing images: of racism, of slavery, of imprisonment, and one of Wong Fei-hung's patients covered in blood (who expires). This is a romantic-melodramatic epic movie, yes, and it's a re-invention of the Wong Fei-hung legend, yes, and it's filled with outrageously inventive action, yes, but it is also stuffed with very grim material: young women in cells taken as slaves, poverty and hunger, multiple deaths, rape, etc.

The violence on-screen is between individuals – that's what drama does. But unlike many movies, which don't go further than that, *Once Upon a Time In China* is loud and clear in bringing out the oppression and the exploitation within the social systems and the political backgrounds (the political stance of *Once Upon a Time In China* is thus liberal and left-wing (as in most of Tsui Hark's films), even tho' its main protagonist, Wong Fei-hung, is a self-confessed and proud conservative, keen to uphold traditions).

The anger of Tsui Hark's two early movies (*Dangerous Encounters – First Kind* and *We're Going To Eat You*) re-surfaces many times in *Once Upon a Time In China* (and sometimes threatens to unbalance the picture). After all, *Wong Fei-hung* is quite clear that the reasons and the under-lying causes behind the degradation, the slavery, and the violence are political and ideological (and capitalist). There are forces at work in *Once Upon a Time In China* which the movie elegantly and vividly places before the viewer, and Wong Fei-hung is caught in the middle of it all.

All of this reminds us, once more, that the *script* of *Once Upon a Time In China* is very fine indeed. Or put it like this: why is *Once Upon a Time In China* a masterpiece movie? Largely because the *conception* and the *script* is excellent.

THE MIDDLE ACTS.

What's also striking about *Once Upon a Time In China* is just how much it pushes its hero into corners and heaps on the obstacles. Wong Fei-hung is on his back foot throughout the second act, as political machinations and gang warfare threaten him and his community from all sides.

It's striking because it departs from your typical action-adventure tale: *Once Upon a Time In China* is not a simple story of good guys and bad guys in a time of political turmoil. Wong Fei-hung and his crew are battling the Shaho gang and their leader Hung, the Governor and his organization, who're aligned with some of the foreigners (the Shaho gang goes to make a deal with the North Americans),[19] and even Iron Robe (plus Leung Foon) turns up to create merry hell.

Once Upon a Time In China is a movie where the hero's home and workplace is burnt in a giant conflagration, in one of the incredible fire sequences in Chinese cinema that seem far, far more dangerous than anything put on the screen in North American cinema. An American production will have corridors of fire allowing for the actors to move, but, when filmed from certain angles, it looks like they're engulfed. Not the Chinese filmmakers! They put fires all around the performers: as with rain scenes, there's no need to act! Burning arrows are shot into the midst of the performers. (One can imagine that representatives from health and safety departments are scarce on a Hong Kong film set! Or at least in the 1980s and 1990s).

The fire sequence in *Once Upon a Time In China* is a major set-piece containing numerous beats within it: of the Shaho mob dressed as ninjas in black, the flaming arrows, the attempts at defending the building, Pork Wing trying to douse the flames, Porky and Kai saving the patients, Wong Fei-hung darting up onto the roof then into an alley to confront the villains, and chasing them on horseback with a burning branch... (the *Wong Fei-hung* films, of all periods, often feature an attack on the Po Chi Lam clinic).

Instead of a single opponent, the *Once Upon a Time In China* movies tend to place Wong Fei-hung in situations where he's up against large groups of people. His powers're pretty much super-human, so it makes sense to pile up the assailants around him (one or two isn't enough). Plus placing precious characters (like Aunt Lee) in jeopardy, so Wong has to save them as well as fight the baddies.

The Peking Opera theatre[20] massacre is a remarkable sequence in *Once Upon a Time In China*, climaxing act two. It is one of the greatest action scenes in Tsui Hark's cinema, a masterpiece of construction, script-wise, and execution as film.

Staged beside the water, the set's a major construction for the crew of wood and bamboo, representing a travelling theatre company. Before the action erupts big-time, the episode starts off with some light-hearted

---

19 This is a recurring theme in movies of the time – how some of the authorities colluded with the foreigners.
20 Lisa Morton notes that it's a black joke on the part of the Americans in setting up an assassination in a theatre (LM, 78).

humour, as Porky Wing and Leung Foon take to the stage in full Peking Opera make-up and costume after Porky accidentally sent the actors on their way as he sits on the gate collecting tickets. The crossdressing sidekicks and plenty of acrobatics on the stage offer a show-within-a-show in *Once Upon a Time In China*, reminding us that this is an extravagant spectacle (theatricality, dressing up and putting on a show are a staple of the New Wave of Hong Kong cinema; of course, the traditions of the Peking Opera are significant here. This is also cinema as pure entertainment, a show just for the sake of a show).

Yes, Tsui Hark stages another of his beloved Peking Opera scenes, as if a whole act of *Peking Opera Blues* was flown in from 1986 and dropped into the second act of *Once Upon a Time In China*. Tsui can't seem to get enough of putting his actors into the extravagant Peking Opera costumes and make-up (and for Yuen Biao, one of the 'Seven Little Fortunes', the Peking Opera troupe, this is home from home).

The comedy is there partly to set-up and contrast with the far more serious sequence where the theatre audience is fired upon by the Governor's troops (the North Americans are also in attendance, and thus are colluding). The scene is yet another demonstration of Western firepower, of the gun vs. the sword, of new technology vs. old ways. That it is Chinese soldiers firing upon Chinese civilians enhances the horror (the main purpose is to kill Wong Fei-hung).

The massacre occurs towards the end of the sequence, which builds from comedy thru rapidfire *kung fu* action (where people're hurt but not killed), to the bloodshed of the deaths of Chinese civilians. That is, the sequence is carefully constructed dramatically, proceeding logically to the point of horror in the massacre (where humour would be inappropriate). Humour's used to defuse dramatic tension sometimes (there's a look between Wong and Peony when she's rather close to him as he rescues her yet again), but not too much. The humour's kept in check because the scene manifests both the gruesome power of Western technology with its guns and weapons, and also the horror of a civil war scenario.[21]

The sequence also shows that Wong Fei-hung is powerless to alter the course of events: he and his entourage are a few against many – especially when some of those (such as the Governor) have aligned themselves with the foreign powers. (The Jesuit Priest throws himself in front of a bullet meant for Wong)

THOSE NASTY WESTERNERS.

The North Americans have hired Chinese to promote work in the gold mines of the American West, reflecting historical events when many Chinese people left for the New World: at a booth rather like something out of the Wild West, hirelings hand out leaflets advertizing a paradise of gold in the Land of the Free.[22] Notice Wong Fei-hung's reaction: he watches the

---

[21] The slow motion evokes Akira Kurosawa (in *The Seven Samurai*) and Sam Peckinpah (in *The Wild Bunch*).
[22] This became a reality in the final *Once Upon a Time In China* movie, when Wong Fei-hung and his entourage headed to the New World.

Chinese clustering around the booth and shakes his head: why would someone from China want to travel halfway around the world?

Meanwhile, behind the scenes, the Shaho gang, working for the Yanks, have kidnapped Chinese women to sell as prostitutes back in the U.S.A. Here, it's the Westerners who are the corrupt, twisted villains (reversing the stereotypical depiction of Asians in similar Western movies). So one of Wong Fei-hung's tasks is not only to defeat the Shaho crew, but the foreigners who've taken Chinese women (including Aunt Lee).

A DARK AND RAINY NIGHT.

Most of act three of *Once Upon a Time In China* is taken up with a lengthy series of episodes set on a dark and rainy night. The highpoint of this sequence, for martial arts fans, is definitely the Wong Fei-hung versus Iron Robe Yim smackdown, situated in the courtyard of the Po Chi Lam clinic in a *mise-en-scène* of hammering rain at night. A truly remarkable feat of choreography, wire-work, lighting, editing and practical effects, this sensational sequence was *hommaged* in 2002's *Hero* (with Jet Li fighting Donnie Yen – and *Hero* was also a tribute to the last time that Li and Yen fought on screen, in *Once Upon a Time In China 2*).

The use of a flying wooden log and of slow motion enhances the grace and ferocity of this smackdown. The choreography includes lightning-quick grappling and open-handed combat, plus the incredible sight of Jet Li motionless in the rain, listening for the movement of the foe he can't see clearly.

Under house arrest, the obstacles are piled high for Wong Fei-hung: he has Iron Robe Yim coming to challenge him, and the Governor and his mob are still trying to pin him down. Which of course leads rapidly to another battle, where Wong exhorts his accomplices to fight. Porky can't believe it – 'fight?' – 'yes, fight!'. So he does.

In the chaos, Wong Fei-hung orders Bucktooth So to take Aunt Lee and a patient away from Po Chi Lam (So is back in his Western garb, and just about to leave for the U.S.A.).[23] And who do they run into? Only the Shaho gang. It's here that brave Aunt Lee takes out a pistol and shoots Hung; alas, it's not a kill shot, and Hung's crew captures our heroine.

Once Upon a Time In China's third act closes with Wong Fei-hung in prison, surrounded by his Po Chi Lam colleagues, plus many poor women unlucky enough to be captured by the Shaho Triads. It's Wong's lowest point, with the odds stacked against him. And it's completely in character that when some of the Governor's men sneak in and offer Wong a chance to escape, he should decline at first, preferring to uphold the laws of the China that he loves.

THE FINALE.

The last act of *Once Upon a Time In China* is incredibly intense: it is one of the greatest sequences in recent Chinese cinema, and certainly an

---

[23] Tho' why So would be leaving in the middle of the night doesn't make sense.

outstanding act in Tsui Hark's *œuvre*.

It features multiple battles and struggles, many of which're depicted in parallel action. Aunt Lee is captured by the Shaho gang and taken, with many other Chinese women, to the vessels in the harbour of Guangdong, where they're going to be shipped to the New World as hookers (they are moved from wooden cells to the ships); Wong Fei-hung breaks out of prison to rush to her aid; Iron Robe fights Ah Foon; Aunt Lee defends herself against the Shaho leader Hung; Iron Robe challenges Wong in a storehouse; Foon tussles with the Shaho Triads; Wong, Porky and Kai battle the Shaho gang; the North Americans at their fort open fire upon the Chinese Governor and his officials; Foon and Bucktooth So sneak onto the ship to rescue Aunt Lee; and in the final *melée*, Wong saves the day and the villains're punished or killed.

In terms of martial arts and action, the storehouse sequence is one of the highlights of *Once Upon a Time In China*, and of recent Hong Kong action cinema. The duel between Wong Fei-hung and Iron Robe Yim is among the finest smackdowns ever put on celluloid – for imagination, speed, staging, ferocity and grace.

Here action directors and choreographers Lau Kar-wing, Yuen Shun-yee, Yuen Cheung-yan, Chia Yung Liu, and Bruce Law shine, letting loose the stunt team, the wire operators, and an army of assistants to create an astonishing display of cinematic virtuosity and imagination. This is what cinema was invented for – flights of fantasy and action which deliver what no other artform can do (sure theatre, concerts and ballet can do many of the same things – but not from so many camera angles! Because, once again, it is the *editing* that is the secret weapon in the huge arsenal of cinematic trickery and effects wielded by the filmmakers. Again and again, you will recognize that no matter what's happening in front of the camera, whether it's John Woo balletic shoot-'em-ups or effects-heavy *wushu* battles, it is the *editing* that orchestrates the real energy and impact. Not only that, editor Marco Mak Chi Sin (a total genius among editors) has interwoven the huge number of fights and action scenes with perfect dramatic logic. Not easy: we've all seen big action movies which mess that up, with too much time spent here, not enough there, and too many gaps or leaps in the narrative flow). And the sound design is amped up from the usual Hong Kong standards – listen to the unreal animal sounds and whooshes that accompany Iron Robe as he descends to a primitive, berserker level.

So in the finale of *Once Upon a Time In China,* it's ladders swinging all over the place (they also seesaw, spin, and break apart – many times), bales of grain being hurled across the building, high falls from towering stacks of produce, pulleys, ropes and weights being flung about (every prop is exploited), and flurries of fists, feet and arms so rapid the camera and the celluloid can barely record them. It's glorious, it's super-intense, it's ridiculous, and it's *way* beyond the demands of the story, the themes or the drama. But it works. You marvel at the sheer genius of achieving these visual effects practically.

Tsui Hark asked Yuen Woo-ping to help out with the action choreography of *Once Upon a Time In China* in its final stages: Yuen worked on the finale in the granary warehouse, where the stunts with the ladders are classic Yuenian choreography (only a handful of people could've pulled the sequence off – and they're all in the Chinese film industry). David Bordwell said there were nearly 300 different shots in the finale. 'Even for hardcore kung fu fans, the warehouse showdown between Wong and Iron Vest Yim (Yen Shi-kwan) is a dazzler', remarked Maggie Lee (2021).

The sequence employs not only every inch of the granary, it also includes every inch of the two bodies, from the hair (both men grasp each other's pigtails), down to their feet (a Yuen Woo-ping speciality). Altho' Iron Robe Yim has his own martial arts style (including a hidden blade in his pigtail), at the end, Wong Fei-hung deploys one of his famous martial arts techniques, the shadowless kick (the signature move is reprised in every subsequent *Wong Fei-hung* movie). The participants are spinning above each other, rolling and sliding along the floor, lurching at each other across great distances as well as grappling each other several times up close.

Talk about 'ecstatic cinema'!

There are numerous mini-highlights in amongst the barrage of images and sounds in the final act of *Once Upon a Time In China*, such as Iron Robe Yim dying in a hail of bullets *à la* Sam Peckinpah (*kung fu* cannot win against the gun, Yim croaks as he expires in Wong Fei-hung's arms, as martial artists in the real Boxer Rebellion hoped); Leung Foon duelling with the U.S. henchmen Tiger (Steve Tartalia) in the rigging of the ship (and hanging him); Foon defending Aunt Lee against a roomful of belligerent Triads; and of course the duel between Wong Fei-hung and Iron Robe (but even that contains countless smaller action units, like the arrival of Porky and Kai to help their *sifu*, and sending their opponents crashing thru the floor). And it's wonderful that Wong isn't using swords or staffs (it's the villains who wield guns), but fighting with his fists and legs and everything else.

ða.

I've seen 100s of Western action movies and Chinese action movies, but I never feel like the Chinese action pictures are milking the finales too much: altho' they are absurdly over-cooked and over-wrought, and altho' the action scenes go on longer than Western equivalents, they are so inventive, they never out-stay their welcome. Whereas, in Western action movies, the action duplicates stunts and situations we've seen so many times before, the conflicts aren't engaging, and the finales tend to drag on too long. And that kills an action movie!

Yes, you want the final showdown between the hero and the villain to be Big and Loud and Intense, but that requires a lot of imagination and skill. Western movies repeat action beats seen elsewhere and set them within conflicts which ultimately don't grip the audience. (It's ironic, but altho' the action itself in a Chinese action flick is longer and filled with more beats and bits of business, it's the Western action finales that drag on and on. North American producers and film studios often commented from the

1980s onwards that Chinese action movies were great but wouldn't play in the U.S.A. (they often said this in relation to Jackie Chan's movies); I find it's the other way around, and it's the Western/ North American action finales that don't play. I find myself getting bored quickly by the final act of a North American/ Western action movie, but never by a Chinese action movie.)

Meanwhile, the finale of a Chinese action movie *rocks*. Not only is the action, the speed and movement, the invention of the moves and the gestures, more compelling than a Western action movie, the Chinese action movie never forgets that this is *entertainment*, that this is movie-making and Show Time. The Chinese action movie builds in pauses, and intimate moments, and pieces of comedy; it creates a *balance* of elements; and it never forgets the *magic* of cinema.

While a Western action movie plays its Big Moments as smug, look-how-clever-we-are scenes (where the hero finally manages to flick the switch to make something awe-inspiring happen), a Chinese action movie emphasizes things like graceful movement or passionate emotion. Look at how beautiful that body moves in slow motion! A Chinese action movie always puts the *body* at the centre of the show, while a Western action movie is obsessed with gadgets, guns, props, big sets, cars, and visual effects (and of course clever, quippy dialogue). The Chinese action movie knows that the greatest visual effect in front of the camera is the human body. Nothing is more fascinating, more compelling.

Another aspect worth noting about the finale of 1991's *Once Upon a Time In China* is just how *brutal* it is. It is very, very vicious. When I saw the movie again recently, I'd forgotten just how violent the treatment of Aunt Lee was at the hands of the Shaho gang and its leader, Hung. He smashes her face and body repeatedly, until he knocks her unconscious; the two are grappling and wrenching each other about. He partially strips her, his wounds drips blood over her front and then back as he gropes her. This is really nasty stuff, a rape scenario which's probably too much, too graphic, and it unbalances the picture (notice how, for instance, the filmmakers rightly drew back from putting Aunt Lee in such horrific jeopardy again in subsequent *Wong Fei-hung* movies. You just don't want to see the heroine beaten so viciously she's knocked out. Or to see actress Rosamund Kwan treated like that. Tsui Hark acknowledged that he was reluctant to go there, 'but that was the natural direction that the story moved' [LM, 82]). And even when the other women captured in the ship shove Hung into a furnace,[24] it's a satisfying demise for this psychopathic villain, true, but it doesn't quite nullify the horrors of the violence against Aunt Lee. (But then, we have to remember that Tsui has not held back from depicting men's aggression against women in his movies: men can be brutes, and Tsui isn't afraid of showing that. Also, Chinese action-adventures movies tend to be more brutal than their counterparts in the West).

A poignant piece of parallel cutting is included here, interweaving the

---

24 What's a furnace like that doing on a wooden ship?!

rape of Aunt Lee with the blood-money scene between Iron Robe, the Shaho gang and Ah Foon. The message is about selling out, about one section of Chinese society selling out and exploiting another. While Foon grapples with his conscience and the money scattered on the ground (while the Shaho thugs chant, 'pick up the money!'), the film cuts repeatedly to Aunt Lee being beaten by Hung. (The message is also *not* for a Western audience, it's for fellow Chinese. The primary audience of *Once Upon a Time In China* is *not* Americans and Europeans, it is *Chinese*).

❖

The furious duel between Iron Robe Yim and Wong Fei-hung would be enough to cap any movie: technically, creatively, imaginatively, it has to be among the most stupendous sequences ever put on film. With its boundless energy, its use of every cinematic trick known to humans, and its forceful beauty, it's like watching a History of Cinema.

But no, there is more in the final ten minutes of *Once Upon a Time In China*: a very important scene, where the Chinese face the insane Westerners. It is played below decks in the Yanks' ship in a *very* over-the-top manner: the mad Yank has guns, the Chinese have fists, and he's stealing their women! It's simplistic but, yes, mercantile capitalism is this simple: it's about pure greed. *You have something I want – I'll buy it; if you won't sell it, I'll take it by force.*

The scene is another simplified, operatic version of the Opium War, of the slave-trading industry, and of Western capitalism: the North Americans, in possessing technology, seem to have the upper hand in the conflict (as usual – whether it's guns, gunboats, helicopters, or Rockwell B-1 bombers).25 Wong Fei-hung takes up some pistols, but they don't work (the Chinese don't know how to use them).26

The scene is filled with Tsui Hark's political subtexts (such as: the villain Jackson has taken the Governor, embodiment of Chinese law, hostage at gun-point).27 Wong Fei-hung dispatches the American slave-trader in a novel manner – by flicking a bullet with his fingers at the guy's skull. (That had already been set up in a piece of foreshadowing so deft you won't notice it: it occurs within the context of a scene where Wong is furious about his inability to find a solution to the political mess, to the alarm of Aunt Lee).

In the *dénouement*, Wong Fei-hung makes a pointed remark (standing next to the Governor on the ship): if there really is gold in the U.S.A., why do Westerners come to China? Maybe, he reckons, we are standing on gold (which's very much Tsui Hark's view).

---

25 Cost: $102 million.
26 Note that Ah Foon is fighting beside Wong now, putting the two stars together.
27 And when the Governor asks Wong and Foon to put down the guns, they obey him. Wong is portrayed as acting within the law.

Once Upon a Time In China (1991). This page and over.

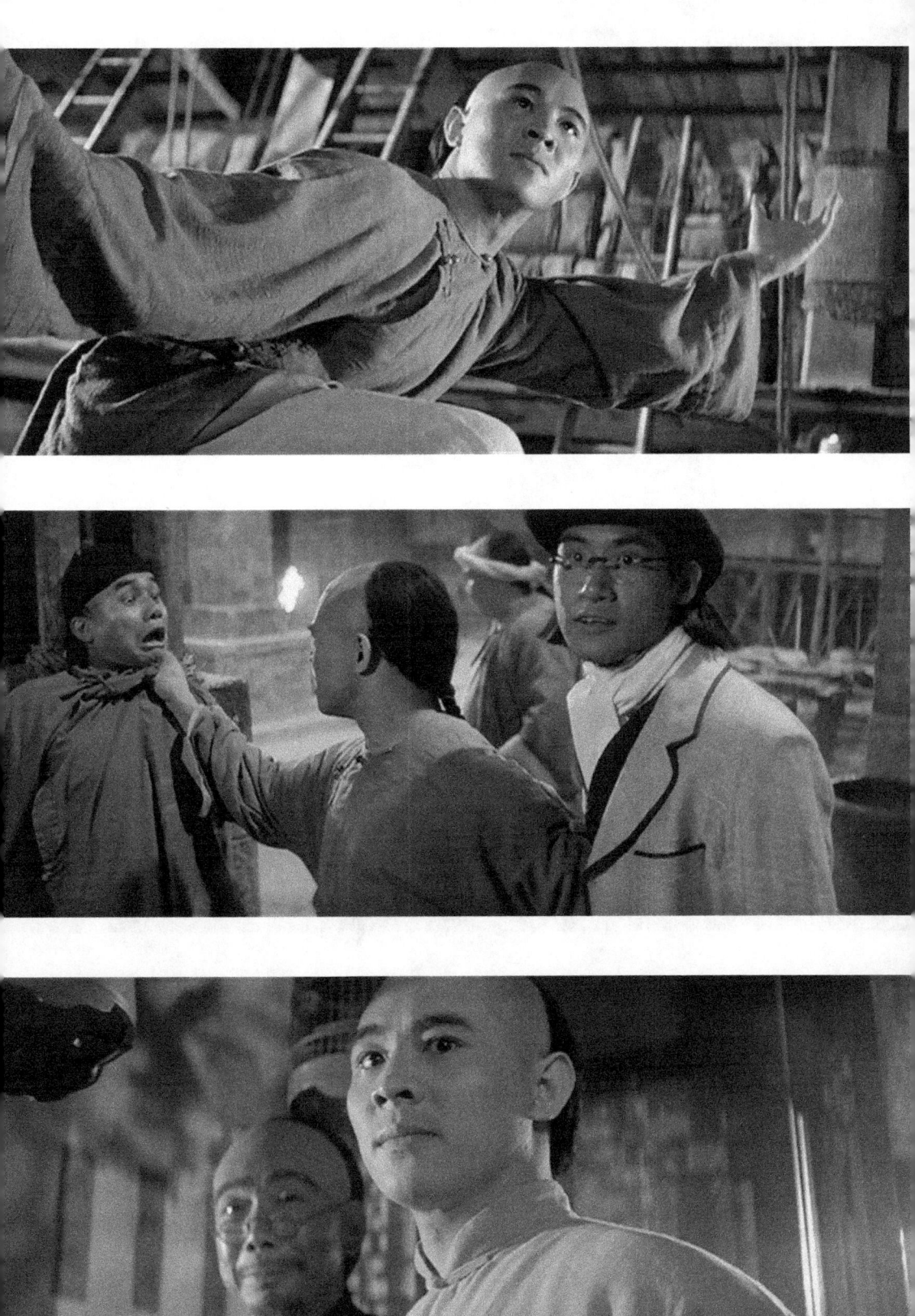

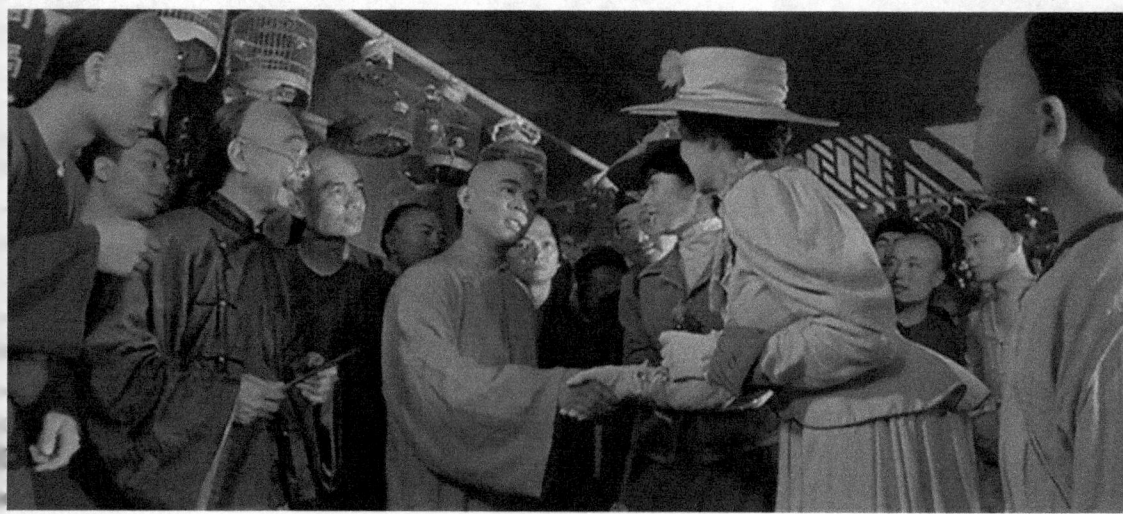

Kwan Tak-hing as Wong fei hung.

13

ONCE UPON A TIME IN CHINA 2

Wong Fei-hung Je Ye – Naam Yi Dong Ji Keung

INTRO.
Once Upon a Time In China 2 (1992, *Feihong Zhi Nam'er Dang Ziqiang* in Mandarin = *Wong Fei-hung 2: Man Should Be Self-Sufficient*) is pure pleasure. This is a movie as entertainment first and foremost, whatever else it might contain. This is an hour and 56 minutes of absolute delight, a perfect piece of cinema made by a Hong Kong film crew for a Hong Kong and Chinese audience. 'It is, to be blunt, an absolutely brilliant sequel to a brilliant first film' (Lisa Morton, 85).

The cast of *Once Upon a Time In China 2* is outstanding – Jet Li, Rosamund Kwan, Max (Benny) Mok Siu-chung, Donnie Yen, Zhang Tielin, Yen Chi Tan, Xiong Xin-xin, Yan Yee-kwan and David Chiang, and the team behind the camera is incredible: Tsui Hark as director, Yuen Woo-ping as action director,[1] Shun-Yee Yuen Tsui and Ng See-Yuen as producers, Marco Mak Chi-sin, Chi Wai Chan and Angie Lam On-yee as editors, Arthur Wong Ngok Tai as DP, Ma Poon-chiu as art director, costumes by Kwok-Sun Chiu, and music[2] by Chow Gam-wing, Johnny Njo and Richard Yuen. Raymond Chow and Golden Harvest as executive producer and distributor (with Jackie Chan singing the theme song). Tsui, Hanson Chan Tin-suen and Carbon Cheung are credited with the script. Released April 16, 1992.[3] 116 minutes.

What's not to like in *Once Upon a Time In China 2*? This is one of the greatest action-adventure series ever made, boasting two of the finest finales in action cinema. Tsui Hark is at his fiercest and most visceral in his 1,0000 miles-an-hour work as director (and co-writer and co-producer),

---

[1] The other action directors were: Huan-Chiu Ku, Shun-Yee Yuen and Donnie Yen.
[2] There are several pieces of Western classical music in *Once Upon a Time In China 2*, including a scene at a society ball where a Chinese orchestra plays Mozart. These are contrasted with the Chinese music – the guy in the restaurant playing the *erhu*, and of course the famous *Wong Fei-hung* music.
[3] Only *8* months after the first *Once Upon a Time In China* movie – and this is a *giant* production! They are *fast* in Hong Kong!

and the production team *really* deliver the goods. These guys are *masters*, they are showmen who know movies and entertainment inside out.

Once Upon a Time In China 2 boasts an enormous cast, and keeping track of the multiple groups of characters and their plotlines is an impressive feat all of its own for the writers (who were Tsui Hark, Hanson Chan and Carbon Cheung). And not only are there many factions to juggle, *Once Upon a Time In China 2* also portrays a very wide cross-section of townspeople, from babies to old folk (so the daily demand for extras for the production was high). It's as if one of the chief ambitions of Tsui Hark and the production team was to deliver a convincing and rich portrait of turn-of-the-century China, a society teeming with people, where life is lived out on the streets.

Set in 1895 against the political background following the first Chinese-Japanese War and the signing of the Shimonoseki Treaty, which sparks demonstrations against the handing over of Formosa (Taiwan) to Japan (a student demonstration against the Treaty is part of act one).

The villains in *Once Upon a Time In China 2* are not the Western powers this time (tho' there is plenty of anti-foreign rhetoric and action on display), but elements of Chinese society: one is the White Lotus Cult, with their nationalistic, anti-Western political movement, and the other is Nap-lan Yun-seut and the military. While the White Lotus Cult (led by Master Kung) is painted in a highly cartoony fashion, the Manchu commander, Lan and his regime is more complexly depicted.[4] However, once Lan throttles the British ambassador (film critic Paul Fonoroff), he has crossed the line into arch movie villainy (from which the way is only, in movie-movie terms, death.[5] And the *Once Upon a Time In China* films are very much movie-movies).

Donnie Yen's Manchu Governor Nap-lan Yun-seut uses the chaos to take control of the British Embassy. He kills the British consulate with a stranglehold, informing him, 'This is China, not England!' Oh, how satisfying moments like that are in Chinese cinema! When, finally, the Westerners are attacked in their enclaves, and the Chinese take control of their destiny.

Apparently, Jet Li walked out of *Once Upon a Time In China 2*, due to disagreements with Golden Harvest over his contract. That left the filmmakers in the lurch, so Tsui Hark had Xiong Xin-xin do what he'd done before: shave his head and double for Jet Li.

THE VISUAL STYLE.

The attention to detail and texture in *Once Upon a Time In China 2* is outstanding. The birds in cages hanging in the stores, the lanterns swinging in the breeze at night, and the food and the restaurants, it's just marvellously rich and visceral. This is a real place filled with real people. There's a *depth* of environmental *mise-en-scène* in the *Once Upon a Time In China* series (and other historical movies produced/ directed by Tsui

---

[4] *Once Upon a Time In China 2* 'may be one of the most compassionate action films ever made', remarked Lisa Morton, on account of its portrayal of race and ethnicity.
[5] Or a year as a movie critic.

Hark) which goes way beyond your average costume picture. These might be film sets, but there's no feeling of costumes and props being rented for the day, or that really stilted aspect of Western historical movies, when that one car from the 1930s or that one horse and carriage that the filmmakers have rented for the day is trotted past the camera.

While we're talking about the cinematography, it should be noted that many scenes in *Once Upon a Time In China 2* take place at night (Tsui Hark is especially fond of night scenes, which're extra-demanding for film crews). These're nights that're lit by hanging lanterns, by candles, by torches, by fires, and by fireworks. *Once Upon a Time In China 2* is a masterwork of *lighting*, as DP Arthur Wong Ngok Tai, his gaffer and what must've been a large crew of sparks fill huge outdoor spaces with light at night (meanwhile, the practical effects crew would've been working non-stop to deliver the smoke, flying leaves, rain, fire, flaming torches and high wind that Tsui likes to include in every exterior shot).

Texture and atmosphere are foregrounded throughout *Once Upon a Time In China 2*. The amount of life presented on screen is hugely impressive. There is a lengthy musical montage focussing on a blind musician playing an *erhu* and singing as the 1992 movie cuts to a very large sequence of vignettes that're beautifully lit and staged. They include an opium smoker, people playing board games, Chinese customs involving ghosts and symbols, the lottery, and of course the Tsui Hark staple: people eating.

THE OPENING SCENES.
Once Upon a Time In China 2 opens with a major production value set-piece as the villains of the film, the White Lotus organization, are displayed in full effect at a mass ritual in their headquarters. It's a giant sequence with acrobatics, fire, bullets, elaborate costumes, many extras and plenty of yelling and leaping about (and it's covered with many formal, carefully composed shots, many using a crane). Master Kung (Xiong Xin-xin) is introduced as the leader of the White Lotus Cult, a group dedicated to ridding China of the foreign devils (Westerners). The White Lotus Cult is a fictionalized version of real historical groups of the early 1900s which hoped to oust foreign powers and influences from China. The ultra-nationalist organizations included martial arts practitioners who believed that they could counter the technological firepower of the *gweilo* ('white devils') with Chinese magic (which's demonstrated vividly in the mass ritual). The sword vs. gun scenario is a staple of Asian action movies, but in the *Once Upon a Time In China* series it's given a blatantly political edge.

The flamboyance and extravagance of the imagery in the White Lotus Cult prologue of *Once Upon a Time In China 2* is typical of Tsui Hark's cinema, which can stage an enormous set-piece with the confidence of a David Lean or an Akira Kurosawa (the filmmakers spent a lot of time and $$$$ on this opening scene). In a symbolic gesture, the White Lotus organization pile a bunch of Western artefacts on the floor and burn them (the mound of stuff is nothing but junk, yet this is what Western capitalism produces – thousands and millions of objects, consumer goods, and trinkets (in the end, every object becomes rubbish). There is of course a clock[6] in the pile of Western crud – in later years, that junk would be computers, cel phones, tablets, DVDs, video games, and of course the ubiquitous, all-conquering television set (the average time spent watching TV in North America is over 4 hours a day).

Once Upon a Time In China 2 also finds mystery and exoticism in the White Lotus sequence, too, with its portrayal of a young girl in traditional costume who sings a pæan to China at the beginning of the ritual (a very Tsui Harkian motif). Filmed in flickering torchlight, the girl looks at the viewer with an enigmatic expression, as if she's the white lotus or the goddess of the white lotus herself (or China, or Chinese magic, or Chinese history).

One of the curious things about Xiong Xin-xin, Tsui Hark recognized, is that nobody can remember him in movies! Even tho' he plays some prominent charas (such as, in *Once Upon a Time In China 2*, the leader of the White Lotus Cult), viewers forget who he is. Tsui's solution to that was typical of Tsui: he had Xiong make himself even uglier,[7] and to walk in deformed manner, so he could play Clubfoot.

When *Once Upon a Time In China 2* combines the pro-nationalist White Lotus ritual sequence with the title sequence, which shows Wong Fei-hung, the most famous hero of recent times in China, travelling by train thru China, it is evoking very powerful political and cultural Chinese elements. The vivid representations of Chinese cultural and political icons are enhanced by the use of the traditional Wong Fei-hung music ('Under the General's Orders'), sung by George Lam, and those striking images of the Black Flag militia training on the beach at sunset (for the end credits, the song is sung by the most famous movie star of the period – Jackie Chan).

The train scene from the credits continues with the introductions of Aunt Lee and Ah Foon, and two of the stars, Rosamund Kwan and Max Mok (Wong Fei-hung has been invited to give a lecture). Foon's characterization is altered (he's still a buffoon, but lacks the stammer – and seriousness – of Jacky Cheung's Foon; in *Once Upon a Time In China 2*, Foon is secretly in love (or lust) with Aunt Lee). The dining car scene is played for comedy, and for more West-meets-East culture clashes (such as trying to eat strange Western food in a juddering railroad carriage).

The train sequence also puts Wong Fei-hung in a different environment: we are not in the Po Chi Lam clinic, and Wong is not surrounded by a large entourage.

Following the scenes where Wong Fei-hung travels on a train to Canton, there is the first fight scene of the 1992 Chinese picture. It's a classic Wong Fei-hung fight, in which he effortlessly trounces a bunch of

---

6 In the medical lecture scene, Wong Fei-hung observes in fascination someone in the audience looking at their pocket watch. In *Once Upon a Time In China 2*, time is a minor theme, with Luk Hao-tung and Sun Yat-sen consulting their watches.
7 Tsui's done that with other actors – such as Lee Fai in *Iron Monkey*.

White Lotus cultists (armed with nothing more'n a fan! – making a change from the usual umbrella!). The brawl – set on the street as Wong, Aunt Lee and Foon make their way from the railroad station to their digs – is of course the movie's finale in miniature (it crystallizes the conflict between the two key rivals in the whole of the 1992 picture: Wong Fei-hung and the White Lotus Cult).

The brawl is staged near one of the targets of the White Lotus crew: the Eastern Extension Australasia and China Telegraph Company, a Western facility. Aunt Lee is also involved when she tries to take a photograph and is set upon by White Lotus men (the camera is more devilish, Western technology). The arrival of Wong Fei-hung is played as the knight in shining armour coming to the rescue of the princess (he flies in across the heads of the crowd).

The medical lecture sequence, where Wong Fei-hung is demonstrating Chinese acupuncture, is in two halves: in the first part, Wong is invited to talk about Chinese medicine (*Once Upon a Time In China 2* features acupuncture in several scenes). The scene contains several East-West topics, such as language and translation, and tradition vs. science. Again, much of the scene is played for comedy (like the Marx Brothers-ish demonstration of the nervous system by tapping Ah Foon's knee). Wong's gentlemanly interpreter is no less than Sun Yat-sen (Zhang Tielin), a fellow Chinese doctor. The second half of the lecture episode has the White Lotus firing burning arrows and messages into the theatre.

Act one (which's short, about 25 minutes), also includes students demonstrating in the streets against the Shimonoseki Treaty, ceding Taiwan to Japan (the procession with banners is a mirror to the scene with the Catholic missionaries in the first film). Plus the introduction of one of the founders of modern China, Sun Yat-sen, in the lecture scene. *Once Upon a Time In China 2* makes several allusions to the founding of the Republic of China – it includes the figure of Sun Yat-sen (d. 1925), who founded the Republic in 1912.

Such scenes announce the much larger political context of the *Once Upon a Time In China* movies compared to many previous Wong Fei-hung films. It's part of a determination to put Wong Fei-hung into situations where major historical events are unfolding – to, no less, portray the founding of modern China.

THE MIDDLE ACTS.

In *Once Upon a Time In China 2*, Wong Fei-hung is up against multiple obstacles. One bad guy simply isn't enough for Wong (or for Jet Li!). Thus, in the second act of *Once Upon a Time In China 2* (which opens with the lengthy *erhu* musical montage), the problems mount as the White Lotus Cult cause trouble throughout the town, and Wong is struggling at first to deal with them. The White Lotus Cult are targetting Western edifices, such as the telegraph building. They assault a lecture of Western doctors. And in the middle point of *Once Upon a Time In China 2,* they burn down a school building (killing the adults, tho' the children hide and survive).

Thus, in the two middle acts of *Once Upon a Time In China 2*, Wong Fei-hung, Aunt Lee and Foon Leung are doing what they can to counter the violent tactics of the White Lotus organization. There is plenty of to-ing and fro-ing as the characters hurry around Canton, helping lost children, and doing what they can against the White Lotus mob (the heroes are thus continually reacting to the villains, and not driving the narrative).

In this section of *Once Upon a Time In China 2*, there is a society ball, where we're introduced to Governor Chung (played by Tsui regular Yan Yee-kwan, who was Iron Robe Yim in the first movie), and to Governor Nap-lan Yun-seut (Donnie Yen). The short scenes are for exposition, to define the behind-closed-doors governance of the area. We see the officials receiving orders from Hong Kong from another new-fangled machine, the telegraph.

As Bey Logan pointed out in his DVD audio commentary, the *Once Upon a Time In China* series works without martial arts: there's enough going on in terms of story and drama that it doesn't need *kung fu* sequences. However, there's no doubt that *kung fu* action enhances the dramatic conflicts in the *Once Upon a Time In China* movies no end. There's a good example of *kung fu* action in the mid-point of *Once Upon a Time In China 2*, when Wong Fei-hung in desperation goes to see the Governor at the courthouse to ask for help with the abandoned children.

The sequence begins with Governor Nap-lan Yun-seut demonstrating his prowess with wooden staff work, and launching himself against Wong Fei-hung when he enters the scene. Then follows a 'fan service' moment – Jet Li versus Donnie Yen (two of the biggest *kung fu* stars of the period – and since). It's fast and furious Shaolin staff action, in the Yuen Woo-ping manner (highly stylized, with plenty of slow motion and punchy insert shots), that of course ends in a stalemate (it's but a taster of the 1992 movie's climax, as the audience can guess. And of course, the outcome in the finale is inevitable, too).

You can have the villain threatening the hero with words, or with a show of strength from one of his henchmen, or with the demonstration of a super-weapon (*à la James Bond*), or you can have them fighting. And when you've got two stars who can move so gracefully, with an enigmatic and compelling speed and beauty, it's far better to have them duelling.

❖

The two middle acts of *Once Upon a Time In China 2* also have time for some mandatory romantic Wong Fei-hung and Aunt Lee scenes: in this one, Wong decides that Lee could do with some self-defence moves of her own. The subtext – Lee's yearning for Wong – is played for wistfulness underneath the comedy (Wong is quite rough, and also shouts at Lee, before apologizing, because that's how he talks to his students).

Aunt Lee, caught in a crouching pose by Wong Fei-hung's arm lock, looks at their shadows projected on a nearby brick wall, and imagines them dancing (so now she's bent over in a dance position). It's a reprise of the scene where Lee kissed Wong's shadow.

❖

In the first half of act three, there are some more modest scenes – such as Ah Foon teaching the children some *kung fu* stances (and getting into a clinch with Aunt Lee, much to Wong Fei-hung's fury); and another Lee-and-Wong romantic beat (filmed in burnished, intense close-up shots), where Lee confesses (some of) her feelings for Wong (to his astonishment).

In a pure Wong Fei-hung scene, the Chinese doctor assists Sun Yat-sen and Mr Luke (Lu Hao-tung – played by David Chiang) in medical operations to patch up the Brits injured in the White Lotus Cult attacks. Here Wong's skill with acupuncture performs the functions of an anæsthetic (which Sun has run out of). There's also a scene where Sun, Lu and Wong are together, and another where Sun and Lu contemplate their pocket watches. 'I never knew time was so important', Wong muses to Ah Foon (but to Tsui Hark, time is *very* important! As the characters say later: 'time is vital').

❖

In the second half of *Once Upon a Time In China 2*, the action comes thick and fast: the nighttime raid on the British Embassy by the White Lotus Cult is one of many set-pieces (it climaxes the third act, using the four-act model). Tsui Hark's genius for conjuring memorable images is to the fore throughout *Once Upon a Time In China 2*: the British Embassy sequences include the burning of a wooden cross (mocking the State religion of Britain), as well as effigies (including, to Aunt Lee's shocked, fainting dismay, one of herself!).

When the White Lotus Cult invade the British Embassy building, it's all-action as the Brits, their guards, Wong Fei-hung, Ah Foon, Aunt Lee, Mr Luke[8] and others defend themselves: this forms the climax of act three of *Once Upon a Time In China 2*. It is a very busy sequence, with action erupting in many settings in and around the Embassy. Continuing the satire on Western religion, Foon grabs a wooden cross and uses it to beat his assailants (something you don't often see in a North American action movie!). The chapel is, suitably enough, where the children hide.

The build-up to the storming contains a lot of action, with injured Westerners finding sanctuary in the Embasssy. This part of *Once Upon a Time In China 2* is a curious mixture of movie clichés (Westerners in a foreign land defending themselves from the angry locals outside); ideological and political subtexts (uneasy coalitions between the Chinese and the Brits; the regressive traditions of the White Lotus group; Wong Fei-hung discovering idealistic Chinese men who've embraced Western ways – Sun Yat-sen and Lung Hao-tung); and Tsui Hark's highly idiosyncratic way of staging all of this (it is thoroughly cinematic). It comes across as a mixture of films of the British overseas in the fading years of the Empire, like *Zulu*, *Gunga Din*,[9] and even a *Carry On* film (particularly

---

[8] With Sun Yat-sen departed on a political mission, Mr Luke (Lu) functions as his representative in the founding-ofChina theme in *Once Upon a Time In China 2*.
[9] Critics such as Stephen Teo have referenced the classic action-adventure *Gunga Din* (1939) in relation to the *Wong Fei-hung* movies. *Gunga Din* was directed by George Stevens, starred Cary Grant, Victor McLagen, Sam Jaffe and Douglas Fairbanks, Jr., and was based on Rudyard Kipling's poem. A wonderful movie, *Gunga Din* is one of those classics that you can watch over and over.

Carry On Up the Khyber, about the British in India), combined with explosive Hong Kong action cinema, and Tsui's own peculiar way of filming historical stories in terms of very heightened and stylized melodrama (as if a Peking Opera troupe were making a film about Wong Fei-hung, but under the guidance of a wilfully eccentric stage director who wants to combine Western adventure flicks such as *Indiana Jones* with a Chinese sensibility).

Among the multiple gags in the storming of the Embasssy sequence are White Lotus Cult soldiers on horseback riding thru the corridors, swinging swords; Wong Fei-hung taking on a bunch of White Lotus men armed with spears on some stairs (a dance of spears); and even Aunt Lee is given a moment to shine, when she wounds a guy in the leg.

As the British Embassy is infiltrated, Governor Lan waits outside for the best chance to turn the tables – he takes advantage of the chaos created by the White Lotus Cult to wrest control from the Brits, who're in disarray. Here he kills the British Consul (witnessed by Aunt Lee, who tells Wong Fei-hung): dramatically, this sets up the finale, when Wong duels with Governor Lan (as Lan is now a murderer, it justifies, in movie-movie terms, Wong taking the fight to the death – plus the fact that Lan is trying to kill him! Repeatedly!). Thematically/ politically, Lan nobbling the Consul proves to Wong that the Chinese authorities are once again corrupting themselves (reprising the portrayal of the Governor in the first *Once Upon a Time In China* film).

THE WHITE LOTUS FINALE.

There are two major action set-pieces that climax *Once Upon a Time In China 2*: both have been signalled early on in the 1992 movie: one is Wong Fei-hung versus the White Lotus Cult, and the second is Wong going up against Governor Lan. Both action set-pieces are state of the art, fearsomely inventive and played with a ferocious, wild energy.

Jet Li is in the spotlight of both action sequences in *China 2*, and he's never looked better, moved more gracefully, or exuded such magnetism and star quality (he was 29 at the time).[10] Li is one of the most fantastically beautiful performers ever to grace the screen. (Li seems to have done far more of his stunts on this movie – on the first *Wong Fei-hung* flick he was injured). But of course, he's not working alone! There is Yuen Woo-ping and his stunt team, and there is Tsui Hark behind the camera! Hell, how can you lose?!

The action in the White Lotus temple in *Once Upon a Time In China 2* is too rapid for storyboarding, and perhaps too long for a North American audience, but any action fan is going to love it. Jet Li's Wong Fei-hung becomes a one-man army against a horde of heavies dressed in white (with some of them going into beserker frenzies). They have swords, Mr Luke has a gun, but Wong is of course unarmed (as always – he *never* walks into a battle with weapons; Wong is always the negotiator first. But when that doesn't work, he resorts to force). He might not carry weapons

---

[10] It's not all action, tho' – Jet Li acts up a storm, in a role he seems to have been born to play.

(well, he has his trusty umbrella!), but Wong does employ everything in the environment against his opponents (such as kicking the wooden platform to shards which are flung at the henchmen, or snapping off the head of one of their spears and using it).

As well as inventing numerous ways in which Wong Fei-hung can dispatch his foes (never have so many heavies been beaten with a brolly!), the action also uses multiple levels – taking the fight up onto a ledge near the roof, onto the pillars, and a stack of tables (a favourite motif in Yuen Woo-ping's form of wire-assisted *kung fu*). The gag of Kung not touching the ground, as part of his sacred function as the leader of the White Lotus Cult who must be worshipped, is exploited to the max (such as, when the tower of tables finally topple, he uses a stretched cloth to stand on an altar).

Xiong Xin-xin plays up the phony pantomime of the leader of the White Lotus Cult with relish, providing a suitably over-the-top villain for Jet Li to battle (Xiong doubles for Li in the *Once Upon a Time In China* series, and also plays Clubfoot.)

The White Lotus temple sequence is a marvel of imaginative filmmaking, a full-on, acrobatic, crowd-pleasing display of outrageous *kung fu*. Wong Fei-hung dispatches numerous henchmen, and then proceeds to duel with Gao Kung on the tables, in the air, on a ledge, on a pillar, on stretched cloth, until every inch of the temple set has been explored. The sheer velocity of physical gags is like watching all of the Marx Brothers' movies squashed into ten minutes.

As with Christianity, the 1992 Chinese movie and its heroes make fun of the more regressive and reactionary forms of Chinese religion. Wong Fei-hung lambasts the White Lotus followers for worshipping a false deity with a fake religion. In one memorable beat, Wong pretends to be taken over by the spirit of the god, standing in front of the altar, with Jet Li executing some of the incredibly rapid *wushu* moves which're one of his specialities (an action star doesn't have catchphrases like a comedian, doesn't sing like a vocalist, but has movements which become part of their signature).

The demise of Master Kung, leader of the White Lotus Cult, is tied to the historical cliché of *kung fu* versus bullets. Kung is revealed to be wearing a breastplate (for the demonstrations of *kung fu* being able to be magically deflect gunfire. Actually, Western movies use bulletproof vests all the time as cheats – usually to bring a character back to life who appears to have been shot). Mr Luke fires at Kung repeatedly, for his crimes. Kung ends up impaled, in 1930s adventure serial style, on the statue behind the altar. (And Wong is the one who hurls him there – in *Once Upon a Time In China 2,* Wong takes care of both villains).

And in the fracas, Mr Luke accidentally but symbolically also shoots the little girl, totem of the White Lotus Cult (the *Wong Fei-hung* movies never put a gun into the hands of Wong – in the films of the 1950s as well as the 1990s. However, *Once Upon a Time In China 1* does have Wong holding a gun, tho' not using it. Instead, he dispatches the slave-trader

Jackson by flicking a bullet at the villain's skull).

THE HERO VS. VILLAIN FINALE.

Foreshadowed earlier in their sparring match with staffs, the confrontation between the chief villain of *Once Upon a Time In China 2*, Nap-lan Yun-seut, and the hero, Wong Fei-hung, does not disappoint: and this is Jet Li versus Donnie Yen, two stars who can move as gracefully as anybody in the entire history of cinema. So as Mr Luke, Ah Foon and Wong hurry to the pier where a ship is about to leave (a classic countdown device, and already used in film one), they are waylaid by Lan and his men. The setting is again a warehouse, and again a place of numerous wooden poles, walkways and multiple levels. The staff duel is absolutely thrilling, filled with so many imaginative flourishes from Yuen Woo-ping and the stunt team, and Tsui Hark's eye for vivid imagery, and Arthur Wong Ngok Tai's gorgeous cinematography – and not forgetting the utterly crucial element of editing (by Marco Mak Chi-sin *et al*).

This is state of the art action cinema, fabulously over-the-top, staged with a technical bravura that few filmmaking teams have matched. In one beat, Wong Fei-hung is way up at the top of the warehouse, stretched between two walkways on outspread legs, using one of the supporting poles[11] (thirty feet long!) to imprison Nap-lan Yun-seut on the ground below like a trapped dog, preventing him from attacking Ah Foon and Mr Luke (there is no scene in Western cinema like this!).

Here the scroll of names is used as the MacGuffin, with Mr Luke hurriedly burning it as the authorities close in; Mr Luke's demise is played as a Big, Dramatic Moment (and he's given a heartfelt eulogy by Sun Yat-sen in the *dénouement*).

The complication-followed-by-complication rule is deployed (being one of the basic rules of drama as well as action), so the staff duel in the warehouse doesn't top the 1992 movie. There is more! Nap-lan Yun-seut pursues Wong Fei-hung and Ah Foon into a back alley, where the action shifts into wet rope weapon territory (Wong has a piece of bamboo, which breaks). The filmmakers excel themselves with hugely inventive scenes of long range combat in a confined space – the rope of cloth speeds thru the air, whistling past Wong (he manages to dodge it), and explodes holes in the nearby walls (clever Wong exploits that, urging Foon to make the hole bigger, and helping himself, in between beating off attacks from Lan).

Nap-lan Yun-seut seems unstoppable, exuding a manic energy. His demise occurs when he's flung the rope around Wong's neck, trapping him, and Wong slides the remains of the bamboo stick along the rope, cutting thru it, back to Lan, and embedding a splinter in Lan's neck. In a nod to samurai movies (including the famous example in *Yojimbo*, 1961), Lan expires in a spray of blood from his neck.

And *that*, folks, is how to stage a hero vs. villain fight! And *that*, folks, is how to make a movie!

Once Upon a Time In China 2 is simply glorious filmmaking, and it

---
11 It smashes into the ground with an ominous thud, to suggest the power of the hero.

might be the finest in the first three *Wong Fei-hung* movies – until, that is, we watch the first one or the third one again!

(The *dénouement* returns to the political theme and the formation of early modern China, with evocations of the revolution, the downfall of the Qing Dynasty, and Sun Yat-sen leaving for Hong Kong, accompanied by Aunt Lee.[12] As Sun Yat-sen unfurls the flag, solemn words are delivered about sacrifice and a better future. Meanwhile, a ship leaving a dock is once again used to close a Tsui Hark movie, with its hints of travel, change, and the future).

---

12 There's a reprise of the grappling hand move, so that Aunt Lee (not Wong Fei-hung) fends off a policeman come to arrest Sun Yat-sen (which she learnt from Wong).

14

ONCE UPON A TIME IN CHINA 3

Wong Fei-hung Ji Saam – Si Wong Jaang Ba

INTRO.
Once Upon a Time In China 3 (1993, Mandarin: *Huang Feihong III Zhi San: Shiwang Zheng Ba = Wong Fei-hung 3: Lion King Struggle For Supremacy*), was filmed in Beijing, not Hong Kong, like the former two installments in the series. Ng Se-yuen and Tsui Hark were producers; Charcoal Cheung Tan, Chan Tin-suen and Tsui were the writers; action directors: Yuen Tak and Yuen Bun; music: Woo Wai-laap, William Hu and Tsui; DPs: Andrew Lau Wai-keung and Chow Man-keung;[13] editing: Marco Mak Chi-sin and Angie Lam On-yee; Sip Gam was production designer; and costumes: Tin-kiu Ching. In the cast were Jet Li, Rosamund Kwan, Max (Benny) Mok, Lau Shun, Xiong Xin-xin, John Wakefield, Chiu Chin, Wong Tak-yan, Meng Jin and Ge Cunzhuang. Released Feb 11, 1993. 105 mins.[14]

Once Upon a Time In China 3 is A Tsui Hark Production – and everyone knows it! But Raymond Chow/ Golden Harvest is an important producing partner in the enterprise, and a movie of this scale can only be produced by drawing on a *lot* of resources and expertise.

THE STORY.
The story and the characters of *Once Upon a Time In China 3* are very familiar if you've seen a few movies from Hong Kong: Wong Fei-hung is the Robin Hood hero, accompanied by Aunt Lee, who's enamoured of the West, foolish but harmless sidekick Leung Foon, Wong's father Wong Kay-ying, and other familiar characters in the Wong universe.

So in the third *Once Upon a Time In China* entry, Wong Fei-hung visits Peking[15] to see his father, to find the place in turmoil over the Lion Dance

---

[13] The film was filmed in Panavision and released in Dolby.
[14] The Taiwanese cut has some 15 minutes more material than the Hong Kong version (there are 26 additions, according to Wikipedia).
[15] The movie recycles the train footage from film two.

competition[16] launched by the Dowager Empress Cixi, for her own political motives (a Lion Dance had opened the whole *Once Upon a Time In China* series). Martial arts groups are pitted against each other, and the bad guys, the Tai-pang Club mob, led by Master Chiu Tin-bak[17] who cackles manically in every single scene), and his henchman Iron Foot or Clubfoot (Xiong Xin-xin), a vicious psychopath, are stirring up trouble (as villains tend to do), aiming to take all of the glory of the competition (by nobbling all of the rival *kung fu* schools, including the Wongs' school).

That's the background and the large-scale story, but that isn't of course what makes *Once Upon a Time In China 3* such a pleasure, such a thoroughly entertaining movie. *Once Upon a Time In China 3* has, for a start, two enormous cinematic presences: Jet Li, one of the most charismatic and all-round beautiful stars of recent cinema, a guy so electric you can't take your eyes off him. The camera loves him, he moves like a dream, with such elegance and speed and imagination, he can act, he can emote, he can carry whole movies, he is *simply amazing!*

And the other giant presence on the production is of course producer-director-writer Tsui Hark (he even has a music co-credit!). And *Once Upon a Time In China 3* has Tsui absolutely at the top of his game, overseeing a huge production with 100s of extras, trucks full of costumes, lavish location shooting, delightful exotic colour and festivities, a vast battery of practical and visual effects, and a deliciously inventive and dynamic cinematic style.

Oh, and incendiary action – this is action filmmaking by the finest team in the world (the action directors were Yuen Tak and Yuen Bun).

Once Upon a Time In China 3 is the movie with the Lion Dances (which had appeared in the first *Once Upon a Time In China* movie) – they open the story with some costly production value scenes filmed in the imperial palaces of Beijing (Wong Fei-hung is representing the Guangdong Association in the tournament). And there's an impressive scene with hundreds of extras in the streets watching the Lion Dance. As Stephen Teo explains:

> The lion dance is, of course, the showpiece in all Chinese festivities. To the Chinese, it is culture in its most popular form, and as a mascot for unity, brings the masses together. (1997, 173)

Once Upon a Time In China 3 is also the movie with the famous fight a-top ladders in the storeroom, a sequence of incredibly fiendish complexity, where Wong Fei-hung faces off against the villains. Another marvellous sequence has Wong going to dinner at Master Chiu Tin-bak's invitation and defending himself against multiple assailants wielding hand axes while slippin' 'n' slidin' in oil on the floor.

As if that's wasn't enough, there is also in *Once Upon a Time In China*

---

16 The Lion Dance is a fantastically lavish sequence, a marvellous recreation of a traditional, Chinese festival. The screen is alive with colour as the paper heads jiggle and bounce thru the streets (meanwhile, at knee and foot level, fights're breaking out between the rival *kung fu* schools).
17 Credited as Chiu Chin or Chunzhong Zhang.

3 a truly charming *lightness* and a *lightheartedness* to the proceedings. This isn't a movie bogged down by being 'weighty' or 'dark' or 'dramatic'. For instance, it's not all internecine battles in the streets and the inns between the bad guys and Wong Fei-hung and his chums, or ponderous musings on East-West geo-politics, there is plenty of romance, and plenty of humour.

THE LOOK AND STYLE.

The cinematography in *Once Upon a Time In China 3* is by Andrew Lau Wai-keung and Chow Man-keung. It is masterclass photography, with juicily saturated colouration, at its richest in the Lion Dance sequences, where the screen's alive with bright reds, yellows, golds, blues and greens. The satin blues of the nighttime scenes, the shimmering backlighting, the wafting smoke and sputtering fires, these are some of the classic images of Chinese, historical movies. Add to that very low angles, often with wide angle lenses, and rapid tracking shots along the ground – the filmmaking approach recalls Orson Welles.

The camera is often tilted in *Once Upon a Time In China 3* : to frame a street procession, the camera operators simply tilt the camera, to include more of the scene, instead of selecting a different angle or shot size. But the Dutch angles don't connote weirdness or a world off-angle, as in many movies, but simply another way of expressing the energy and freedom of the filmmaking.

Once Upon a Time In China 3 was filmed without sync sound, and was dubbed in the studio (the usual practice in Hong Kong movies. It was a long time before Chinese movies, and especially action movies, took up direct sound in significant numbers).

SUBPLOTS AND THEMES.

Romance: the lovely Rosamund Kwan once again carries the romantic subplot as Cousin/ Aunt Lee, continuing the will-they-won't-they? romance plot of the *Once Upon a Time In China* series. The self-conscious naïvety and simplicity of the romance between Aunt Lee and Wong Fei-hung is very appealing. It's a romance that has everything to do with literature and cinema, and happily sidesteps any notions of 'realism' or 'naturalism'. It is also, unlike in some other Tsui Hark movies, chaste and restrained. These are potential lovers who rarely even embrace (and when the Russian Tomanovsky (John Wakefield) kisses Aunt Lee's hand, Wong Fei-hung is outraged, and calls it unsanitary!). And yet the real Wong was married 4 times.

The motif of shadowplay is part of the romantic subplot in *Once Upon a Time In China 3*: in the previous movies, Peony imagines herself dancing with Wong Fei-hung's shadow; in the third movie, the shadows reflect the reality of Wong and Peony embracing. (And now they are seriously discussing marriage; and there's another comical moment when Ah Foon and the boys hurry in and Lee and Wong break apart, embarrassed).

That romance and eroticism is a key element in Tsui Hark's cinema often goes unremarked. And the lighthearted romances are just as much a part of Tsui's cinema as the more melodramatic or intense relationships. In *Once Upon a Time In China 3*, the courtship of Wong Fei-hung and Aunt Lee is essential to the movie, at the thematic as well as psychological and emotional level.

The romance of Wong Fei-hung and Aunt Lee is exploited many times throughout *Once Upon a Time In China 3*. In some scenes, the whole *kung fu* school is involved, like the great moment when Wong is anxious when Aunt Lee goes missing, and, re-united, he hugs her, while everybody stands there in a row, gawping (Tsui Hark is very fond of scenes where onlookers provide comical reactions).

Another subplot in *Once Upon a Time In China 3* is the Western technologies and *mœurs* that Aunt Lee brings with her (and embodies), plus items such as the steam engine. Again, the confrontations with Western science and politics are played lightly as well as seriously and dramatically. There are humorous scenes, for instance, where Aunt Lee is using an early, wind-up film camera,[18] and making a movie. During the Lion Dance sequence, the camera falls on its side, and when the *kung fu* school view the footage at a screening with a 🎞, they all have their necks bent over (a classic Tsui Hark sight gag involving a crowd, recalling the gag with the street sign in *Shanghai Blues*). The celluloid becomes part of the nefarious plots of the Russians (to kill Premier Li Hongzhang), which Aunt Lee uncovers with a little detective work. (It is of course ironic that cinema itself is a Western/ European invention, and was imported into China).

The movie camera also captures Ah Foon and Wong Fei-hung going thru some *kung fu* moves. Aunt Lee calls 'action!' and Wong does nothing (yes, a female film director!), doesn't realize what's going on. Meanwhile, Foon is monopolizing the camera, performing in front of it, while everyone else waits for their turn.

Another subplot involves Iron Foot: he's introduced as Master Chiu's chief bruiser, a formidable opponent with a nasty flying kick fighting style (Iron Foot is played by Xiong Xin-xin, Tsui Hark's regular stunt director in the 1990s, as well as a stunt double for Jet Li). But when he's injured, Iron Foot becomes the laughing stock of the Chiu mob, and is cast down some stairs. The images of Iron Foot crawling on the ground are striking, and the scene where he arrives at the Wong Fei-hung residence and is eventually helped by the doctor are moving. In cascades of heavy rain, Wong goes out to Iron Foot who spurns the sympathy of the Wong clan.[19]

Few critics foreground the elements of comedy and humour in the cinema of Tsui Hark, but it's clearly hugely important. Lengthy sections of Tsui's movies are actually lighthearted and comical (and when Tsui performs cameos, in his own or in other movies, it's often, as with Alfred Hitchcock, in a comical role).

---

18 A movie camera also features in the Lion Dance prologue.
19 It's also a reprise of the scenes of Iron Robe in the rain in film one, and Porky Wing in the rain in film two.

THE ACTS.

The opening act of *Once Upon a Time In China 3*, as in the other *Once Upon a Time In China* movies, is the whole movie in condensed form. It introduces all of the main plots, and culminates with a giant action sequence. Following the impressive production value scene of the Lion Dance in the Imperial Palace, and the introduction of the Dowager Empress (Meng Chin) and her minister, Governor Li Hongzhang (Ge Cunzhang), the movie shifts to the hero and his entourage arriving in a bustling Peking. We see the three biggest stars in *Once Upon a Time In China 3* (Li, Kwan and Mok), and some of their customary light-hearted banter (part of which involves East-West contrasts – such as Aunt Lee causing a commotion in her Western clothes, and a foreigner (the Russian man Tomanovsky) kissing Lee's hand – and also the Lee-and-Wong romance).

The confrontation between Wong Fei-hung and some locals (in which Wong effortlessly dominates them) outside the railroad station, is a prelude to several scenes in the opening act which repeat that scenario. So at the halfway mark in act one, Wong dives into a fray in the streets (literally – he leaps from the upper story of a building onto the street below). The martial arts groups are fighting over supremacy in the upcoming Lion Dance competition, and Wong plays the peace-maker, tho' by beating sense into the tussling groups. Wong is not armed, once again, and doesn't even have his trademark umbrella. So how is he going to subdue 100s of angry guys, many of whom are armed with swords? Simple – he takes off his jacket and uses it as a weapon to whack the fighters on all sides. It's another of Jet Li's familiar taking-on-all-comers action scenes, in which nobody is a match for him.

One of delights of the first act of *Once Upon a Time In China 3* is to see Xiong Xin-xin as Clubfoot in a major smackdown with Wong Fei-hung's father, Wong Kay-ying, played by Lau Shun. The setting – the Cantonese Association, where Wong senior and his colleagues are putting together (and painting) the Lion Dance masks – is once again a very traditional and very Chinese *milieu*. It's as if Tsui Hark and the team are trying to encourage their audiences not to forget Chinese traditions and customs – as well as to entertain and thrill them.

The action sequence draws on the White Lotus scenes in *Once Upon a Time In China 2* and the Embassy scenes in *Once Upon a Time In China 1*, as a local gang led by a venal commander (Master Chiu) arrives to cause trouble. The issue is simple: Chiu wants to be the sole team entering the Lion Dance competition. So he sends in his chief bruiser Clubfoot to rough up Wong senior's cohorts. The fight itself is another very acrobatic sequence, with Iron Foot parodying the famous shadowless kick of Wong Fei-hung by flying towards his opponents and kicking (including racing across the floor and up the walls, feet first).

Act one also introduces the will-they-could-they-should-they? romance plot between Aunt Lee and Wong Fei-hung. Marriage is on the cards – at least from Aunt Lee's view of things. Once again much comical juice is squeezed out of one half of a romantic couple being uptight, repressed, indignant. The scene between Wong and his father (and the misunderstanding about the marriage) is coupled with a scene featuring devilish Western technology (a steam engine), where Lee steals a kiss from Wong.

❖

The second act of *Once Upon a Time In China 3* includes several action scenes, such as Wong Fei-hung and Clubfoot battling it out in the crowded streets of Peking: Wong is chasing the rickshaw which's taken Aunt Lee off in the wrong direction, and Clubfoot is trying to stop him. It's a delight, as in film two, to see Jet Li and Xiong Xin-xin duking it out – by this time, they have worked together so often, they move with assurance and incredible high speed. They are running up walls, dancing across the top of people's heads, and performing multiple kicks as they soar through the air.

The second act of *Once Upon a Time In China 3* climaxes with a massive outdoor scene of the Lion Dance competition, in the preliminary part of the competition (thus, this is essentially a forerunner of the finale, which's set at night). These noisy, busy scenes, filmed on crowded streets filled with Lion Dancers and spectators, fireworks and smoke, might be a documentary on traditional, Chinese customs. In few other films do so many Lion Dance costumes and dancers fill the screen, in shot after shot (many shots are in slight slo-mo).

It's gloriously colourful, and extended far beyond the necessities of the drama. Tho' there *are* dramatic elements: the romantic rivalry that the Russian Tomanovsky represents, for instance (he insists on coming over to see Aunt Lee), Master Chiu's bully boys creating havoc in the Lion Dance with knives and swords, and the MacGuffin of the movie camera.

The sequence runs on and on, and includes Ah Foon being chased by Iron Foot (across the rooftops), Aunt Lee getting lost in the mob, and a stampede of horses, until finally Wong Fei-hung takes control: he rounds up the horses, and puts the Lion Dancers in their place. How? By beating them with staffs – yes, it's another example of Jet Li's astonishing ability to control long, wooden poles (two this time!), and flail them with lightning speed.[20]

The third act of *Once Upon a Time In China 3* keeps several plot strands spinning in the air, which have already been a part of acts one and two: the romance/ marriage plot (Aunt Lee looking on as Wong Fei-hung confides in his father and tells him that he's marrying Cousin Lee); more Westernization (Aunt Lee teaching Wong some English words, including 'man', 'woman' and 'I love you'); the scene where Clubfoot is ostracized from the Tai-pang gang; and a moving sequence where Clubfoot rejects the help of Wong and co., until he relents.

Act three climaxes with one of the great sequences in the *Once Upon a Time In China* series: Wong Fei-hung visiting Master Chiu for dinner, which rapidly descends into an elaborate bust-up with the gimmick of an oil-slicked floor, which has everybody skidding helplessly all over it (in a

---

[20] He also uses the poles like stilts, hopping over the Lion Dancers.

fun gag, the Tai-pang heavies have spiked shoes, so they can grip in the sea of oil). Dodging flying axes and flailing swords, this is another scene of Jet Li taking on all comers, and triumphing, accompanied, inevitably, by the *Wong Fei-hung* signature music.

The fight moves out onto the streets, as the Po Chi Lam brigade run down Master Chiu, who's revealed to be a mean martial artist. As Chiu departs, chuckling as always, across the roofs, there is another 'to be continued' hung in the air, which leads us directly into the finale.

THE FINALE – THE LION DANCE COMPETITION.

The finale of *Once Upon a Time In China 3* is of course the Lion Dance competition, a giant action sequence set at night involving the Lion Dance teams competing for the trophy, overseen by Governor Li Hongzhang and numerous officials (plus the foreign – Russian – contingent). The Russians want to kill Governor Li over the treaty which will cede the Liandong Peninsula to Japan.

The Lion Dance sequence begins with stately festivities,[21] but gradually escalates into in-fighting down at the level of the dancers, and ultimately all-out fight scenes as Master Chiu and his Tai-pang mob take on Wong Fei-hung and Iron Foot (Ah Foon gets injured early on, and has to wait out the fight). Wong and Iron Foot work together to win the competition, while fighting off henchmen on all sides (they're armed with swords, small shooting spears, and banners fitted with blades at the top).

In the Lion Dance finale the assassination plot also plays out. The Russian Tomanovsky confronts Aunt Lee about the movie camera in a dark alley, which rounds off the subplot of flirtation between Lee and Tomanovsky (he commands her to return the footage she filmed, then he decides that he'll have to kill her). Tomanovsky foolishly raises his pistol to shoot the Governor himself, when the assassination plot is foiled, and is killed by his own side (they tell the Chinese officials that he was a Japanese spy). Here, Lee voices the familiar nationalistic mantra: China is for the Chinese, and it can sort out its own problems, without foreign intervention.

In amongst the colourful dancing lion masks and bodies, Wong Fei-hung's Lion Dance mask is white, like most of his costumes, which makes it stand out. Master Chiu, meanwhile, of course has the largest lion head in the competition (four times as big as the others).

The centrepiece of the competition is a tall, wooden tower, decorated with red cloth (similar to the one in *Fong Sai-yuk*, 1993). The winner is the one who snaffles the golden trophy. As expected, it's soon tottering, with wooden poles being snapped or kicked across the square as missiles. Much of the action occurs on top, inside or halfway up the tower – a very challenging sequence for the stunt team, filming over many nights. Jet Li and Xiong Xin-xin are very fine here, with Xiong generously giving all of the glory to Li (tho' he has his own moments to shine).

After an impressive duel with Master Chiu amid twirling staffs and

---

[21] Wong Fei-hung handles the exposition, to explain how the Lion Dance competition works.

banners, Wong Fei-hung saves the day, as usual, and gets to say his piece about peace to the Governor (who has nothing to offer in reply). In the finale of *Once Upon a Time In China 3*, as Stefan Hammond and Mike Wilkins sum up, Wong does everything:

> enters the Lion Dance competition in order to win the crown, defeat Chiu, frustrate the Russian assassination, produce more film evidence against the Russians, and lecture President Li on how his policies are dividing the country. (87)

❖

This is filmmaking that simply bursts out all over the place with energy. The dynamism of this 1993 movie, and much of Hong Kong New Wave cinema, is breathtaking: the camera is all over the place, but it's always moving with a function. Altho' it seems showy (well, it *is*!), it is also utterly unlike MTV or pop promo or commercials filmmaking in the West, or the Western movies trumpeted with the meaningless word 'stylish',[22] where the camera moves independently of the action and the drama, has little real dramatic value other than offering a different (and pointless) view of the same action (like the over-editing of Western movies, where four different shots will be used of a single action, for no other reason than using a variety of images of the same thing, in a desperate attempt at making something more interesting. The rapid editing and the multiple, brief views of the same action disguise the fact that the *storytelling* and the *pacing* are pretty much the same as they're always been in Western cinema. It seems 'faster', but it *isn't*. For ex, acts *still* run to 25-30 minutes, as usual in cinema since the 1920s, and there *aren't* more characters than in previous cinema, and the stories are often *exactly* the same. Sure, there might be more scenes, and more events, or action within scenes, but the storytelling isn't quicker – indeed, you can argue, with Hollywood movies now regularly running to two hours, or 140 mins, that storytelling today is *slower* than in earlier films. Certainly many movies today are longer than the average feature in the Classical Hollywood era).

Chinese action filmmaking is completely different: it is tied in to the action to an incredibly strong degree. Even tho' the filmmakers are using the same tools – cameras, tripods, microphones, dollies, cranes, Kodak film stock, etc – their approach to filmmaking is so different.

Once Upon a Time In China 3 celebrates the body in space, the body in movement, the body beautiful. The very low angle tracking shots, with a wide angle lens, across a row of people watching a Lion Dance... the tilted camera views of the fights, as Wong Fei-hung batters the participants in a street fight between rival martial arts organizations using his clothes as a weapon... the compositions that emphasize the huge, blue bowl of the sky... *Once Upon a Time In China 3* is a dream of a movie, a marvellous succession of colourful images.

Again, in looking at *Once Upon a Time In China 3*, I'm struck by the feeling that *anything can happen!* That a scene could move in all sorts of directions, with the same openness towards drama that the movie shows

---

22 All art, nay, everything has a 'style'.

towards movement and bodies. Even tho' the tale the movie's telling is familiar and genre-based, and very much drawing on the Wong Fei-hung legend, and even tho' the characters're predictable and as familiar as character types in any genre fiction, there's still a feeling of total freedom.

And it's this emphasis on freedom that makes *Once Upon a Time In China 3* and Hong Kong New Wave cinema, and so much of Chinese action cinema, so appealing. Even when you've seen these movies many times, they still manage to surprise you each time. These movies really are as light on their feet as their characters. The way the figures leap onto a table as if it's the easiest thing in the world, or suddenly strike a memorable pose (how does Jet Li crouch down to the floor, with his legs spread wide and almost parallel with it, *so* quickly?!), is reflected by the 1993 movie itself, by its graceful and quickfire motion, its ability to sketch in a scene with a few elegant brushstrokes (now we're in a moonlit street, now we're in the upstairs room of an inn), and by its seemingly boundless ability to re-invent itself as it goes along.

A movie like this is surely what cinema was invented for. This is true cinema, the total opposite of 'filmed theatre' or 'talking heads', which comprises most cinema and all television.

15

ONCE UPON A TIME IN CHINA 4

Wong Fei-hung Ji Sei – Wong Je Ji Fung

INTRO.

The fourth installment in the *Once Upon a Time In China* series was released the same year as the third movie – 1993 (this was a period when the Hong Kong film industry was in a massive renaissance – look at how many movies the actors and filmmakers were working on in 1993! Did they ever sleep?!).

Once Upon a Time In China 4 (1993, Mandarin: *Huang Fei Hong Zhi Si: Zhe Zhi Feng*), was produced by Tsui Hark and 'N.G.' (Ng See Yuen) for Film Workshop/ Paragon Films Ltd.; Tsui and Tang Pik-yin scripted; and Yuen Bun directed (and was action choreographer). Music was by William Hu; the DPs were Arthur Wong Ngok Tai, Ko Chiu-lam, Chow Man-keung and Cheung Man-po. Edited by Marco Mak Chi-sin. Hong Kong gross: HK $11,301,790.00. Released only 4 months after *Once Upon a Time In China 3*: June 10, 1993. 101 minutes.

Among the cast were Vincent Zhao as Wong Fei-hung, Jean Wang as 14th Aunt, Max Mok as Ah Foon, Xiong Xin-xin as Clubfoot, Billy Chow as Iron Fist, Chin Kar-lok as Tuen Tin-lui, Lau Shun as Wong's father, Wong Kei-ying, Louis Roth as Father Thomas, and Wang Zhiwen as the deputy Governor.[23]

Once Upon a Time In China 4 was the first *Once Upon a Time In China* movie which changed the actor playing the title role – Jet Li stepped out, to pursue other projects (Li made a *lot* of movies in 1993), and Vincent Zhao (also known as Zhao Wenzhou, a.k.a. Chin Man Chuek, b. 1972) was hired.[24]

There was talk about Jet Li in the first *Once Upon a Time In China*

---

[23] You can see in numerous scenes that it was *very* cold during the making of *Once Upon a Time In China 4*, and that even many of the interiors, filled with lights, were still cold (partly because many scenes were filmed at night).
[24] Vincent Zhao was apparently discovered by Corey Yuen Kwai in a martial arts school in Beijing. But director Ann Hui claims that she discovered Zhao (F. Dannen, 90).

picture, wondering if he was too young to play the much-loved character of Wong Fei-hung (who had been played in the *Wong Fei-hung* series by a much older actor, Kwan Tak Hing). Well, Vincent Zhao looks even younger than Li (he was only 21). And he is, you have to admit, a less appealing actor all-round (tho' he moves like a dream in the action scenes). Zhao is superb (very wonderful in *The Blade*), but he doesn't heat up the screen like a superstar such as Jet Li.[25] Zhao also seems uncomfortable in the scenes which require real acting, including the comical scenes and the romantic scenes[26] – both vital ingredients in the *Once Upon a Time In China* franchise. (However, as the villain Governor Oryeetor in *Fong Sai-yuk*, filmed the same year, where Zhao goes up against Jet Li, Zhao was more impressive. And, to be fair, Zhao did have the challenge of following a big star like Li, and in movies which had been very successful locally).

Fortunately, in *Once Upon a Time In China 4* Vincent Zhao is surrounded by a host of familiar and dependable Chinese actors, many of whom are part of the *Once Upon a Time In China* family: Max Mok, Xiong Xin-xin,[27] Lau Shun, etc. So that even if Zhao is somewhat wooden, he has many people around him who can deliver the goods.

Once again, *Once Upon a Time In China 4* is a gorgeous production photographically. But then, with the DPs being headed up by Arthur Wong Ngok Tai, it's going to look great (plus Ko Chiu-lam, Chow Man-keung and Cheung Man-po). Of course, you can't lose visually with so many luxurious costumes and colours in the Lion Dances, the Red Lantern Society, and the outfits of early, modern China.

Tsui Hark's input in *Once Upon a Time In China 4* included production and co-writing (plus it was produced by his company, Film Workshop – along with Paragon Films and Golden Harvest). *Once Upon a Time In China 4* is wholly A Tsui Hark Movie in pretty much every respect, despite him handing over the directorial reins to Yuen Bun (one of Tsui's regular action choreographers). Not least because it is the fourth entry in a series which had been directed and produced and co-written (and, crucially, *conceived*) by Tsui. That is, Tsui's stamp is all over the first three *Once Upon a Time In China* films, and the fourth film is actually directed – by Yuen Bun – like Tsui (right down to the movement of the camera).

YUEN BUN.

Director Yuen Bun (b. 1954) is an actor who has been in pretty much everything, and an action director who has worked with Tsui Hark on many productions, as well as numerous Hong Kong classics. Yuen was one of the 'Seven Little Fortunes', the Peking Opera School group that included future Hong Kong legends such as Jackie Chan, Sammo Hung, Yuen Wah, Corey Yuen Kwai and Yuen Ting.

By 2014, Yuen Bun had action director credits on 102 films! (Going back to 1974, a remarkable career). Plus 107 acting credits. However,

---

[25] And those thick eyebrows! Oh dear. Where were the make-up girl's scissors?!
[26] Zhao 'seems completely at sea when it comes to the right Wong mix of stoicism and emotion', complained Lisa Morton (LM, 196).
[27] Clubfoot is a much cleaned-up, much less angry guy from the third *Once Upon a Time In China* movie.

Yuen has only directed three films,[28] preferring to work as a choreographer or actor: *Once Upon a Time in China 4* (1993), *Tough Beauty and the Sloppy Slop* (1995) and *Fearful 24 Hours* (2004).

Yuen Bun is without question one of the great action directors of recent times, with a list of credits that includes many masterpieces (and Yuen's contribution, in choreographing the action, is absolutely pivotal to those films being masterpieces): such as, for Tsui Hark: *Time and Tide, Dragon Gate Inn, Swordsman 2, The Blade, Flying Swords of Dragon Gate* and the three *Detective Dee* movies.

Yuen Bun is one of the unsung heroes of Hong Kong action cinema. The limelight is hogged by other action directors – Yuen Woo-ping, Tony Ching, Corey Yuen Kwai and Jackie Chan, but Yuen has choreographed some of the greatest action in all Hong Kong cinema (and therefore all world cinema).

In sum, the collaborations between Yuen Bun and Tsui Hark have been among the finest in action cinema: they clearly work well together (you've got be *really* good to keep up with a director as amazing as Tsui).

THE STORY, ACT-BY-ACT.

Once Upon a Time In China 4 opens with two lengthy prologue/ title sequences (one wonders if these were included to bump up the running time): Wong Fei-hung practising kung fu in an Imperial China setting (with the customary 'Under the General's Orders' march music, to introduce the new star), followed by the main titles (set against the Lion Dance competition footage, which climaxed the previous *Once Upon a Time In China* film – a cheap option, and a standard tactic for increasing the running time).

Once Upon a Time In China 4 seems like a chronological continuation of *Once Upon a Time In China 3* (and from the Lion Dance finale of *Once Upon a Time In China 3*): the first act contains many scenes of Lion Dances and colourful parades (production value scenes, yes, and also scenes asserting Chinese national culture, a particular passion for Tsui Hark).

Once again, nationalist politics, national cultures, and the conflicts between nations are foregrounded in *Once Upon a Time In China 4*, emphasizing yet again just how intensely *political* the *Once Upon a Time In China* series is. Altho' they are movies about a great Chinese hero, and they're colourful action movies, it's surprising just how much of their setting and background is ideological, cultural and political. *Once Upon a Time In China 4* is set in 1900.

Once again, any group or individual that's 'foreign' is negatively typed: here, it's Germans and Brits. And the battleground? Only another Lion Dance competition! (How can any group from outside China possibly be victorious in a traditional, Chinese event like a Lion Dance?! Especially when Wong Fei-hung is involved!). But the Lion Dance competition is a mere sideshow to the Eight Nation Alliance, which's moving against China.

---

28 It might've been daunting to follow Tsui Hark in directing his first film, and having his first film as director being a big picture and part of a successful franchise.

Meanwhile, the organization within China that's shifting too far towards radicalism or nationalism in *Once Upon a Time In China 4* is a group of nationalistic feminists, the Red Lantern Society. The *Once Upon a Time In China* series doesn't create narratives where only 'foreigners' are rivals/ enemies – there is always a group inside China which is descending into a radical ideology which unbalances the status quo. The *Once Upon a Time In China* series doesn't side with rebels or activists – its politics are ultimately conservative and pro-State.

After all, let's not forget that the hero of the 1990s *Wong Fei-hung* movies is... Wong Fei-hung! That is, an upright citizen of society, if ever there was one! Wong is almost too perfect, too righteous. And he needs big villains, whole organizations, not single individuals (because an individual, even if they're played by martial arts masters like Donnie Yen or Xiong Xin-xin, are ultimately no match for Wong).

Thus, in the action climax of act one of *Once Upon a Time In China 4* – a terrorist attack on a German church by the Red Lantern Society – it's Wong Fei-hung defending law and order. Well, that's the over-arching, political setting – but the filmic reality is actually one young man beating off a whole troupe of female martial artists! Bang goes the taboo against hitting women! (And yet, there are differences between the way this scene is filmed – no blood, for a start, and Wong beats the women with a piece of rolled-up cloth, not swords or spears).

The Red Lantern Society are very likely wholly created by Tsui Hark. A band of young women who're taking nationalistic fervour to terrorist extremes is a classic, Tsuian motif. Radical feminism plus terrorism plus martial arts! – it's the perfect combination for Tsui! In terms of action and choreography and staging, the Red Lantern Society sequences are predictable – it is, after all, young women kicking ass, which Hong Kong cinema has been trotting out for decades. They throw lanterns filled with ether (which explode like fire-bombs), and they have an attractive leader, Miao (played by Elaine Lui Siu-Ling). In the procession sequence, the leader somersaults down from a human pyramid to have a little time in amongst the crowds with Wong Fei-hung (with a little moment of rivalry with 14th Aunt).

But beyond the cheesy action cinema trappings, politically and ideologically, the Red Lantern Society is fascinating. *Once Upon a Time In China 4* is clearly aiming to evoke some deeper undercurrents in contemporary Chinese society and politics. And in this quasi-historical setting (rather than a fantasy context), seeing a group of women acting so aggressively in public, and in a very patriarchal and traditional society like China *circa* 1900, is very unusual.

❖

Act one of *Once Upon a Time In China 4* includes the aftermath of the Lion Dance competition from the third film (with much self-congratulation), the invitation to participate in another Lion Dance festival, a procession and Lion Dance in the streets, and the finale: the procession from the Red Lantern Society followed by the raid on the German church.

Act one also contains the requisite comical scenes from Ah Foon, and the introduction of the romantic interest (in the second part of act one): with Rosamund Kwan stepping down, her role is now taken up by Jean Wang, playing what is essentially the same character. As well as the romantic elements (one-sided, as usual – Wong Fei-hung is not interested in 14th Aunt like that – yet), the scenes also feature the character's fascination with Western technology (here, it's printing presses).29 But Wang's 14th Aunt has little to do in *Once Upon a Time In China 4,* and doesn't contribute to the plot as much as 13th Aunt did in the previous installments. One wonders if more was filmed but left out, due to Vincent Zhao coming across as uncomfortable in the romantic scenes.

❖

Act two includes two stunning sequences featuring the nationalistic feminists of the Red Lantern Society. Like the White Lotus Cult in film two of the *Once Upon a Time In China* series, the Red Lantern Society is very fond of putting over their ideological messages using pageantry and co-ordinated acrobatics. The twist here in *China 4* is seeing an all-women team, clad in matching white costumes (with red trimming). So we know, for a start, that when the fighting starts (as it must!), there will be no murders (tho' the women will be pushed, kicked and battered about).

The two set-pieces are staged at the Po Chi Lam clinic at night, when the Wong Fei-hung group returns (minus Wong, however), to find that the Red Lantern Society have overwhelmed the building with their banners and deadly lanterns (the Red Lantern Society certainly have an eye for decoration). The inevitable bust-up is spectacular, intense, and wildly acrobatic, like the Cirque du Soleil meets Peking Opera. If there's a circus trick to be used, the *Once Upon a Time In China* series will use it (they include a lengthy duel on wires, a call-back to the White Lotus Cult sequence, where touching the ground is avoided, and the famous ladders scene in the first *Once Upon a Time In China* movie).

In the first Red Lantern Society set-piece, our heroes are overcome by the powder wielded by the warriors in their lanterns (no one is immune to it). In the second set-piece, Wong Fei-hung turns up (accompanied by Miao Sanniang), having escaped jail. The scene involves an over-elaborate game of dominoes,30 using large blocks of wood (again with balancing and not touching the ground as a rule, as in a children's game), and the staple of the *Once Upon a Time In China* series: Wong Fei-hung versus numerous assailants. The second part is a highwire act, with Wong going up against Miao, the leader of the Red Lantern Society (cue close-ups of feet on wires, and the commander being kicked to the ground. Oh no, we couldn't have Wong being bested by a woman!).

There's no shortage of ideas here – or energy: indeed, these movies look like the filmmakers could go on and on coming up with new moves, new twirls, new ways of using wires, or new ways of nobbling an opponent. I bet if they were allowed to, Hong Kong action directors could fill out an

---

29 But 14th Aunt isn't such a passionate proponent of Western science as 13th Aunt.
30 Plenty of celluloid is reversed to provide the trick shots of the domino pieces being returned upright by Wong Fei-hung.

entire movie with tumbling, jumping, slashing and flying. This is movie-making as a Peking Opera performance. The stamina seems endless – these guys and girls just don't quit! – and the use of the body in space is without equal anywhere on the planet.

❖

With so much of *Once Upon a Time In China 4* taking place during Lion Dances or street processions, it's like watching a travelogue about Chinese folklore and customs: cinema of course adores festivals, carnivals, fairgrounds, anything where there's a multitude of people, colour, movement, performance, rides, etc. The *Once Upon a Time In China* series contains a striking amount of theatre and performance, of processions thru the old town set, or from the tumbling acrobats of the Red Lantern team at the Po Chi Lam clinic. Indeed, one of Wong Fei-hung's alternative careers is as a Lion Dancer and street performer (of course, Wong turns out to be the finest of all Lion Dancers, and always does something heroic at a Lion Dance show. Sometimes, Wong seems like an expert and famous Lion Dancer who just happens to run a clinic and be a martial arts star, too).

Thus, *Once Upon a Time In China 4* contains not only several Lion Dances, but also a street procession from the Red Lantern Society, a funeral for General Chengdu, and even Ah Foon performs to a crowd. The *Once Upon a Time In China* series is very fond of combining the pageantry and tradition of China (in the Lion Dances) with martial arts choreography: thus, as in previous *Once Upon a Time In China* outings, the Lion Dance staged by the Eight-Nation Alliance in Peking is an excuse for the foreigners to attack the General and his team (with new-fangled technology – a Gatling gun). So, once again, it's the foreigners inside China who turn on the Chinese and assault them.

❖

As usual in the *Once Upon a Time In China* series, there isn't a single sequence for the finale in *Once Upon a Time In China 4*, but several. The first climax rounds off the Red Lantern Society plot: once again, it's those nasty foreigners (here, Germans) who are the villains, firing on the Red Lantern Society girls with rifles. Well, we know that *kung fu* and swords are no match for firearms (which are, as Akira Kurosawa noted, too easy – you just stand there and shoot).

The violence exerted against women is striking in *Once Upon a Time In China 4* (one of the members of the Red Lantern Society, for instance, is lacerated with bullets like Sonny Corleone in *The Godfather*, and the leader is decapitated, much to her followers' dismay). These acts are carried out by the two heavies (Tuen Tin-lui (Chin Kar-lok) and Iron Fist (Billy Chow)) hired by the foreign powers to deal with the locals. (One of the henchmen (Iron Fist) is given the ability to punch out a horse (a staple of the cowboy genre) – Clubfoot encounters these guys on horseback, and only just manages to get away).

There is re-match of the Lion Dance competition back in the capital, with Wong Fei-hung, Clubfoot, Wong senior and their chums turning out victorious (of course). This supplies the setting for the last part of the finale of *Once Upon a Time In China 4*, which's fantastically chaotic and visceral – everybody is being flung around in the dust of the parade ground (right into the night). In the finale, the stunt team stage every gag they can think of – the screen is frantic with fighters in festival costumes leaping about, amazing images of lions, eagles, centipedes, bulls and crabs,[31] guns blazing and swords flashing (Wong chooses a walking stick this time). Quite rightly, the movie depicts the clashes of animals among the Lion Dancers as if they are real, mythical creatures – thus, the lion heads attack the bodies of the birds, crabs and centipedes, as if this is a smackdown between huge, Japanese monsters (*kaiju*).

For action fans, some of the finest moments are in the closing minutes, when Wong Fei-hung and Clubfoot go up against the two bruisers sent by the foreign powers, Iron Fist and Tuen Tin-lui (here, Vincent Zhao's strength as a *wushu* performer pays off. Zhao and Xiong make a great team – the highlight of their collaboration being the truly extraordinary duel that closes *The Blade*, two years later).

Once Upon a Time In China 4 does suffer from the downsides of sequelizing – that we have seen all of this before: the same sort of characters, the same sort of action, the same sort of spectacle and effects, the same sort of romance, and the same sort of comedy. Part of the feeling of *déja vu* comes from the use of the Lion Dance motif – which ran throughout the third *Once Upon a Time In China* movie (and featured in the first movies, too); film four thus not only continues the Lion Dance theme of the third movie, it feels like a remake of it.

Starting a Wong Fei-hung movie with some new actors in the lead roles (such as Wong Fei-hung and 14th Aunt) might've been better served with a different *milieu* for the story. (Being released 4 months after film three maybe didn't leave time to develop new material).

---

31 The Lion Dance costumes are a delight.

Once Upon a Time In China 2 (1992).

Once Upon a Time
In China 3 (1993).
This page and over.

Once Upon a Time In China 4 (1993). This page and over.

16

ONCE UPON A TIME IN CHINA 5

Wong Fei-hung Ji Ng Lung Sing Chin Ba

Once Upon a Time In China 5 (1994, *Shiàonián Huáng Feihóng Zhi Tie Maliú* in Mandarin = *Wong Fei-hung 5: Dragon City's Exterminator Tyrant*), was produced by Tsui Hark and Ng See-yuen. It was written by Tsui, Lau Daai-muk and Lam Kee-to. The DPs were: Ko Chiu-Lam, Derek Wan, Peter Pau Tak-Hai, Tom Lau Moon-tong and Andy Lam. Art dir. by Bill Lui. Costumes: Kwok-Sun Chui. Action dir.: Yuen Bun. Edited by Marco Mak Chi-sin. Music by William Hu. It was produced by Film Workshop/ Paragon Films Ltd. (The home box office was disappointing – HK $4,902,426, compared to the HK $11 million-plus of *Once Upon a Time In China 4,* and it's disappointing for a Tsui Hark movie, and a *Once Upon a Time In China* movie). Released November 17, 1994. 101 minutes.

In the cast of *Once Upon a Time In China 5* were the full compliment of Wong Fei-hung regulars: Vincent Zhao as Wong Fei-hung, Rosamund Kwan as 13th Aunt, Max Mok as Leung Foon, Kent Cheng as Porky Wing, Roger Kwok as 'Bucktooth' So, Xiong Xin-xin as Clubfoot, Jean Wang as 14th Aunt, Lau Shun as Wong Kei-ying, Tam Bing-man as Boss, Yee Tin-hung as Devil Cheung, Elaine Lui Siu-Ling as 'Single-eyed' Ying, Zhang Tie-lin[1] as Chief Constable, Stephen Tung as Junior Cheung, and Dion Lam as Flying Monkey.

Music: as with *Once Upon a Time In China 4*, you have to admit that some of the music composed and produced for *Once Upon a Time In China 5* is rather generic and so-so (it is credited to William Hu and Tsui Hark). And too much of it is cheaply and cheesily orchestral – using synthesizers to emulate strings in an orchestra, but not in an impressive or imaginative manner. Visuals and set-pieces this grand really do demand (and deserve) a higher grade of musical composition.

---

[1] He played Sun Yat-sen in *Once Upon a Time In China 2*.

Once Upon a Time In China 5 is Tsui Hark's pirate[2] movie.[3] The 1994 movie goes all-out in its depictions of pirates at work and play. Battles on ships, treasure chests, a treasure horde, cascading gold, bandoleros, etc. From the Prologue, where pirates menace a hapless petty criminal, Once Upon a Time In China 5 celebrates movie-movie pirates – the more grizzled, belligerent and OTT the better. Nobody can do a pirate movie straight since, well, probably the 1940s: Once Upon a Time In China 5 is no different (but this time combines the pirate genre with the kung fu genre). The pirate genre is sent up while it's exalted (and yet, pirating perfectly describes the aggression and rampant capitalism of new economies like Hong Kong and the Pacific Rim, where real pirates, in the form of organized syndicates, flourish; and pirates still prey on ships today). Tsui is especially fond of no-goods with a scuzzy, eccentric appearance – he enjoys villains and rebels with a punky or post-punk look (they crop up in New Dragon Gate Inn, The Blade and Seven Swords for instance. Indeed, parts of Once Upon a Time In China 5 look like a dry run for the teeming scenes of rough-and-ready banditos in The Blade).

The comedy in Once Upon a Time In China 5, which takes up a *lot* of screentime (the first act contains several purely comical scenes), is largely carried by the four goofs who surround Wong Fei-hung: Ah Foon, Porky Wing, Bucktooth So and Clubfoot. In numerous scenes this foursome of hapless, accident-prone fools delivers comical business, under-cutting the action and the drama, lightening the narrative, and reminding us, once again, that *comedy* is actually one of Tsui Hark's major concerns. And you can see that Tsui enjoyed the interplay of the four actors (Max Mok, Kent Cheng, Xiong Xin-xin and Roger Kwok), dwelling on their humorous antics at length.

In the 1990s conception of the Wong Fei-hung Legend, the group that gathers around the Robin Hood figure of Wong is absolutely fundamental. They are simple-minded, naïve, brave and utterly devoted to Wong. When Wong enters the room, squabbling ceases instantly, and things become serious.

Once Upon a Time In China 5 seems to be an attempt at a different kind of Wong Fei-hung movie, or a self-conscious departure by the filmmakers from the pattern already established. Thus, the visual approach steps away from the bright, colourful images of the first three movies, and into a much murkier, shadowier realm. The first act takes place, for instance, largely at night, or in reduced light, with the customary oranges and blues of night scenes in Hong Kong movies taken way down (actors play scenes with their faces moving into shadow. The low levels of light also mean that Wong seems interchangeable now with the many members of his coterie who look similar).

Once Upon a Time In China 5 delivers the familiar Tsui Hark visual

---

2 The pirate setting allows our heroes to dress up differently, as pirates (all in black), as they go in disguise.
3 Pirates had appeared in Jackie Chan's Project A movies, among other Hong Kong pictures.

flourishes – like the rainstorm in the opening scenes, with the first Big Fight occurring at night in a heavy downpour, and the rapidly mobile camera, the shadowplay, and penchant for capturing unusual camera angles, or telling close-ups and insert shots. (Despite five DPs being credited, *Once Upon a Time In China 5* has a seamless look).

Once Upon a Time In China 5 continues Tsui Hark's penchant for staging scenes in a *tableau* format with lengthy takes: he and his DPs will frame a bunch of actors (typically grouped around Wong Fei-hung), and keep the camera on them without cutting, while they deliver the dialogue.

There is a larger group of characters surrounding Wong Fei-hung in this movie – such as Porky Wing (Kent Cheung), Ah Foon (Max Mok), Bucktooth So (Roger Kwok) and Clubfoot (Xiong Xin-xin). 14th Aunt (Jean Wang) is retained from the previous *Once Upon a Time In China* movie, but Rosamund Kwan is back as 13th Aunt. (This is largely the cast that appeared in the 1996 *Once Upon a Time In China* TV series).

Sometimes, *Once Upon a Time In China 5* looks as if it's more of a team format than a Wong Fei-hung format – it's Wong Fei-hung plus his four trusty fighting assistants: Porky Wing, Foon Leung, Bucktooth So and Clubfoot. Wong is still the commander, leading the team into battle, and making all of the key decisions, but often he's offscreen, and we're watching Mok, Cheng, Kwok and Xiong do their stuff as four martial artists.

It's true that *Once Upon a Time In China 5* doesn't have the grandly political sweep of the earlier *Once Upon a Time In China* movies. *Once Upon a Time In China 5* is much more like a television episode, or a small-scale film, in which the heroes tackle a single foe (here, it's pirates).

❖

Once Upon a Time In China 5 opens with action that continues directly from the ending of *Once Upon a Time In China 4*, where our heroes were travelling away from Peking after the Lion Dance competition (the movie even uses the main titles sequence wholesale from *Once Upon a Time In China 4*). They are travelling to Foshan, a step away from moving to Hong Kong. So, at the start of *Once Upon a Time In China 5*, they are waylaid on their trip, in a similar manner to the beginning of *Once Upon a Time In China 4* (and also *Once Upon a Time In China and America*).

The world of China evoked in *Once Upon a Time In China 5* is a more troubled place than in previous *Once Upon a Time In China* films. Food is scarce, and people are hungry (many scenes in the first act are set at meal times, and in a food store). The sombre tone is evoked in the opening action scene involving pirates (led by Stephen Tung), where a victim's hands're whipped off by the villains. Not long after this archetypal piece of Chinese horror (which doesn't really fit in the *Once Upon a Time In China* series), a chest of human fingers is delivered by the pirates to the food store.

It's in this atmosphere of socio-economic unrest that Wong Fei-hung and his entourage arrive, and are ambushed by the guys from the food store (of course, they are no match for Wong, Clubfoot, Foon and co.). This begins the story in *Once Upon a Time In China 5* – with Wong acting in his guise as Robin Hood, the Hero of the Oppressed.

The first act of *Once Upon a Time In China 5* also features the other regular ingredients of a *Wong Fei-hung* outing: several comical scenes (often at Ah Foon's expense), the romantic subplots, and the introduction of the principal groups or communities (the pirate gang, the Chief Constable and his team, the food store employees, etc).

A romantic triangle is set up in the first act of *Once Upon a Time In China 5*, between the two Aunts (the 14th and the 13th Aunts), played by Jean Wang and Rosamund Kwan[4] (once again, Vincent Zhao doesn't look quite at home in the romantic scenes, and Jet Li's portrayal in the romantic scenes was lighter and more playful). The erotic rivalry is of course between the two women – it's the women who're desiring Wong Fei-hung, not the other way around. Because in the 1990s *Once Upon a Time In China* series, Wong is fairly indifferent to matters of the heart. Or at least, to playing the romantic heartthrob in a romantic melodrama (or anyway, in pursuing women, whereas the real Wong had four wives).

❖

Opening act two of *Once Upon a Time In China 5* is a *lot* of comedy exploring the romantic triangle, using the motif that Tsui Hark and the filmmakers had developed for the romance in the first three *Once Upon a Time In China* movies: shadowplay. So we have the bunch of Wong Fei-hung's followers (Porky Wing, Ah Foon, Clubfoot *et al*) seeing what appears to be some romantic goings-on in a nearby room between Wong and the 14th Aunt (in fact, they are picking up a pearl necklace that's Daddy Wong's broken and scattered on the floor). The 13th Aunt also turns up and sees what appears to be a kiss (and maybe more) with her beloved Wong and 14th Aunt next door.

The comical interplay in the romantic triangle carries over into the following scene, where pirates're sneaking around town at night brandishing swords, up to no good. Aunt Yeo storms out in a huff, and in her anger she's able to easily overcome the pirates who intimidate her (this offers a welcome bit of action for Rosamund Kwan – it reprises the grappling hand move that Wong Fei-hung taught her in film two). Earlier, a two-hander scene had Aunt Yeo persuading Wong Fei-hung to exchange rings, in preparation for a Western-style marriage (Aunt Yeo already has the confetti, too. The soundtrack plays Felix Mendelssohn's *Wedding March*, which Aunt Yeo also hums). Needless to say, Wong is baffled, as ever, with Aunt Yeo's romantic overtures.

Act two of *Once Upon a Time In China 5* properly begins, however, with the commencement of the pirate theme, as Wong Fei-hung and co. decide to take some action against the bandits disrupting Southern China. There are scenes at the port of Foshan, with our heroes in disguise, as they manœuvre into place to pin down the pirates.

Some movies sag in their middle acts like bloated bellies full of beer and burgers. Not *Once Upon a Time In China 5* – this is a trim, agile movie that leaps about from foot to hand to toe to finger to elbow and back again.

---

4 Kwan's introduction receives a *big* build-up; 14th Aunt looks on jealously as 13th Aunt embraces Wong closely.

Thus, following the comical scenes in the kitchen, involving the romantic triangle and Aunt Yeo's huff, *Once Upon a Time In China 5* explodes into two (really three) absolutely outstanding action sequences (with a short training scene, where our heroes try their hand at firing guns – with, of course, comical results. Bucktooth So, unexpectedly, turns out to a crackshot, and performs two-gun acrobatics, in a send-up of John Woo's films, a bit of the kooky humour from the *Aces Go Places* and *All the Wrong Clues* series).

The first action sequence takes place on boats at sea: this is Tsui Hark's version of the swashbucklers and action-adventure movies he loved as a youth (Oriental ones as well as Western ones). If Tsui were directing the *Pirates of the Caribbean* movies (if only!), this is what they would look like. The stunts and action choreography are glorious – again the feeling of freedom, of movement into any area of the frame, from any direction, is pure delight. (Tsui explored this territory in the *Detective Dee* series).

(The girls are left behind now: true, *Once Upon a Time In China 5* brings the romantic subplots and the action plots together, but not as convincingly as in previous *Once Upon a Time In China* outings. This time, the men and the women are separated, and it's the boys who go into battle).

The pirate den sequence is really two action sequences smashed together. *Once Upon a Time In China 5* revels in putting cartoon-like outcasts and criminals on screen, drinking and carousing.[5] It's another saloon/ nightclub/ restaurant scene where the heroes enter in disguise, and you know there's going to be a Giant Fight. It takes place in one of the densely layered sets that regularly turn up in Tsui Hark's movies (the lighting job by one of the five cinematographers is outstanding and very intricate). The set is crammed with stuff – principally, of course, for the stunt team to bounce around in, manipulate on wires (boxes and poles are thrown around all over the place), and smash to bits. It seems as if every wooden chest, every suitcase, and every box in Hong Kong was carted in just for this scene.

Our heroes (Wong Fei-hung, Clubfoot, Ah Foon, Porky Wing and Bucktooth So) are up against countless pirates in this sequence, which segues into the treasure trove scene. Notice how the filmmakers concentrate completely on the five heroes, always shooting action from their point-of-view, with the opponents being piled up one after another as henchmen to be dispatched in countless imaginative ways. The pirates aren't personalized at all (beyond generic, piratey carousing) – except for the female pirate ('Single-eyed' Ying) that Wong encounters.

Yes, *Once Upon a Time In China 5* pits Wong Fei-hung against a formidable woman pirate (played by Elaine Lui Siu-Ling, the Red Lantern Society heroine Miao Sanniang in the previous film). And the setting eroticizes their relationship, with 'Single-eyed' Ying leading Wong into her

---

[5] There is some comedy before the bust-up: the drink (beer?) tastes disgusting and is spat out, and our heroes are clad in cool black costumes that seem much more like the 1990s than the 1900s.

boudoir. As the clinch seems about to take place, of course the action starts up (no, not even a kiss with the wrong woman for the ever-chaste Wong! The movie always sticks to the formula!).

The struggle on the bed between Wong Fei-hung and 'Single-eyed' Ying recalls the equally amazing scene in *New Dragon Gate Inn* between Jade and Yuan Mo-ya. The bed fitted with a variety of weaponry (like spikes and rows of spears, which suddenly burst upwards phallically) is reminiscent of an early *James Bond* movie. The choreography has a rapidity and invention which is never seen in Western movies – it's love-making as action as dance.

The final section of the seemingly continuous action sequence in the middle of *Once Upon a Time In China 5* involves a remnant from another era, Flying Monkey (Dion Lam). This is Tsui Hark putting a bit of the Monkey King on screen (which he's always wanted to do – and finally did in *Journey To the West*). So Flying Monkey is a mandarin who can leap about and is beyond the capabilities of anybody among the heroes, except for – yes – Wong Fei-hung.

Once again, the duel employs gravity-defying stuntwork and reprises the motif of not touching the ground. This time, the participants are balancing atop large vases, which teeter-totter like the wooden dominoes in film four and the ladders in film one. It's marvellous stuff, purely – solely – crowd-pleasing, a movie as a circus act in which the audience can admire the stunts and agility of the performers, gasp when Wong Fei-hung is hit, boo-hiss the villain, and cheer when Flying Monkey disappears under an avalanche of chests, vases, and treasure.

❖

The climactic action sequence of *Once Upon a Time In China 5* is essentially a reprise of previous action scenes in the movie: it's Wong Fei-hung and his cohorts going up against the pirates (the bunch from the opening scenes). There are battles and duels all over the place, entirely filmed at night (Tsui Hark is especially fond of filming at night – one imagines that film crews find this exhausting, but Tsui, with his boundless energy, keeps them enthused thru the night).

The finale is given a suitably lengthy build-up, with the filmmakers taking their time in covering the preparations that Wong Fei-hung and company have made to counter the attack of the pirates (for example, going to the lengths of staging a Lion Dance on wires, but without people, to fool the pirates, and to set off fireworks, to make the pirates think they're out celebrating. Meanwhile, our heroes have set up gun emplacements with sandbags, as if they're staging a war. It's *The Seven Samurai* narrative format again, preparing to defend a village).

The action sequences run thru numerous outdoor spaces (such as Porky Wing's mob, with their canons), all over the roofs (several times), across the festive decorations on a balcony, in the upper levels of the warehouse (and the jail), and back onto the streets, with the filmmakers exploiting every inch of the sets. Again, there is that feeling that the filmmakers can and will zoom their actors and stunt guys into any part of the frame and any corner of the set. Total freedom of movement – if a pirate grabs a rope and skitters upwards like a monkey onto the roofs, then the heroes will follow him instantly (there are incredible scenes where Wong Fei-hung and Clubfoot are leaping from pillar to wall to roof, kicking off from one wall to fly thru the air to land on a post, then launching themselves upwards).

'Single-eyed' Ying escapes from prison by unpicking the locks on her wrists using her feet *through* the cell bars (she is a very flexible girl), a guy has a gun hidden in a spear, and everybody is running and flying about like crazy. The movie comes up with surprising elements and textures – billowing gunpowder, cascades of rice, sacks of food hurled across the set. Ying is dispatched with a gunshot to the head (the *Battleship Potemkin* shot thru the glasses), and a victim receives a cannon ball at close range (it's Wong Fei-hung, of course, who kicks the cannon round).

Part of the finale culminates in the food storehouse – an elaborate set that contains multiple levels and plenty of props to throw about (boxes and sacks of rice), and plenty of wooden structures to smash. Instead of sand or dust, rice is used (by Wong Fei-hung) to hurl at the enemy to temporarily blind them. Very impressive fire effects are employed again, as the warehouse burns down; actors are set on fire; when the action moves outside, gunpowder is bursting over the performers (from out of a barrel), and filling the air, with a guy clambering about trying to reach a lamp to ignite it (and everyone trying to stop him).

It really is astonishing cinema – purely in terms of the orchestration of movement in space in conjunction with outstanding camerawork, gorgeous and *very* intricate lighting, razor-sharp editing and pacing, and a total confidence in exploiting the technical weaponry of modern cinema.

17

ONCE UPON A TIME IN CHINA AND AMERICA

Wong Feihong Ji Sai Wik Hung Si

INTRO.
Sammo Hung + Tsui Hark + Jet Li + an idea supposedly stolen from Jackie Chan! It can't fail, can it?! For this 1997 *Wong Fei-hung* outing, the sixth in the *Once Upon a Time In China* movie series, Tsui opted for the producer role (but we know for Tsui that can mean co-direction!), and asked his friend Hung Kam-bo to helm a 'Chinaman in America' story,6 complete with cowboys, Native Americans, guns, shoot-outs, horses, one-street towns, saloons, deserts, dust, sunsets, Sherrifs and Mayors, and just about everything else from the mythical American West that the Chinese filmmakers had imbibed back in Hong Kong as kids.

Actually, an 'Eastern Western' – a Chinaman in the Wild West – wasn't original to Jackie Chan. Bruce Lee, for example, had pitched an 'Eastern Western' called *The Warrior* to Warners in 1971, with himself in the lead role:

> It's a really freaky adventure series about a Chinese guy who winds up in the American West in 1860 [Lee explained]. Can you dig that? All these cowboys on horses with guns and me with a long, green hunk of bamboo, right?7

But according to Bruce Lee's biographer Matthew Polly, Lee didn't originate the idea: it was Ed Spielman and Howard Friedlander, two New York comedy writers, who developed the concept of a Shaolin monk who comes to America in the 1880s in a Western.8

The sixth *Once Upon a Time In China* (*Huang Feihong Zhi Xiyu*

---
6 *Once Upon a Time In China and America* is also an early 20th century version of another Tsui Hark 'Chinaman in America' story, *The Master* (which also starred Jet Li).
7 Quoted in M. Polly, 334.
8 Ibid., 277f.

Hongshi in Mandarin = *Wong Fei-hung: West Territory Mighty Lion*), brought Jet Li back to the series with a tale that went to the U.S.A. The concept apparently came from Jackie Chan, who had told Sammo Hung Kam-bo, his former Peking Opera buddy, about it years before. *Shanghai Noon* (2000) was Chan's version of the Chinaman in the American Old West idea (with Owen Wilson playing the Yank he teams up with).

Roy Szeto Cheuk-hon, Shut Mei-yee, Sharon Hui Sa-long, Philip Kwok and So Man-Sing co-wrote the script of *Once Upon a Time In China and America*; Tsui Hark and Dick Cho Kin-nam produced, thru Film Workshop (Lau Kar-wing is sometimes credited with co-direction, and/ or second unit direction);[9] the DPs were Walter Gregg, Lam Fai-tai and Koo Kwok-wah; Marco Mak Chi-sIn and Angie Lam On-yee edited; and music was by Lowell Lo.[10] The 98-minute movie grossed a healthy HK $30,268,415 in Hong Kong (it was shot quickly in time for a traditional, Chinese New Year release (Feb 1, 1997) – you can see how cold it was on location in Texas). The budget was very high for a Hong Kong movie (some $8 million (no doubt due to filming in the U.S.A.)

The crew of *Once Upon a Time In China and America* was largely from Hong Kong – *Once Upon a Time In China and America* is very much a Chinese movie made in the U.S.A. (based in Texas, filming at the Alamo Village, built for the movie *The Alamo*).[11] The cast, headed up by Jet Li and Rosamund Kwan, included Xiong Xin-xin (a big part of the *Once Upon a Time In China* franchise), back as Clubfoot (a.k.a. Seven), Power Chan (Chan Kwok Pong) as Bucktooth So, Richard Ng as Han, Jeff Wolfe as Billy, Joe Sayah as a Mexican bandit, and T.J. Storm as a Native American brave. Plus Mars, Lau Kar-wing, Patrick Lung, Ron Ring, Crystal Bell, Ryon Marshall, Freddy Joe, and William Fung.

Tsui Hark had wanted to do a Western, and *Once Upon a Time In China and America* was a golden opportunity. The whole Old West mythology is thrown into the mix, and totally in a movie-movie manner. (Of course, the *Once Upon a Time In China* movies draw on plenty of American Western movies which the filmmakers grew up watching – *Once Upon a Time In China and America* is another of Tsui's movie-movies).

Hong Kong cinema had already produced Westerns in China, or *kung fu* and historical movies which took motifs from American Western movies: *Blood Money* (1974) and *Kung Fu Brothers In the Wild West* (1973), for example. In the 1990s, Chow Yun-fat had starred in *The Peace Hotel* (1995), and later there was *Warriors of Heaven and Earth* (Ping He, 2003). However, Hong Kong productions which went to the U.S.A. to film *kung fu*/ Western hybrids were much rarer (partly because of cost).

Once Upon a Time In China and America is filmed in the textured, rough-and-ready style of Hong Kong filmmaking: plenty of smoke and rain, and an emphasis on visceral, rough-and-tumble action.[12] With Sammo

---
9 Lau Kar-wing also played a Lion Dance Drummer.
10 Lowell Lo delivered some impressive versions of Native American-ish music – even the famous *Wong Fei-hung* cue in a percussive, Native American style.
11 In the entertaining 'making of' documentary, every actor and crew member notes how cold it was filming in Texas in December, 1996, for a Chinese New Year's release.
12 In some scenes, Jet Li moves thru many fighting styles – from *wushu* to Northern mantis to chen tai chi.

Hung Kam-bo holding the directorial reins, *Once Upon a Time In China and America* inevitably displays Hung's penchant for martial arts action which stays close to the ground, involves lots of fists and kicks, and is what a human could realistically achieve (however, there is wirework a-plenty). Action choreographers were Hung, plus Cho Wing and Xiong Xin-xin. Visual effects, as usual in a Tsui Hark movie (or any Hong Kong action movie), are everywhere, from exploding glasses of beer to vats of water that blow up.

THE SCRIPT.

In terms of plot and character, *Once Upon a Time In China and America* is certainly a less engaging outing in the *Once Upon a Time In China* series than the earlier movies. Many of the characters are either types or one-dimensional (they coast along on characterizations already created in the earlier films), and the white Americans are relentlessly caricatured as ugly, violent, racist bores. The 1997 movie also runs thru similar scenarios to the previous five movies (inevitable, really, for the sixth outing in a series). And it does seem, despite the colossal talents involved, a lesser work than the earlier *Once Upon a Time In China* flicks. (But that's only, really, if you compare the movie to the earlier pictures. On its own terms, *China and America* is rousing stuff).

There *is* a story in *Once Upon a Time In China and America*, but the movie is more about exploiting the clash of cultures, in mining the action (and the comedy) of throwing a bunch of Chinese guys in amongst some (mainly unfriendly) North Americans. Five writers are credited (Roy Szeto Cheuk-hon, Shut Mei-yee, Sharon Hui Sa-long, Philip Kwok and So Man-Sing), and you'd have to add Sammo Hung and Tsui Hark, artists who aren't shy about adding their own input.

Critics complained that *Once Upon a Time In China and America* was largely 'plotless'. Not true, of course: but *Once Upon a Time In China and America* does lack an over-arching plot, or a series of clearly-defined goals which the heroes have to achieve. Rather, *Once Upon a Time In China and America* is episodic, it's a 'Wong Fei-hung's Adventures in the U.S.A.' story: there's 'the Wong Fei-hung Among the Native Americans' in the first act of *Once Upon a Time In China and America*; there's 'Chinese In the Old West' in the first two acts; and there's the 'Robbery and Imprisonment of the Heroes' plot in the third act. Those episodes are not quite melded together satisfactorily, but they all fit under the over-arching 'Chinese folk in America' story, which's what *Once Upon a Time In China and America* is at heart.

In defence of the screenwriting of *Once Upon a Time In China and America*, some of the characters *do* under-go 'story arcs', that favourite narrative device of North American screenwriting gurus (and film studios). Thus, Billy, down on his luck in the 1997's movie's opening scene (he's just about to kill himself), becomes the Mayor of the town by the end of the movie. (Billy, as played by Jeff Wolfe, is a rather plastic version of a do-gooder cowboy. With his blond locks, tho', and very contemporary acting style, he is clear forerunner of Owen Wilson in *Shanghai Noon*. But Wolfe moves well, and blends in with the ensemble nicely).

The 1997 movie, however, does sideline Wong Fei-hung for too long, and we miss Jet Li when he's not on screen. The script also doesn't find much for Aunt Yeo to do in the third act of *Once Upon a Time In China and America* (other than be tossed into jail along with all of the other Chinese folk). Aunt Yeo does get involved in some of the action sequences, tho' (she's thrown around in a galloping coach, for instance, and performs several versions of the Wongian shadowless kick), and she's a fetching sight in her Chinese version of a cowgirl costume (Rosamund Kwan as a cowgirl? What's not to like!?).

POLITICS.

For the critics and theorists who like to analyze everything that comes out of the Hong Kong film industry in terms of politics and ideology, *Once Upon a Time In China and America* could be seen as another rumination on the 1997 Hand-over (it was released several months b4 the Hand-over), with its evocations of Chinese immigrants in the American West of the early 20th century (thus, Wong Fei-hung literally becomes an 'Overseas Chinese', a social/ national identity that has consumed quite a bit of Tsui Hark's interest – being one himself. And we recall that of course Tsui had studied cinema in two universities where the movie was filmed – good ol' Texas, back in the Seventies – the 1970s, that is, not the 1870s!).

The xenophobia of the American West is brought out very strongly and crudely in *Once Upon a Time In China and America* in the early scenes involving the Chinese doctor Bucktooth So and his chums. The (white) Americans are portrayed as ultra-violent thugs, who'll whip out a pistol at the slightest provocation: they shoot out the glass of beer that Bucktooth So holds in a bar (given to him by one of the ladies of the saloon); they draw guns on the doctor and his pal when they put up posters for Wong Fei-hung; and they manhandle Aunt Yeo really roughly. Yup, pardner, no Chinamen are allowed in the saloon, and they cain't drink beer, neither – hell, not anywhere in the goddam town, outside-a their own alley!

Once Upon a Time In China and America delights in portraying the racism that seethes everywhere in the U.S.A. – then as now. The xenophobia is depicted with many comedic touches, but there's no denying the intensity of it, and what the filmmakers think of the bigoted, intolerant (and corrupt) Sheriff and the Mayor. (Even so, racism and classism was also a key ingredient of the *Wong Fei-hung* movies based in China, with different sections of the Chinese community being set against each other. However, the North Americans were also vividly derided as slave-traders and aggressive oiks).

Meanwhile, one of the aims of the *Once Upon a Time In China* series was to cover or allude to historical events: *Once Upon a Time In China and America* is notable for *not* making much of North American politics or history (other than the generic, Old West context). *Once Upon a Time In China and America* isn't much interested in North America or the American people (and the Native Americans, too, are really just generalizations). Instead, the Americans of all types are simply cast as 'foreigners' (intolerant, crude, corrupt), as far as the Chinese within the movie, and the Chinese in the primary audience for the movie in Hong Kong, are concerned.

In their book on Hong Kong cinema, L. Stokes and M. Hoover remind us that Chinese were forbidden to be naturalized citizens in the U.S.A. until 1952, and that they were prohibited from entering the country in a 1882 law (which was in place until 1943).

Yes – the 1882 Chinese Exclusion Act aimed to control Chinese immigration and fears of the 'Yellow[13] Peril'. Chinese came to the U.S.A. for many reasons – one was the rigours of the Qing dynasty; another was the lure of the California Gold Rush.

COMEDY AND ROMANCE.

Once Upon a Time In China and America contains more of the gentle comedy that Tsui Hark explores many times in his cinema deriving from cultural differences. So there's a lengthy sequence in the stagecoach at the beginning where Wong Fei-hung once again attempts to understand another language (English). And once again lovely Aunt Yeo is on hand to correct him. And when Wong sits down to talk with Billy at a rest-stop, he smiles and pretends to understand him, as people have done for thousands of years. You nod, you smile, you say the only words you know in the language (like 'yeah!'), and you get by.

Once Upon a Time In China and America also contains other examples of Tsui Hark's sense of humour: a scene where a bunch of Chinese workers huddle round a doorway, looking in awe at Aunt Yeo – it's a *woman*! (There are very few Chinese women Out West).

Much comedy (very much of the Tsui Harkian kind) is squeezed out of Wong Fei-hung losing his memory: Jet Li's talent for humour is often unappreciated by film critics. It *is* funny seeing Jet Li as a Native American. Not as funny as Mel Brooks or Woody Allen, admittedly (!), but still amusing. Certainly, he's a much finer comic actor than many action stars in the West. The view that Li is too often too serious and stoic isn't true – if you look at movies he made around this time, such as *Tai Chi Master, Fong Sai-yuk, Last Hero In China* and the *Once Upon a Time In China* series, there are many humorous scenes (and Li has a beautiful smile, which pops out of the screen). For action fans, maybe the comical scenes – like the romantic scenes – slow the movies down. But they are vital in maintaining an appealing mix: this is one of Tsui's fundamental formulas of movie-making – his form of entertainment (like Wong Jing's) is designed to take in romance and comedy as well as action and thrills.

Among the Native Americans, there is a teensy hint of a mild flirtation btn an attractive, young woman, Sarah (Chrysta Bell Eucht) and Wong Fei-hung. However, in keeping with Tsui Hark's characterization of Wong (and that of Wong in the movies and TV in general), it is a very chaste,

---

13 Wong Fei-hung is given the name 'Yellow' by the Native Americans.

restrained and barely evoked liaison (and it's mostly from the woman's point-of-view. She is much fonder of 'Yellow', as she calls him, than he is of her. He gives her a ring in jest, but it means more to her (and to Aunt Yeo later on). Jackie Chan's relations with white women in the *Shanghai Noon* films were much racier, in keeping with Chan's screen image. And Chan wasn't playing Wong Fei-hung, of course).

The romantic subplot plays into the Wong-losing-his-memory subplot, with Aunt Yeo sinking into a huff when she discovers that Wong as 'Yellow' and the Native American woman Sarah seem to have a relationship (the rings are used as a token of love). Even when Wong Fei-hung recovers his memory, and claims he doesn't remember anything that happened, Aunt Yeo is not convinced.

ACTION.

The first Big Action Sequence in *Once Upon a Time In China and America* is not the Chinese versus the Americans, but an attack on the Chinese as they travel in the desert by some Native Americans. (Made in 1997, *Once Upon a Time In China and America* might've been responding to movies such as *Dances With Wolves* (1990), in portraying Native Americans in a more sympathetic light. But in a way the Native Americans are caricatured just as simplistically as the white Americans). For a Chinese audience (the primary audience for this movie), they are all *gweilo*, 'foreign', whether they're white Americans, or Native Americans, or Mexicans, or African Americans.

But nothing much changes, either, when it's a North American production depicting Chinese immigrant workers in the American West – in *The Lone Ranger* (2013), a giant ($215m) Walt Disney movie produced by Jerry Bruckheimer (where the Chinese are depicted from a white, American perspective). However, American movies are sometimes more careful about offending audiences overseas (partly because such a huge amount of their revenue is made in foreign territories). The Chinese immigrants issue would be reprised in *Shanghai Noon*.

Anyhoo, *Once Upon a Time In China and America* takes up one of the staples of the revisionist Western genre – the white hero who holes up with a Native American community (which, of course, lives in teepees in a rural setting, evoked in several formal crane shots worthy of *Heaven's Gate*, 1981). It worked for *Dances With Wolves*[14] (1990) and *The Last of the Mohicans* (1992), and before that, *Little Big Man* (1970) and *Buffalo Bill and the Indians* (1976). But this time, it's a Chinese guy in amongst the Native Americans, not a white guy from back East (with the added gimmick of it being the most famous Chinese hero of all, Wong Fei-hung, and of Wong having lost his memory, which handily delays his reunion with his Chinese chums).

With Jet Li's Wong Fei-hung spending half of the 1997 movie in the Native American village, much of the action back in town is handled by

---

[14] David Chou called *Once Upon a Time In China and America* 'a noodle Western' – like 'the original *King Fu* series colliding head on with *Blazing Saddles* and *Dances With Wolves*' ("*Once Upon a Time In China and America*", *S.M.R. Home Theatre*, Nov, 1998.

Clubfoot, Aunt Yeo and Bucktooth So, as they come into constant conflict with the boorish, backward Yanks.

Once Upon a Time In China and America delivers more of the martial-arts-versus-the-gun theme, the aggressive manifestation of the West v.s East issue that the *Once Upon a Time In China* series has explored (along the very simple ideological lines of: West = guns = bad, and East = martial arts = good). Notice that no Chinese fire a gun in this movie (handily, they have Billy on their side to do that – Billy's invited to be a deputy). Instead, they use *kung fu* and athletic prowess to run rings around the Yanks (and as the white Americans're all depicted as burly cowboys who seem to spend all of their time slouching about in the saloon, drinking and smoking, that isn't difficult).

There's a satisfying Chinese/ Hong Kong version of the stereotypical bar-room brawl in a Western movie where Clubfoot (a.k.a. Seven) takes on not one but all of the no-goods loitering there. Here, a single, small Chinese guy fights all of the hulking cowboys and knocks them flat. It's doubly satisfying, because in the dramatic build-up, poor Aunt Yeo is pretty harshly treated (she is pushed about, insulted, and has alcohol poured over her before Clubfoot and Bucktooth So come to the rescue).

Xiong Xin-xin is superb as Clubfoot (you can see why he doubled Jet Li for so long, and why he is an accomplished action director himself) – he is given a *lot* of screentime. Indeed, after making such an impact as Clubfoot in the second installment of *Once Upon a Time In China*, Xiong was given more prominence (and in the *Wong Fei-hung* TV series, too).

One of the highlights of *Once Upon a Time In China and America* is a lengthy duel between Jet Li and Xiong Xin-xin, with Clubfoot trying to encourage Wong Fei-hung to remember who he is.

The robbery is a clichéd piece of dramatic business which's not interesting in the slightest: it's there to provide the impetus for the finale of *Once Upon a Time In China and America*. What it does do, tho', is offer a context for yet more racism and brutality from the Yanks. To the point where the Chinese at the Po Chi Lam clinic are raided, searched and imprisoned. Once again, Westerners are depicted as crooked all the way through: in this town, both the Mayor and the Sherrif are dishonest. The blackmailing (it's a fellow Chinaman who plants the sacks of money in the clinic), allows for more malicious treatment of the poor, innocent Chinese by the crude, horrible Americans. (In *Once Upon a Time In China and America*, the Chinese are portrayed as hard-working, close-knit, compassionate, with only small-scale gambling[15] as their vice[16]).

THE FINALE.

Once Upon a Time In China and America creates a rather preposterous villain in the figure of the Mexican bandit (Joe Sayah): he's the classic cowboy bad guy dressed in black out of Spaghetti Westerns and post-1960s horse operas. He has razor-sharp spurs which he uses to

---

15 But even Wong Fei-hung joins in (when he's still hazy after his regaining his memory).
16 However, in the *dénouement*, there's a new arrival in town: a hooker, which delights the Chinese guys. That gag seems very Tsui-ian.

slice open victims. In his absurd introductory scene, the bandito is loitering in the woods at night (as you do); he sees a pack of wolves approaching; he slashes open his chest, to let the animals smell the fresh blood; when they attack, he demolishes one hound, and the others flee.

Well, anyway, the Mexican bandito is created solely for Jet Li to have someone suitably accomplished as a warrior to duel in the finale (that Signor Mexico is a nasty piece of work all-round – he kills several people, including unnecessarily and in cold blood – is par for the course).

Thus, the finale is exactly as expected, and the same as all of the previous *Wong Fei-hung* movies: a Big Battle, with the centrepiece being a Long Duel between the hero and the villain. The prelude to the smackdown has our heroes about to be executed: Wong Fei-hung and the Po Chi Lam crew are strung up with nooses around their necks on a wooden scaffold, a particularly gruesome sight (Wong escapes using his martial arts skills).

The action in the finale includes the usual elements (lightning kicks, stuff smashing to bits, brief pauses, slo-mo, high falls, height and a wooden tower, etc). The camerawork is especially wild, careening off the horizontal all over the place. To address the vexed issue of guns versus fists, the 1997 movie includes some visual effects to portray how the Chinese martial artists could elude bullets. And, much cheaper than effects and opticals, simple cuts are employed to suggest that Wong Fei-hung can move *very* fast.

Everyone gets their moment to shine in *Once Upon a Time In China and America*, with pride of place being given to Jet Li and Joe Sayah. By this point in the *Once Upon a Time In China* franchise (film six, plus the TV series), it was very challenging topping the finales in the previous movies (indeed, the benchmark was set impossibly high in the first *China* movie, with the fight on ladders in the warehouse). Not to mention the endings in the other *Once Upon* flicks – the Lion Dance competition finale, the White Lotus Cult finale, the pirate ships finale, etc). As this is Sammo Hung Kam-bo in the director's chair, the action is wonderful.

In the duel in *Once Upon a Time In China and America*, Wong Fei-hung is depicted as never being in serious trouble – the Mexican bandit is no match for him in any respect, really (morally, spiritually, ethically, politically, socially, culturally). Now it's all about Wong teaching the villain the true meaning of Chinese *kung fu*, of training for years, of being effortlessly brilliant.

Also, the finale of *Once Upon a Time In China and America* is smaller in scale, and doesn't have the big, political-ideological cargo of the previous *Once Upon a Time In China* films. The vicious racism of the Yanks has been exposed throughout the movie, and hardly needs embellishing in the action of the finale. So there are no extra dramatic elements, apart from Wong Fei-hung needing to beat the Mexican bandit to clear his name of the crime of the bank robbery. And with Aunt Yeo gone to fetch the Native Americans to help out, there are no princesses to be rescued, either (that gives Aunt Yeo something to do in the finale, but also cleverly takes her away from danger. But, shoot, it's nice to see the Native

American characters brought back for their curtain call).

As is customary in the *Once Upon a Time In China* series, *Once Upon a Time In China and America* closes with an affirmation of Chinese values and traditional, Chinese culture – with a favourite Tsui Hark motif, the Lion Dance[17] (to celebrate the establishment of a Chinatown in the community). Wong Fei-hung performs the dance, as usual (being the finest Lion Dancer in history), and the *Wong Fei-hung* music sounds off. (A Lion Dance is the perfect scene for a movie released in China during Chinese New Year, of course). And after that, Wong, Aunt Yeo, Clubfoot and co. are heading back home, to Guangdong.

---

[17] Lau Kar-wing has a cameo as a Lion Dancer.

Once Upon a Time In China 5 (1994).

Once Upon a Time In China and America (1997).
This page and over.

18

TWIN DRAGONS
Seong Lung Wiu

We go back in time to continue our look at Tsui Hark's film career. *Twin Dragons* (1992, a.k.a. *Double Dragons, Brother vs. Brother, When Dragons Collide, Duel of Dragons, Dragon Duo* and *When Dragons Meet; Shuang Long Hui* in Mandarin, *Seong Lung Wui* in Cantonese = *Double Dragon, Brother vs. Brother*), was exec. prod. by Ng See-yuen, produced by Teddy Robin Kwan, co-directed with Ringo Lam Ling-tung, co-written by Teddy Robin, Barry Long, Tung Cho Cheung, Wong Yik and Tsui Hark, music by Michael Wandmacher and Lowell Lo, DPs: Wong Wing-hang and Arthur Wong, editor: Marco Mak Chi-sin, costumes: Che Leung Chong, special effects and car stunts: Bruce Law, action choreographers: Tony Ching Siu-tung, Chris Lee, Siu-Hung Leung, Siu Ming Tsui, Wei Tung, Yuen Woo-ping and Jackie Chan.

Twin Dragons featured Jackie Chan, Maggie Cheung Man-yuk, Teddy Robin, Nina Li-chi, Philip Chan, David Chiang, Guy Lai Ying Chau, Jamie Luk Kim Ming, James Wong Jim, Johnny Wang, Sylvia Chang, Mars, Eddie Fong, Kirk Wong and many others. Production by the Hong Kong Director's Guild/ Paragon Films/ Golden Harvest. Released: Jan 25, 1992. 100 mins.[1]

Twin Dragons was a benefit movie – this time for the Hong Kong Directors' Union,[2] who needed to buy land for a new HQ.[3] Consequently, it includes cameos from almost every Hong Kong film director,[4] including Kirk Wong, Teddy Robin, Clara Law, Raymond Lee, Ringo Lam, Gordon Chan, Lau Kar-leung, Wong Jing, Eric Tsang, John Woo[5] and many others. Several other movies had been made in the era for benefits, charities, etc, including *The Banquet*.

One of the delights of *Twin Dragons* for Hong Kong cinema fans is playing Spot The Cameo – tho' for a global audience, the level of

---

[1] The U.S. cut of 1999, from Dimension, had about 16 minutes left out.
[2] *Twin Dragons* is also a re-make of *Double Impact* (1991), a Jean-Claude van Damme picture.
[3] By 1997, the headquarters for the directors still hadn't been built.
[4] Tsui has a cameo, along with Ringo Lam and producer Ng See-yuen, playing cards.
[5] Playing a priest, of course.

recognition is probably low (once again, this is a movie for a local audience: it's filmed in Hong Kong, it's filled with Hong Kongers, and the jokey cameos are from people in the Hong Kong film industry).

Tsui Hark said that Ringo Lam Ling-tung had directed most of the action in *Twin Dragons* (tho' no doubt Jackie Chan contributed, too, as he always does). Lam said he directed the second unit material. When Chan came aboard, the film shifted from action to comedy (B. Logan, 77).

✪

Twin Dragons is very much a Jackie Chan movie, rather than a Tsui Hark movie, or a Ringo Lam Ling-tung movie, or even a Hong Kong action comedy movie. Once Chan is headlining a movie, the productions always seem to become Jackie Chan Movies through and through. Chan is one of those performers who puts his stamp all over the movies he stars in (rather than taking a cameo). In *Twin Dragons* Chan is everywhere.

At this time in his career, Jackie Chan was an enormous star, able to command big budgets for his increasingly ambitious productions (he had recently completed the very costly, over-schedule and over-budget[6] *Armor of God 2: Operation Condor*). Chan's influence is all over the action, as expected: *Twin Dragons* is very much based in Chan's 'realistic' style of action choreography – that is, what can be achieved by the human body unaided by wires, trampolines and tricks (tho' of course, there *is* wire-work, and tricks all over). The action is big and loud; it's centred around Chan; Chan doesn't use guns; he employs numerous props; he tries to avoid confrontation, too; it includes Chan's distinctive form of comical action, where pain and suffering are emphasized, where Chan isn't always the best fighter, where Chan undergoes numerous setbacks.

✪

The working-class Jackie Chan in *Twin Dragons* is teamed up with a sidekick, Tarzan, played by the famous Hong Kong celebrity Teddy Robin Kwan (who appeared in *All the Wrong Clues,* and who directed one of the sequels, which Tsui Hark produced). When Maggie Cheung Man-yuk[7] turns up in the first action scene, it's like a re-run of the *Police Story* films (where Cheung was the long-suffering girlfriend May of Chan's cop Ka-Kui). A scene's included to play to the Japanese market (Jackie Chan performs some rough-and-tumble stunts in front of a group of young, Japanese girls).

Notice how, once he's performed his sidekick role, and the twins plot kicks in, Teddy Robin's Tarzan exits the picture (using the old staple of being chucked into hospital). Tarzan reappears in the finale, as the princess who must be rescued (he spends most of the finale hiding in cars).

✪

In *Twin Dragons*, we have one of the longest pieces of black-and-white photography in Tsui Hark's œuvre, depicting the back-story of the twin Jackie Chans in the prologue which opens the 1992 movie. Here, Tsui

---
6 Rumoured to have cost $12-15 million.
7 Even in an under-developed role as 'the Girlfriend of the Hero', Cheung lights up the screen.

goes back to the 1960s (to 1965),[8] instead of his more usual decades of the 1930s and 1940s, or back to the period of the *Once Upon a Time In China* movies (1890s-1910s). The prologue portrays the usual switch or loss (i.e., separation) of the twins in a twins narrative. So one boy grows up middle-class, affable, intellectual, artistic (the pianist and conductor), and one is a street tough, involved in minor crime, as well as working as a car mechanic.

The first act of *Twin Dragons* contains three big action sequences, with Jackie Chan front and centre in the second two: the first takes place in the prologue when the force that separates our heroes is a criminal who runs amok in a hospital. It's here that Bok Min (Wan Ma)[9] is discovered by a woman called Tsui (Wei Tung, portrayed as a good-time girl, first seen drunk).

The second action sequence is a typical Hong Kong action movie routine: one man against a mob of mobsters (set in a swanky hotel). We've seen this sort of caper many times – it is one of the default positions of the Hong Kong action movie, after all, and it appears throughout Tsui Hark's career as well as that of Jackie Chan (plenty of scenes in the whole *Once Upon a Time In China* series are just that: Jet Li or Vincent Zhao surrounded by bad guys). Glass tables which smash, TV sets hurled at hoods, a mic stand as a Shaolin Temple spear – it's Jackie Chan 101.

The third action sequence is a much bigger, more complex and more dangerous affair, which rounds off act one of *Twin Dragons*: a boat chase in Hong Kong harbour. The action sequence is mounted in the style of the Stanley Tong-helmed Jackie Chan pictures (such as *Rumble In the Bronx* or *Supercop 2*): *James Bond*-scale action of our heroes in a speed boat being pursued by henchmen in speed boats, while their boss yells into a cel phone, egging them on from a car following the chase (Bruce Law likely oversaw this scene).

●

Act two means complications, right? Two of the key complications in the narrative are Bok Min and Ma Yau switching round, so that Bok Min ends up conducting an orchestra for a prestigious concert, and Ma Yau is commanded to act as a getaway driver as the mob from earlier try to spring their boss from a cop wagon. This forms the big action set-piece which climaxes act two of *Twin Dragons* – it's a classic, Hong Kong action movie car and bus chase, with the cops closing in and Ma trying to do all he can to escape.

The second complication revolves around romance: it might be Tsui Hark's influence on this script, which clearly has many hands stirring the narrative pot, that two women – Maggie Cheung and Nina Li[10] – are foregrounded. While the romantic plots in an action comedy are, as usual, subplots, they are deftly handled by the filmmakers. For ex, consider the

---

[8] The 1960s? Thus the movie shaves off eight or so years of Jackie Chan's age.
[9] The U.S. cut has different names: John Ma and Boomer for the twins, Tammy for Tong Sum, Tyson for Tarzan, etc.
[10] Nina Li-chi was Butterfly in the third *Chinese Ghost Story*.

significance of music, as Ma woos Barbara by playing some Ludwig van Beethoven music at a grand piano, on the concert stage, while Cheung plays Barbara as a goofy girl who's swept away by music. Meanwhile, the more strait-laced and prim Tong Sum, Ma's girlfriend, enjoys some R. & R. with Bok Min. Action's included in the romantic subplots, too, as Nina Li's Neanderthal ex-boyfriend[11] turns up to make a fuss, and Chan's Bok Min shows his stuff once again (the shopping mall setting is a call-back to *Police Story*, 1985).

❂

The finale of *Twin Dragons* is the customary smackdown between the heroes and the villains, Hong Kong action movie-style: it's Jackie Chan and Jackie Chan versus countless hoods, with his sidekick Tarzan acting as the weasel who needs protecting. The first part of the finale is staged in a *milieu* we've seen plenty of times in Hong Kong flicks: the harbour. Which provides plenty of opportunity for gags with ropes, nets, boats, cranes, shipping containers, water, and of course men in suits running about wielding guns.

Jackie Chan and Tony Ching (and the many action directors) have been here before, and will revisit exactly the same territory again. And again.

The second part of the finale of *Twin Dragons* takes place in another staple of Hong Kong actioners: the warehouse/ factory (and, as it's a car testing centre, it combines the garage with the warehouse). The action is lengthy, intricate, fast, inventive and almost unduly complicated (how many times are Ma Yau or Bok Min going to run in and out of the rain room and the hot room, switching places, one a great fighter, the other a coward?).

After that, the short *dénouement* is a double wedding to the two lovely girls, while the twins threaten to do a runner. Well, with multiple directors, producers, writers and the like, what did you expect? *Twin Dragons* is not the finest outing for anybody concerned in the production team, or among the cast, but so what? It's a pleasant enough hundred minutes.

❂

Western critics found *Twin Dragons* a lesser Jackie Chan movie,[12] enjoying the visual effects and the stunts, but not so much the comedy (the clunky U.S. English dub (1999) doesn't help, even tho' Chan was dubbing himself into English – or 'Changlish', you could call it – Jackie speaks his own brand of English).

Anyway, in Hong Kong, *Twin Dragons* did great business at Chinese New Year in 1992 – HK $33,225,134.

---

11 Don't ask why the daddy's girl Nina Li would date a gorilla.
12 Chan himself wasn't happy with *Twin Dragons* – he found the comedy wasn't as funny as it should've been, and was disappointed with the visual effects (which he thought he oughta be good coming from Tsui Hark and co.).

19

GREEN SNAKE

Ceng Ji

The Legend of the White Snake (*Bai She Zhuan,* a.k.a. *Madame White Snake*), by Lillian Lee Bik-dut, has been the source for several Chinese movies, and the story it drew on – *The Tale of the White Snake*, developed in the Tang Dynasty (618-907 A.D.). As well as *Green Snake* (1993, *Ceng Ji* in Cantonese, *Qing She* in Mandarin, a.k.a. *Blue Snake, White Snake*), there have been two TV series of the mythology, plus other live-action versions,[13] including the awesome *The Sorceror and the White Snake*,[14] directed by Tony Ching Siu-tung, who's often worked with Tsui Hark, and starring one of Tsui's favourite actors, Jet Li. The 1980 film *Legend of the White* sold an incredible 700 million tickets in China. Meanwhile, one of the early Japanese *anime* movies, a landmark in animation, was *The Tale of the White Serpent* (a.k.a. *Panda and the White Serpent,* Taiji Yubushita & Kazuhiko Okabe, 1958), another version of the folktale. *The Tale of the White Serpent* greatly impressed the greatest animator of recent times, Hayao Miyazaki, when he saw it as a 17 year-old youth.[15]

Green Snake was produced by Ng See-yuen, Benzheng Yu and Tsui Hark; Lillian Lee (Pik Wah Lee) and Tsui have script credit; William Cheung and Ng Po-ling did the costumes and make-up (hugely important in this movie); James Wong Jim and Mark Lui Cung Dak composed the music;[16] Bill Lui was art director; action dirs.: Yuen Bun and Tong Gaai; edited by Ah Hik; DP: Giu Chiu Lam. In the cast were Joey Wong Jo-yin, Maggie Cheung Man-yuk, Vincent Zhao, Feng Tien, Hsing-Kuo Wu, Ma Cheng-miu,

---

[13] Such as *Phantom of Snake* (2000), movies in 2019 and 2021, and *Madam White Snake* (1962).
[14] *The Sorceror and the White Snake* could be regarded as a remake of 1993's *Green Snake* – the depiction of the Buddhist monk Fahai draws on the depiction of Fat Hoi in *Green Snake* (as played by Vincent Zhao, who had replaced Jet Li in the *Once Upon a Time In China* series). Meanwhile, some of the action set-pieces in *The Sorcerer and the White Snake* (such as the battle on the canal) seem to employ the scene in *Green Snake*.
[15] Miyazaki recalled: 'I can still remember the pangs of emotion I felt at the sight of the incredibly beautiful, young female character, Bai-Nang, and how I went to see the film over and over as a result. It was like being in love, and Bai-Nang became a surrogate girlfriend for me at a time when I had none.' (*Starting Point, 1979-1996,* tr. B. Cary & F. Schodt, Viz Media/ Shogakukan, San Francisco, CA, 2009, 19)
[16] With vocals by Shu-Hua Chen and Winnie Hsin.

Chan Dung-Mooi. Kong Lau, Lau Shun and Nagma. Released: Nov 4, 1993. 99 minutes.

Lillian Lee Bik-dut (b. 1959) is a Chinese novelist best-known for *Farewell My Concubine*; her fiction has provided the basis for several projects from Tsui Hark, including *Green Snake* and *A Terracotta Warrior*. Lee adapted her novel *Green Snake* into a ballet in 2001. Other Lee books have been adapted, including *Reincarnation of the Golden Lotus, Temptation of a Monk, Red and Black, Sheng Si Qiao* and *Tales From the Dark*.

Green Snake is one of my favourite Tsui Hark movies. It's a full-on fantasy adventure in which sexual desire is foregrounded in a direct and sensual manner. 'Positively heady in its beauty, *Green Snake* is a film that celebrates all of the rich sensuality of everyday life', enthused Lisa Morton; it's her favourite film by Tsui Hark (103).

Green Snake is a very sexy movie (by far Tsui's sexiest), featuring two beautiful stars, two of the biggest female stars of the Hong Kong New Wave cinema – Maggie Cheung Man-yuk[17] and Joey Wong Jo-yin – slidin' an' slitherin' through a fantastical, mythical world of a China that never existed (but should have existed!).

Green Snake is a spot-on mix of almost every element in the cinema of Tsui Hark: Chinese mythology; historical settings; women in the lead roles; romance; magic and the supernatural (and fantasy and horror); visual effects and tricks; a heightened visual style; Peking Opera performance; humour; (traditional) music; and movie references.

This kind of movie goes back to the Shaw Brothers movies of the 1950s and 1960s, which were based on myths and legends, and often adapted into operas. The romance btn a lady and a feminized scholar was a staple.[18]

Joey Wong Jo-yin (as Bai Suzhen = White Snake) is one of the principal female stars of the New Wave of Hong Kong cinema. Appropriately for *Green Snake*, Wong is known for playing supernatural women – such as in *Portrait of a Nymph, A Chinese Ghost Story* and *The Reincarnation of Golden Lotus*. Lovely to look at, Wong has the coy, curious allure of a magical being down to a 'T' (not everyone can carry off playing a supernatural creature like this, but Wong has a wistful, spiritual aspect to her screen persona which suits otherworldly characters perfectly).[19]

Maggie Cheung Man-yuk (playing Xiaoqing/ Ceng Ji = Green Snake) is perhaps the biggest female star in recent Chinese cinema. A stunning performer who can do anything, Cheung throws herself into her roles wholeheartedly (what's the point of holding back in a Hong Kong movie?! Nobody else in the production does!).

Maggie Cheung Man-yuk has appeared alongside most of the great

---

17 Maggie Cheung in Cantonese is Jeung Maan-yuk, and Zhang Manyu in Mandarin. Howard Hampton noted that Maggie Cheung in *Green Snake* 'blissfully slithers away with the picture' (F. Dannen, 342).
18 S. Teo, 1997, 77.
19 Wong is 'sweetly seductive, regal and, lastly, heartwrenchingly tragic' as White, remarked Lisa Morton, while Cheung 'makes Green vibrantly funny, curious, confused, jealous and very alive' (LM, 107).

Chinese actors, including Jackie Chan (in the *Police Story* movies), Jet Li (in *Hero*), Tony Leung (in *In the Mood For Love*), and Jacky Cheung (in *Flying Dagger*). In *Project A, Part 2*, Cheung is radiant and incredible, and in *New Dragon Gate Inn*, produced by Tsui Hark, Cheung delivers an extraordinary performance which out-shines every other actor (not easy in the middle of that sensational cast!).

It's easy to see why Maggie Cheung Man-yuk and Joey Wong Jo-yin would leap at the chance to play the snake-deities in *Green Snake*: parts like this don't come along very often! We are *long ways* from being 'stay-at-home wife of the hero' or 'boring girlfriend of the sidekick'. The girls rock in *Green Snake* – they are battling monks in the sky, beating off magical cranes, and causing floods and devastation in towns.

Green Snake is in essence the same sort of folktale as *A Chinese Ghost Story* – a hapless, young man and a supernatural woman; and there's even a Taoist monk hunting down the monsters. However, in *A Chinese Ghost Story*, the villains (the Tree-Demon and Black Mountain), are nasty pieces of work, domineering and vicious, but the spirits in *Green Snake* – Green Snake and White Snake – aren't evil at all. Indeed, they are the heroines of the piece.

What a delight *Green Snake* is, what deliciously sensual material.

It is one of those movies which creates its own world. You can recognize the constituent parts (the familiar outdoor street sets used in every Hong Kong production of the period, for instance, and the greenery and watersides of the New Territories), but each element is mixed together to produce a coherent and pungent mix.

There are four major characters in *Green Snake*:
• Two spirits/ snake-women: White Snake and Green Snake.
And two human men:
• a Taoist scholar and teacher, Hsui Xien (Wu Hsing-kuo),
• and a monk, Fat-hoi (Vincent Zhao).

You could agree with Lisa Morton that Hsing-Kuo Wu is a little miscast as the scholar, and wish that Leslie Cheung or Nicky Wu had been cast (Wu doesn't have the charisma that persuades us to believe that the women would fall for him) (LM, 107).

Certainly, Nicky Wu, in *The Lovers* of the following year, is a more satisfying scholar character, and Leslie Cheung is, well, the undisputed genius of portraying hapless, clumsy but fantastically gorgeous young men.

Tsui Hark said he focussed on the Buddhist monk maybe too much, but the monk character interested him (LM, 109). The story from the Tang Dynasty concentrates on White Snake, but the filmmakers shifted the emphasis to Green Snake, and then to the monk. True – but each of the four main characters gets their chance to shine, and we see the movie from their perspective many times.

Green Snake is a *lot* of fun, produced when Tsui Hark was at his productive peak – this was the period when Tsui was directing two movies per year (!), and producing other movies, too (did he ever sleep?!). At this time, Tsui was producing the *Swordsman* movies, *Once Upon a Time In China 4*, and *Dragon Gate Inn*, while also directing, in 1993, *Once Upon a Time In China 3* (another giant movie) – he must've been racing around Hong Kong, Taiwan and Mainland China like a madman.

Green Snake is a visual effects extravaganza: right from the outset, *Green Snake* never lets up with including a whole marauding army of visual effects, practical effects, trick shots, wire-work, and optical effects, plus the arsenal of on-set effects that're mandatory in every Tsui Hark movie: smoke (and more smoke), fire, explosions, wind (*high* wind) and rain (*heavy* rain).

Parts of *Green Snake* look like an ancient, Chinese scroll being unrolled on a desk: it has the flattened look (filming with long lenses against screens and veils), the colourful props, the settings of Chinese landscape painting, the delicacy of romantic etiquette, and numerous superstitions.[20]

A bamboo forest, mountains, rivers, a waterfall, a harbour, a town on a lake with canals, a Buddhist temple, a water-enclosed villa – *Green Snake* is a marvel of exotic locations.

Cherry blossom petals, snowflakes and Autumnal leaves are also drifting across the screen. *Green Snake* is another of Tsui Hark's pæans to the seasons, as in *The Lovers* (which's a kind of follow-up to *Green Snake*). This is a vision of traditional Chinese culture and art, with lotuses, arched bridges, waterways, and drapes.

There are marvellous touches to the costumes, hair and make-up – how the hair stylist Chung Wai-shing has created snake-shaped waves of hair which're wetted and arranged on the skin of the two actresses, for instance (Hsui Xien is embarrassed when he notices a strand of hair which winds down White Snake's neck and between her breasts). The hair and make-up is perfect, enabling Joey Wong and Maggie Cheung to look astonishing even in the midst of tumultuous, action-packed scenes where they're having 100 of gallons of freezing water hurled at them, and being battered by ten wind machines.

Meanwhile, Bobo Ng Po-ling's costumes cleverly exploit the properties of very thin pieces of cloth to emulate the look of snakes (and the *movement* of snakes – cloth is pulled around pillars and over surfaces to suggest serpents.[21] Once again, attention is drawn in Chinese cinema to the *motion* of clothing, and the *sound* of that motion, one of the very distinctive features of Chinese films).

Humour's squeezed out of snakey attributes, like feeling drowsy when it's too hot, or being unable to resist flicking out a tongue to trap a bug, or walking like a snake.

Altho' the 1993 Chinese movie spends time with each character, the tale is slanted towards Green Snake (rather than, as is usual in adaptations of the Madame White Snake folk tale, focussing on White

---

[20] *Green Snake* is full of charming traditional, Chinese rituals and superstitions.
[21] The women are perpetually either undressing or getting dressed or they're partially dressed.

Snake). Green Snake is thus portrayed as the younger sister to White Snake's older sister: Green Snake's the younger, goofier, more immature type, who isn't as used to the ways of the human world like White Snake. She's curious, wants to learn, but also is mischievous, and impulsive, and sometimes can't stop her snakey spirit coming through.

Green Snake opens with Vincent Zhao (a.k.a. Chin Man Chuek) as the demon-hunting monk Fat-hoi on the tail of a spider spirit (who transforms into a wizened, old guy (Feng Tien) with a beard).[22] (Zhao was one of Tsui Hark's leading men of the mid-1990s, appearing as the lead in *The Blade* and the two later *Once Upon a Time In China* movies). This truly remarkable sequence in the first ten-minute reel of celluloid of *Green Snake* introduces the heightened fantasy of the piece, as well as its fabulously rich look and design.

Forget the cool blues and deep reds of 1980s Hong Kong, urban thrillers, *Green Snake* is lit with rainbow-hued lights that slide across actors' faces (in bars of light), with coloured filters on the camera lens turning the skies gold and orange and red and purple, and with superimpositions that further layer colour onto the screen. It's self-consciously over-rich, a Pop Art version of a Chinese folktale. It's a wild, comicbook approach which revels in extravagance and artifice.

The cinematography experimented with more filters than most other Tsui Hark movies: Tsui said there were sometimes five or six filters in front of the camera (LM, 110). And the filters aren't only used for the skies, they are at the bottom of the frame, too. For *Green Snake*, cinematographer Giu Chiu Lam developed a remarkable *mise-en-scène* – this movie doesn't look like any others, and it is certainly one of the masterpieces of Chinese cinema in terms of its cinematography. (Consider, in addition to the use of fog, dry ice and smoke, and back-lighting, the remarkable attention to detail in the veils and screens, with silhouettes conjured on them, a favourite Tsui Hark motif – the shadows of plants, of the women, and of the giant snakes).

As well as the DP Giu Chiu Lam, production designer Bill Lui should be credited for creating the unique look, as well as William Cheung and Ng Po-ling (costumes and make-up). The production design in *Green Snake* is outstanding: marvellous touches include the white drapes that surround the snake-spirits' pavilion; the pond of pink lilies; and the use of water.

The deploying of smoke and dry ice is unique too – no other filmmaking industry is so inventive in its use of smoke. In *Green Snake*, smoke and fog don't simply drift across scenes, to add texture, as in most movies; they are included in the action, enveloping the actors in particular ways.[23] How the smoke is manipulated into shapes is very impressive.

Water is a major motif in *Green Snake*: the snake-women's pavilion has a large pool, filled with lilies (and a square, indoor bath). The snakes swim in the canals of the lakeside town. They can create rain and storms

---

[22] Reminiscent of Sammo Hung's patriarch wizard in *Zu: Warriors From the Magic Mountain*. .
[23] The stagehands controlling the fans and the smoke are geniuses.

(and it's raining in many scenes). Green Snake seduces Fat-hoi at a waterfall (and they're partially submerged). Floods rise in the town. Water and birth; water and sex; wet snakes, wet women. A seduction scene in a boat.[24] In the finale of *Green Snake*, water is everywhere, from surging floods and waves, to rain, to underwater scenes.

And the water effects are remarkable – it's as if the filmmakers can orchestrate water and smoke, wind and rain, just like the serpent-spirits themselves. Water is one of the great challenges in visual effects – everybody knows how it moves, what it looks like, but reproducing water effects on a grand scale is a tough task (scale is a giveaway). Somehow, in *Green Snake*, the water effects are not simply evoking floods, or depicting water where it's usually found – searching for the lowest point. Oh no, in *Green Snake*, water is not tamely resting at the bottom of the frame, it's spaying across the screen, it's shooting *up*, it's surging *sideways* (enveloping the monks in the Golden Temple), and it creates water spouts which turn into giant snakes.

James Wong and Mark Lui Cung Dak composed what 'may be the finest score to ever grace a Hong Kong film' (Lisa Morton, 108). It's a soundtrack of women's voices (actress Joey Wong sings many times), and includes Cantopop, traditional, Chinese music, and, more daringly, some Indian themes. As in many Tsui Hark movies, the music is allowed to run throughout some scenes, which're cut to the music as montages.

The opening reel of *Green Snake* includes chases and duels in the grandiose, high fantasy style of Chinese movies, which manifest the dramatic conflicts and themes is a spectacular manner. You can do this with two people sitting at a table drinking green tea, but I'd rather see monks flying through bamboo forests hurling bolts of fire at giant snakes!

As well as putting fantasy action, Buddhist religion, monster chases and duels and rainbow colours into the mix, the opening reel of *Green Snake* also includes another staple audience-pleasing ingredient: nudity (from Joey Wong). A woman gives birth in a bamboo grove, while the giant snakes above shelter her from the rain. (Parts of *Green Snake* look like a Japanese *animé* – not only the motifs, and the *very* over-the-top storytelling, but also the colourful, highly stylized approach. In this same period Tsui Hark was producing *The Wicked City* from a Japanese *manga*).

Nudity and sex and women – the scene also introduces the theme of the Buddhist monk's battle with erotic feelings. Monk Fat-hoi turns away and walks off, pauses, then continues. Not long afterwards, he's beset by primal urges as he meditates in a temple presided over by a huge statue of Buddha. This is another all-out action sequence, again delivered more with playfulness than genuine threat or scares. Here, erotic desires are embodied as young, devilish women dressed up as white monkeys – it's delightfully theatrical, another Peking Opera moment in a movie stuffed with them.

---

24 The seduction scene between the scholar Hsui and White Snake, on her boat, evokes similar scenes in the *Chinese Ghost Story* movies (when it was also Joey Wong in the seductive role), and also Asia the Invincible in the *Swordsman* movies.

Much is made, too, of the two women as snakes walking on land with legs, but emphasizing their sexuality as much as exploiting the comedy of the scenario (for instance, the two women slink and waggle along the sidewalk, in a cartoony send-up of a sexy walk,[25] and Green Snake fools around with fake legs).

Both Joey Wong and Maggie Cheung flirt shamelessly with the camera, giggling and pouting, happy in the knowledge that they are radiantly beautiful. With the rain spattering their gleaming skin, and their flawless make-up (deep red lipstick and pale skin and jet black hair), they might be appearing a commercial for skincare products, or a music video for a J-pop band, or a softcore porn flick.

What's also wonderful about *Green Snake* is that it puts two women at the heart of the movie: it's *their* desires which drive the plot, their yearning to find out more about humans, and to fall in love with men. This is a movie where women are pursing men, *and* out-pacing them, and out-distancing them. Once again, it's striking how much of Tsui Hark's cinema is about women, and how they negotiate the very patriarchal society of historical as well as contemporary China.

And with Joey Wong Jo-yin and Maggie Cheung Man-yuk, you have two strikingly attractive as well as strong actresses. This is their movie, and they grasp the opportunity to play magical beings fully, playing up the coquettish, frisky side of the snake spirits, as well as their wistful, introspective aspects. The picture wouldn't work so well if you didn't identify with these characters.

And it's the women who're the protagonists, driving the plot: what happens in *Green Snake* comes from their desires. But this is a supernatural movie from the monsters' point-of-view. Thus, because they are partly monsters, they can also be regarded as the rivals or the antagonists, with the Buddhist monk and the scholar representing repressive patriarchal society. The monk, for instance, has appointed himself as a censor, policing monsters in the public arena. The moral condemnation of the snake-women is couched inside Buddhist religion. These are not just regarded as monsters who will disrupt society, they are women whose erotic appetites threaten more than the lives of a scholar or two.

The first act of *Green Snake* also includes several scenes where women're the object of (masculine) admiration and desire – the snake-women (several times), and the belly dancers, the monkey demons, and the woman giving birth.

So *Green Snake*, taking a second wave feminist stance, is another fairy tale about women with too much desire, too much agency, too much life – all of which is seen as a threat to the patriarchal status quo. Incidentally, Western fairy tales have a story about a green snake – in *Green Serpent* by Madame D'Aulnoy.

The eroticism of the snake-women and their desires is introduced in the opening act, where they appear on the roof of a building in thundering

---

25 While men gawp and fall out of boats.

rain while an exotic troupe of Indian belly dancers shimmy and slink below. It's an unforgettable introduction for the serpents, as they giggle and writhe orgasmically on the roof, getting aroused by the dancing and carousing below. The lesbian undertones of these sensuous sisters doesn't need to be highlighted – the movie does all of that. For instance, Green Snake joins the party below, falling thru the roof and materializing naked on the dance floor, and gigglingly joining in the dance, wrapping herself around the lead dancer (Nagma).

The first act of *Green Snake* is busy with scenes: as well as the Indian dance and party, and the introduction of the snake-women, and Fat-hoi fending off monkey girls, and the monk witnessing monstrous births in bamboo forests (and chasing down giant spiders), there are also scenes of White Snake turning her attention to the scholars in their school-room, and the seduction of Hsui Xien on the boat. Indeed, *Green Snake* begins at such a high velocity, it is some twenty minutes before anything resembling regular film narration appears (when we finally meet Green Snake and White Snake together, by day, talking). Before that, for 20 minutes we're either racing thru the tree tops following Fat-hoi, or battling monkey demons, or writhing in lesbian clinches on rain-soaked roofs, or dancing with wiggling belly dancers.

And the succession of imagery in act one is awe-inspiring, as is the self-conscious theatricality of the movie. *Green Snake* revels in the tricks and gimmickery of cinema: this is fully-realized fantasy cinema where almost every shot is a trick shot. For example, when Fat-hoi's running alongside the spider-man, the actors are running on the spot while stage hands out of shot move branches behind them to simulate the background in motion.

The emphasis on theatricality evokes Western filmmakers such as Orson Welles, Jean Cocteau, Walerian Borowczyk, Vincente Minnelli and Francis Coppola – filmmakers who often foregrounded the mechanism of movie-making.

Even if *Green Snake* underwhelmed many critics and viewers, there is so much going on it doesn't matter.

The first act includes a scene where women on one side and men on the other are setting lanterns afloat on the canals, an exotic and lyrical scene which helps to foreground the theme of romance, and the interplay between the genders. (Even here there's a tiny sub-subplot, as one of the girls hopes to connect with Hsui Xien, but doesn't; later, during the Dragon Boat Festival, we see her embracing a lover).

Act two of *Green Snake* includes complications, plus additions and variations on the themes established in act one. There are more romantic and seduction scenes (act two climaxes – literally – with two love scenes cut together in parallel); more scenes of Hsui Xien as a teacher; more scenes where Fat-hoi challenges the snake-women; more scenes of the girls bathing (they spend *a lot* of time in that sunken, square pool!); and more comedic scenes where the snakes try to hide their true nature from Hsui.

A further complication in act 2 has the already-weakened Hsui Xien fainting away at the sight of Green Snake fully transformed: consequently, White Snake opts to travel to the Kwun-lun Mountain to fetch a special remedy.

Now in act two the authorities ranged against the two snake-women increase (as if the monk Fat-hoi wasn't enough): first, a blind Taoist priest (Kong Lau) and his aides try to tackle them; secondly, there's a wave of anti-snake charms and anti-snake weapons being sold at the Dragon Boat Festival.[26]

A marvellous ingredient in *Green Snake* is the blind Taoist demon-hunter, aided by two youths (who've stepped right out of a Peking Opera School). There's a terrific scene (early in act 2) where the team stake out the snake-women's home, setting out powdered sulphur around the perimeter. But the spirits can conjure (torrential) rain (with a cup of water flicked at the sky), which dissolves the sulphur. In the second action scene, the Taoist priest and the lads enter the white house, only to be repelled again.

The blind Taoist and his accomplices provide one of several action sequences in act two: there's an outstanding canal sequence,[27] where characters're flying thru the air, landing on boats, and using tiny bells to scare off their prey (Green Snake is not impressed – she manages to grapple the priest underwater). Flying scenes over water are one of the recurring motifs of movies of the period – as if the filmmakers're demonstrating that they can stage incredible stunt work anywhere, including in the middle of oceans or rivers or waterfalls.

The Dragon Boat Festival is pure Tsui Hark – it's not a Tsui Hark historical picture unless there are one or two very big scenes of bustling streets. Every historical movie should have at least one big production scene teeming with extras in costume. The festival is humorously punctuated by the citizens preparing to defend themselves against snakes (with charms, potions and of course big knives). Meanwhile, poor Hsui Xien is feeling very sick, vomits and gets drunk. He mutters darkly about giant snakes.

A big scene occurs in the second act when Green Snake and White Snake travel to a mythical realm to obtain a magical plant which can revive the scholar Hsui Xien (with Fat-hoi in pursuit). So the narrative has a woman working to save her man. Here Green Snake seduces Fat-hoi, as well as duelling with him, which's filmed in a travel brochure waterfall location (which pops up in other Hong Kong movies). Maggie Cheung is at her pixieish and slinkiest in these scenes, sliding all over Fat-hoi: these scenes are cut in parallel action with White Snake making love with Hsui Xien in her pavilion (their gestures seem linked, like those of the two Jackie Chans in *Twin Dragons*). It's the love-making that forms the finale of act two of *Green Snake*, not the supernatural duelling between Fat-hoi

26 Some of the jokes play into the Chinese use of snakes.
27 The scene was replayed in *The Sorcerer and the White Snake*, 2011.

and Green Snake (which would be the case if this was an action movie).

The final act of *Green Snake* is absolutely sensational, an all-out and epic slice of fantasy filmmaking. There are hundreds of visual effects and trick shots, with an extensive use of models.[28] Fire, smoke, rain, wind machines, explosions, optical superimpositions, animatronics, puppetry, and animation are all employed, along with every possible trick that cinema is capable of. It's all achieved in a high fantasy manner, reminiscent of Ray Harryhausen's mythological movies.

Monk Fat-hoi unfurls a monk's surplice which grows to the size of a red, Maoist banner hundreds of yards long, billowing in the wind (he floats in the centre of the huge acreage of red cloth). The snake-women conjure a colossal storm and flood. Water is spraying everywhere, flowing along the town's streets, battering down bridges, and smashing against cliffs and temples (actresses Maggie Cheung and Joey Wong are completely drenched in many scenes – they are real troupers).

The image-making in the finale of *Green Snake* is stupendous, and so rapid you can barely keep up with it. Everything the filmmakers can get hold of (can beg, steal or borrow), is chucked into the mix. Yet the imagery, beautiful and hypnotizing as much of it is, is locked into the dramatic issues and telling the story: Fat-hoi the monk is battling the snake-women, Green Snake is trying to save her husband Hsui Xien, and White Snake, right in the middle of the mælstrom, gives birth (echoing the birth in the bamboo forest at the beginning of the picture).[29]

The finale of *Green Snake* is not only sound and fury – it is playing out the emotional and psychological conflicts and themes of the story, with the urge to become human (and be accepted as human) on one side, and the acceptance of love and sex as part of being human on the other.

And there are many changes in the tone in the finale of *Green Snake* – it's not all rollercoaster action. The scenes in the Buddhist temple, for instance, are played for a ghostly atmosphere, of dusty blues and greys (it's a markedly austere, less colourful world than the realm of the serpent-spirits). Here the sound mixers take the sound down to eerie throbs and drones, as the narrative moves into a spiritual form of storytelling (we are beyond the senses – the monks cover their eyes, ears, mouths, etc. Tsui Hark is fond of those aspects of Buddhism and Oriental religion – remember the waggling ears of the priest Bai Yun in *A Chinese Ghost Story*).

As the Buddhist monks try to keep out the rampaging spirits of nature, and fail, Green Snake materializes inside the Golden Temple to find Hsui Xien, to bring him back to the ailing White Snake. The sequence is mysterious and thoroughly Oriental: there are no scenes like this in Western cinema: Green Snake floats at waist height over the chanting,

---

[28] Miniatures are all over the place in the finale of *Green Snake*, from the temple to the cliffs to the town. Water scenes are of course some of the toughest to do in visual effects, and with models. As if to make things extra difficult for themselves, the filmmakers shoot in full daylight (night scenes can hide a multitude of visual effects sins), and with water not just calmly lapping a shore, but gushing about everywhere.

[29] The monk Fat-hoi is astonished: if a demon can give birth to a human baby, then it has perhaps become fully human.

meditating monks, searching for Hsui. The camera looms into extreme close-ups of shaven-headed men, repeatedly, with fades to black. When Green Snake discovers Hsui (now he's one of hundreds of monks), the narration features a succession of enigmatic close-ups of Green Snake (Maggie Cheuung has her nose right up against the lens).

Here you're watching an old, Chinese folk tale being brought to life, a true fairy tale and fantasy from ancient times, wittily and skilfully updated for a contemporary (1990s) audience, and played for sheer entertainment. The imagery is super-heightened, as far from Western cinema's slavish devotion to 'realism' as possible, and it works wonders. The *tone* is perfect, hitting just the right balance between playing it straight, and delighting in the total silliness of it all. Monks flying thru the sky duelling giant serpents is completely mad, but it's such fun. (Tsui Hark revisited similar territory of fantastical battles at sea in the second *Detective Dee* movie, and *The Legend of Zu* is full of this sort of spectacle, tho' with much more digital trickery added).

For a contemporary audience in the 2000s and after, some of the visual effects in *Green Snake* might appear 'dated'. But that's not the way to look at *Green Snake* at all, and in fact the visual effects are part of the charm. *Everything* in a movie is fake, whether it's achieved with computers, pixels, models, paintings, puppets, animation, animatronics, or actors.

It can't end well in *Green Snake,* and it doesn't: like thousands of fairy tales and folk tales and mythological tales of humans falling for monsters or demons or spirits or ghosts, the lovers wind up torn apart, or destroyed. Monk Fat-hoi, at least, learns that he has been over-zealous in his pursuit of demons, and his condemnation of them (seeing White Snake give birth shows how she has achieved humanity). Green Snake learns that her kind can never mix with humans. Everybody learns that being alive is dangerous, whether it's pursuing the ascetic life of a meditating monk, or trying to attain humanity thru engaging in love and sex. White Snake expires, lost at sea, and Green Snake kills Hsui Xien in retribution. giving us our tragic ending to this beasts-and-humans tale.

For Tony Rayns, *Green Snake* was 'Tsui Hark's nadir, and Maggie Cheuung's most undignified screen moments'.[30] People who don't enjoy *Green Snake* (it polarizes viewers), draw attention to the visual effects, but that's always a side issue: what they are really complaining about, perhaps, is the women-centred focus, the emphasis on sisterhood, how both males are flawed and less than appealing, and how the men are seen from the women's point-of-view.[31] Plus, this is a very *Chinese* story, made in a very *Chinese* style; also, it makes many leaps into fantasy, with snakes who're women, which depart from the Western models (a Westernized, Disneyfied approach would be radically different – consider

---

30 Quoted in F. Dannen, 398.
31 Lisa Morton suggests that the structure is part of the problem: it's two-parts 'intimate, small-scale, gentle fantasy and one-part cast-of-thousands epic swordplay' (LM, 107). Morton prefers the snakes-as-sisters central section of *Green Snake*, not the opening or the ending (she recommends watching the film from 11m 30s onwards, and missing out the ending).

how Disney has filmed human-beast tales). And *Green Snake* doesn't make concessions to an international or Western audience – there are no witty sidekicks offering clever quips to explain the story, no framing story (as in *Zu: Warriors From the Magic Mountain*), and no Westernized audience identification figures.

Better perhaps to think of *Green Snake* as a musical – a musical version of a supernatural story. *Green Snake* has all of the hallmarks of a musical, without being one (tho' the music is beautiful). It's Fairy Tale Time, where you're encouraged to succumb to the magic. It's Tsui Hark's rendition of *Beauty and the Beast*, tho' seen from the Beast's point-of-view, and the Beast is female (and there are two of them!).

20

THE LOVERS

Leung Juk

INTRODUCTION.
The Lovers (a.k.a. *The Butterfly Lovers* – *Liáng Zhù* in Mandarin, *Leung Juk* in Cantonese = *Leung & Chuk*, 1994) is one of the reasons why Tsui Hark is one of the great directors of recent times. It is a hugely enjoyable and very accomplished piece of entertainment. In fact, I'd class it as a masterpiece. True, it's over-shadowed by the big Tsui Hark movies like *Once Upon a Time In China* and *Peking Opera Blues* and *Zu: Warriors From the Magic Mountain*, but *The Lovers* is perfectly formed; it delivers, and it's pitched at just the right note.

The Lovers was directed, produced and co-written by Tsui Hark. In the cast were Charlie Yeung (as Zhu Yingtai/ Chuk Ying-toi), pop singer Nicky Wu (Ng Kei-lung) (as Liang Shanbo/ Shan-pak), Carrie Ng Ka-lai (as Yingtai's mom, Sin Yuk-ting), Elvis Tsui Kam-kong (as Yingtai's father, Master Chuk), Lau Shun (as a servant, Chung Kwai) and Sun Xing as a monk. Also in the cast were: Linda Lau as Madam Yuen, Hau Bing-ying as Ingenue, Yuen Sam as Mr Ching, Shum Hoi-yung as Madam Leung and Peter Ho as Ting Mong-chun.

Sharon Hui Sa-long was co-writer with Tsui Hark. It was produced by Tsui Hark for Film Workshop/ Paragon Films, and distributed by Golden Harvest. The DP was David Chung Chi-man, the score was by William Hu, Mark Lui Chung-pak, James Wong Jim and Raymond Wong. Art direction by William Chang and Cheong Kwok-wing. Costumes by Cheung Kam-Kam. Make-up by Gwok Yim-Gwan and Chin Ai-Lan. The editors were Marco Mak Chi-sin and Wong Jing-chang. A.D.: Chien-ching Chu. Sound recordists: Chin-yung Chou and Shao Lung Chou. Sound mixer: Chia-lun Liang. Dubbing editor: Hung Lu (Cantonese). (Many in the team also worked on Tsui's previous movie, *Green Snake*).

Tsui Hark recalled that the schedule for making *The Lovers* was very short – a month, which also included the preparation (thus, many of the sets were from other productions). Released on Aug 13, 1994. 104 mins.

The source of *The Lovers* is an oft-filmed tale, *The Story of a Tragic Love,* one of the *Four Great Tales of China.* It was written in the Northern and Southern Dynasties (42-581 A.D.), and in the Tang Dynasty. The legend is known as the Chinese *Romeo and Juliet*. It has been filmed many times before in cinema and television (as well as operas and stage plays).

The Lovers was another instance of Tsui Hark following in the footsteps of King Wu: Wu had worked on a version of the *Butterfly Lovers* legend in 1963 (as *Love Eternal*).

The ancient story was altered in *The Lovers* – class was an issue, for example – it was another case of the poor man and the princess. The pressure from the parents was another alteration. And Tsui Hark felt that Zhu Yingtai should be isolated (tho' she has people helping her at the school). The changes were made so the story would be more amenable (or believable) for a modern audience.

The Lovers moves away from the norm by delivering what amounts to a 'chick flick'. Yes, this is a romantic comedy which takes the woman's point-of-view: Zhu Yingtai is the character first introduced, we follow her progress from home thru the scene with the parents to the college. *The Lovers* spends quite some time establishing Yingtai's personality, how she is rather dreamy,[32] awkward, clumsy and hapless, until she meets Liang Shanbo, her lover (some 20 minutes into the movie).

The Lovers is a comedy movie as well as a romantic tragedy – I haven't seen the film with a Chinese audience, but one can imagine many scenes here amusing them. One of the best's in the first act, where Yingtai is interviewed by her parents in a formal setting. The topic of discussion is marriage, and the prospect of Yingtai being a suitable mate. Grooming, education – Yingtai tries reciting a poem and fails, tries making up a poem and freezes, tries her hand at calligraphy and is hopeless, and she manages to make a lyre sound like a wooden box falling down stairs.

The Lovers is a delightful romantic comedy (or comical romance), with a light touch that never labours the romance or the comedy, the characters or the settings (comedy, that is, until the tale takes a turn into tragedy, in the final third). Known as an over-cooked and over-done film director (like Steven Spielberg or Orson Welles), who'll chuck in everything into every movie (if he's allowed to! – and he seems to get his own way quite often!), *The Lovers* proves otherwise (as with other Tsui Hark flicks, such as *Dangerous Encounters – First Kind*). Yes, it's true that *The Lovers* is a fantastic *style* piece, with an emphasis on the look and the style which would threaten to overwhelm the story and the characters (we've all seen movies like that, where style wins out over substance).[33] But no, *The Lovers* always keeps the two lovers in the foreground, and is always charting the development of their relationship, and tracking the narrative.

The Lovers is a highly accomplished delivery of an updating of ancient, Chinese tales, and it develops convincing and poetic ways of

---

32 She is introduced as a dreamer, looning about on her own up on the roof.
33 Among Western filmmakers, Michael Bay, Ridley Scott, Tony Scott, Paul S. Anderson and Guy Ritchie come to mind.

using well-worn symbols and motifs, such as butterflies, music, Buddhism, arranged marriages, etc.

The Lovers is a love story. Yes, it's not an action movie with a love story as the secondary plot, or a boysy fantasy adventure with a love story cynically attached to it, and it's not a love story couched inside a thriller or urban or gangster narrative.[34] No, the romance is the central spine of this 1994 movie. (Many of the great and celebrated filmmakers in the contemporary era have *not* made an out-and-out romantic movie like this: they'll use romance as a secondary plot, or to target a section of the global audience (i.e., women), but romance as the primary plot? Not many).

To make a movie as charming and witty as *The Lovers* takes some guts and some talent – especially in this ultra-cynical age, when everything has been done/ seen/ made, and bored audiences have Seen It All Before. Because in *The Lovers* there is humour and comical business between the lovers that's as lightweight and sappy as a Disney cartoon. But, somehow, the movie gets away with it, and carries the audience along – by its energy, its invention, and its light touch.

The Lovers is pure delight – and one of the chief reasons for this is that it doesn't rush the crucial early scenes, which introduce the two principals. Rush those scenes, and the audience won't've had time to get to know Zhu Yingtai and her predicament in being put forward for marriage by her vain (and somewhat bullying) parents. (It makes things a little easier for us to sympathize with Yingtai when her father is portrayed as a vain fool, tho' her mother, Sin Yuk-ting, is more practical and understanding of Yingtai's predicament. Both Elvis Tsui and Carrie Ng, Tsui Hark regulars, are excellent).

▶

Zhu Yingtai is a sweet, innocent, awkward but gutsy character, and she is winningly played by Charlie Yeung (a.k.a. Young). Born in Tapei on May 23, 1974, the 20 year-old Yeung grabs this role and runs with it (the chance to star in a romantic tale made by filmmakers this celebrated is a rarity): she is a great comedienne, and the screen loves her (the 1994 movie made her a star, and she became much in demand in the subsequent years (appearing in *Ashes of Time, Fallen Angels, The Wedding Days, Dr Wai, Task Force*, etc), before retiring in 1997 (she appeared later in *Seven Swords, New Police Story, Kung Fu Jungle, Cold War, Sleepwalker, Floating City, Wind Blast, 37, Bangkok Dangerous, Christmas Rose, Catching Monkey* and *All About Love*). Nicky Wu is a superb foil for Yeung, and the two have great chemistry together.

Much of the impact of *The Lovers* stems from Charlie Yeung and Nicky Wu – after all, the camera is right in their faces throughout the movie. They are both charming, lending the story an irresistible appeal.

Everything about *The Lovers* is traditional and shamelessly indulgent: this is a romantic comedy which does not intend to offer any major overhauling of old, well-worn chestnuts of the romantic comedy genre like

---
[34] Where 'cool', flashy visuals and smug acting mask what is basically a traditional romance.

mistaken identity, disguise, gender-bending, and blossoming love in a strictly hierarchical setting (here, a college). And it's another romance where the woman is in drag, a perennial Tsui Hark motif.

Tsui Hark was quizzed by gay director Stanley Kwan about his move to normalize the relationship of the lovers by bringing it back to heterosexual norms in the documentary *Yang and Yin*. Tsui didn't really have an answer (this was in 1997). He said he related *The Lovers* to his own experience of first love.

From its relaxed opening (some 2.5 minutes of languourous establishing shots of lovely landscapes and Ye Olde Chinese wooden buildings sprinkled with cherry blossom), *The Lovers* announces itself as a candy box romantic comedy, a reworking of a classic, Chinese tale in a self-consciously nostalgic manner. Yet *The Lovers* is also a movie of the 1990s, of the New Wave of Hong Kong, and of Hong Kong's renaissance of the early Nineties. A movie of its time, despite its ancient, classical subject matter. (But it is also one of Tsui Hark's most old-fashioned and conservative pictures – a case of 'old stories with new actors').

There are many scenes evoking traditional, Chinese pursuits of calligraphy, music, reciting poetry (and, for Zhu Yingtai, carrying herself properly as a woman – small steps, with her ankles tied). Magic hour photography captures the elegant, hierarchical home life of Yingtai, with cherry blossom drifting thru the air, white roses blooming in front of the house, and Yingtai is first seen doing nothing more'n lounging on the roof with butterflies captured in a glass jar.

The Lovers is in short a skilful updating of an olde worlde romance, a yarn in which nothing surprises or startles the audience, but plenty amuses and moves them. *The Lovers* is no different from 10 million other romantic stories in being fundamentally conservative and restrained, enshrining institutions such as heterosexuality, marriage, the family, the law and the community, and concepts such as finding a mate, and doing the right thing (a biggie for Tsui Hark).

The Lovers is thus yet another instance of Tsui Hark taking up an old and much-used story/ source/ form, and updating it for the contemporary era. Tsui enjoys delivering his own take on a well-known story. In some scenes, the lovers simply gawp at each other fondly – it's amazing that the filmmakers reckon they can get away with such adolescent behaviour; yet they do. Getting the tone and the attitude right here is crucial, which *The Lovers* achieves (it looks effortless, but it isn't – that's the trick).[35]

In *The Lovers*, Zhu Yingtai is a woman masquerading as a boy in order to study at a college (thus neatly exposing the ingrained sexism of ancient, patriarchal China, where women were presumably not allowed to study at a school like this). The gender-bending is amusing and delicately done (the comedy in *The Lovers* is gentle, avoiding the obvious crudities which a movie set in contemporary times would feel obliged to include). Some comedy is also squeezed out of Liang Shanbo wondering if he's gay. Yet altho' the main character is a woman, and the 1994 movie takes the

---

[35] Bringing the audience along with you, so they buy into this cheese, is also crucial.

woman's point-of-view, the social codes are entirely patriarchal and anti-feminist. The college is all-boys, the teachers are men (i.e., crusty, old coots), and even maids are not allowed to accompany their masters.

Patriarchy rules OK here, with the double standards of sexism firmly in place: Zhu Yingtai may be at the college to educate herself (according to her parents' wishes), but with the chief intention of turning Yingtai into an educated woman, so that she'll be a more promising mate for marriage. For second wave feminists, women are commodities that're traded in marriage between men in a patriarchal society, and *The Lovers* embodies that completely (as do most romantic stories, West or East).

LOOK AND STYLE.

Style-wise, *The Lovers* is a masterpiece of cinematography, production design, costume design, hair and make-up. It is ravishing to look at, a highly poetic concoction of elegant, wooden buildings, lush forests and valleys, and gorgeous, Chinese gardens (complete with rocks and pools). It is, once again, the myth and the dream of Ancient China, a world that never existed, but *should* have existed. There's a lovely moment when Zhu Yingtai and her maid leave the home and look with delight at the wooded hills of China. (Yes, it's true that the love story doesn't require quite this high level of production value, but the tiny budget of *The Lovers* is of course made to look like US $20-40 million, by Western standards, of the 1994 period). Chinese films are real wonders of taking a budget of US $1.2 million (average in the early 1990s) and turning it into a widescreen extravaganza which can stand beside any epic movie in the history of cinema.

The photography (David Chung was DP,[36] one of Tsui Hark's regular DPs of the era), is ravishing in *The Lovers*. As this is a sweet, tender tale of romance, the *mise-en-scène* is suitably poetic and indulgent. The daytime scenes are lit with a subtle, soft light (augmented by filters). Indeed, much of the film seems lit to approximate to magic hour photography, with golden side-lighting to emulate sunset. And the firelight, lamplight and candlelight offers the kind of lighting that cinematographers love to recreate. 'Of course, it's visually stunning. But all of Tsui's films are stunning', opined Thomas Weisser (123).

Indeed, just to present to the audience a collection of music, of costumes, of traditional buildings, of ancient, Chinese arts might be enough for Tsui Hark, regardless of the story or the characters. This is a movie where the *mise-en-scène* and the production values are as important as the story: and yet, as in the finest movies, they are all in the service of the story, and *The Lovers* is always telling a story.

MUSIC.

Music is one of the major ingredients in *The Lovers*, and contributes *enormously* to its success. The film generously allows music to dominate in several scenes. Four composers are credited in *The Lovers*, including

---
[36] With lighting by Chow Wai-Kuen.

William Hu, Mark Lui Chung-pak, James Wong Jim and Raymond Wong (all regulars in Tsui Hark's *œuvre*; Wong won the Music Award at the 14th Hong Kong Film Awards).

Music is playing pretty much throughout *The Lovers*[37] – not continuously, but in most scenes (not continuously, that is, in the recent Hollywood manner of having music burbling under every single scene, as if North American film studios and producers are terrified that an audience cannot possibly stand a scene without music. 'Playing through' a scene they call it; music reduced to muzak). No – in *The Lovers*, the music is shamelessly emotional and romantic, enhancing the romance at the heart of the picture ('romantic is the most key word in everything' for Tsui Hark [LM, 22]). There are many scenes which use music and play without dialogue. Some of these are music video-style scenes, evoking the growing friendship btn the lovers. Some are musical montages, where time's compressed, and the scenes describe events over several days. Some scenes foreground the playing of musical instruments. And quite a few scenes use music to push the emotion up to very intense levels – especially in the final third of *The Lovers*, where the tragic story kicks in big time. In this part of *The Lovers*, the score becomes positively operatic, as the movie shifts into a place that Chinese cinema adores to explore: high emotion, hysteria, and grand opera.

Music is also deployed as a motif that connects the lovers: when they first see each other, Liang Shanbo is part of a music class for the lyre (in a chocolate box scene in woodland dappled with sunlight). She sees him, and he sees her (as she arrives with her entourage. In fact, other guys look round before he does, but she has already selected him as the object of her affection, and waits for him to turn and look at her). The teacher ironically prates about playing music with feelings (deriding his pupils, and wondering if they have any idea what he means). Later, when Shanbo and Zhu Yingtai are punished following an incident of fooling around in the music class (and another, where a lyre is broken), Shanbo plays for Yingtai (she has to stand in one place as punishment, holding up her broken instrument). This is one of the loveliest montages in *The Lovers*, with the music given full prominence in the 1994 movie, while characters're depicted listening to it (including the music teacher – it's the pay-off of music being performed with feeling – here, it's love, as Shanbo encourages Yingtai to win thru with his performance). And Yingtai does the same in another music class, reversing the roles (only she's not as accomplished a player, and she gives up and weeps).

STRUCTURE AND THEMES.

Structurally, *The Lovers* is divided into two sections: love and tragedy (or comedy and tragedy). Love takes up roughly the first two-thirds, and tragedy the last third. You can also divide *The Lovers* into four sections: in the first section, we are introduced to Zhu Yingtai (20 minutes). In the second section, the fascination of the potential romance begins ('the

---

[37] At least four pieces of music are included in the first 3 minutes.

fascination' is a term that Thomas Hardy employs for erotic attraction in *Tess of the d'Urbervilles*). The third section develops the romance up to its consummation in a cave. The fourth section of *The Lovers* is the tragedy, as Zhu Yingtai is called back to her family home to be presented in marriage, and Liang Shanbo is beaten and dies, ending in the deaths of the lovers. The ending was reworked from the ancient, Tang Dynasty tale, to make it more amenable to a modern audience (for instance, the death of the man).

There are subplots introduced in the second act of *The Lovers* (using a three-act model), where the lovers encounter a monk (Sun Sing), who turns out to have had an affair with Zhu Yingtai's mother Sin Yuk-ting, when she too studied at the college in the disguise of a boy. (Actually, Tsui Hark says he's an intellectual who's shaved his head, not a monk, but he is another societal outsider).[38]

Love/ sex and religion are counterpointed in *The Lovers* using the motif of Buddhism: the lovers consummate their relationship sheltering from a storm in a cave near a Buddhist temple;[39] the early scenes emphasize Buddhist temples; there are references to Confucian ethics, etc.

In *The Lovers*, marriage is presented in the familiar terms of economy and exchange: as patriarch Master Chuk explains, the family needs this marriage to survive financially. The pressure on Zhu Yingtai is immense, and her parents are somewhat cool and domineering (they are also sent up – particularly Chuk, with his vanity and use of make-up to mask ageing – a common motif applied to Chinese Emperors). The mother (Carrie Ng), is rather imperious and implacable when she needs to be (particularly in the finale act, where she exerts her influence over Yingtai to marry).

THE FINALE.

So in the final section of *The Lovers*, the comedy is put to one side (tho' not entirely), and the tragic aspects of erotic relationships kicks in (the third act is announced clearly when the movie cuts back to Zhu Yingtai's home, and of course to her parents, now fretting about the arranged marriage).

For the finale, the 1994 picture makes a massive shift in tone and attitude from comedy to drama, from light-hearted banter and blossom-pink, dreamy imagery to full-on, operatic and hysterical intensity. Now the screen is boiling with heavy rain and thunderous wind (when Zhu Yingtai dutifully performs her calligraphy for her now-stern parents, lightning is thrashing continuously and violently). There are huge close-ups of teary faces, as the emotions are screwed up to hysterical heights (the parents are satirized with unflattering and too-close close-ups).

This is an area of filmmaking that Chinese cinema has made its own – no other cinema can quite do over-the-top emotions like Chinese cinema. Especially when it's enhanced by lavish filmmaking (the rain machines, the

---

38 The setting for the encounter – a beautiful waterfall in Mainland China – acts as a breather from the college setting.
39 Where the figure of Buddha seems to bless their union.

smoke machines and the wind machines are going full-blast, with the gaffer flashing the lamps on and off for lightning, with the props guys throwing leaves and debris into the camera from above and the side, and the actors can barely stand in the gale-force winds).

In *The Lovers*, when love goes wrong, it *really* goes wrong: the Heavens and the Earth contribute with shifting mounds of soil and boiling clouds and hurricane winds. It is a classical form of storytelling, using the familiar and ancient tropes of love and poetry: where love is potentially as fierce as a tornado or an earthquake. Did the Earth move for you? Here, it literally does – swallowing up the distraught Zhu Yingtai at Liang Shanbo's grave.

The ending of *The Lovers* is spectacular, filled with the impressive visual effects which Tsui Hark enjoys so much, but always in the service of the story and the characters. But this is not effects for effects' sake: the lovers and the narrative are always kept centre stage. This form of filmmaking we've seen many a time in the action-based finales of martial arts movies (particularly the ones of the 1980s and 1990s, the time of *The Lovers*, when Buddhist monks or Wong Fei-hung are flying thru the air while winds howl and everything appears apocalyptic). To use this form in a love story takes the narrative into a whole other place. It wouldn't work if the characters and the strength of their romance hadn't been firmly established (and the supporting players, particularly Chung Kwai and Ingenue, are helping plenty with their sorrowful, concerned reactions).

And the finale of *The Lovers* is *milked* to the max by the production team. Scenes are played at a manic pitch, sequences are revisited to make sure we've *really* got the point, and, most important of all, the music – oh, that music! – is sawing with the strings, and blasting with the brass, and pounding with the percussion, to ram home the emotion, the emotion, oh, that crazy emotion!

Yes, the ending of *The Lovers* would still play powerfully without the music (there are sounds mixed high of wind, rain, thunder, etc), but it's that miraculous, invisible artform, music, which turns the finale into a symphony, or the final act of an opera.

The imagery milks the predicaments of the lovers to an equally over-the-top degree as the music does: Zhu Yingtai is placed in a room like a butterfly in a cage, hammering at the doors to get out and rejoin her lover; the cutting emphasizes the nearness and the distance between the lovers; there are the inevitable montages of happier times for the lovers; Liang Shanbo expires after writing his last message to Yingtai – blood spilled on parchment; Sin Yuk-ting continues to be as implacable and immovable as ever as the imperious mother (there's *no way* she will allow her daughter to marry Shanbo), even tho' she also appears sympathetic.

The scenes at Liang Shanbo's graveside on the hill are suitably operatic – it's the finale of a tragic, Peking Opera performance, when the main characters expire. The staging and the orchestration of the action is masterful here, a beautiful and convincing demonstration of Tsui Hark's control of romantic symbols and tropes. The 1994 movie enters a fantastical mode of narration to evoke the high drama of the emotions (centred around Zhu Yingtai kneeling before the grave), with loud, elemental sounds, shaking camera, coloured filters, wind machines, Charlie Yeng emoting, and strident music.

And finally the intellectual, quasi-monk Sun Sing finds Zhu Yingtai's drawing of butterflies and sets them to fly in the air (they flutter into the sunset in the final shot). There shouldn't be a dry eye in the house.

Tsui Hark was surprised that so many people cried when they watched *The Lovers*; he thought he was making a happy, romantic picture. Some wept, he said, because they knew what was coming.

SEX AND ZEN 2 AND *THE LOVERS*

Sex and Zen 2 was produced by Wong Jing for Golden Harvest and Wong Jing's Workshop Ltd., wr. by Elvis Tsui and dir. by Chin Man-kay. In the cast were Loletta Lee, Lok Tat-wah, Tsui Kam-kong, Wong Yat-fei and Shu Qi. Released: May 17, 1996. 89 mins.

Wong Jing has producer credit, and *Sex and Zen 2* is very much a Wongian sort of movie, but actually it was written by actor Elvis Tsui (who's been in everything in Hong Kong, including several Tsui Hark productions), and it's Tsui's patriarch Sai-moon who steals many scenes. (Tsui was the patriarch in *The Lovers*, too).

The domineering patriarch Sai-moon, ever the old goat, takes a shine to his idiot son's bride, Siu-Tsiu, and tups her (after waiting outside the bridal chamber in a fretful mood for his son to do the duty). The bride is really the mysterious villain of the piece, Mirage Lady, played by Shu Qi, a Category III actress.

Using the magical scroll *The Secret of Virginity*, Mirage Lady is able to suck out the life of her victims during sex. Sai-moon is killed by Mirage Lady, with a poison that attacks his libido and penis. In the finale, Mirage Lady couples with the heroine, Yau, in an extended sex scene that has Mirage Lady performing as a hermaphroditic creature (that old favourite of porn, a girl with a member).

Loletta Lee plays the lead role, Yau, the patriarch's daughter (she was in *Shanghai Blues*), and is a delightful incarnation of the innocent, crossdressing girl played by Charlie Yeung in the 1994 movie.

The bawdy humour in *Sex and Zen 2* includes phallic jokes, replacement penises, chastity belts which shred weeners, lesbian sex, masturbation (male and female), group sex, etc. The charas are the familiar ones from the rest of the *Sex and Zen* series, and many other Chinese Category III comedies: the eager, young scholars, inquisitive, young women, pervy, old coots, slinky *femme fatales*, etc.

Sex and Zen 2 is a studio-bound movie, and parts of it look low budget. But it does also feature the familiar smoke-filled, backlit photography of all Hong Kong pictures. (For some reason, DP Cheung Man Po has almost every shot off-kilter. Hong Kong movies use Dutch tilts from time to time, but in *Sex and Zen 2* they're everywhere).

ಜಿ

The Lovers (1994) is crudely tho' amusingly sent up in the 1996 movie *Sex and Zen 2*. In true Wong Jing style, *Sex and Zen 2* happily brings out all of the more subtle innuendo and allusion in *The Lovers*. *Sex and Zen 2* also draws on the basis for *The Lovers, Butterfly Lovers*, and *The Golden Lotus* and *The Water Margin*.

Sex and Zen 2 features the scene from *The Lovers* where the scholars're studying outside. Yau joins them. This time, however, the lads are masturbating off *en masse,* in a crude competition (to see how far they can ejaculate). *Sex and Zen 2* thus happily brings out the phallic subtext, the homoerotic aspects, of the male bonding and brotherhoods in Chinese cinema.

In the scene in *The Lovers* where Zhu Yingtai and Liang Shanbo are sleeping in the library, *Sex and Zen 2* has Yau having a wet dream, masturbating, while Fa Do wakes and looks on agape. Here, the hero has his penis mauled by Yau's chastity belt (which's fitted with anti-male gadgets by her stern father, Sai-moon). In a version from the horse penis transplant in film one, Fa Do gets his member replaced by a mechanical sex toy which can spin and expand. (The Happy Taoist, Wong Yat-fei (also from film one), performs the unlikely operation).

As it's obviously mechanical, the penis can be seen on camera, but in the double standards of the rest of the *Sex and Zen* films, and in movies everywhere in general, shots of the male member are withheld, tho' women are fully nude and on display.

THE BUTTERFLY LOVERS

The Butterfly Lovers (a.k.a. *Jian Die* and *The Assassin's Blade*, 2008) was a remake of the 1994 Tsui Hark movie. *The Butterfly Lovers* saw Tony Ching working as the action choreographer on a *wuxia pian* interpretation of the Ancient Chinese legend of the doomed lovers Liang Shanbo and Zhu Yingtai.

The Butterfly Lovers was helmed by Jingle Ma Choh-shing (a Hong Kong director and cinematographer – *Mulan, Tokyo Raiders, Prison On Fire, Fong Sai-yuk, Viva Erotica* and several Jackie Chan pictures),[40] prod. by Catherine Hun Ga-jan for Brilliant Idea Group/ China Film Co-Production Corp./ Different Digital Design Ltd./ Xian Mei Ah Culture Communication Ltd, and wr. by Chris Ng Ka-keung, Yeung Sin-ling, Wong Nga-man, Jingle

---

[40] Jingle Ma filmed several Jackie Chan movies, including *First Strike, Drunken Master 2* and *Rumble In the Bronx*.

Ma and Chan Po-chun.

Some of the cast and crew had worked with Tsui Hark (and Tony Ching) before – such as Xiong Xin-xin (here playing a tough *sifu* at the *dojo*, costume designer Bruce Yu, and Ti Lung from *A Better Tomorrow* and a zillion other Hong Kong movies). In the cast were Charlene Choi Cheuk-yin, Wu Chun, Hu Ge, Ti Lung, Harlem YuChing-hing, Li Qunqin and Xiong Xin-xin. Released: Oct 9, 2008. 102 mins.

The approach in the 2008 interpretation was in part a remake of the 1994 movie *The Lovers,* directed by Tsui Hark (the characterization of Zhu Yingtai, for example, clearly draws on the way the character was played by Charlie Yeung). Like *The Lovers*, *The Butterfly Lovers* mounted much of the story as lighthearted comedy (in the first half, before the tale becomes tragic), making much of the crossdressing of Yingtai (with the usual misunderstandings and embarrassments stemming from a girl dressing up as a guy).

Charlene Choi Cheuk-yin steals the 2008 movie as Zhu Yingtai – she plays Yingtai as Charlie Yeung performed the character – a naïve, vulnerable but plucky, young girl. Harlmen Yu as the herbalist (Teacher Herbal Head) provides solid support as a kindly guide for both Yingtai and Liang Shanbo. Choi appeared in another folktale 3 years later, *The Sorcerer and the White Snake* (2011), as Green Snake.

As you'd expect from a director who was (and still is) a cinematographer, *The Butterfly Lovers* looks wonderful: it features many camera techniques which photographers are fond of, such as mounting long scenes in two shots, and using selective focus to shift attention from one actor to another (in *The Butterfly Lovers,* several scenes are staged with both actors facing the camera, but with one actor with their back to the other).

As *The Butterfly Lovers* was a *wuxia pian* approach to the *Romeo and Juliet* legend, there were many action scenes – even though the story didn't quite need them, being at its heart a tale of tragic love. Thus Tony Ching was hired to stage some of his famous martial arts choreography – and Chingian choreography fits in perfectly with a romantic drama clad in period costumes.

The Butterfly Lovers is not a movie to fight – it's pointless trying to resist, or trying to turn it into a different movie. It's entertainment, and it's entertaining. Maybe it should have more of *this*, or less of *that*. Maybe it should be more lighthearted, or maybe it should be more dramatic. Maybe it shouldn't include so much action. Maybe it should've cast *this* actor instead of *that* one. Maybe – but you can always go and make your own version of the legend of Liang Shanbo and Zhu Yingtai, can't you?

The Butterfly Lovers is a confection, and you have to submit to it. *The Butterfly Lovers* is a handsome production, with some appealing actors and performances. The action sequences and swordplay are not essential, but they add some thrills and rapid pacing to the romance and the tragedy.

21

LOVE IN THE TIME OF TWILIGHT

Huayue Jiaqi

1995's *Love In the Time of Twilight* (great title!) was a sequel of sorts to *The Lovers* (Hong Kong cinema produces sequels often in the same year – no waiting 3 or 4 years (or 15 years) for them! And in this same year, 1995, Tsui also directed *The Chinese Feast* and *The Blade*! Did he ever sleep?!).

Love In the Time of Twilight (*Huayue Jiaqi* in Mandarin = *Flower Moon Wedding Day*), was directed by Tsui Hark, produced by Tsui for Era Pictures/ Golden Harvest/ Film Workshop, written by Tsui with Sharon Hui Sa-long and Roy Szeto Cheuk-hon. DP: Peter Pau. Action director: Yuen Bun. Released: Apl 13, 1995. 99 mins.

The two charming lovers were back – Charlie Yeung and Nicky Wu, supported by a marvellous ensemble of Chinese actors, many of them regulars in the Tsui Hark Circus, and many were regulars in the Hong Kong movie industry: Lau Shun, William Ho, Cheung Ting, Eric Kot, Peter Lai Bei Tak, Raymond Lee Wai Man and Wong Yat Fei, etc.

A sequel of sorts – because *Love In the Time of Twilight* is actually a different sort of film, in a different form, tho' it does retain some of the key elements of *The Lovers* (but switched around). So, yes, the sequel focusses on Charlie Yeung's character again (called Hung Yan Yan or So So), and we take her point-of-view in the proceedings (yes, this is another movie with a female lead, and it's that rare item, a comedy with a young woman in the main role). But the romance is very different: now Yan Yan and Kong Gai-wai[41] are bickering in 1930s, screwball comedy style (as soon as they meet), with Yan Yan insisting that she isn't really attracted to Kong at all (she works in her father's theatre, he works in a bank). Yes, there is a father figure (this time played by Lau Shun, who was the servant in *The Lovers*, and is one of Tsui Hark's favourite actors), whose daughter exasperates him, like the father in *Peking Opera Blues* (most of Tsui's female characters are father complex girls, for all the obvious reasons.

---
[41] Tsui gives the main character his own name (before he changed it).

And they are in most mainstream movies – for all the obvious reasons).

The form that *Love In the Time of Twilight* employs is a delightful and classy mixture – the romantic comedy is blended with parts of the backstage comedy (and the backstage musical), plus some Chinese ghost story elements (played largely for laughs), plus a time travel plot, and a doubles/ twins plot, and some melodrama. Lisa Morton sees *Love In the Time of Twilight* as a movie that crossbreeds *Ghost* (lovers) with *The Mask* (visual effects), a time travel adventure, and a gross-out comedy (LM, 205).

Set in the early 20th century, the background of *Love In the Time of Twilight* is a theatre and its players – so that *Love In the Time of Twilight* seems more a sequel to *Peking Opera Blues* than *The Lovers*. There is also a film studio in there, too – thus, *Love In the Time of Twilight* also comes across as a heightened, romanticized portrait of the Hong Kong film industry itself.

Wait – did I mention Peking Opera?! Once again, Tsui Hark and co. are filling the screen with busy-busy Peking Opera scenes: we're backstage at a Peking Opera theatre company, as in films such as *Peking Opera Blues* and *Once Upon a Time In China*, a realm where Tsui feels right at home. Tsui can't get enough of the actors with the elaborate headdresses and the rouged cheeks, the hustle and bustle of backstage life, the bitchy quips, and the out-size characters with their child-like demands. One imagines that Tsui is either a frustrated Peking Opera player himself, or he could have a second (or third or fourth) career directing Peking Opera revivals in Beijing).

The ghost story elements in *Love In the Time of Twilight* are a clever way of using the Butterfly Lovers mythology of *The Lovers* and updating it (with hints of reincarnation), plus some gender reversal (the typical Chinese ghost is usually female, appearing to the man, as in *A Chinese Ghost Story*). So the lover (Kong Gai-wai) dies, but doesn't – he comes back as a ghost, then the two of them are travelling back in time.

A surprising amount of *Love In the Time of Twilight* uses Chinese superstitions and customs – which Tsui Hark adores. Much of the first act of *Love In the Time of Twilight*, for example, takes place at a festival ('Affinity Day') where hopeful petitioners visit the match-maker temple, or see oracles, in order to conjure up a suitable lover. (It's as if Tsui is sneaking a documentary about Chinese superstitions and religious beliefs (related to the theme of 'seeking a mate') into each of his movies of this period. Tsui is such a ballsy director when it comes to including all sorts of odd bits of business in his movies – you can almost hear the film crew wondering, why the hell does he want us to do *that*? Yet it works, when it's edited (by Marco Mak) into the flow of images. There are times when you simply have to trust your director – and, as Tsui is a filmmaker of legendary status, that's easy to do).

On the Love Hong Kong Film website, a critic called 'Kozo' points out, *pace Love In the Time of Twilight*, that Tsui Hark plays by his own rules narratively:

He's an incredibly opaque storyteller, but he infuses his pictures with an energy and cinematic charm that's infectious and even beguiling. There's a creative energy to Tsui's cinema that's simultaneously quick to please, yet suddenly uncompromising. When watching a Tsui Hark film, it's clear that you're operating by his rules, and not some handbook for quickie box office hits.

The first act of *Love In the Time of Twilight* is Tsui Hark's cinema at its very best: light-hearted (nothing is taken too seriously or solemnly), very swift on its feet (the camera – like the actors – is everywhere), very colourful and child-like (the production design emphasizes rainbow hues), dazzlingly choreographed (the screen is teeming with action and extras), and pro-feminist (it takes Hung Yan Yan's point-of-view). As feminist, that is, as you can be in a movie set in early modern China! But there are numerous quips about finding a decent man, and how all of them are no good. They're all wolves, Yan Yan complains (women have probably complaining about that for, like, 100,000 years at least). Act one climaxes with the revelation that Kong Gai-wai has come back from the dead, when he appears (repeatedly) to Yan Yan (who avoids him until it's impossible).

And, yet again, Tsui Hark manages to get away with lovers acting like silly kids – pushing each other into water, getting covered in incense dust, stealing the other's seat, and generally horsing around. The 1995 movie relies quite a bit on the charisma of actress Charlie Yeung – but she really sells it, and the audience goes along with it (you can think of 1,000s of other actresses where this sort of of naïve foolery wouldn't work). Yeung is a great comic actress – and for a 21 year-old to carry a big, busy movie like this, that really is something. (Yeung's chemistry with Nicky Wu is terrific, too: they make a very fine comical couple).

Slapstick humour, toilet humour (vomit gags), screwball comedy exchanges of dialogue – *Love In the Time of Twilight* is like watching a wealth of comedies of Hollywood's golden age filtered through Chinese eyes and one of the strangest, visionary minds in contemporary cinema. Tsui Hark is happiest when he has a film studio stuffed with actors in period costume, some lightweight and silly action to shoot (lovers who irritate each other), two appealing leads (Charlie Yeung and Nicky Wu), and all of the toys of cinema to play with (with visual effects and lighting foregrounded).

A single act in a Tsui Hark movie has enough going on in it for a whole movie anywhere else – and the first act of *Love In the Time of Twilight* certainly is that. Don't try to track the narrative and the characters in great detail, don't try to work out who's who and catch their names and their relationships – just enjoy the dazzling, bubbling energy of this cinematic candy (when you start watching this film, you can't stop). If you think of Hong Kong the city, with its fast pace, its blazing neons, and its noisy, teeming streets, *Love In the Time of Twilight* makes perfect sense: it's a perfect date movie that you go to see in Kowloon on a Saturday night; it's as quick and disposable as a bowl of noodles (cheap! hot!), eaten at a stall on the street near the theatre, in amongst the crowds.

Tsui Hark's cinema has that form of entertainment cinema down to a 'T'. It's candy. It's popcorn. It's froth and bubbles. Tsui is a master showman, a Cecil B. DeMille or a D.W. Griffith of new Chinese film (but his narrative are *faster* than anything in those great, founding fathers of cinema. Indeed, Tsui has always worked very much in the tradition of the founding force of fantasy film – Géorges Méliès, who you can imagine enjoying Tsui's films at their throwaway, fluffy best).

In the second act of Love In the Time of Twilight, several fantasy elements are introduced big time: not only is there a ghost story (with Kong Gai-wai returning to haunt Hung Yan Yan), but also a time travel ingredient. Here, using the new fangled technology of electricity and light bulbs (yet another evocation of the old and the new and the modernization of China in Tsui's cinema), the lovers are able to go back in time to right wrongs (Kong was strangled with an electrical cable by mobster Devil King (William Ho), which links him to the lightbulb. A *lot* of comical mileage is squeezed out of the lightbulb being plugged in and switched on). This part of Love In the Time of Twilight resembles Western time travel comedies of the 1980s such as Peggy Sue Got Married and the biggie, Back To the Future[42] (and, like those comedies, Love In the Time of Twilight doesn't quite make sense if you think about it too much). As if all of this wasn't enough, writers Tsui, Sharon Hui Sa-long and Roy Szeto Cheuk-hon also include a doubles/twins motif, with Yan Yan and Kong encountering themselves numerous times.

There's also a crime subplot in The Lovers, in which mob lord Devil King uses Kong Gai-wai, who works at a bank, as an unsuspecting insider in a bank robbery. Devil King is one of those gangsters who kills his accomplices once he's got his mitts on the swag (so Kong is strangled by electrical wire in an alley). Yet another subplot in Love In the Time of Twilight involves the hapless fool Little Shrimp (Eric Kot) and his unrequited lerrrve for Yan Yan.

The middle acts of Love In the Time of Twilight are so convoluted, so intricately-woven, and so busy with bits of business, they are in the end rather over-stuffed. Much as Jean-Luc Godard complained about James Bond movies – why do they have to be so *complicated?* (so that even a simple A-to-B journey is filled with ultimately pointless details) – Love In the Time of Twilight creates a dazzling but also confusing and superfluous wealth of action: there's to-ing and fro-ing all over the theatre, the canal and the surrounding streets • there's hiding behind stage curtains • there's encountering one's double then hiding • there's asking the same question multiple times • there's Kong Gai-wai wearing a black mask so he won't be seen by his former self • and there's plenty of juggling with suitcases (of guns).

Needlessly complicated? Very. Tracking the action in Love In the Time of Twilight demands that the audience keep up and concentrate. The

---

[42] 'A half-baked Back To the Future rip-off' was Thomas Weisser's opinion (122).

form of the middle acts is essentially a farce[43] – a stagey farce, where characters're rushing about, trying to get here, to avoid that, to dodge this, to grab that. It *is* funny, even tho', inevitably, some of the jokes're lost in (cultural) translation.

Once again, altho' the media image of Tsui Hark is of a restless mind, a technically savvy and cinematically brilliant *auteur*, whose most well-known movies are historical martial arts epics (the *Once Upon a Time In China* films or *Zu: Warriors From the Magic Mountain*) or thrillers (*Time and Tide*), it is *comedy* that takes up a significant proportion of Tsui's output. Comedy – with farce as a fundamental form. Even the films with a more 'serious' content, such as *Peking Opera Blues* or *The Master* or *Time and Tide*, have plenty of farcical moments, where characters are hurrying about and bumping into each other in a comical manner.

So, in *Love In the Time of Twilight*, as in *Twin Dragons* of three years earlier, Hung Yan Yan and Kong Gai-wai spend a lot of time encountering their doubles, with the expected amusing results. Charlie Yeung's comic timing meshes with the Tsui Hark machine gun editing (the movie, as with *The Lovers,* relishes Yeung's considerable talents as a comedienne).

2∙

The finale of *Love In the Time of Twilight* ups the ante with some broad action and supernatural events – the visual effects are coming as thick and fast as the stunts, the rushing around, and the camera bowling in for yet another close-up of an agonized character.

Love In the Time of Twilight is a giant visual effects movie, containing the full arsenal of visual effects that Tsui Hark celebrates throughout his career. Added to the vast battery of physical and in-front-of-camera effects are new digital effects (with digital[44] distortions and faces and bodies similar to those in *The Mask*, the 1994 Jim Carrey vehicle, which it seems to consciously evoke).[45]

Love In the Time of Twilight becomes very cartoony in its finale, with long, extendible arms grasping throats, doubles crashing into each other, and Hung Yan Yan and Kong Gai-wai winding up in a scary netherworld where all is topsy-turvy *à la Alice's Adventures In Wonderland* (one of the best scenes has Yan Yan losing her mouth and hand when she moves too quickly).[46]

2∙

The secret ingredient that's withheld, after Hung Yan Yan and Kong Gai-wai have tried everything they can think of, is of course lerrrve. Saved 'til last, the romance blossoming into an affirmation of love, and that longest two weeks ever is melted away in a kiss.

Love In the Time of Twilight is indeed a romantic fantasy comedy which enshrines love as one of the ultimate experiences, and one of the

---

[43] As with many Tsui Hark films – *Shanghai Blues, All the Wrong Clues, A Chinese Ghost Story*, etc.
[44] Cinefex employ a FLINT system for the first time, which allowed for digital compositing in real time.
[45] Though millions of dollars cheaper than the vfx of Industrial Light & Magic, which pushed up the budget of *The Mask* considerably, much to New Line Cinema's dismay.
[46] 'The limbo scenes are stunningly surreal, easily the equal of anything in the work of Luis Buñuel or David Lynch' (LM, 205).

foundations of life. For all his postmodern creative moves, his cultural, transnational/ multi-national sophistication, and his status as a genius *auteur* of the contemporary era, Tsui Hark is an old softie at heart. His movies often put love forward as an absolutely primary force.

Is that simply because Tsui Hark wants to sell tickets, and is giving the audience 'what they want'? That he reckons that audiences hanker after love stories? Partly – after all, Tsui is a filmmaker *acutely* conscious of the need to make money in order to survive and to produce more movies. And, yes, love relationships are at the core of cinema (as Jean-Luc Godard pointed out). And, yes, erotic stories have been part of literature and storytelling since, like, forever.

But there is more to it than that: Tsui Hark doesn't 'need' to have directed and produced so many love stories in his career (some directors *never* do that, and always relegate love and romance to the subplots). But he does.

Twin Dragons (1992).

Green Snake (1993).

The Lovers (1994).

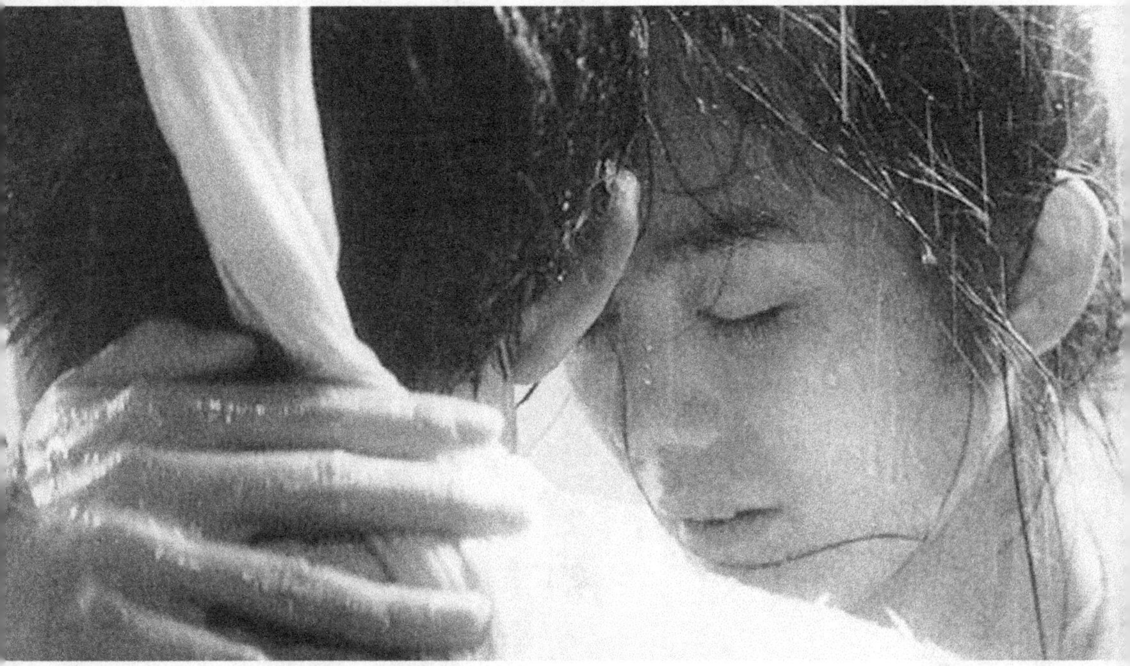

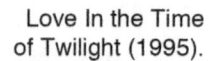

Love In the Time of Twilight (1995).

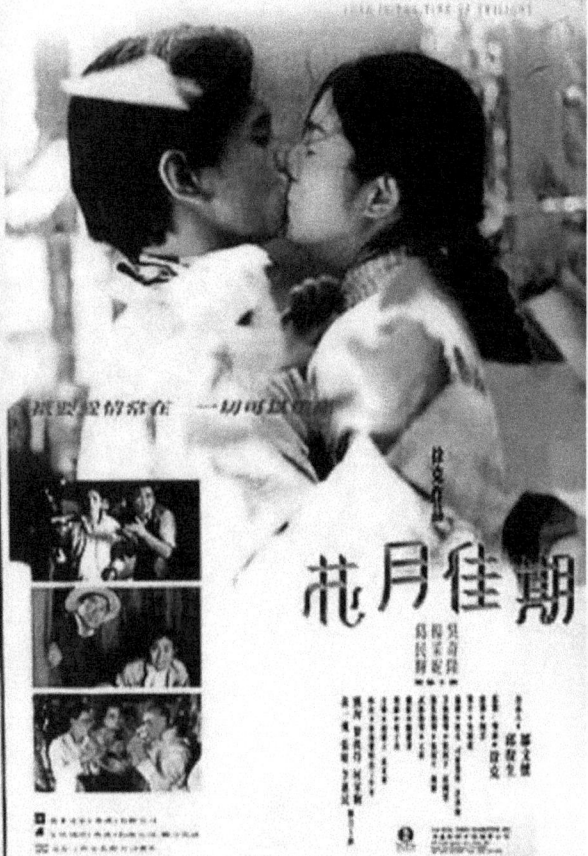

22

THE BLADE

Diy

INTRO.

The Blade (*Dao* in Mandarin, 1995) is a New Wave of Hong Kong cinema production, made towards the end of the New Wave era of the mid-Nineties, and helmed by the superstar director of the New Wave period, Tsui Hark. Vincent Zhao (a.k.a. Zhao Wenzhou, a.k.a. Chin Man Chuek) stars (he played Wong Fei-hung in the *Once Upon a Time In China* series after Jet Li left), along with Xiong Xin-xin, Song Lei, Moses Chan, Austin Wai, Chung Bik-ha, Michael Tse, Chan Wing-chung, Chin Tsi-ang, Suet Nei and Valerie Chow.

Tsui Hark produced with Raymond Chow for Paragon Films/ Film Workshop;[1] co-writers with Tsui were Hui Nyn (Koan Hui On) and Siu Man-sing; Gam Sing and Venus Keung were DPs; William Cheung, Bill Lui and Yau Wai-ming were art directors; Gam Ma was editor (with Tsui); Woo Wai-laap and Wong Ying-wah composed the score; action choreographers were Yuen Bun, Mang Hoi, Xiong Xin-xin and Stephen Tung. Category IIB. Released Dec 21, 1995. 101 minutes.

The Blade:
Wow!
One word sums it up:
Intense.
The Blade rocks, big time, from the opening frames onwards.

The feeling for texture, for atmosphere, for light, for colour, for movement, for costume, for make-up, for music, for sound – *The Blade* is just marvellous. It's a 100% authentic slice of *cinema*. Not filmed theatre (which's most movies), not filmed radio (most movies), not a movie version of a TV show (most movies), but *pure, 100% cinema.*

Pure cinema in the sense of the poetry of cinema. Yes, in the sense of

---

[1] Part of *The Blade* was filmed at a studio Tsui Hark had in the New Territories (tho' later the authorities said they couldn't use the land as a studio).

the poetry of cinema of Pier Palo Pasolini[2] (he would *love* Tsui Hark's movies!), Jean Cocteau (probably a tad *too* violent for Cocteau!), or Orson Welles (Welles would admire the rapid cutting: he hated s-l-o-w movies! As for the camerawork in *The Blade*, it truly is Wellesian).

Orson Welles and Tsui Hark: why not? Of the many filmmakers who're compared with Welles, Tsui is one of the *very few* who can properly and justly be placed beside the towering giant of cinema that is Welles. Just look at the way that Tsui stages scenes, or uses the camera,[3] or employs music and sound, or deploys editing! (And critics such as Lisa Morton have compared Welles' début movie with Tsui's, *The Butterfly Murders*, as an example of an impressive first film).

It's an *astonishingly* sensual and visceral form of cinema. The feeling for sensuality, for atmospheres and textures, for instance, is one of the most impressive elements (among 100s) of Tsui Hark's cinema. The movies he directs are filled with flickering flames and billowing smoke, with saturated reds and blues, with a heightened sense of dirt, skin, water, and light (purely photographically, Tsui's films are the equal of any of the great directors of light, from Erich von Stroheim and F.W. Murnau to Steven Spielberg and Hayao Miyazaki).

Tsui Hark knows that one of cinema's most appealing aspects is to create a whole world, and to entice the viewer into that world. There is no *distance*: the camera that's wielded (by DPs Venus Keung and Gam Sing) puts the audience right into this fictional world, and right up against the actors.

This is down-and-dirty, in-your-face filmmaking: the audience is right there, in amongst the actors (with so much wild handheld work, there must be outtakes in every Chinese action movie where actors are being whacked by the camera, or camera operators are tripping over the actors).

> ...in *The Blade*, I tried to do something authentic or realistic in a way; less shots with supernatural movements like jumping off the ground to an exaggerated height. (2011)

That's only partially true, because in *The Blade* the camera is flying high above the roofs, to crane down rapidly into a fight.

In a Tsui Hark movie or a Chinese action movie, you don't stand back and film the drama with a long lens (which happens so often in Western and Hollywood movies): you are right there, on the set, two inches from the actor's face with a wide angle lens.

The Blade is thus passionately visceral filmmaking, and it's fearless. Tsui Hark encourages the production team to try anything, to see if it works. You get the impression very strongly that ideas are cooked up on the spur of the moment on a Tsui movie, and tried there and then. It's filmmaking at fever pitch. It's gutsy. It's ballsy. It's wild!

---

[2] Certainly the costumes and the look of *The Blade* evoke several Pasolini movies, including his famous 'trilogy of life' films (where the chunky, textured, flamboyant and earthy costumes were designed by the remarkable Danilo Donati).
[3] The boom shots are worthy of Welles – a director who created some of cinema's great crane shots.

Let's try anything! – like, during the lengthy nighttime confrontations in the bamboo structure, as On tries to defend Ling against countless henchmen, the hero's rolling on the ground, grappling a guy. And the camera rolls with him, over and over. It's mad!

The camera is fixed to the actors in some shots, in others they are riding a dolly with the camera, in others the camera's pulled along the ground behind an actor (how many cameras did the production smash in this movie?! Don't rent out a camera to Tsui Hark – you'll never get it back in one piece!).[4]

You know what you're going to see in a swordplay movie, in a genre movie, in a Chinese action movie – yes, story-wise, that is true (in the main). But you *don't know* what Tsui Hark and the team are going to try in telling that story! They are going to give you crane shots swooping over roofs for seconds before they tilt down to reveal the fighting on the crowded streets below. They are going to give you scenes dimming down to near-darkness, and expect you to follow the story (and you can!). And they are going to cut the movie at a cracking pace, even while they keep the story fresh and lively, and the storytelling clear.

'You're not fast enough!'

taunts the hero to Flying Dragon in *The Blade* (reversing the taunt that Flying Dragon hurls at opponents); the challenge certainly applies to Tsui Hark's cinema!

▶

Howard Hampton wrote that *The Blade* 'reinvents the sword-opera as a pageant of grim, crazed hunger for sex and revenge'.[5]

However, altho' a masterpiece, *The Blade* did not fare well on local turf. The lack of success of *The Blade* may have been its timing: it was released after the wave of *kung fu* movies was nearly over (*Drunken Master 2*, of 1994, is regarded as one of the last successes of the cycle). Vincent Zhao, while superb, doesn't quite have the marquee value of Jet Li (or Donnie Yen). But altho' Zhao isn't everybody's favourite Hong Kong star, and he can be rather wooden in dramatic scenes, there's no doubting his committment to this production, where he's smashed about, burnt, drenched and hung upside-down. It is a *very* physical role, very demanding, the sort of part you can only play if you are very fit (and very patient – these incredible effects take a long time to set up and deliver).

Tsui Hark acknowledged that lack of star power may be one reason for *The Blade*'s poor performance (in Hong Kong, at least). And he realized that the approach was again, as in his early films, probably too savage for many viewers.

It's probable that Jet Li would've starred as the one-armed swordsman, but he and Golden Harvest fell out over the *Once Upon a Time In China* movies. Indeed, the star of *The Blade*, Vincent Zhao, stepped in to play Wong Fei-hung in the *Once Upon a Time In China* series. (One can't

---

4 Or to Werner Herzog – you won't get it back at all! Herzog famously 'borrowed' a film camera from the Munich Institute for Film Research. 'Under these circumstances,' Herzog said, 'I think it was right to appropriate the means of production' (in T. Elsaesser. *New German Cinema: A History*, Macmillan, London, 1989, 91).
5 Quoted in F. Dannen, 340.

help noticing that the villain in *The Blade*, Fei Lung, resembles Jet Li, as if Tsui's having a sly dig at his star. Actually, no[6] – because Tsui worked with Li on *Black Mask*, a 1996 sci-fi actioner, not longer after *The Blade*, and the villain is played by Li's regular stunt double, Xiong Xin-xin).

TECHNICAL ASPECTS.

The costume, hair and make-up design in *The Blade* is outstanding: it creates a thoroughly convincing pre-modern China that might also be any period in history from 10,000 years ago to the 20th century. The make-up includes scars, tattoos, dirt and blood for seemingly every actor, and chunky jewellery; the clothing features fabrics that're thick and rough; the sets are wood, bamboo, irregular, with trimmings in red or blue for hangings.

China? Maybe – as Stephen Teo wrote of *The Blade*:

Tsui gives us a vision of China that has never looked so multicultural or so alien to the mythical conception of a homogeneous Han China most often depicted in the genre. (1998, 145).

Indeed, this is the mythical martial arts world that never existed in the first place taken even further into prehistoric myth. The costumes include elements from the Middle East, from Central Asia, and from Africa (as well as China). Altho' the historical era is meant to be the late 19th century, there are consciously few attributes of that epoch. No electricity, no electric lamps, no modern gadgets like clocks or watches, no trains, no horse carriages, and none of the Western artefacts that were celebrated in the *Once Upon a Time In China* movies.

Another technical aspect immediately pops out of *The Blade*: the music (by Woo Wai-laap and Wong Ying-wah) is no longer the swishy, plangent, traditional Chinese singing that Tsui Hark often favours for historical stories. Instead, it's back to the scores of his early films, aided by an extensive use of percussion. (Again, it seems as if Tsui and co. have gone in the *opposite direction* from historical movies such as *Once Upon a Time In China* and *The Lovers*, which they'd recently made).

The Blade certainly comes across as a self-conscious antidote to the kind of swordplay pictures that Tsui Hark and co. had been making[7] – from the fantasy of the *Swordsman* series or the supernatural whimsy and quaint horror of the *Chinese Ghost Story* series. And *The Blade* is the flipside of the *Once Upon a Time In China* cycle, the brutish, ugly side of patriarchal hierarchies: there are no genteel discussions about Western medicine vs. Chinese acupuncture here!

And yet, at the same time, *The Blade* is also purveying *exactly the same stuff* we've already seen in *Once Upon a Time In China, The Swordsman, A Chinese Ghost Story*, etc. What's different is the degree of bitterness, of cynicism, of brutality, and the filmmaking style is a

---

[6] The disagreement was with the Golden Harvest studio.
[7] The aim with *The Blade* was to produce a new sort of *wuxia pian*, a film with an earthy, *verité* look.

conscious departure from the sweet prettiness of many previous swordplay flix.

Tsui Hark didn't want wires in *The Blade*, he wanted action that was achievable by actors without assistance or special effects. Yes, but there are still 100s of practical effects in *The Blade*, and the trickery of cinema – editing, sound, camera angles, etc – is simply another sort of trick from wires.

Tsui Hark returned to some of the style of *The Blade* in *Seven Swords*, but with a much bigger budget, that allowed him to stage bandits in the mountains on a larger scale. but it's the same rough-and-ready approach.

The Blade begins with an almost documentary approach to the portrayal of the *jiangzhu*, the martial arts world. Instead of the grand, formal shots to depict epic, Chinese vistas, we are in close with shaky shots of bandits in the dust and a girl looking out from a workroom. Instantly, *The Blade* announces a radical stylistic departure from the traditional *wuxia pian*.

Every scene has smoke billowing through it. The wind is always blowing across the actors' costume and hair. Fires are flickering outside and inside. It is a totally convincing reality, the polar opposite of the Hollywood approach, where glossy, slick visuals do little to persuade the audience that these characters really live in those places.

The Blade's editing style, coupled with the photographic style, represents a search for a new approach to staging action in a swordplay picture. The cuts are not always clean, they don't always match, the editors include parts of shots that most editors would automatically leave out, the cuts don't come in at the beginning of a camera move, or where one would normally expect them.

Nothing new here, of course – cinema had already done this in the 1910s and 1920s. But when it's coupled with such high speed in the performance (and really aggressive, fierce fighting), and so many different styles in the camerawork (running from formal crane shots to handheld shots), plus numerous editing effects (freeze frames, washes to red or white), it has a terrific, visceral impact.

The Blade was a tough shoot – there were problems with Vincent Zhao; he fell in love with Anita Mui (not difficult to do!), and Tsui Hark found Zhao distracted and too busy pursuing his personal life.

CINEMATIC ALLUSIONS.

The Blade evokes numerous movies: obvious references are revisionist cowboy pictures of the 1960s onwards, which emphasized the violence simmering underneath the old, mythical West (from the *Fistful of Dollars* films and Sam Peckinpah's Westerns onwards). *The Blade* has the same dusty, earthy texture, the gung-ho bandits, the internecine warfare between clans or groups, and the desperate urge towards survival at all costs.

Spartacus might be another reference – the tough regime of the Sharp

Factory, with its oiled, half-naked men and its air of rebellion have affinities with *Spartacus* and similar, Greek and Roman-themed films.

'In the end, *The Blade* may be as much a tribute to Tsui's idol Akira Kurosawa as to any of the Chinese filmmakers', remarked Lisa Morton (LM, 125). Absolutely: many scenes are pure Kurosawa: the fights at night in the rain (plus copious amounts of fire, smoke, fog, mud, and other textures); the evocation of a rough-and-ready martial arts world; the fiercely-enforced patriarchal structure of the Sharp Factory; the siege on the foundry by the bandits; women as victims who are caught up in the struggles of men, etc. It's clear that Tsui Hark and the team were thinking of Kurosawa's masterpieces such as *The Seven Samurai, Yojimbo* and *The Hidden Fortress*. Indeed, the follow-up to *The Blade, Seven Swords*, is itself in part a reworking of *The Seven Samurai*.

THE STORY.

There are three main characters in *The Blade*:

On Man (Vincent Zhao)

Iron Head (Moses Chan)

Siu Ling or Blackie (Song Lei)

The world of *The Blade* is the late 19th century: it's a patriarchal world which has its harsh aspects. Apart from Ling (Song Lei) and the grandmother figure (Chin Tsi-ang), this is a boysy movie. A brotherhood movie. A fathers-and-sons movie. These are staples of the action movie genre, and especially of the Chinese action genre (where the brotherhood issues of loyalty, devotion to the gang or family, are absolutely paramount).

Thus, in *The Blade*, Iron Head (Moses Chan) and On Man (Vincent Zhao) are the brothers at the centre of the story. They work for the stern patriarch the Master (Austin Wai) in a sword-making factory (cue plenty of sweaty, naked torsos as the guys hammer weaponry at anvils).

Both Chan and Zhao are playing below their age – they seem meant to be about 18 or 19. Meanwhile, Flying Dragon (played by Xiong Xin-xin) hasn't aged much in the 20 or so years since the back-story.

The Blade opens with several twists on the conventional martial arts or swordplay movie. Firstly, the 1995 movie is narrated not by On Man, the obvious choice, but by Ling. So, we're in a very macho realm, of tough guys being tough guys, and who is our observer and narrator figure? A young girl. That automatically sets *The Blade* apart from most *wuxia* flicks.

Secondly, we are considering the main character, On Man, from the perspective of Ling; so that, even tho' Ling has far less agency within this particular world (there is no question whatsoever that this is a brutal and very patriarchal realm, and that women are most definitely second class citizens), she is raised from the role of observer figure and narrator to a participant. True, Ling still plays the Princess Who Must Be Rescued (as in the finale to act one), but is also a woman who acts on her desire (rather naïvely at times – as when she brings soup to both Iron Head and On Man. Ling's grandmother points out that it won't work).

Thirdly, we are often looking with Ling at the men in the sword foundry (peeping thru wooden slats): it's a woman looking at men with sexual desire, which objectifies them (reversing the usual network of looks in cinema). Ling is depicted spying on the men bathing naked; it's the male body, not the female, that's on display here. (Within her dark room, Ling is like a fairy tale character from the West – the princess in the tower who weaves with an old crone, who looks longingly out at the world. Ling's position echoes that of Zhu Yingtai in *The Lovers* of the year before).

A later scene in *The Blade* has Iron Head capturing a prostitute and Ling, and having his wicked way with the hooker (Ling explodes in indignation). Tsui Hark's movies are never shy of depicting how men exploit women, often sexually. In his Category IIB ('R' rated) movies, there are often whores, and men who use whores: in Tsui's cinema, prostitutes are treated roughly by men, including being beaten. It's not pretty: in fact, it's very nasty. But it's not gratuitous: this is not sleazy exploitation cinema (there is some nudity, for instance, but no full-body nudity). It's about how patriarchal societies enshrine the exploitation of women as sex objects. In his movies, Tsui is keen to depict the brutal aspects of the worlds he and his teams have created. (The prostitute informs Ling of how men really are: she has a thoroughly *un*romantic, practical view of how life is).

The homoeroticism that runs underneath *The Blade* hardly needs to mentioned, it's so in-your-face. For Barry Long, *The Blade* was 'the most homoerotic film to come from Hong Kong', with the perspective being that of a woman so that the male body 'becomes pure spectacle'.[8] Yet it is not the veiled homoeroticism of the brotherhood movies helmed by John Woo, it's clear to see. (Thus, *The Blade* is a sort of counterpoint to films like *Green Snake*, which had foregrounded women together with eroticized, lesbian scenes).

NEW BRUTALITY.

It's a film where characters scream in rage in huge close-ups.

It's a film where shiny, new blades tinkle in close-up (repeatedly), ready to be grabbed and stuck in the nearest hunk of flesh.

The Blade is a movie where life is cheap – no, it's worth nothing. The bestial logic runs thus: if you can stand, you can wield a sword. If you can wield a sword, you can kill. Indeed, you *must* kill. Not 'kill or be killed', but killing for the sheer hell of it.

Fei Lung and other characters spout the bleakest of views: that humans are animals, they're pigs, they're worthless. Thus, they can be killed and skinned and hung up like slabs of meat (which's what happens to On Man's father Fong Lai, and to On).

This is beyond even Nazism – it's not about cleansing the German nation of racial impurities, or of other religious and ethnic groups, such as Jews – it's a murderous, cannibalistic outlook which reduces humans to pigs and meat.

---

[8] Quoted in F. Dannen, 364.

The Blade depicts one of those worlds where nobody's happy, where everyone's looking for a fight, where nowhere is safe, where thugs roam the lands, where everyone's a thief, a bandit, a gangster, a warlord, a bully, a merchant struggling to get by, or one of the victims.9 If you haven't got any money you're rudely shoved out of the store. And when one group of bandits or misfits is left behind, the narrative simply invents a new one. (Thus, there are several bandit collectives, and wherever the three characters travel, they run into them).

The brutality of the world in *The Blade* is harsh and in-your-face. There are many vicious, bloody fights. There are scenes where the patriarch of the Sharp Foundry, the Master, whips his workers. They line up, bare their asses, and the Master repeatedly beats them until he draws blood, while he lectures them. The scene goes on and on! On Man complains, but is yelled at and told to kneel, while Iron Head struggles to refuse to give the Master the pleasure of seeing him wilt.

The world of *The Blade* is so savage it goes beyond those post-apocalyptic dystopias, where everybody is a potential enemy, and bandits roam the land, as the *Road Warrior* or *Escape To* or *Terminator* movies.

Raping, pillaging and looting – it's Viking Time, it's Pirate Time.

From the outset of *The Blade*, it's obvious that Tsui Hark has gone back to the approach of his early movies, in particular the cruel worlds of *We're Going To Eat You* and *Dangerous Encounter – 1st Kind* (Wan Chu from *Dangerous Encounter* and the cannibals from *We're Going To Eat You* would be right at home in the *milieu* of *The Blade*).

ACT ONE.

The first act of *The Blade* is remarkable in many respects: the storytelling is at 1,000 miles-per-hour, the look and the texture is dazzling, the lighting and colour is a ravishing mix of hot colours, the world is violent and earthy, there are several incredible action sequences, and of all of the technical elements, it is once again the *editing* that impresses most of all.

The first act of *The Blade* is very long for a Tsui Hark movie – 36 minutes. We know that Tsui likes to jam the first acts of his films to the brim, and this one contains a welter of information. Unusually also for a Tsui Hark movie, there is a ton of back-story played out in the first act (concerning On Man and his father Fong Lai and the Master) – all of this will pay off in the climax.

The motif of the mantrap is introduced in the first minute of *The Blade* – with Ling telling us that if you want something, you have be will to pay the price. The motif is illustrated with the bandits laying a trap of meat for a dog. The dog can't resist, and SNAP! goes the trap. The scene (covered with glimpses thru long lenses), neatly alerts the audience to several things: this is a brutal world; everyone is in a trap; and no one will be spared, because even dogs – yes, dogs! the most beloved of all animals on the silver screen! – will be sacrificed (we know that in the hierarchy of dramatic logic concerning death and sacrifice in movies, you can kill any

9 Putting Ling, an innocent and naïve girl, into this violent world creates an enormous contrast.

number of henchmen, but never a dawg!).

By the end of act one, both Ling and On Man have been caught in man-traps. The motif explains how On loses his arm, in a very graphic sequence.

From the man-trap and dog sequence, the 1995 film rapidly introduces the dusty, tough *jiangzhu,* and also the harsh, patriarchal world of the Sword Factory, the two rivals (Iron Head and On Man), Ling as a dreamer in a man's world, and includes the first big action sequence: the monk (Chan Wing-chung) taking on all comers as he saves a young woman being menaced by the bandits. The scene, which comes after the mandatory Bustling Market Scene in every historical movie (including all of Tsui Hark's films), also introduces us to the new style of action developed for *The Blade*: gone are the carefully rehearsed combinations of camera and stunt/ movement; now we have the cameras capturing the action (still well-rehearsed, of course) in a much looser fashion. And it's the *editing* that really sells the new approach to action: instead of neat cuts, there are many abrupt cuts, and cuts which don't match.

The action scene in the village also demonstrates that even a great warrior like the monk (who pounds every bandit into submission, and seems invincible), will not be safe in this cruel world: the dog was killed in the man-trap, and so is the monk. In a back street, the bandits gang up on him, and the monk is attacked, beaten and later beheaded. Usually this sort of character, particularly in the martial arts and swordplay movies that preceded it in 1995, isn't killed, and in such a gruesome fashion. (However, this act does galvanize Iron Head and the lads at the Sharp Factory, even after the Master has berated them and whipped them.)

Act one of *The Blade* includes a lengthy dive into On Man's ancestry: now we see he's on a father quest, and beginning the search for the identity of his father Fong Lai. The back-story includes a fierce smackdown in pouring rain at night, where the Master and On's father Fong Lai take on the man with the tattoos, Fei Lung. We see how incredible the villain is, and we see On as a baby being protected.

Back in the present tense, the scene between the Master and On Man is played at a similarly hysterical level: there's a thunderstorm, lightning flashes, and On Man loudly demands that the Master tell him about his father Fong Lai.

The scene introduces the audience to another key factor in *The Blade*: performances are going to be *loud,* and *wild,* and *hysterical!* The youth and the patriarch could perform this scene sitting down for a quiet cup of tea (as Wong Fei-hung might do): but no! not here! The scene involves two actors yelling at each other, while lightning flashes, thunder rumbles, and shadows flicker.

ACT TWO.

Tumbling over a cliff into an abyss, On Man is given up for dead (yet there are scenes where the Sharp Foundry pays its respects to On Man, and the Master too prays in vain). Act two takes our hero into another world: it's the mythical descent and return of the hero of Joseph Campbell and his Jungian acolytes. Using subjective camerawork, On Man is nursed back to life by an unlikely saviour.

In every way, On Man is not having a great time: he's lost his arm (and rages mightily at its loss). Now he's an outcast, following the calamitous confrontation with the bandits. He recovers in the remote rural home of Siu Ling (a.k.a. Blackie), a damaged, nervy, near-hysterical soul herself (a brilliant, kinetic performance by Chung Bik-ha). That the hero is tended back to life by someone who's equally wounded or just plain strange is part of the action-adventure genre (typically it's a wizard or shaman figure, in Chinese martial arts. Not here – the Buddhist monk was decapitated in the first reel!).

On Man works in a restaurant, where the patrons demean him. Here he sees Iron Head and Siu Ling passing thru town, but opts to hide instead; and when Flying Dragon rolls through town, On Man is determined to take him on, but we know that this has to be delayed.

Every scene in *The Blade* seems to be played at a pitch of operatic intensity. Scenes that would be simple two-handers in other movies are in *The Blade* filled with anxiety and movement. For ex, many scenes involving On Man and Blackie are fraught with fractious, bickering behaviour, snarls and grimaces, and lots of physical acting, where the performers are grappling each other, so that a simple conversation between two actors is turned into a life-and-death tussle.

Here's another example: when Iron Head visits Siu Ling, to ask her if she would accompany him to search for On Man (at the start of act two), the scene's played like a rape scenario, with Ling backing off and Iron Head looming towards her, so she grabs a sword and scurries to the other side of the room. Meanwhile, to emphasize the desperation, the camera tracks rapidly to follow the movement of the actors.

Actors adore this sort of performance style – it's a million miles away from the usual style of most drama and nearly all television: actors standing around reciting their lines. In Tsui Hark's films, and in Hong Kong cinema in general, the performance style includes imaginative staging and blocking, physical acting, and of course Peking Opera moves. There's no need for subtitles often, because the dialogue only carries a small part of the dramatic impact.

In a chaotic, sprawling brothel and carousing scene, brilliantly staged, a prostitute is threatened and manhandled by a thug (while Iron Head looks on from a balcony, becoming more and more outraged, until he leaps into action, starting yet another brawl. In *The Blade*, everybody is busting for a fight, and they need the slightest provocation). Meanwhile, Siu Ling hides in her room, terrified (yes, it is a little artificial that Ling would accompany Iron Head on this venture – the Master or her grandmother wouldn't allow it).

During a nighttime raid, a bunch of bandits set fire to Blackie's house, hang On upside-down[10] and beat him with flaming torches. And the music

---

10 The motif reprises the disturbing image of his father, naked, upside-down and dead.

is pounding throughout the scene, enhancing its savagery and anti-humanity. At the close of the scene, with the whole building exploding in flames, the soundtrack becomes a rhythmic, smashing thud, which sounds like a demon pounding on the side of a warship with a Thor-sized hammer.

The raid and torture of On Man, which climaxes act two, is narratively simply a repetition of the climax of act one (even down to the inclusion of a young, female character that needs to be protected). This is thus another injustice that On Man experiences and needs to pay back (which he does).

And, to show just how nasty this new set of villains are, we see them portrayed as ruthless gangsters demanding protection money. And when the local villagers can't come up with the coins, what do these guys do? Slaughter them all!, in another scene of widespread devastation, again caught in rapid dolly shots as everybody flees for their lives and is mercilessly cut down.

It's another example of pointless barbarity in *The Blade* – the massacre serves no purpose (other than perhaps looting). If you want to extort money and resources from people, you keep them alive! You don't kill them all! (Some of the women are roped together and retained, however).

In *The Blade*, the *jiangzhu* is at its most lawless and degenerate – as gangs terrorize the world, everything boils down to the basest of desires and needs: hunger, money, sex, power, violence. Instant gratification – victims are beaten for the fun of it, not only because humans are vile freaks, but just because it's possible.

No wonder, then, that the consequence of the homestead raid is that On Man decides he's going to do something. Well, he *is* the hero, after all. After another nervy, bitter scene between Blackie and On Man (where the *kung fu* book is discovered), we shift into the lengthy training sequence, one of the recurring ingredients in the martial arts genre. Here, On learns how to wield the special sword from the Sharp Foundry (dug up from his father's grave) with one hand (using a spinning and leaping technique). Which sets us up for the third act.

ACT THREE.

So when the bandits return to attack the re-built house again, On Man is ready for them. He tells Blackie to hide herself (which she does – like an animal, in a hole in the ground!), then sets about taking on an entire troupe of bad guys on horseback on his own. What an action scene! Filmed at night (with the mandatory flames and smoke), plus flashes of lightning, and in slushy mud (it looks like it was an absolute nightmare to shoot), it is a crunching, full-on slice of Chinese action and swordplay. The speed of the edits, the rapidity of the action, the inventiveness of the outstanding work of the stunt co-ordinators and choreographers and the recklessness of the stunt team as they throw themselves into the fray, are all marvellous to behold. This is down-and-dirty fighting: a real, palpable, dragon-like energy is whipped up in the combination of the spinning, hurling technique that On employs, the slashing of the sword, and the numerous variations on falls, injuries and deaths that the brigands undergo. The bandits' commander is nobbled by being kicked headfirst into mud that seems to swallow him up. The image of On Man in the midst of horses and warriors, spinning, cutting down beasts as well as men, is truly remarkable.

It's stupendous. It's the kind of scene that only Chinese action cinema can deliver. And yet, this sequence is topped in the finale! Hard to believe, but the climax of *The Blade* goes beyond this nighttime siege, to create a scene of extraordinary aggression and violence.

Before the final smackdown, which has been advertized in neon throughout the movie (the groundwork was laid in the back-story sequence halfway thru *The Blade*'s first act), there are further action sequences (tho' what we've seen already would be plenty for any action movie, and certainly enough to satisfy the demands of the narrative).

First, On Man and Blackie opt to leave her birthplace in the wilds, and to travel the *jiangzhu* (in an ironic moment, they leave just as the locals have gathered to pay their respects to the hero who vanquished the black-clothed bandits).

They end up in the basement of the same hotel where Siu Ling has been tied up with the prostitute. Yes, the subplot of Ling and Iron Head on their own journey takes a bizarre and alarming turn when Iron Head decides that his idea of rescuing a woman and loving her is to tie her up while he goes to get cleaned up! (This is after the tussle with more no-goods). It's another scene played at near-hysteria by all three actors (Valerie Chow, Moses Chan and Song Lei), and again set in a shadowy, wooden room lit by candles and what might be the fires of Hell (which turn up shortly after this!).

Everyone's yelling at everyone else, and the hooker laughs in despair. Iron Head tups the prostitute, which infuriates Siu Ling so much she hurls herself at him. So he ties both women up (Iron Head is an almost Mel Brooksian send-up of a Stone Age, very stupid man frfom *A History of the World*).

Not dramatic enough for you? How about *another* raid by sword-wielding, teeth-gnashing, be-masked bandits? How about another bout of louts rushing in to snatch the women and beat up the men? The collateral damage in this fevered ruckus is the prostitute, slashed – with heavy irony – by On Man in the basement, thinking she is another assailant.

Masking himself, like the bandits (and like *Black Mask* the following year), On Man sets about the thugs, and is revealed to both Iron Head and Siu Ling. In a classic piece of Existential philosophy, or Oriental nihilism, On Man regards himself as a 'no man', damaged, wounded, not whole anymore; his identity has been burned away, perhaps, by too much suffering. And so he disappears (with Ling, another bruised soul).[11]

Prior to the unique, apocalyptic duel, there is a raid on the Sharp Foundry, which brings together all of the main characters. It's a mini siege of Troy, with the bandits tricking their way inside (previously, a scene

---

[11] The scene is significant narratively, because it helps to explain how On Man shows up at the Sharp Factory in the finale.

featured Flying Dragon and the commander of the bandits discussed eliminating the regime at the foundry). One of the men climbs down a rope to check that the group of seemingly injured men (plus Uncle Wah – Szema Wah Lung) are unarmed. Well, they don't need to bring weapons: an unmotivated tracking shot reveals gleaming, new weapons on display in the factory).

Once inside, it is pure Hell. The sequence is striking for its bone-crunching vehemence and its blood. This is 'R' rated material, with the participants soaked in blood by the end of it (every participant has blood sloshed all over them – the white shirts are drenched in it).

And look at the displays of anger and emotion: nobody does *rage* like the Chinese in their action movies! Every actor and extra in *The Blade* seems infused with fury – of betrayal, of righteousness, of injustice. This has always struck me about Chinese action movies (you see it also in Japanese *animé* and *manga*): how the characters are consumed by absolute outrage. In a Chinese action movie, characters go from calm to fury in 0.2 seconds. There is no in-between! They are either calm as Buddhas underneath the bo tree, or they are drawing their swords and glaring at their opponents (or, in *The Blade*, swinging them wildly and chop-chop-chopping!).

The finale of *The Blade* is played at fever pitch, as arch villain Fei Lung, a.k.a. Flying Dragon (the tattooed father-killer) invades the Sword Factory to create merry Hell (entering after, of course, the other banditos have dispatched most of the opponents – which's when the super-villain tends to make his entrance. This is one of Xiong Xin-xin finest roles in a Tsui Hark flick – alongside his manic leader of the White Lotus clan in the second *Once Upon a Time In China* movie).

Everyone is yelling at everyone else, and On Man appears. Siu Ling's delight at seeing On is lovely to see (actress Song Lei has a beautiful smile) – a ray of light in amongst the macho, testosterone-heavy confrontations.

Although the Master and Iron Head are close by, and are partially involved,[12] the finale of *The Blade* can only be On Man pitted against his key adversary, the man who killed his father, Fei Lung. The spinning technique becomes the key signature of this incendiary, visceral duel to the death, with both warriors spinning at alarming speeds, kicking up dust (with power powder emphasizing their moves), and crashing into another forest of bamboo sticks. Fei Lung wields double blades, some with trick knives in their handles (Tsui Hark is very fond of gadgets and tricks). Chains are also an important element – the swords are on chains, (a scene earlier depicted On Man practising with spinning his sword). And there's a call-back to the man-traps (where On Man lost his arm) – now he can dodge them, and also use one as a weapon against Fei Lung.

Can the filmmakers top everything they've done before in *The Blade*? Well, they're going to have a really good try! The duel is astonishing – it's awesome in its speed and energy, becoming a literal vortex of whirling

---

12 Iron Head runs in but is smashed aside by Fei Lung.

blades, chains, hooks, daggers, staring eyes, bloody limbs, sweat, and pounding music.

And instead of the customary pauses and interludes of your usual duel in a Chinese action movie, the editors (Gam Sing and Tsui Hark) cut the conflict in large chunks of fierce fighting (tho' there *are* pauses for breath – so that Fei Lung can deliver his vocal detestation of the heroes, boasting about skinning the pig that was Fong Lai, On Man's father). Stephen Teo remarked that

> This duel sequence is one of the most extraordinary in martial arts cinema, its effect and significance perhaps second only to the final sequence in King Hu's *The Valiant Ones* (1975). (1998, 146)

The Blade's *dénouement* is a curious *mélange* of narrative elements: perhaps because the film has been so bleak and has depicted humanity at their most despicable and violent, there is a lighter side to the ending. Once again, it is narrated by Siu Ling, but now from middle age (where she's now played by Suet Nei). Ling relates that On Man and Iron Head visit her at the now-defunct Sharp Factory (the Master, her father, also expired in the finale). We see images of a Big Hug between On Man and Ling at the gates of the foundry; so it's sunny, it's smiles all-round. But the movie shifts into middle-age for Ling, which might be twenty years later; now she's waiting and waiting for the one who loves her to come, and lying back and smoking opium.

It's a mixed bag of emotions, then, at the end of *The Blade*, of regret and loss, and, crucially, separation: the characters are not together (except for that brief, once-a-year embrace), and of all people, it's Siu Ling who is alone.

THE ONE-ARMED SWORDSMAN.

The One-Armed Swordsman (1967) is a classic *wuxia* picture from the heyday of swordplay movies in Hong Kong. *The One-Armed Swordsman* is a solid, confident and occasionally flamboyant piece of filmmaking, with enough action, exotic locales, restaurant bust-ups and glaring looks for several martial art movies.

The One-Armed Swordsman starred Jimmy Wang Yu, Pen Yinzi, Guk Fung, Wong Chung-shun and Tin Fung, and was directed by Chang Cheh. There are a few one-armed swordsmen striding through this 1967 movie – the plot revolves around inter-clan rivalries, teachers and father figures, and the mystery of a criminal who committed thirteen robberies.

The One-Armed Swordsman resembles an American Western picture at many points – this is the Chinese *jiangzhu*, but it might be a horse opera filmed in Arizona or New Mexico in the 1950s or 1960s (the influence of the *Fistful of Dollars* movies is plain to see in *The One-Armed Swordsman*).

The One-Armed Swordsman is a very manly movie, featuring several one-armed swordsmen, plus their victims, *sifus*, Shaolin monks, etc, with only two significant female characters (played by Lisa Chiao-chiao and

Violet Pan-yingzi). Typically, Tsui Hark and the writers Hui Nyn and Siu Man-sing changed the emphasis for *The Blade*, building up the character of Ling,[13] as well as the prostitute.

While some of Tsui Hark's remakes are founded on rather skimpy artistic foundations (where they're described as respectful reworkings of the original film, but are actually shameless remakes), *The Blade* is certainly an incredible updating of the mythology of the one-armed swordsman for a contemporary audience.

---

[13] *The Blade* strengthened the character of Ling, giving her more influence on the plot.

23

DOUBLE TEAM

PRODUCTION.
Double Team (1997) was the first of Tsui Hark's 'North American' productions (it was distributed by Sony/ Columbia), and the first of his two collaborations with second tier action star Jean-Claude van Damme (Columbia/ TriStar have been involved with releasing many Asian movies in the West).

Double Team (a.k.a. *The Colony*) was produced by Moshe Diamant[14] (he has prominent billing, and extensive credits in TV and cinema), Nanshun Shi Nan-sheng, Rick Nathanson and David Rodgers, written by Don Jakoby and Paul Mones (from a story by Jakoby), photographed by Peter Pau,[15] edited by Bill Pankow, production design by Marek Dobrowolski, with music by Gary Chang.[16] casting by Illana Diamant and Penny Perry, prod. des. by Marek Dobrowolski, art dir. by Damien Lanfranchi, costumes by Magali Guidasci, make-up by the Eleks, sound designers were Jonathan Miller and Steven Ticknor, and vfx supervisor: Joe Bauer. (Many of the significant positions in the crew were taken up by Chinese, but the crews also drew on French and Italian crew).

It starred Jean-Claude van Damme, Dennis Rodman, Mickey Rourke, Paul Freeman, Natacha Lindlinger, Valeria Cavalli, Jay Benedict, Joëlle Devaux-Vullion, Bruno Bilotta, Mario Opinato, Grant Russell, William Dunn and Asher Tzarfati. The budget was U.S. $30 million (some say $40m), and was filmed mainly in Europe. Released on May 8, 1997. 93 minutes.

It's easy to see that *Double Team* was very likely *not* a script that Tsui Hark developed from scratch, and was probably a project that he was offered to direct. It has the look and feel of a script that might've been offered to many other film directors and film stars of the 1990s (for example, in the mid-1990s, other North American movies covering similar territory included *The Peacemaker, Bad Boys, Under Siege, Mission: Impossible, Eraser, Daylight, Broken Arrow, Con Air, Enemy of the State, Snake Eyes, The Saint,* and of course the *Die Hard* and *Lethal Weapon*

---

14 It was Diamant who oversaw van Damme working in Hong Kong cinema.
15 Peter Pau's (b. 1951) credits include *Crouching Tiger, Hidden Dragon, The Bride With White Hair* and *Forbidden Kingdom*.
16 There are songs by Joey Schwartz, Leareo Gianferrari and Crystal Waters.

series. One can imagine Mel or Tom or Bruce stepping into the role of Jack Quinn with ease). And yet *Double Team* is also very Tsui-ian – it has a *James Bond* vibe throughout, which Tsui had already explored in the *Aces Go Places* series. There are numerous Tsui-ian motifs in *Double Team* – tigers, butterflies, rain, water (and underwater scenes), funfairs, motorbikes, ancient history,[17] etc.

Thrillers are products that Hong Kong, like Hollywood (and TV companies the world over), can churn out in its sleep. After all, the default position of Hollywood and Hong Kong cinema product is a thriller or crime movie, is men running around with guns (drive along Sunset Boulevard any time between now and 2030, and I bet you'll see billboards featuring men waving their phallic substitutes, guns).

Or put it like this: as long as the Hollywood and Hong Kong film industries exist, there will be thrillers. Which means that audiences must enjoy thrillers, even stories they've sat through 56,000[10] times before.

So in discussing *Double Team* in relation to Tsui Hark's cinema, it's worth reminding ourselves that:
• Tsui Hark did not originate the script, the concept or the characters;
• Tsui Hark did not write the movie;
• Tsui Hark doesn't have a producer credit;
• Tsui Hark did not cast some of the key roles.

And while there are Chinese among the crew and the cast, *Double Team* is one of the few movies directed by Tsui Hark which doesn't include scenes set in China; and it's one of the very few Tsui movies without Chinese in the main roles. (This latter item is perhaps the most significant of all: the hero of *Double Team* is a white, European guy).

Double Team is Tsui Hark's *European* movie: the team filmed significant portions in the capital of two dead empires – Rome (the Catholic Empire and the Roman Empire), plus sequences in Belgium (Antwerp), and France (in Nîmes[18] and Arles). *Double Team* is one of the few Tsui movies to take place entirely outside of China, like *Aces Go Places 3*, which visited Paris and London.

With a budget of U.S. $30/ 40 million, Tsui Hark and the team make it look like $150 million. (But there's plenty of product placement in *Double Team*, as in *James Bond* movies – such as Omega watches, Nokia, and Coke – it was released by Columbia, and Coca Cola often features in their flicks.[19] So there are scenes featuring Coke machines, piles of Coke cans scattering, a Coke can is used in Quinn's escape, etc).

Double Team received one of the worst reactions for a Tsui Hark-directed movie in his career, with complaints about the story, the characters, and the acting. The box office was disappointing (U.S. gross was $11.4m). And Tsui found working with a part-U.S. crew had its

---

17 For instance, the finale takes places at the Colosseum, and there are some Catholic monks who're also computer whizzes, aiding Yaz and Jack with intel in the bowels of a monastery (shades of *Black Mask*).
18 Nîmes was used for its very impressive amphitheatre, to stand in for the Colosseum in Roma.
19 In the 1980s, the Coca-Cola Company owned Columbia Pictures Entertainment (as it became). Sony bought Columbia in 1989 and renamed it Sony Pictures Entertainment in 1991.

problems (unionization, for instance).

JEAN-CLAUDE VAN DAMME.

Jean-Claude van Damme (Jean-Claude Camille François Van Varenberg in Berchem-Sainte-Agath,)[20] born on Oct 18, 1960, Brussels), known as the 'Muscles From Brussels', is a second tier action star in the West (like Steven Seagal and Dolph Lungren, with whom van Damme is often lumped). Van Damme moves well, is convincing and competent in fight scenes,[21] but always seems to be rather wooden in talky scenes (when you find out that van Damme is appearing in a Tsui Hark movie, you do sort of prepare yourself for the worst). You wouldn't hire van Damme to play Oedipus or Othello, for instance! Like Christopher Lambert or Vin Diesel, van Damme is more like a coathanger on which a movie can hang its narrative elements, which it isn't really interested in. In *Double Team*, van Damme's characterization is given depth and back-story, but that doesn't count for much, and hardly affects the central narrative, which is one action sequence followed by another. (Prior to *Double Team*, van Damme was known for action movies such as *Universal Soldier, Replicant, Last Action Hero, Streetfighter, The Quest* and *Kickboxer*.[22] He appeared in *No Retreat, No Surrender* (1986), produced by Ng See-yuen (one of the important producers of the cinema of Tsui) and directed by Corey Yuen Kwai. Van Damme often played villains in his early films. One of his biggest hits was *Timecop* (1994), an amusing sci-fi actioner. He also appeared in *Death Warrant, Legionnaire, Derailed, The Order, Sudden Death, A.W.O.L. Black Eagle* and *Predator*. Van Damme has also been in several Asian movies, including *No Retreat, No Surrender, Bloodsport* (1987),[23] and *Hard Target* (1993) directed by John Woo. Van Damme's biggest successes were in the early-to-mid 1990s, after that, his movies received decreasing revenue, and some went straight to video).

When you find out that Jean-Claude van Damme is appearing in not one but two Tsui Hark movies, it does make you wonder. No Jet Li?! No Maggie Cheung or Brigitte Lin?! However, both *Knockoff* and *Double Team* are far more enjoyable than you might expect (and certainly far superior to most of the other movies that van Damme has starred in). And once you forget about van Damme, and about the formulaic scripts, there is plenty to enjoy.

Mickey Rourke plays the Bad Guy, Stavros, one of those brilliant-at-everything villains who can out-smart everybody (but what is that accent Rourke's attempting? Greek?! Rourke takes Marlon Brando mumbling to new heights/ depths here). Paul Freeman (great as always) is the helper/ older adviser figure Alex Goldsmythe (at the Colony), whose main function is to rattle off pages of exposition (combining the roles of 'Q' and 'M' from *James Bond*). Natacha Lindlinger plays Kathryn Quinn, the wife of the hero

---
20 His website is jcvdworld.com.
21 Fight fans who don't like van Damme complain that he only has a few moves, which he uses again and again (like kickboxing).
22 The *Kickboxer* series, like the *Universal Soldier* films, continues to recent times, with movies in 2016 and 2017.
23 *Bloodsport* was filmed in Hong Kong at Clearwater Bay; it was produced by Cannon.

(in the usual unrewarding role of the Hero's Wife).

THE STORY.

Story-wise, *Double Team* is delightfully dumb and formulaic: it's basically cops and robbers, good guys and bad guys, or in this case, anti-terrorist guys versus nasty terrorists. But then, most of Hong Kong movies are similarly 'formulaic', script-wise – and so are Tsui Hark's movies. (There is some unsettling footage which foreshadows 9/11 – a 747 airliner blowing up over Korea, apparently by North Korea;[24] but, it turns out, the atrocity was committed by the U.S. government using Korea as a cover).

As with some of Tsui Hark's other contemporary-set movies, and with his thrillers, film critics derided the story of *Double Team* as formulaic and silly. Well, yes – but pretty much every thriller you've seen in the past 20 years – hell, the past *100* years! – has been formulaic and stupid.

In fact, I dare you to cite any of the great thrillers and crime movies of recent times which seem to be complex and 'deep', and I bet you'll find a ridiculous story with unbelievable characters. Yes, because most thrillers, murder mysteries and crime stories boil down to cat and mouse narratives, with the bad guys or the serial killer or the rogue agent always one step ahead of the heroes or the authorities.

This is the narrative structure of *Double Team.* As written by Don Jakoby and Paul Mones, it's a thoroughly familiar chase and cat and mouse scenario (all thrillers – and many action and adventure movies – can be boiled down to chases).

So Jean-Claude van Damme plays Jack Quinn, an agent who's retired from hunting down terrorists following an incident involving stolen plutonium (which Quinn managed to steal back from Stavros in Croatia, in a hi-octane chase along mountain roads). He's holed up in the South of France (he has a nice house[25] overlooking the ocean *à la* Malibu, swimming pool, attractive wife,[26] baby on the way), when the obligatory messenger from the government comes to visit to ask/ persuade/ demand that Quinn take up the task of hunting down Stavros (the *Hot Shots!* movies (of 1991 and 1993) delivered a great spoof of this regular feature of action movies, the reluctant hero being given his assignment, with Charlie Sheen taking refuge in a teepee!).

JAMES BOND.

Double Team is Tsui Hark's second most *James Bond*-a-like movie – a return to the *Bond*-ian territory of *Aces Go Places 3. Double Team* takes numerous elements from the *James Bond* series; there's even an amusing select club for retired secret agents (called the Colony – well, this flick was made around the time of the Hong Kong Hand-over!). This bunch of grizzled, war-weary guys lounges about on an island in the Mediterranean

---
[24] *James Bond* movies have also used North Korea – in *Die Another Day* (2001), for instance.
[25] That lovely house and garden and swimming pool on the Côte d'Azur is blown to pieces – as Jack Quinn somehow manages to get the better of a slew of henchmen.
[26] Butterflies, a Tsui Hark motif, are one of the symbols of the couple.

Sea (which looks like a resort hotel), and are called upon by world governments as a think-tank to sort out tough situations when the Central Intelligence Agency, Mossad, the former K.G.B. and M.I.6 falter. It's where James Bond will go when he's retired (and it's where Quinn is taken after nearly dying in a bomb blast courtesy of Stavros). And, as in *The Prisoner* TV show or *The Count of Monte Cristo*, the denizens isn't allowed to escape (the sea is fitted out with lasers).[27] And, as in *The Count of Monte Cristo*, our hero Quinn stages a daring escape[28] (which features very *James Bond*-like stunts, including a fight underwater with a diver (one of Quinn's rivals, and his 'guardian'), and Quinn grabbing onto some cargo in a net trailed from a passing supply plane. (The same gag was employed in the finale of *The Living Daylights*, the 1987 *James Bond* movie.) The sequence doesn't stop with that, however: there are impressive aerial stunts, as Quinn battles guards on board the plane, hurling his victims out into the big blue.)

The aircraft stunts in *Double Team* are astonishing, tho' with his fear of heights, it's unlikely that Tsui Hark personally oversaw any of the sequences up in the air. The close-ups of the principal actors are tricked out in the studio, of course (no one but Jackie Chan would fancy hanging out of a plane for real!), but the second unit photography is remarkable.

(The Colony briefing room sequence contains some of the most sophisticated visual effects in a Tsui Hark movie – there are digital animations, superimpositions, burn-ins, TV and computer screens, edited into a dense collage of information.)

CAMP AND COMEDY.

Critics couldn't abide Dennis Rodman as Jack Quinn's buddy Yaz in *Double Team:* a big, black basketball player decked out in wild, Euro-trash fashions (Jean-Paul Gaultier mixed with bondage gear, plus tattoos, plus neon-bright, dyed hair, that changes colour in every scene!). The bad boy of baskbetball, Rodman's media image is self-consciously camp, glam, bisexual and ridiculous. Costume designer Magali Guidasci and Rodman have great fun with Yaz's clothing and accessories (Rodman will happily wear *anything!*). It's hilarious – especially the introduction of Yaz wearing shiny silver pants in Antwerp's sleazy downtown,[29] with its drag queens and clubbers dressed for the Berlin Love Parade (meanwhile, the desperate-to-be-trendy nightclub has divers in water tanks situated around the dance floor, instead of the usual semi-naked, dancing girls). It was certainly unusual to have the hero's buddy played in such an out-there, ostentatiously gay/ queer manner (camp/ gay/ queer characters in the ultra-macho action genre are typically comical sidekicks (at best), or caricature cameos. To include a wildly camp character as the hero's buddy

---

27 Lasers in the ocean? Sounds crazy? No it isn't! Western powers have all sorts of warning systems in place in the oceans of the world (to warn of submarines, for instance).
28 Which includes spy movie business like cutting off his thumbprint (and, improbably, attaching it to a swinging pencil – which again uses a Coke can). Meanwhile, the training sequences are right out of martial arts cinema, where the downtrodden hero betters himself to fight back.
29 Jean-Claude van Damme is from Brussels, of course. The movie seems to tap more into Holland's rep as a progressive, alternative nation.

– and also his fixer and weapons specialist – is much more unusual. And it's guaranteed to wind up action fans as well as film critics. But we can also recall that Chinese (action) cinema often plays gender games, with women dressing up as men, and vice versa, plus of course magical transgenderizations).

How any critic or viewer could take any of this seriously is scary – nothing in *Double Team* is meant to be taken literally or seriously. This is a popcorn thrill ride movie – you either go along for the ride, or you don't. I mean, critics complained that Dennis Rodman stood out in *Double Team* – well, *duh*, yes!

▸

I would imagine that another aspect of *Double Team* (and some of Tsui Hark's other contemporary-set movies) that perplexes or irritates Western critics and audiences is its *tone*. As with Japanese animation, Western audiences find it difficult to accept comedy or lightheartedness in the midst of supposedly serious scenes. The *tone* of *Double Team* is playful *as well as* delivering action and drama. But it's not playful always in the manner of an *Indiana Jones* or *James Bond* flick, which have clearly signposted comical moments. *Double Team*, like many of Tsui's movies as director, regards everything as somewhat playful or even downright ridiculous. *Double Team*, like *Knockoff* and *Time and Tide,* is thus a cartoon, and is more cartoon-like than many comicbook movies and superhero movies in the West (just prior to *Double Team*, Tsui had produced *Black Mask*, of course).

No intelligent filmmaker would produce movies like *Double Team* or *Knockoff* and pretend that they're making something 'worthy' or 'meaningful' or 'important'. They and we all know that this is a piece of fluff, like a *James Bond, Batman* or *Avengers* flick, something to enjoy for an hour-and-a-half then completely forget.

The greatest film directors, however, can deliver a fantastic action movie but also do Something More. Howard Hawks, D.W. Griffith and Sam Peckinpah in North America, for instance, and Tsui Hark, Tony Ching Siu-tung, John Woo and Akira Kurosawa in the East.

Double Team in the end doesn't really contain that Something More. But it's not nearly as bad as the critical reception makes out (tho' one can understand why it didn't set alight the theatrical box office). Part of the problem is that the character of Jack Quinn isn't especially riveting, and neither is the way that the 'Muscles From Brussels' plays him. Quinn is the straight-jawed, do-right hero we've seen so many times before. (Like the Harrison Fords and Tom Cruises who play heroes who're just too good, too wholesome, too smart and too talented to be true.) Another is that the story of super-smart terrorists and personal vendettas is a plot we've seen a million times before. I reckon the cast of secondary characters could've been kookier and crazier (altho' Dennis Rodman's wardrobe goes some way in providing wackiness).

VFX.

Double Team is also a visual effects extravaganza – if someone gives Tsui Hark and his team thirty million dollars, you can bet that some of those green bills will be spent on visual fx. By now, tho', the sleight of hand and trickery is so sophisticated, you don't notice many of the visual effects and special effects. The pyrotechnics guys find new ways of blowing stuff up (it usually is *guys* who blow stuff up); the visual fx create miniatures and mattes (and models which also blow up, of course!); the post-production crew add opticals and digital animation (for the hi-tech briefing room in the Colony); and the practical effects team deliver smoke, fire, fog, rain and everything else environmental and atmospheric that the Maestro likes to put in every single movie he directs. It's not a Tsui Hark movie unless there's rain slanting thru the scene, or smoke billowing across a shadowy bridge in the background, or exaggerated water reflection light effects on the underside of bridges (go back and look at *Double Team* for its cinematography by Peter Pau – it's beautiful. And of course, it doesn't 'need' to be that superlative, for a formulaic actioner. But it is).

Again, there is a striking emphasis on water in a Tsui Hark movie: Jack Quinn lives next to the Med (and has a swimming pool – the setting for a tender scene between husband and wife following the prologue, where we discover that Kathryn Quinn is pregnant); Kathryn loons in the rain (she's been told that Quinn is dead); the Colony has a luxurious pool and is on a small island; the nightclub in Belgium features scuba divers as entertainment; Quinn trains holding his breath in a bath; Quinn takes cover from explosions in a pool; and there are several scenes set in water. (You could forge links between the preponderance of water imagery and the emphasis on mothers and babies in the emotional subtext of *Double Team* – pools as wombs, water as amniotic fluid, etc).

ACTION.

One of the stunt directors was Xiong Xin-xin, one of Tsui Hark's regular stunt directors in the 1990s and 2000s (he was Clubfoot in the *Once Upon a Time In China* movies). He has a terrific cameo as one of the henchmen that Jack Quin battles in a hotel suite in Rome (the fight, which includes plenty of breaking glass and splintering wood, allows for some more traditional, Chinese *kung fu* moves.[30] Xiong, as usual, goes for it big-time – remember him as Club Foot in *Once Upon a Time In China*, a terrific cameo? Or as the fearsome villain in *The Blade*? Xiong is one of those actors who gets the tone dead-on – straight/ serious, but, hell, not *too* darn serious!).

Sammo Hung and Charlie Picerni are also credited as action directors. Rémy Julienne did the car stunts. 2nd unit dirs. were Allan Graf and Charlie Picerni.

Double Team is stuffed with action sequences. One after another –

---
30 As Lisa Morton remarked, 'Xiong's presence in the film is utterly inexplicable, but when a knife pops out from between his toes as he whirls around Quinn, who cares?' (LM, 218).

they keep coming. If you insist on harping on about the *story* in a Chinese action movie, or the *characters*, boy, you have really missed the point. In the first act, we have an explosive chase in mountains, a giant gun battle in a theme park in Antwerp at night, and a bust-up in a children's hospital.

The chase in the prologue is very much in the *James Bond* mold: it occurs three years earlier, and is a self-contained sequence: our hero (introduced in shot one), drives a huge truck to freedom, while battling numerous opponents on curving mountain highways. Multiple explosions, machine gunfire, cars crashing, and plenty of stunts – the prologue culminates with a classic 'look-at-us!' gag: the truck leaping over and smashing thru a moving freight train at a railroad crossing.

The Antwerp fairground fire-fight humanizes the villain Stavros by having his six year-old child dying in a hail of bullets (plus his girlfriend/ wife). So now he has a strong motivation to get some payback on Jack Quinn. (Unfortunately, their deaths have a limited dramatic impact, because we've only just met them. The movie really requires an additional scene of the villain with his family. Yes, but, Stavros is also a mass murderer! He puts a bomb in a baby's crib! He kills a C.I.A. agent in Rome when we first meet him. And his henchmen fire on unarmed, civilian women).

The funfair action sequence in *Double Team* segues for no particular reason into a hospital which's full of newborn babies in cots – seemingly abandoned, with not a nurse in sight! So we've got the hero versus villain smackdown in amongst crying tots (is this a nod to 1992's *Hard-Boiled*?). Yes, it's true that sometimes the issue close to Tsui Hark's heart – of mothers and babies/ children – is woven into Tsui's movies a little awkwardly – here you've got guns and babies, which don't mix! (That Quinn's wife Kathryn is expecting, and that Stavros has just lost his six year-old boy, plays into the drama. But it's still very contrived).

But it *is* a significant minor theme in Tsui Hark's cinema – *Double Team* is not an isolated incident of evoking issues such as motherhood and babies in Tsui's output (it's in *Time and Tide*). In *Hard-Boiled,* for example, Chow Yun-fat wields a baby like a lucky mascot (no way can he die with a baby in his arms!); in Tsui's work, there is a far greater investment dramatically in 'women's issues', compared to the thoroughly macho, brotherhood make-up of John Woo's movies.

The action in *Double Team* is very much in the Hong Kong action cinema manner, tho' with a bigger budget to stage some larger stunts. The fights are visceral, with plenty of breakaway glass, and the use of props and every part of a setting. One area of *Double Team* displays the North American influence: ærial stunts. Hong Kong action cinema might rule the world on the ground, and up to 100 feet (with cranes), but it seldom features such elaborate stunts as guys hanging outside planes thousands of feet in the air.

Then there's the *Monte Cristo* break-out from the Colony... a wild fire-fight at Jack Quinn's South France home... an outstanding martial arts duel in a hotel suite... and an incredible action sequence right in the centre of Rome...

The Eternal City has been used in 1000s of movies, of course (and by visiting productions since the 1950s), but it's not often you see a *Chinese* production setting up shop in one of Rome's famous squares, Piazza Navona (and moving on to the equally famous Termini railroad station),[31] and delivering a fantastic action sequence which includes a wedding, horses, carriages, galloping riders,[32] snipers, machine guns, cars, and a host of agents from around the world. This is a long way from Federico Fellini or Pier Paolo Pasolini! (Because for them, this scene would be simply another ordinary day in Rome!).

And while film critics would be right in drawing attention to some of the deficiencies of the story and the characters and the themes and the issues in *Double Team* (a regular criticism of all action movies, of course), there's no doubting that the directorial control exerted by Tsui Hark and his team is very impressive. Once again, Tsui's boundless energy for creating memorable images soars throughout *Double Team* (courtesy of Oscar-winning DP Peter Pau). Couple that with the blazing, forceful editing (by Bill Pankow), and you have a tremendously effective creative combination.

Again and again, we can see that it is the *editing*, above perhaps *all other technical elements*, that distinguishes Chinese action cinema from any other cinemas. Other cinemas can deliver exploding cars, stunt guys crashing through glass windows, or fist fights, but only Chinese filmmakers can stage and shoot action scenes like this, and only they can cut them together like this.

The *flow of action* in a Chinese action movie is spellbinding. The form of cinema created by Chinese filmmakers has a *spatial awareness*, a *sensuality* and a *texture*, a *speed* and a *timing*, and an *inventiveness* that no other cinema around the world can match. Give Chinese filmmakers a chair, a table and a room and they will be able to come up with a really imaginative action scene. They don't need anything else! Give them the budget for some breakaway glass and a squib or two, and they're away!

(Ironically, altho' *Double Team* was backed by N. American money, it was shorter – at 93 mins – than N. American equivalents: had *Double Team* been made with a U.S. director (and a U.S. star who liked to wield their influence on the script), it might run to 120 mins or longer. But with Tsui Hark's super-heated nerves at the helm, it's a 93-minute movie – the perfect length for an action movie. For any movie).

MOTHERS AND BABIES.

Double Team is a boys' movie, once again, so that Kathryn Quinn (Natacha Lindlinger) plays the damsel in distress. Thus, *Double Team* isn't one of Tsui Hark's great movies for feminism, or proto-feminism (in fact, with its depiction of Yaz as a flamboyant dandy of a guy first seen hanging out with drag queens, if you want to look for interesting sexual politics in

---

[31] Here Denis Rodman performs some basketball moves – inevitably chucking a guy like a basketball (thru the window of a van, outside the Termini station).
[32] Stavros is a particularly venal villain – the guy on horseback, who seems to be working for him, sprays a machine gun all over Piazza Navona, hitting many civilians.

Double Team, it's there).

But there is a minor motif of mothers and babies in *Double Team* (which also cropped up in *Time and Tide*). Jack Quinn is happily married to Kathryn, and they're having a baby: is Tsui Hark getting soft in his old age? Certainly there's an emphasis on parents and babies/ children in some of Tsui's later works (even the villain gets to play the heartbroken daddy when his son's killed in the first act at the theme park).

Sexual politics – there is also a clear macho/ phallic battle going on in *Double Team,* between the hero Jack Quinn and the villain Stavros. Because the hero's wife Kathryn is expecting a baby, and Stavros kidnaps her close to her time, thus pushing aside Quinn, and playing the father role. The villain often uses the hero's girl as a pawn in his scheme to rule the world in action cinema: in this case, the displacement of Quinn in his fatherly role is a kind of castration. So that one of Quinn's goals is to take back his masculine identity – his manhood, you might say, which Stavros has destabilized).[33] (A mother, a baby, and two guys, one the 'good father' and the other the 'bad father' – there's plenty of material here for a Freudian or Kristevan or Lacanian exploration of sexual politics, of fetishism, of castration, and of gender).

THE FINALE.

So the finale of *Double Team* is a gladiatorial duel set in the Roman Colosseum[34] (tho' much of it was filmed in Nîmes, in the S. of France), complete with a tiger![35] (A famous fight was set in the Colosseum in the Bruce Lee picture *Way of the Dragon*, a.k.a. *Return of the Draon*, 1972, between Lee and Colt.) Mickey Rourke strips to the waist in black pants,[36] Jean-Claude van Damme glowers (still wearing that furry, hippy jacket), Dennis Rodman's Yaz scurries into the fray on a motorbike to snatch up the baby,[37] and everybody tries to avoid the tiger and the landmines that Stavros has thoughtfully set in the dust.

All in all, the finale of *Double Team* is a long, punchy and exciting sequence, which culminates with the Colosseum blowing up (reminiscent of a Ray Harryhausen or 1970s disaster movie). The tiger is employed to great effect – not, as is usual with lions and tigers, for a few shots, but in a lengthy pursuit sequence, where it hunts Jack Quinn up the terraces and down the stone and sand corridors of the Colosseum. These are spectacular scenes in a tough environment for animal wrangling (an ancient building at night). Quinn escapes the tiger, but hapless henchmen are chomped. Yaz is busy tackling more henchmen, and offering his buddy some assistance in the fight against Stavros.

---

33 Thus you can regard *Double Team* as another of the many 'male identity crisis' movies of the 1980s and 1990s, movies where the hero's masculinity and identity were under scrutiny.
34 Which has been used in numerous movies.
35 Is it a tiger as a piece of Asia? Asia in Europe? The 'tiger' economies? Tigers of course crop up in *Taking Tiger Mountain*.
36 Mickey Rourke, tho' he has a boxer's moves, doesn't come out too well in the finale. You need to possess more than a gym-honed body and a good punch to flourish in a finale created by Chinese action filmmakers. Rourke fared better as the disgruntled Russian inventor in the second *Iron Man* flick.
37 To take the child out of the equation very soon.

Yet you have to admit that the climactic scenes of *Double Team* aren't quite as satisfying as other action scenes in the 1997 flick. And altho' you've got the Colosseum in Rome exploding,[38] somehow it's not big enough (what, the Colosseum blowing up isn't 'big enough' for you?!). Or maybe not big enough for the ending of a Tsui Hark actioner! (*Black Mask 2* revisits a stadium for the finale).

The action is also a little samey and repetitive, and it doesn't quite flow as smoothly or as logically (or poetically logically) as in the finest Chinese action movies finales. It has the look, too, of too many people putting their oar in – you've got Stavros and Quinn, plus the baby, plus Yaz, plus henchmen, plus a tiger, plus land mines, plus the labyrinthine passageways of the Colosseum (and it's fitting that Alex Goldsmythe is brought back at the end). Compared to the climaxes of the *Once Upon a Time In China* movies, or *The Blade*, or *Black Mask 2*, all of which Tsui Hark and co. worked on not long before *Double Team,* this is underwhelming.

---

[38] With our heroes shielding themselves against the fire with a Coke machine! Again with the Coca Cola in a Columbia movie!

24

KNOCKOFF

INTRO.

Knockoff (1998) is usually described as one of Tsui Hark's North American movies, or a movie financed by North American money.[39] But how 'American' is *Knockoff*? It's set in Hong Kong during the Hand-over of 1997,[40] so it possesses a very Chinese as well as international setting and political context (and not especially 'American', or even something that American audiences would find riveting). The main character, Marcus Ray, is played by Jean-Claude van Damme, the 'Muscles From Brussels', who's teamed up with a Yank, Tommy Hendricks (played by Rob Schneider). There are two other Americans among the principal cast (Paul Sorvino and Lela Rochon), playing Americans, but many of the secondary characters are either Chinese or Russian (including Michael Fitzgerald Wong, Carman Lee Yeuk-tung, Glen Chin, Wyman Wong, and Moses Chan, and all of the extras are Chinese. It was filmed in Hong Kong, probably by a largely Chinese film crew (most of the heads of the technical departments seem to be Chinese).

So *Knockoff* is not particularly 'American' – 'international' might be a more accurate term, or a Chinese version of an 'American' movie (which Hong Kongers have been making for decades). However, *Knockoff* is principally an action movie – a North American genre – and it's conceived and written and produced in an 'American' style, right down to the buddy relationship at the heart of it, and numerous aspects of the American thriller and gangster picture.

Knockoff was written by Steve de Souza,[41] produced by Nanshun Shi Nan-sheng and Tsui Hark's own Film Workshop (and M.D.P. Worldwide), and distributed by TriStar (like its predecessor, *Double Team*). Arthur Wong was DP; Marco Mak Chi-sin was editor; Yuen Bun and Sammo Hung were action choreographers (Hung is among the assistant directors); music by Ron and Russell Mael (Sparks); and costumes by William Fung

---

[39] Apparently, Francis Coppola contemplated filming *Knockoff*.
[40] *Knockoff* was the only Western production that was allowed to shoot during the Hand-over celebrations.
[41] De Souza's credits include *Commando, 48 Hrs, Die Hard, The Running Man, Hudson Hawk* and *The Flintstones*. Perfect (and impressive) credentials for *Knockoff*.

Kwun-Man, Mabel Kwan Mei-Bo and Ben Luk Man-Wah. The budget was around U.S. $35 million[42] (i.e., one of the biggest budgets that Tsui had worked with up to that time). Released Sept 6, 1998.[43] 87 minutes.

Meanwhile, the teaming up of Jean-Claude van Damme with actor and *Saturday Night Live* comedian Rob Schneider isn't wholly successful, and not as funny as it wants to be. Schneider's Hendricks is the familiar shorter, weasley, neurotic, fast-talkin' buddy to the troubled hero. There are some good humorous moments, but not as many as you might expect, tho' Schneider and van Damme do work well together. (Jeff Yang reckoned that *Knockoff* 'had the stupidest plot ever conceived for an action film' [2003, 100]).

On a minor note – the music in *Knockoff* is composed by Ron and Russell Mael: Sparks! Remember 'This Town Ain't Big Enough', their smash hit of 1974? And of course 'Number One Song In Heaven'. Sparks were a superb duo who made a big splash at the tail-end of the glam rock era (no one can forget Ron Mael on TV, sitting at a keyboard with staring eyes and an Adolf Hitler moustache!). The Maels had persuaded Tsui to record some banter for their song 'Tsui Hark', on the album *Gratuitous Sax and Senseless Violins* (1995). 'I was fooling around with my voice,' Tsui recalled. 'We became very good friends. That's why I was curious to use them on a movie' (LM, 133).

The first time I saw *Knockoff,* I had no idea who composed the soundtrack. In fact, there are a couple of scenes where I reckoned the music was simply burbling along underneath a too-long scene (a type of undistinguished, bland under-scoring which I loathe, because it's a crime against the magic of music, and demonstrates that the inspiration in the storytelling is declining into mush). But seeing the Mael brothers in the end credits makes me want to go back and listen closer to the soundtrack! (One motif that the Maels employ are very low percussive booms, which add an ominous atmosphere).

Knockoff is a joke on action movies, too – it's a 'knockoff' of action flicks. And it's a joke on 'Made In Hong Kong' and 'Made In China'. And a joke on copies and rip-offs – where, in the Hong Kong film industry, successes are immediately copied (Tsui Hark had already explored this theme in *The Swordsman 3*, where there are multiple replicas of Asia).

The story of *Knockoff,* its themes and its political context, are only vaguely interesting, and certainly not emotionally or psychologically compelling at all. The viewer couldn't care less about any of the characters or what happens to them. (The betrayals and double-crossings, tho' part of the genre, are rather tiresome: *Knockoff* is one of those movies where nobody is what they seem at first, and everybody is hiding something). Meanwhile, the villain, Harry Johannson (Paul Sorvino), seems to die twice: once in the giant, *James Bond* explosion during the climax of the finale, and in the Buddha explosion, too. Finally, during the Hand-over festivities and fireworks, when Marcus Ray, in possession of the remote control device, activates it, he dies again, in a ball of green flame. We

---
42 The same as the $35 million budget of another van Damme movie of 1998, *Legionnaire*.
43 One of the widest releases for a Tsui Hark picture in the U.S.A. – 1,800 screens.

hope. Because he's a villainous villain).

Yes, there are issues in *Knockoff* which address the anxieties of global capitalism and politics – like the 1997 Hong Kong Hand-over setting, or the issue of ripped-off brand names ('Pumma' instead of 'Puma') and crappy merchandize (jeans and sneakers that fall apart), with Asia creating goods for the West (the familiar racist angsting over products being 'Made In China'). And there are groups of characters which play into global politics: the post-Cold War, Russian gangsters, the Yanks and the Central Intelligence Agency, with the Chinese in the new Hong Kong in the middle (themes and politics which Tsui Hark has explored in other movies). The fractious relations between N. Americans, Russians and Chinese (plus Hong and Mainland China), form part of the political context of *Knockoff* (but then, *Knockoff* has made the 1997 Hand-over a central issue).

But that's not why audiences come to *Knockoff,* or why *Knockoff* is enjoyable. *Knockoff* is not a history lesson, not a lecture on post-1997, Chinese politics, and not a film-essay on the anxieties of living in a postmodern, hyper-capitalist world. *Knockoff* is an action movie, and it's a Tsui Hark movie.

'A Tsui Hark movie': yes, the great man directed this action thriller which, let's face it, is *way* below his talents and his potential. This is a filmmaker who can do *anything*, so in some ways it's a shame to see him taking on something he could deliver in his sleep.

ENERGY AND EDITING.

That aside, *Knockoff* is stuffed with Tsui Harkisms: it is filmed with a dynamism and vitality that few filmmakers can sustain beyond one-minute bursts; the energy bouncing off the screen is simply stupendous; it contains several outstanding action sequences (worth the ticket price alone!); it features many marvellous scenes of texture and atmosphere; and it is a technical marvel (powered with the usual battery of visual effects – the pyrotechnics, the practical effects, the miniatures, the multiple film speeds, and the extraordinary action choreography which we've come to expect from Tsui).

There's no doubt that Tsui Hark was on fire when he directed *Knockoff*. If you put aside the story (which takes in many clichés of contemporary thrillers), and the rather routine characters, you can see that Tsui was very inspired.

It's the *storytelling*, the way the story is being told, that is at a higher, punchier, faster level than Western or North American action movies or thrillers. The editing is only part of that – it's how the scenes're blocked, how the action is staged and how it flows, how the action moves within each shot and relates to the shots before and after. The material might be clichéd and hokey at times, but *Knockoff* itself, as movie-making, is ecstatic.

Ecstatic?! Surely that is going too far for a Jean-Claude van Damme flick?! But actually, *Knockoff is* ecstatic. And it's feverish, it's hysterical, it's over-the-top, it's baroque, it's wild.

If Tsui Hark is going to take on a run-of-the-mill action thriller, you hope he's going to do something special with it. He does. There are scenes filmed from angles that boggle the mind (how did they film a scene where the camera's hurtling down to the ground from ten stories high?).

The intense feeling for texture and visuals makes *Knockoff* seem like a Tsui Hark documentary on contemporary Hong Kong – you could select hundreds of shots from *Knockoff* (missing out the fight and action scenes), and cut together a fascinating portrait of the South China city of 1997. A close-up of frogs in a restaurant... a food factory... a street of crummy food stalls in the scuzzy side of town... It's a marvellous, even magical representation of the speeding city of the future.

At times, *Knockoff* seems like Tsui Hark's response to the critical success of the films of Wong Kar-wai, which had critics in the West oohing and ahhing. *Knockoff* gives Wong's movies like *Chungking Express* and *Happy Together* a run for their money in terms of rapid, allusive editing and poetic visions of the postmodern city of Hong Kong.

This is a movie which opens with a giant close-up of a doll floating underwater – a typically surreal, Tsuian image (dolls are part of the counterfeit goods). There's even a point-of-view shot of a foot sliding into a shoe[44] (because the counterfeit 'Pumma' shoes are part of the plot). Close-ups of frogs. Of fish in an aquarium (a Tsui Hark fave – goldfish crop up in *Shanghai Blues* and *Detective Dee*).

And there are cutaway shots – to the inside of the Pumma sneaker, for instance (to show it falling apart). A phone call becomes a hi-energy rush (using vfx) along the millions of miles of cables connecting one human ear to another.

As to editing, *Knockoff* is remarkable (Marco Mak Chi-sin was editor): in the middle of some scenes, as well as the usual step-motion, true slow motion, and over-cranked shots, there are sudden freeze frames, and also multiple freeze frames dissolved together. Who else would judder an action scene to a halt with multiple freeze frames, run together with dissolves?!

Knockoff is not just a superb example of Tsui Hark's later film editing style, which's one of the hallmarks of his cinema (*nobody else* edits movies like this!), it is also an example of a filmmaker trying out all manner of experiments with the editing. Tsui is incredible in his editing also because he and his editors will use parts of a shot you wouldn't expect (that is, not always the section of a shot which everyone else would use), and he will also hold on a shot longer than expected (even tho' he's known for his extremely rapid cutting style).

There's a whole other level to the energy of the editing in a Tsui Hark movie, and in a movie such as *Knockoff*. If you come to *Knockoff* after looking at other movies, even celebrated action movies, you have your senses jammed into an electric socket and powered up to dangerous

---

[44] 'Even the mere act of putting on a shoe becomes a bobsled ride as Tsui ably demonstrates why he may be the best visual stylist in the film world today' (Lisa Morton, 131).

degrees. This is a movie rated 'T' – for 'Tsuian'. Speed – acceleration – cocaine – amphetamine – you can use all sorts of images or comparisons to evoke the rush of images that flow out of *Knockoff*.

And yet this is *not* rapid editing in the North American/ Western manner, which's used in many contemporary TV dramas and movies, where you have five angles of someone performing an action that would usually be covered in one shot. That form of over-cutting is used by producers to spice up a boring piece of television or cinema. (And it's *horrible!*).

Thus, those five shots still portray the same action. So the *storytelling* is still just as *draggy*. So *slow!* Western and N. American TV dramas and cinema are *so slow* in terms of storytelling! In a Tsui Hark movie, the editing creates a new high voltage, super-fast form of storytelling. Instead of five shots of the same action, there is one shot of the action (but achieved quicker), followed by four shots which take in all sorts of unusual details, or a new view of a familiar object, or a camera move which enhances the energy of the scene.

Damon Houx has written a humorous reappraisal of *Knockoff*; Houx noted that Tsui Hark

> decided he didn't want a single shot in the movie to be boring and so every place he puts the camera is interesting and surprising... it's as if Hark was using the film not as an audition piece, but as a chance to try everything he ever wanted to do with a camera.

On the downside, *Knockoff* is marred a little by a couple of too lengthy and too talky scenes (around the beginning of the second act). Too talky for Tsui Hark's style of cinema, that is. From any other movie-maker, they might not stand out. But when a Tsui Hark movie slows down for a *long* conversation, you really notice it (there are justifications, of course – there is a *lot* of exposition to get through. Also, the script was by Steve de Souza, not Tsui). Or maybe it's that, in a movie with so many action sequences, the talky scenes pop out as stodgy.

The settings and set-pieces in *Knockoff,* too, are clichés: the finale, for instance, takes place at a dockside and on a ship in Hong Kong harbour. So we've got metal ship containers, and giant cranes, and boats, and explosions, and gun battles (the kind of non-residential, industrial, macho *mise-en-scène* that action movies, East and West, love). There's a warehouse battle, a face-off on a downtown rooftop, a superb van chase (the vehicle smashes into a store thru the front window), a duel in a hotel, a stunning car chase in a concrete car lot, a racy boat chase in the opening sequence, and a truck chase thru festival streets.

The critical reception of *Knockoff* wasn't great, and the movie only made around $10 mil in the U.S.A. in theatres (but then, N. American critics don't react well to Chinese action movies. While American action movies are just as dumb and crude, many of the main U.S. critics just don't get Chinese actioners). I would imagine that *Knockoff* has done good business on video and DVD, however: it's a perfectly enjoyable action movie if you don't expect too much, don't hope that Tsui Hark is going to make *Seven Swords* or *Once Upon a Time In China* every single time, and try to forget that Jean-Claude van Damme is the star. (And let's not forget that Tsui *didn't* write *Knockoff* – Steven De Souza did).

And once you put aside those considerations, *Knockoff* comes across as a wonderfully energetic piece of filmmaking. Even, as I've suggested, ecstatic. Any film which boasts scenes like the factory chase, the rickshaw race, the boat chase, the truck fight, the car lot fight, and Lola Rochon as a kick-ass action heroine has got to be worth seeing.

In David West's otherwise excellent book on martial arts movies (*Chasing Dragons*), he talks utter rubbish about Tsui Hark's movies *Double Team* and *Knockoff* which, he claims, 'contain none of the trademarks or flair normally associated with Tsui' (194). No, no, they are *stuffed* with Tsui-ian trademarks! (Mothers and babies, tigers, butterflies, rain, water, funfairs, etc).

THE ACTION SCENES.

Knockoff opens with two action sequences: in the first, there's an underwater operation involving counterfeit goods which escalates into several explosions and a frantic boat chase (the explosions announce the nano-bombs gimmick – in *Knockoff*, terrorists are going to blow up Westerners by selling counterfeit goods to the Occident with nano-bombs sewn into them. A suitably bonkers, *James Bond*-ian gimmick). Within four minutes, *Knockoff* has staged enough stunts and gags for a *James Bond* teaser (which it out-does). It's got explosions, grenades, fire-fights, speedboats, the lot. Han (Michael Wong) is a Hong Kong cop in hot pursuit by boat of the crooks (who get away). There are two outrageous boat crashes (reminiscent of the boat gags in *Live and Let Die*, 1973). The sequence is punched home with an editing style that is jittery with energy.

James Bond is cited in the dialogue of *Knockoff* – the *James Bond* franchise had been revived in 1995 (with *Goldeneye*), followed by *Tomorrow Never Dies* (1997), which of course starred one of Hong Kong cinema's finest stars, Michelle Yeoh (who has worked with Tsui Hark, and everybody else in Hong Kong).

In the second action sequence, a comical race between rickshaws of local businesses (including our heroes from V-6 Jeans, Marcus Ray and Hendricks), escalates into a battle between the villains and the heroes (and it introduces the hero, Ray, in full effect). The models from the V-6 Jeans company provide the mandatory babe quotient in a hi-tech thriller (being models, they can be presented in several states of undress). As if to please the American investors in the movie, the girls are put into cheerleader costumes for the rickshaw race (the setting is the 1997 celebrations in H.K., so there are production value crowd scenes and a festive atmosphere).

The rickshaw race, tho' played for laughs, looks incredibly risky, with actors and stunt guys being hurled down steep concrete stairways (the useless sneakers play a role here, falling apart as Ray runs). Again and again, in a Hong Kong action movie, the impression of physicality and movement is light years ahead of Western counterparts.

When a van nabs one of Marcus Ray's rival competitors, the thriller element kicks in again – and now Ray is chasing the van because he thinks his chum Eddie Wang (Wyman Wong) is in there (Eddie performed a switch, to get him ahead of Ray in the race). Hendricks whips Ray's ass with an eel. The van crashes into a convenience store (an incredible stunt), where the filmmakers stage a remarkable series of gags and moves – to show off Jean-Claude van Damme as the hero, of course, but also Tsui regular Carman Lee Yeuk-tung as the Chinese cop Ling Ho. This scene alone, for action fans, is amazing; the invention of the choreographers Yuen Bun, Sammo Hung and the stunt team seems boundless. Not to mention the use of props (like cans of food), plus of course Tsui Hark's eye for startling details and views.

Among the other outstanding action sequences in *Knockoff* are a running battle in a food warehouse between the heroes and a horde of furious, knife-wielding guys, intent on revenge (Tsui Hark is very fond of mobs on the war-path, or crowds reacting comically in unison. Here, the motivation is that Eddie Wang is killed by the Russians, who've wired his safe with nothing less than a missile! So the mob thinks our heroes killed Eddie). The sequence is incredibly visceral and physical, with our heroes being bashed, pushed, thrown and hauled around. Action choreographers Sammo Hung and Yuen Bun conjures up 100s of mini-beats and bits of business which delight the audience: Hendricks sliding down a staircase on a trolley (and crashing into piles of fruit in trays); Ray wielding a chain as a makeshift weapon; and our heroes bursting thru a second storey window onto an awning above a market (a Chinese action movie staple).

Knockoff delivers the entire *James Bond* arsenal of stunt scenes: cars hurtling out of upper windows onto the street, our heroes diving out of windows, a fist fight atop a moving truck, knife fights, running gun battles, cops pursuing villains in a boat, and of course giant explosions (there are many of these, including a scene where the C.I.A.'s secret base, underneath the famous, giant Buddha statue[45] at the top of Lantau Island, is blown to bits. Well, a model of it is).

Discovering that his buddy Tommy Hendricks is a spy (for the Central Intelligence Agency), Marcus Ray elicits information by literally pushing Hendricks nearly over the edge of a six-storey building (there's an enormous hoarding for Coca-Cola here, too – a shameless piece of product placement. Coke often appears in movies released by Columbia; you also see Coke product placement in Japanese animation released through Sony-Columbia).

The truck chase is terrific – it starts with the truck blasting out of a building, and continues with the cop Han and Ray fighting henchmen atop

---

[45] Putting the C.I.A. underneath a statue of Buddha is a very *James Bond*-ian concept, recalling movies such as *The Man With the Golden Gun* (1975), where an outpost of the British secret service is housed inside the *R.M.S. Queen Elizabeth* ship, which's run aground in Hong Kong.

and beside the truck.

The mid-movie car lot fight and chase is another marvellous sequence, with the action choreographers inventively employing the concrete pillars (so that Marcus Ray climbs up them, to out-smart the henchmen). Jamming Skinny Wang (the very tubby crime lord) into the car, Ray out-manœuvres the enemy by slamming the car through a huge billboard and a wall. A truly epic stunt, rightly caught in a long, slo-mo shot (where you can see stunt guys diving for cover as the car crashes down from above).

The proto-feminism which runs throughout Tsui Hark's cinema is at work in *Knockoff:* the female lead is Karen Leigh, a Central Intelligence Agency operative who can handle herself, including wielding a gun, kickboxing and fighting the two heroes in a hotel room (where it takes the guys quite a long time to gain the upper hand. In many other action flicks, that fight would be over much quicker). The bust-up is pre-figured by a typical piece of Tsui-ian comedy, when Hendricks is handcuffed by Leigh, after she's pretended to seduce him (to extract more information), tending his wounds pressed against him.

Karen Leigh is played by the lovely Lela Rochon (she was in *Waiting To Exhale*, 1995) as a feisty, independent young woman who doesn't accept sauce from a guy and will hit him.[46] There is another strong female character, the cop in the first act, Ling Ho (unfortunately, she soon disappears from view).

While the finale of *Knockoff* is clichéd narratively, that isn't wholly why we watch Hong Kong action movies! This isn't Chekhov or Bergman, charting the so-subtle changes in a priest having a crisis of conscience because he's experiencing the first glimmers of a suggestion of a hint of the possibility that he might doubt God and his faith!

Oh no, this is men running around with blammy guns like 5 year-old boys. Bang! You're dead! Bang! You fall splayed out against a metal container. Bang! A winch releases a box that crushes you. Bang! A lamp smashes in a shower of glass over you. Bang! Blood spurts from your chest just when you thought you'd got the heroine in your sights.

And so on. The complexity and invention of the action in the finale of *Knockoff,* however, is marvellous to behold. *Knockoff* not only has the shipping containers[47] being used like ammo (slamming into each other, with our heroes only just managing to escape), it orchestrates a dazzling array of props – cables, ropes, netting, winches, cranes, pulleys, windows, lamps, boats, etc.

There are rain-wet decks for sliding along (while shooting), ropes to slide down using belts, ladders to slide down, windows to dive out of (and plenty of other windows to smash), netting to yank to topple an opponent, and containers to squish the baddies.

There's an endless supply of henchmen (as in a *James Bond* movie), so there's always plenty of things for the four heroes to do. And when it

---

[46] When Karen Leigh berates Ray and Hendricks, the camera cranes up, as if Leigh has become a giant teacher, and the guys are kids again (back in skool).
[47] Jackie Chan used containers in *Thunderbolt*.

comes to destroying stuff, and to blowing stuff up, in live-action there are no competitors for Chinese filmmakers.

Of course, Hong Kong action cinema has employed ships many times for action scenes (as has Tsui Hark, in movies such as the *Once Upon a Time in China* series). They're perfect: multiple levels for staging action, a bunch of props strewn about (with a genuine reason for being there), ropes and masts to clamber over, the sea all around for villains to topple into, and they're self-contained, so the action has to stay on the ship.

Happily action co-ordinators Yuen Bun and Sammo Hung also give Lela Rochon stuff to do – so we have cop Karen Leigh firing machine guns, sliding down ladders, diving onto departing vessels, kicking a bottle of acid at Harry Johannson, and cleverly frying the villain using the nano-bombs – all in a day's work for an actress on a Tsui Hark film set! (Johannson is a nasty guy – he smashes Leigh in the face (and, prior to this, Leigh has been tormented with a henchman armed with a bottle of acid).)

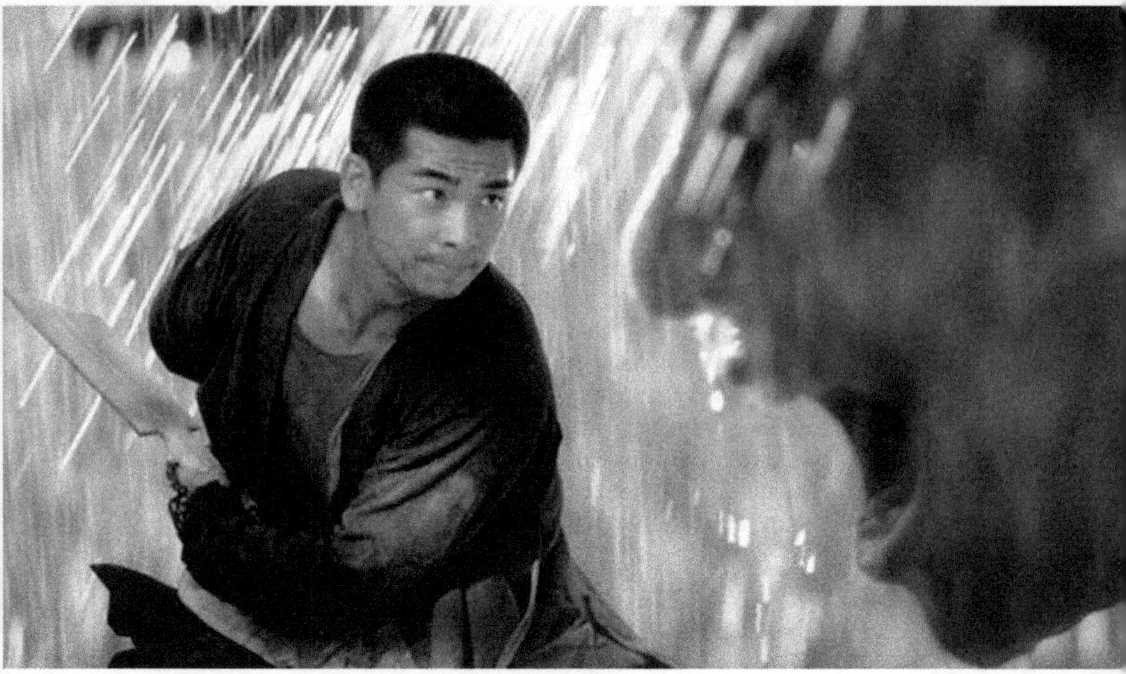

Blade (1995).

WING ZHAO
「ダブルチーム」ツイ・ハーク監督作品
THE BLADE
ブレード
刀
TSUI HARK
TSUI HARK

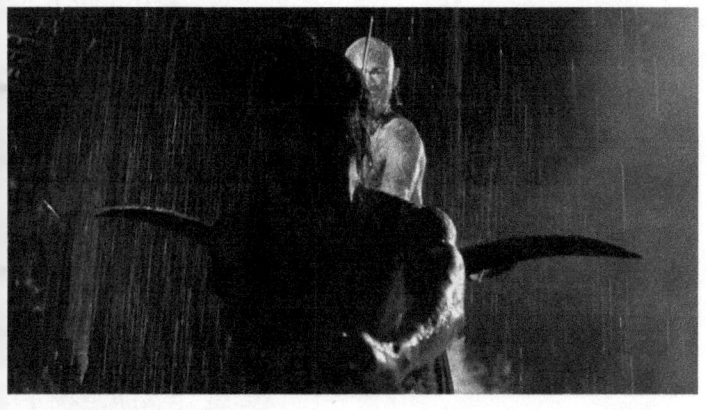

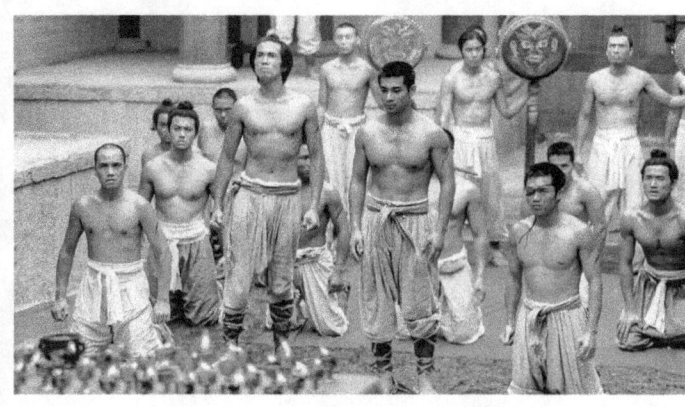

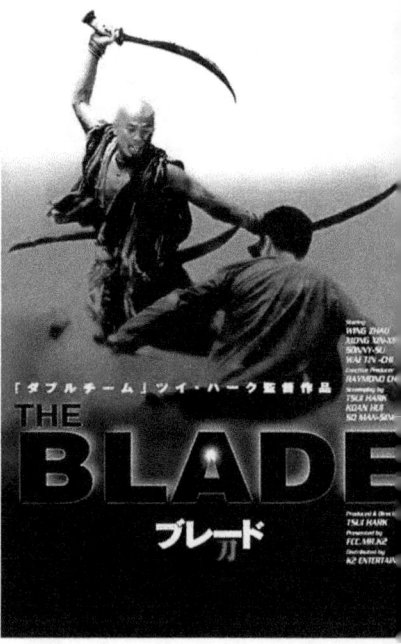

Double Team (1997).

Knock Off (1998).

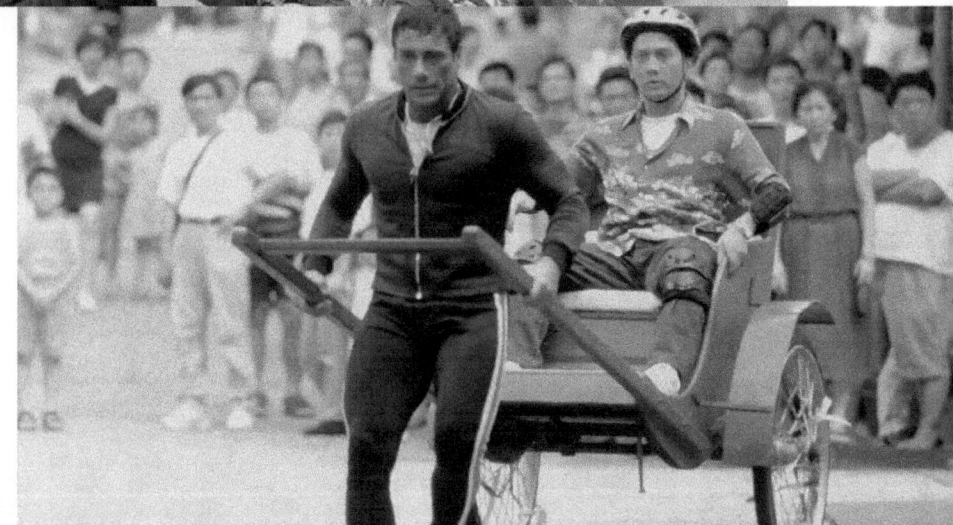

25

TIME AND TIDE

Shun Lau Yik Lau

INTRO.
Time and Tide (2000, *Shùnliú Nìliú* in Mandarin) continues the career of the unstoppable force of nature that is Tsui Hark. This is a movie where it looks as if everybody was just trying to keep up with the 50 year-old director, and he was out-stripping them all. *Time and Tide* was co-written, produced and directed by Tsui, so it's presumably another movie, like *Once Upon a Time In China* or *Seven Swords*, that was close to Tsui's heart. Nicholas Tse (at the time a Cantopop star), Wu Bai (real name Wu Chin-lin, from pop band Wu Bai and China Blue), Anthony Wong,[1] Joventino Couto Remotigue, Candy Lo Hau-yam and Cathy Tsui (Chui) starred. Koan Hui-on was co-writer (and 2nd unit director and sound designer); Tommy Wai composed the music; the DPs were Ko Chiu-lam, Baf Sjamsuddin and Herman Yau Lai-to (William Yim, Davy Tsou Lin-yau and Puccini Yu Kwok-bing were assistants); Marco Mak Chi-sin was editor; and Xiong Xin-xin was action dir. Released Oct 19, 2000. 112/ 116 minutes.

Time and Tide was the first production backed by a N. American company to be filmed wholly in Hong Kong. It was produced by Film Workshop and Film Production Asia, Columbia's new arm in the Orient. The budget for *Time and Tide* was HK $25 million (= U.S. $3.5 million – much lower than the U.S. $35m for *Knockoff*).[2]

Altho' *Time and Tide* is flawed in parts (in its script, its concepts, aspects of its characterizations, its lack of humour, and its clichés), as an action movie, there are sections of *Time and Tide* that are works of art. As if Tsui Hark and his teams, having refined their presentation of action in flashy, contemporary settings with *Knockoff* and *Double Team*, were now able to stage simply extraordinary action sequences. (*Time and Tide*

---
[1] Anthony Wong is a very familiar actor – he has appeared in just about everything in Hong Kong cinema.
[2] At that price, the music couldn't be licensed, but had to be bought. Also, the film couldn't use brand names (LM, 219).

seems like a remake of *Double Team,* as if Tsui Hark and co. decided to make good the poor reception oft *Double Team. Time and Tide* contains several elements from *Double Team,* including the rivalry, the *James Bond*-ian motifs, terrorism, the fire-fights, both heroes're called Jack, the outrageous stunts, and the theme of mothers and babies. Indeed, *Time and Tide* replays the scenario of a woman about to give birth being harassed by henchmen from *Double Team* very closely. And in case you don't get the point, the motif is doubled, with two pregnant women and two couples).

On first screening, *Time and Tide* was the first movie helmed by Tsui Hark that I thought was less than stellar (tho' I hadn't seen the disappointing *Triangle* then!). With some filmmakers, such as Stanley Kubrick or Andrei Tarkovsky, you expect a little *more* when they tackle a genre movie (Kubrick with the horror genre in *The Shining*, for example, or Tarkovsky with the sci-fi- genre in *Solaris*). If *Time and Tide* had been directed by anybody else, it might be celebrated as a formidable movie, but altho' *Time and Tide* is a powerful action thriller, it doesn't quite have the Tsui magic. No, that's not true: better to say that *Time and Tide* doesn't have the grandeur and craziness of Tsui's finest works.

Time and Tide is also a movie that we have all seen thousands of times before. Yes, action thrillers and gangster pictures are staples of Hong Kong cinema, and have been for many decades (indeed, contemporary thrillers and dramas have kept the Hong Kong movie business afloat in lean times: it's a (relatively) cheap genre: you use existing, contemporary locations and contemporary costumes (plus the mandatory sharp suits and shades), add a few guns and cars, and some by-the-numbers action sequences). But we expect more from a filmmaker of Tsui Hark's calibre. Or maybe it's me: unless a crime or gangster picture is as good as *The Godfather* or *Cowboy Bebop*, I find them the least inspiring of any genre.

Taking Tsui Hark out of the loop, and setting aside some of the predictable characterizations, and the boring crime genre elements, *Time and Tide* is certainly a formidable work on many levels: the action is brutal and crunching (Xin-xin Xiong was action director – he was Clubfoot in *Once Upon a Time In China 3*, and Jet Li's double in the earlier *Once Upon a Time In China* movies), the editing is as rapid and light-stepping as ever (Marco Mak Chi-sin was editor), and the storytelling and pace are pushed along with Tsui's customary nervous energy.

But *Time and Tide* gets better with every viewing – the flaws and clichés dissolve amidst the truly remarkable imagery, the outstanding action sequences, and the thrilling momentum of the cutting.

Parts of *Time and Tide* seem full of the energy and naïvety of a first film, as if the director has just watched a Jean Luc-Godard movie of the 1960s for the first time, and decides to put some of the French genius's famous, irreverent verve onto the screen. For ex, the scene in the supermarket featuring the two couples in *Time and Tide* is very Godardian – from the setting (ultra-capitalism), the antsy relationship between Ah Jo and Tyler (when she sees him standing next to the very pregnant Ah Hui), to the characters throwing things to each other (such as condoms – and they're shown next to the tampons and diapers).

On further viewings, *Time and Tide* seems even more impressive: it comes across as a superbly engaging action thriller powered by lightning-fast editing, and filled with truly extraordinary imagery and camerawork (to the point where the camera operators (Herman Yau Lai-to, Chiu-lam Ko and Baf Sjamsuddin were DPs; William Yim and Puccini Yu Kwok-bing were 2nd unit DPs; Lien-you Tsouand Jan-wah Yuen were assistant DPs) are among the stars of the 2000 picture. This is camerawork where the operators are so closely involved in the action they are dancing around the performers more intimately than most marriages). But there's no doubt about who's in charge on this show – it's A Tsui Hark Production through and through.

In *Time Asia*, Richard Corliss enthused:

> surely the movie-est movie of the year. Like graffiti written in blood, it spells out Tsui's message to the industry he left in 1996: I'm back, lean and mean, gun blazing.

▶

In *Time and Tide*, we follow the exploits of Tyler (Nicholas Tse), a bit of a drifter who moves up from being a barman to a bodyguard with Uncle Ji's (Anthony Wong) somewhat ramshackle outfit.[3] He pairs up with Jack (Wu Bai). *Time and Tide* is narrated by Tyler. (The two leads are both Asian pop stars, but they are more successful than some Western pop stars we could name who moved into movies. Indeed, it's commonplace for the Chinese film industry to cast pop stars, and Tsui Hark has done it several times – most impressively with Leslie Cheung).

Tyler is a young guy trying to earn some money to help out the woman he got pregnant during a drunken one-night stand (Ah Jo – who happens to be a lesbian cop). With his floppy fringe, smart suit and quick grins, he might've walked off stage from a boy band concert in Kowloon in front of 20,000 screaming teenyboppers. Nicholas Tse doesn't wholly convince as a wannabe man of the streets, or a guy who could be a bodyguard, but he does throw himself wholly into the role (which's the best thing to do in a Tsui Hark movie! No point holding back!).

Tyler shows his colours early on when, given the job of escorting a portly and irritating woman to the airport, he opts to take the journey in reverse – by hurtling the car thru the streets backwards. It's played for comedy (the plump woman bounces around in the car, whimpering), and the filmmakers don't bother to hide the crowds watching the film crew from the sidewalks.

Guns, gangsters, cars, suits, betrayals, posh hotels, sunglasses – *Time and Tide* has most of the clichés of the action crime genre. And this is partly the problem with *Time and Tide* at a genre and dramatic level – it *is* too clichéd, too standard, too close to the norms of the genre.

There is also the boring emphasis on cool in *Time and Tide*, on looking

---

3 A classic piece of Tsui-ism has Uncle Ji refusing to give Tyler a gun (a castration motif); Tyler buys himself a plastic BB replica instead (in a store where he first meets Jack Chow).

cool, on acting cool, that turns so many recent gangster and crime pictures into smugfests. The main characters, Tyler and Jack Chow, seem so desperate to appear cool and nonchalant and swaggering and mean, they come over as arrogant (Tyler especially). For instance, during an intense fire-fight in a heist/ ambush scene, Miguel hides behind a counter, drinking a can of beer and smiling smugly to himself. Oh, look, he is *so* cool, even in the middle of heavy machine gun fire and knife-edge proximity to death, he's got time to sip beer and grin.

I don't buy it, and I don't buy the main character, Tyler.

▶

I also had the impression that in *Time and Tide* Tsui Hark was looking too much over his shoulder – at other filmmakers. So you can spot Tsui doing his version of the contemporary, urban movies of Wong Kar-wai in *Time and Tide,* as also in *Knockoff* (such as *Chungking Express* or *Happy Together*), or his version of John Woo (which Tsui had already done in *A Better Tomorrow 3*), or his version of a North American action thriller *à la* Paul Thomas Anderson, Quentin Tarantino or Martin Scorsese (and their many imitators), those urban movies which're *always* described by reviewers as 'dark' and 'edgy' and 'stylish' (my three most hated phrases in film reviewing).

However, on further viewings of *Time and Tide*, no, Tsui Hark isn't imitating anybody – after all, he is his own genre! This is simply the way that Tsui makes movies! When people complained to Orson Welles about his baroque camerawork, he replied that it just seemed natural to him. Doesn't everyone film like that? Welles wondered. To Welles, putting the camera way down low and tracking with the actors along a corridor wasn't showing off, it just seemed like the right way to film a scene.

Anyhoo, Tsui Hark doesn't need to 'imitate' anybody – he can do everything that everybody else does anyway (indeed, the influence goes the other way, more often, with Western film producers being influenced by Hong Kong filmmakers all the time).

EDITING.

According to some reports, *Time and Tide* was changed quite a bit in the editing. I mean more than usual, to the point where subplots and the point-of-view was altered. *Time and Tide* apparently came in at three hours in the first cut, which was too long and slow for Tsui Hark. The movie was tightened up (as is often the case), and subplots involving Uncle Ji were ditched. (A pity – because Anthony Wong is always worth watching, and the uneasy father-and-son relationship between Uncle Ji and Tyler is central to *Time and Tide*).

It's also a little disorientating when you come to *Time and Tide* after watching many of Tsui Hark's historical and fantasy pictures. After seeing *Green Snake*, *Once Upon a Time In China*, *The Blade* and others, I kept wondering when a character was going to fly across the room, or when someone was going to initiate a sword fight.

Because, let's face it, another flaw with *Time and Tide* is that it's rather humourless. Comedy is I think an absolutely vital ingredient of the Tsui Hark School of Cinema, and in *Time and Tide* it's thin on the ground. Tyler is a grinning, apparently affable but actually quite empty and unappealing personality, so there aren't many laughs there. The women Ah Hui and Ah Jo are so sour and angry with their lot in life, they can barely speak.[4] Uncle Ji (Anthony Wong),[5] who runs the dodgy bodyguard business, also plays it straight (despite Wong being known for his wacko roles), as do, *inevitably*, every single one of the mobsters and Triads.

THE GIRLS.

Meanwhile, *Time and Tide* is much more interesting when it leaves the desperate-to-be-cool boys and middle-aged men and joins the girls. Two young women're introduced early on in *Time and Tide* as lesbian lovers. One of them is a cop Ah Jo (played by the 18 year-old Cathy Tsui),[6] and she spends a drink-fuelled night with Tyler, resulting in pregnancy. (*Time and Tide* includes several images of women vomiting – this is not your usual movie!).

What's far more entertaining in *Time and Tide* than Tyler and adolescent desires to be a wise guy or hoodlum *à la* Chow Yun-fat or Al Pacino, are the early scenes when the two women are allowed to really let rip and lose their tempers (when they argue in the bar where Tyler works). There's a great scene where Ah Jo's lover attacks him on a street at night with a metal pipe (!), yelling that he's stolen her lover and got her pregnant. It's not often that actresses get to scream and bellow like this, and beat the main star about the face with a pipe! (The vehemence and physicality of the performance recalls the 1960s movies of Jean-Luc Godard, when characters snipe and nudge and hit each other).

The morning-after scene, between Tyler and Ah Jo, is a *tour-de-force* of physical acting and in-your-face camerawork, as the actors slide and career around a small apartment strewn with clothes. Coupled with the razor-sharp, 180 m.p.h. editing, the domestic scenes in *Time and Tide* have an intensity that makes Western movies look like fat slobs who can barely get up off the couch. The filmmakers encourage the actors to *really* let fly (which actors *love* to do!), and Cathy Tsui and Nicholas Tse really deliver.

Unfortunately, that tremendous energy seeps away a little in later scenes in *Time and Tide*,[7] and the women, interacting with the male characters, return to the default position of all contemporary thrillers and contemporary dramas, which is that sarcastic, weary attitude and communication. It's what you see in every North American/ Western TV drama show, cop show and military show, where actors stand and talk and snipe at each other in a cynical fashion. That isn't acting, it's merely delivering your dialogue by numbers. A two-shot, bang bang, an over-the-

---

[4] However, Candy Lo as Ah Hui does goof around a little – look at the facial expressions she pulls in the supermarket scene, which seems to have been a particularly playful and silly day of filming.
[5] Anthony Wong is known for his out-there performances, but here he keeps it toned down.
[6] Cathy Tsui embarked on a high profile wedding in Martin Lee to 2006.
[7] The editing also slows down a tad after the opening ten minutes, before the ambush involving the Angels.

shoulder close-up, bang bang, a final close-up, bang bang.

▶

Time and Tide is a testosterone, macho feast – the only two prominent female charas, Ah Jo and Ah Hui, do not drive the plot, nor are they the focus of attention. The entire second half of *Time and Tide,* for instance, is a *Boy's Own* affair, and Candy Lo (as Ah Hui) plays a woman in peril role (not only that, but in the midst of a fierce siege and fire-fight, she is giving birth!). Yes, but there *are* scenes, in between the action, where both Ah Hui and Ah Jo at least makes an impression: Jack takes his wife Ah Hui to her (estranged) father's place, for her protection (even when she's turned up at their apartment, after he's warned her not to); and Tyler has an awkward-but-kind-of-sweet make-up meeting with Ah Jo in a road (after she's tried to bail him out when he's been arrested, but didn't have the money). Afterwards, Ah Jo drives off and smiles to herself (as does Tyler – the movie allows itself a brief romantic montage of superimposed images to music here).

TECHNICAL ASPECTS.

At a technical level, *Time and Tide* is another of Tsui Hark's *tour-de-force* directing jobs, with his facility for making images as energetic and imaginative as ever, punched along with express train editing, and a host of quirky elements (bizarre point-of-view shots,[8] very low, tilted tracking shots across floors, sudden blips and judders in the editing, incredible freeze frames, abrupt whip pans, step-motion, adjusted colour, etc). An important plus point with *Time and Tide* is that it uses (some) direct sound – you can see and hear the difference it makes straight away. To go back and loop all of *Time and Tide* would deaden the liveliness of the picture so much.[9]

It's true that Tsui Hark makes it all look so easy, as if he's simply arrived at a hotel or on a street with a couple of cameras, and shot the scenes on the wing, without rehearsal. *Time and Tide* does have an appealing immediacy and urgency, as if life is about to end at any moment, and the quicker you get on with living the better.

Tsui Hark is certainly a filmmaker you could give a camera to and some raw film stock (or some video tape or hard drives), and he could film something memorable anywhere. A street, a hotel, a car, an airport, a garbage dump... Tsui is such a natural filmmaker, a filmmaker with an incredible talent for creating images and telling stories.

Time and Tide is an effects-heavy movie – apart from the battery of practical effects, which're mandatory in any Chinese action movie (fire, smoke, fog, squibs, bullet hits, smashed glass and of course explosions), there are digital effects throughout *Time and Tide.* Many of the vfx are self-conscious, look-at-me images – like the camera travelling down the barrel of a gun and out the other side, into an E.C.U of an eye, or a C.U. of a spinning grenade. We are always conscious that we are watching a

---

[8] Inside a washing machine, inside a gun, giant close-ups of eyes freezing from a fire extinguisher.
[9] Altho' plenty of *Time and Tide* is also looped.

movie: *Time and Tide* never lets us forget that.

And the camera never stops moving in *Time and Tide* – but the movements have a poetic logic, a spontaneity which's delightful.10 *Time and Tide* is as lively as any movie I can think of for instilling a freshness and vitality in the movement of the camera. This goes way beyond using Steadicams, or being handheld – there's a freedom of movement in the cinema of Tsui Hark which's very appealing, and at times intoxicating.

The use of locations in *Time and Tide* is another striking aspect of the production, which filmed in many existing locations. *Time and Tide* takes you not only into the usual stairwells and elevators and underground car lots of an action thriller, but right thru kitchens, service corridors, locker rooms, ducts, etc. The use of space is so inventive – look at the choreography of the lengthy scuffle between Tyler and the rogue waiter, in amongst piles of stacked chairs and tables (a very unglamorous setting!).11 Nobody can match Hong Kong filmmakers for the use of props in action scenes.

There are running motifs/ gags involving cigarette lighters (stolen), musical boxes, cheap Hong Kong merchandize (Hong Kong is derided as 'Cockroach City'), guns (and fake guns), and characters throwing things to each other (very Godardian). *Time and Tide* contains many of Tsui Hark's familiar motifs (tigers, fish, animals, food, restaurants, babies, etc),

SOUND.

The *sound* is another outstanding, technical ingredient in *Time and Tide* (Koan Hui-on was sound designer, Dave Terman and Martin Chappell were sound editors): there is a score, of course (by Tommy Wai), but it is striking just how often the movie plays *without* music, and relies on *sound effects*. Also, the sound of *Time and Tide* appears at times as if the filmmakers were trying something that goes *against* the usual Action Movie Soundtrack. Without a score, the filmmakers use sound effects, but much more muted and low volume sound effects than you expect to hear in a movie of this type. Thus, while the screen is filled with incredible action, and the camerawork is dazzling you *again* and *again* with *truly remarkable* framing and movement, the sounds you hear are actually mixed low and are often minimal. (The whole apartment block action sequence plays without music).

A Western action movie typically includes the sounds of pretty much everything you will see on screen: if someone runs, you hear footsteps, creaks of clothing, the clatter of weaponry, the creak of leather or webbing, panting/ breathing, plus background atmos. Not in *Time and Tide*, where the sound editors (Terman and Chappell) pick out maybe two sounds, and use them, forgetting about everything else. Yet the result is curiously mesmerizing, with its own reality and clarity.

If someone's running down a corridor carrying a gun, would you hear

---
10 But it isn't the simulation of 'handheld' camerawork found in North American TV shows, where the camera's wobbled with that fake, 'reality TV' effect.
11 The choreography has many of the hallmarks of a Xiong Xin-xion action scene, where the movements are rough-and-tumble, inelegant, and involve lots of grappling.

absolutely everything clearly? Probably not: sound in a Hong Kong action movie is much more *psychological* or *atmospheric* than a Western action movie (Western movies are of course dedicated to 'realism', or what they think of as 'realism', than Oriental movies).

One thing's for sure – more recent movies from Hong Kong have spent more time on the soundtrack and the sound effects than movies in the 1960s or 1970s or 1980s (which were entirely dubbed, and the practice continues today). Tsui Hark's movies are certainly very sophisticated in terms of sound editing, mixing and sound effects. (For ex, *Time and Tide* contains numerous uses of whooshes and breathy sounds which accompany camera moves past objects, or sudden changes in the editing. which are used in Western action cinema: these noises are not music, but act in the same way as music, to emphasize elements of the movie.)

The narration (from Tyler) adds another layer to *Time and Tide* – the voiceover extends beyond the usual demands of exposition, to add characterization and detail. For ex, we don't need to know *that* much about Uncle Ji – casting Anthony Wong is all that's required. (However, the subplot involving Uncle Ji was cut back – the voiceover thus describes dialogue aspects of Uncle Ji without needing to show them).

THE ACTION.

However, ignore the cheesy grins of some of the actors, and just look at that fire-fight as the Angels[12] perform their ambush! Wow! It's another example of how Hong Kong action cinema bests everyone else on the planet in live-action. It has a bone-crunching ferocity, with bullets smashing into metal doors, filmed with outrageous camera moves and visceral choreography. It's loud, it's exciting, and it's wildly over-the-top. Like many Hong Kong movies, *Time and Tide* is unashamed of being a movie, of being movie-movie-ish, of putting on a show. The ambush climaxes with enormous explosions (courtesy of a ridiculous number of grenades).

Back in Hong Kong, we see Uncle Ji's outfit in operation as they act as security for a big shot at his birthday celebration in a swanky hotel downtown with 100s of guests. Marco Mak Chi-sin's editing is ziiipping so fast thru multiple (and parallel) action beats, it makes most other action thrillers seem as a lively as a coma victim in cryogenic freeze. Tyler, once again, is at the centre of this party – going after suspect waiters (and getting the wrong guy), and driving Uncle Ji nuts.

Jack and Tyler are a duo who go up against a mob of professional assassins, the South American Angels, whom they've trounced in a spectacular heist. The Angels never give up, tho', and the warfare that develops is relentless. It's not about the classic MacGuffin of thrillers, the suitcase full of money, anymore, but about honour, and payback, and cold-blooded revenge (and 'face' – male ego, male vanity, and male

---

[12] The leader of the Angels, Miguel (Joventino Couto Remotigue), with his dreadlocks and sun glasses, has wandered out of a Quentin Tarantino or *Matrix* movie (Miguel doesn't convince – he is also guilty of being too smug, and the ropey looping of his lines doesn't help).

vulnerability). The authorities, as in many gangster pictures, are only glimpsed on the fringes, and the cops always turn up too late. Even when the Special Weapons and Tactics team arrive at Kowloon Station, to clean up the mess, the Angels are ahead of them, and have their own uniforms and gas masks.

Jack Chow fleeing from the hit is another extraordinary action sequence – again, the filmmakers take the action into corridors, elevators, storage rooms and kitchens (plus the mandatory ducts and service walkways).

There is also a superb car chase inside a multi-level parking lot – very *James Bond* (there was a good one in *Tomorrow Never Dies*), but entertaining, too. There's a feeling for the high impact hits from machine guns and pistols as they blast into car doors or grills, for the crunch of metal as cars slam into concrete, that elevates Hong Kong action scenes far above their Western counterparts.

The whole second half of *Time and Tide* is wall-to-wall action that makes any of the recent *James Bond* movies, or any Western action movie, look like geriatrics on their deathbeds. Disregarding the characters and the issues/ motives/ goals at stake, what most of *Time and Tide* boils down to, and all of the second half, is good guys versus bad guys. That's all it is (or one group of guys vs. another group of guys). The cat and mouse games are nothing more'n glorified and excessive versions of the games that kids play: cops and robbers, cowboys and Indians, the Yanks versus the Krauts (this applies to most action movies of the commercial kind, anywhere).

Yes, you can talk about 'political allegory', you can talk about post-1997 Hong Kong, or about transnational, pan-global capitalism and market economies, or about the 'abstract nationalism' in Tsui Hark's cinema, or you can wheel in philosophers like Paul Virilio, Jean Baudrillard and Frederic Jameson, but, come on folks, what *Time and Tide* boils down to is *huge* action sequences in which boys (sorry, I mean, *men* – big, beefy, so-macho *men*), run around with guns, blasting away at each other, leaping over bannisters, crashing thru glass windows, hiding on ceilings ninja-style, pulling victims down stairways with ropes,[13] sliding down escalators (can't walk down, right? – too slow!), yelling into cel phones and mics, banging away with more machine guns, tossing hand grenades, kicking each other in the shins, slicing up throats, sliding across floors under rows of seats,[14] flipping up from the ground or on top of guys' shoulders, Peking Opera-style, punching each other, hanging off walkways 100s of feet in the air, and abseiling down the side of tall buildings...

It's pretty darn extraordinary, as an action movie, and if action was the sole requirement of an action movie then, well, *Time and Tide* would surely be among the masterpieces of contemporary cinema. Perhaps it is: as a style piece, a bodies-in-motion piece, a sound-and-light piece, it *is* remarkable. The ingenuity of the stunt team, the action directors, the

---
13 Would that even work? The filmmakers make it work!
14 There is some parkour-style action in *Time and Tide*. When the 2006 *James Bond* movie *Casino Royale* tried 'free running', it was utterly dreadful. Here, it's blissful.

camera teams, the practical effects guys and everybody else, is marvellous to behold. This is filmmaking as a giant train set with Tsui Hark and his cohorts gleefully conjuring up one impossible but stunning scenario after another.

If the actors (or their stunt doubles) are abseiling down a building, why, then, so does the cameraman! In amongst ten thousand gags and stunts in *Time and Tide,* the abseiling sequence and the running across roofs and balconies sequence takes some beating. In *Time and Tide,* the camera's on wires, on remote arms, on giant cranes... In some sequences, the camera soars out over the side of rooftops, capturing the sort of shots you see in mountaineering documentaries. (How many stuntmen were harmed in the making of this movie? There's isn't a gag reel at the end as in a Jackie Chan picture, but you can bet that someone got injured some time!).

If Tyler is the goofy sidekick, Jack Chow is James Bond, the all-knowing, always-prepared warrior, who's ready for every eventuality. So while *Time and Tide* aims for a sort of verisimilitude of contemporary Hong Kong, it forgets about that when it depicts Jack performing one incredible stunt after another (and Jack is also a master of disguise – he has numerous changes of clothing when he's fleeing from his hit).

But *Time and Tide* is at least more'n a run-of-the-mill action/ crime/ gangster/ thriller picture. It is a wild action movie, and sometimes a wilfully eccentric one. It's just not possible for Tsui Hark to deliver a routine picture, or for him to place his camera in the expected position.

▶

The extended action sequences that soak up the second half of *Time and Tide* begin in an enormous tenement building (when Tyler goes to Jack's apartment, which the Angels have staked out), then to Kowloon Station, and then to the Colosseum (a giant arena).

In the midst of all the childish but hugely enjoyable bang--bang-you're-dead fun and games, the suitcase full of money is swiftly ditched. Now it's all about payback: the Angels are expending a *huge* amount of effort just to kill Jack Chow (and Tyler gets in the way, as usual).

How many ways can you think of to stage chases and gun battles in the corridors, stairwells and balconies of a housing tenement? Well, the filmmakers certainly deliver stunts and gags that seem 'new' (even if they aren't 'new'). For instance, taking a guy *and* the camera right out of a window and down the side of the building on ropes. Incredible!

There's no question that when it comes to wirework and flying stunt guys everywhere (such as all the way across the face of a building), Hong Kong filmmakers are supreme. There is a feeling of freedom of movement, that a performer can move anywhere at any time, but in real space, and in real time.

Tyler has his own very lengthy bust-up with a heavy in Jack Chow's apartment (which's lit in sun-orange hues). By the end of this fight, action choreographer Xin-xin Xiong seems to have used every space, every prop, every piece of furniture in the entire apartment (taking the fight into the bathroom (the shower), the bedroom, the kitchen, etc). Tyler manages to survive by climbing inside a fridge as the place explodes in a gas blow-out (with the filmmakers adding plenty of self-conscious visual effects).

Also, it is a brilliant example of film editing and sound editing. The sound in the tenement sequence is dense with radio cross-talk, which cleverly acts as voiceover to explain what's happening elsewhere. The editor (Marco Mak Chi-sin) is orchestrating numerous little pieces of parallel action. Coupled with the way that the camera operators cover everything by keeping the camera moving (even the most mundane shot is off-kilter), it might be confusing, but it isn't. The orchestration by the editors of space, of moving characters through spaces, of making the action clear and readable, is simply astonishing.

And there's another remarkable thing about the tenement action sequence in *Time and Tide:* it's musicless. The temptation to put music into at least some of this sort of sequence is difficult to resist: instead, the sequence is a *tour-de-force* of sound effects editing and sound mixing. And instead of battling the music, and fighting with the dialogue, as in the typical action sequence, the sound team can happily hog the stage, adding only explanatory voiceover (dubbed afterwards).

▶

Kowloon Station is the setting for the first half of the finale of *Time and Tide* – with both Jack Chow and Tyler having their own adventures. Tyler is given the task of recovering the bag of money – but that job is soon supplanted by protecting Ah Hui, who's going into labour. Tyler and Hui are caught in the midst of the running battle between the Angels and the Special Weapons and Tactics teams. In amongst shadows obscured by smoke canisters, the filmmakers stage intricate cat-and-mouse games.

Tyler escorts Ah Hui into the basement, and assists her in delivering her baby. To round off Tyler's side of the crime plot, he has a visceral bust-up with one of the Angels gang. Once again, the invention of the action choreography is remarkable, as if, altho' it's the final reel of the movie, there's no indication that the filmmakers are running out of ideas. Instead, they put babies and pregnant women into a fierce duel (with the baby inevitably being thrown about, to protect it). In the movie's proto-feminism, the kill shot is given to Ah Hui, as she unloads a gun into the Angels' henchman (why use one bullet when six will do?!).

Jack Chow, meanwhile, finishes his business with the Angels mob, by going up against Miguel in the customary heroes vs. villains fight and finale. For no particular reason, the action is shifted from Kowloon Station into the nearby Colosseum (where, in true *James Bond*-style, a big event is taking place to a packed house). No need to rewrite the action genre from scratch at this point in *Time and Tide* – so the fight is set, inevitably, on the gantries high above the stadium floor and the audience (which Tsui Hark and others in Hong Kong cinema have used before – in, for exmaple, the Jet Li actioner *My Father Is a Hero*, 1995). Action director Xiong Xin-xin employs his familiar style of grappling bodies (where participants grab each other with their legs, not arms), and Peking Opera tumbling. Miguel has booby-trapped the steel walkways with grenades and wires, but that is his undoing in the end, when Jack manages to kick a grenade in the air back to Miguel, which explodes.

The finale of *Time and Tide* contains the expected outrageous stunts and gags; like most Hong Kong action movies, the climax contains numerous mini-scenes within the overall structure. One section, for instance, concerns a staple of action cinema – a train heading towards the locked-down station which can't be stopped. The fire-fight on the railroad tracks is just one ingredient in the finale (narratively, the scene reverses the power games, because Jack saves the commander's life).

WOMEN, BABIES AND THE ENDING.

The 2000 movie features two guys and two women, but altho' one of the women (Ah Jo) is a cop, she disappears for long sections of the story. Like a John Woo movie, *Time and Tide* instead focusses on the brotherhood of Tyler and Jack, and their on-going and hyper-intense war with the Angels mob.

The subplot of women and children is important, however, and this is thus *not* a John Woo-style narrative – tho' more at a thematic and spiritual level. The lesbian cop Ah Jo gives birth, tho' she resents Tyler and her one-night stand enormously (he keeps giving her money,[15] which she pointedly ignores or returns). Gradually, Jo softens a little, and the movie closes with them reunited, at the hospital, looking at their baby in the next room.

Candy Lo's Ah Hui, meanwhile, goes into labour during the climactic battle of *Time and Tide*. So she is what is at stake in *Time and Tide,* what the guys have to protect, and she's the hope for the future. The motif of imminent birth has been used many times in action movies, adding layers of jeopardy and melodrama to the proceedings. Yes, it's far-fetched and highly contrived, but *Time and Tide* sort of gets away with it – partly by being so ballsy with its clichés. The filmmakers are not inventing the wheel here, and they know it. They're not adding anything 'new' or 'original' in particular to the action and crime genre (hell, who does? Who can?). But they are delivering slambang pyrotechnics of motion and threat which destroy the competition from thousands of other action and gangster movies.

So *Time and Tide* closes on a note of hope, with two births, two babies, and two sort of couples. 'Sort of' couples, because Jack Chow has to part from his wife, Ah Hui (he's allowed to leave by the head of the S.W.A.T. team), and Tyler is an immature and rather hapless youth who's had a child with a lesbian cop. Yes, but look at the framing: in a typically eccentric Tsui Hark style, the camera, at floor level, takes a picture of Tyler and Jo standing next to each other in the corridor of the hospital, but only shows their shoes and legs! So it's Tsuian eccentricity (a totally bizarre camera angle!), yet the two charas are filmed in the *same shot*, one of the giveaways that these two folks'll be connected after the movie ends

---

15 Pushed under her front door.

(this is the final shot – modest but hopeful – in a movie crammed with truly extraordinary images).

Meanwhile, Tyler's naïve but sweet ruminations on the Creation myth from the *Bible* offer a religious/ spiritual layer to the mix, lending a grand element to the 2000 movie (the seven days of Creation are introduced early in the picture – in the opening scene, with heavily ironic imagery to illustrate what Jehovah created on each day). When Tyler (in the voiceover) talks about the creation by God of humans, we cut to a close-up of his baby in its crib. Cute! Babies! New Life! Hope!

Time and Tide (2000).

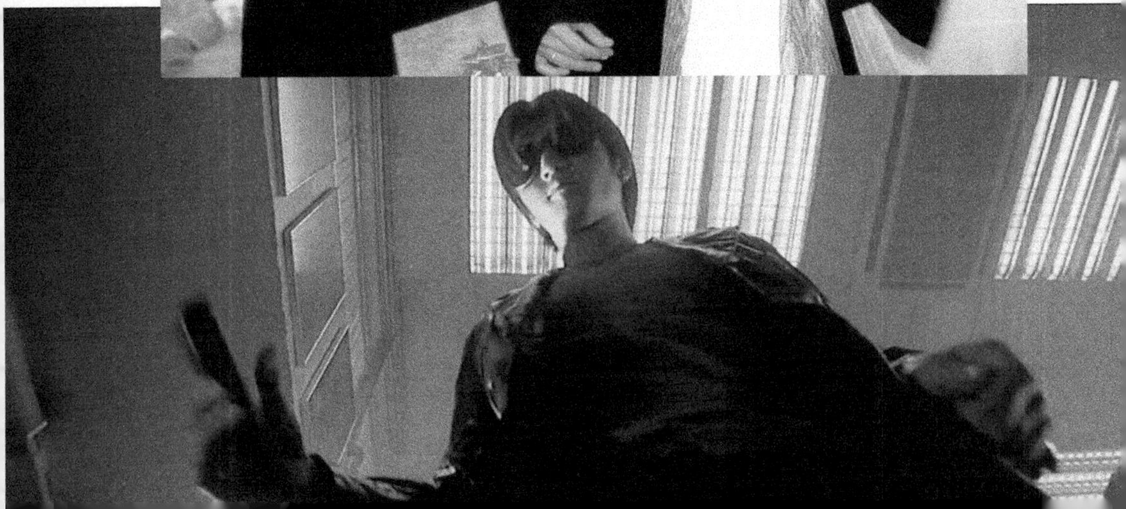

FILMOGRAPHY

MOVIES AS DIRECTOR

The Butterfly Murders, 1979
We're Going To Eat You, 1980
Dangerous Encounters of the First Kind, 1980
All the Wrong Clues, 1981
Zu: Warriors From the Magic Mountain, 1983
Search For the Gods, 1983
Aces Go Places 3, 1984
Shanghai Blues, 1984
Working Class, 1985
Peking Opera Blues, 1986
Spirit Chaser Aisha, 1986
The Master, 1989
A Better Tomorrow 3, 1989
The Swordsman, 1990
Once Upon a Time in China, 1991
The Banquet, 1991
The Raid, 1991
Once Upon a Time in China 2, 1992
Twin Dragons, 1992
Once Upon a Time in China 3, 1993
Green Snake, 1993
Once Upon a Time in China 5, 1994
The Lovers, 1994
The Chinese Feast, 1995
Love In the Time of Twilight, 1995
The Blade, 1995
Tristar, 1996
Double Team, 1997
Knock Off, 1998
Time and Tide, 2000
The Legend of Zu, 2001
Black Mask 2: City of Masks, 2002
In The Blue, 2005
Seven Swords, 2005
The Warrior, 2006
Triangle, 2007
Missing, 2008
All About Women, 2008
Detective Dee and the Mystery of the Phantom Flame, 2010
The Flying Swords of Dragon Gate, 2011

Young Detective Dee: Rise of the Sea Dragon, 2013
Catching Monkey 3-D, 2013
The Taking of Tiger Mountain, 2014
Journey To the West: The Demons Strike Back, 2017
Detective Dee and the Four Heavenly Kings, 2018
The Battle At Lake Changjin, 2021
The Battle At Lake Changjin 2, 2022
The Legend of the Condor Heroes: The Great Hero, 2025

MOVIES AS PRODUCER

All the Wrong Spies, 1983
A Better Tomorrow, 1986
The Laser Man, 1986
A Chinese Ghost Story, 1987
A Better Tomorrow 2, 1987
The Big Heat, 1988
Gunmen, 1988
Diary of a Big Man, 1988
The King of Chess, 1988/ 1992
The Master, 1989
A Better Tomorrow 3, 1989
The Killer, 1989
Just Heroes, 1989
The Terracotta Warrior, 1989
The Swordsman, 1990
A Chinese Ghost Story 2, 1990
A Chinese Ghost Story 3, 1991
New Dragon Gate Inn, 1992
The Swordsman 2, 1992
The Wicked City, 1992
Once Upon a Time in China 2, 1992
Once Upon a Time in China 3, 1993
Green Snake, 1993
The Swordsman 3/ The East Is Red, 1993
Once Upon a Time in China 4, 1993
Once Upon a Time in China 5, 1994
The Lovers, 1994
Burning Paradise, 1994
The Chinese Feast, 1995
The Blade, 1995
Shanghai Grand, 1996
A Chinese Ghost Story: The Tsui Hark Animation, 1997
Once Upon a Time in China and America, 1997
Time and Tide, 2000
The Legend of Zu, 2001
Old Master Q, 2001
Tsui Hark's Vampire Hunters, 2002
Black Mask 2: City of Masks, 2002
Xanda, 2004
Seven Swords, 2005
Triangle, 2006
Missing, 2008
All About Women, 2008

Detective Dee and the Mystery of the Phantom Flame, 2010
The Flying Swords of Dragon Gate, 2011
Young Detective Dee: Rise of the Sea Dragon, 2013
Christmas Rose, 2013
The Taking of Tiger Mountain, 2014
Sword Master, 2016
The Thousand Faces of Dunjia, 2017
Journey To the West: The Demons Strike Back, 2017
Detective Dee and the Four Heavenly Kings, 2018
The Climbers, 2019
The Battle At Lake Changjin, 2021
The Battle At Lake Changjin 2, 2022

RECOMMENDED BOOKS AND WEBSITES

One of the finest general introductions to the history of Hong Kong cinema, and a great place to start, is *Hong Kong Cinema* (1997) by Stephen Teo. David Bordwell and Kristin Thompson are consistently excellent commentators on film, in books such as *Film History: An Introduction* (2010) and Bordwell's account of Hong Kong cinema, *Planet Hong Kong: Popular Cinema and the Art of Entertainment* (2000).

Bey Logan's *Hong Kong Action Cinema* (1995) is an entertaining introduction to the action side of Hong Kong cinema (with many valuable illustrations). *Kung-fu Cult Masters: From Bruce Lee To 'Crouching Tiger'* (2003) takes a more theoretical approach to the same subject.

For surveys of films, Jeff Yang's *Once Upon a Time In China* (2003) is superb, as is *Hong Kong Babylon* (1997) by F. Dannen & B. Long (this book also features many interviews with the key players in the Hong Kong industry). Lisa Morton's *The Cinema of Tsui Hark* (2001) is an important early study.

Jackie Chan has attracted many studies and biographies, including *Jackie Chan* by C. Gentry (1997), *The Essential Jackie Chan Sourcebook* by J. Rovin & K. Tracy (1997), and *Dying For Action: The Life and Times of Jackie Chan* by R. Witterstaetter (1997). And Chan's own memoirs: *I Am Jackie Chan* (1998) and *Never Grow Up* (2018).

Among critical essays, I would recommend *At Full Speed: Hong Kong Cinema In a Borderless World* (1998, edited by E.C.M. Yau) and *The Cinema of Hong Kong* (2002), edited by P. Fu & D. Desser.

WEBSITES

Hong Kong Movie Database
Love Hong Kong Film
Hong Kong Cinemagic
Film Workshop
Jet Li   jetli.com

BIBLIOGRAPHY

ON TSUI HARK

B. Accomando. "Army of Darkness: Hong Kong Director Tsui Hark Takes On the West", *Giant Robot*, 8, 1997
G. Hendrix. "Tsui Hark: Great Directors", *Senses of Cinema*, July, 2013
Howard Hampton. "Once Upon a Time In Hong Kong", *Film Comment*, 33, 1997
Hal Hinson. "*Peking Opera Blues*," *Washington Post*, Oct 14, 1988
D. Houx. "The Underrated Insanity of Tsui Hark and Jean-Claude van Damme's *Knock Off*', *Badass Digest*, 2014
A. Hwang. "The Irresistible: Hong Kong Movie *Once Upon a Time In China* Series", *Asian Cinema*, 10, 1, 1998
Y. Lee. "Artist Provocateur – On Tsui Hark", Hong Kong International Film Festival, 23, 1999
P. Macias. "Animerica Interview: Tsui Hark", *Animerica*, 7, 10
The Making of A Chinese Ghost Story: The Tsui Hark Animation, Hong Kong, 1997
L. Morton. *The Cinema of Tsui Hark*, McFarland, Jefferson, North Carolina, 2001
C. Reid. "Interview With Tsui Hark", *Film Quarterly*, 48, 3, 1995
S. Short. "Tsui Hark", interview, *Time*, CNN, 2000
Chuck Stephens. "Tsui Hark's Planet Hong Kong", *Village Voice*, May 1, 2001
S. Tan. "Ban(g)! Ban(g)! *Dangerous Encounter – 1st Kind*', *Asian Cinema*, 8, 1, 1996
Stephen Teo. "Tsui Hark: Filmography", *Senses of Cinema* 17, Nov, 2011
Tsui Hark. Interview, in F. Dannen, 1997
Ben Umstead. "An Interview With Tsui Hark", *Twitch/* N.Y.A.F.F., 2011, July 11, 2011

OTHERS

A. Abbas. *Hong Kong*, University of Minnoestoa Press, Minneapolis, 1997
J. Abert. *A Knight At the Movies: Medieval History On Film,* Routledge, London, 2003
G. Adair. *Vietnam on Film*, Proteus, New York, NY, 1981
—. *Hollywood's Vietnam*, Heinemann, London, 1989
R.C. Allen, ed. *Channels of Discourse: Television and Contemporary Criticism*, Methuen, London, 1987
R. Altman, ed. *Sound Theory, Sound Practice*, Routledge, London, 1992
—. *Film/ Genre*, British Film Institute, London, 1999
M. Anderegg, ed. *Inventing Vietnam*, Temple University Press, Philadelphia, PA, 1991
G. Andrew. *The Film Handbook*, Longman, London, 1989
—. *Stranger Than Paradise: Maverick Filmmakers In Recent American Cinema*, Prion, 1998
J. Arroyo. *Action/ Spectacle Cinema*, British Film Institute, London, 2000
A. Assister & A. Carol, eds. *Bad Girls and Dirty Pictures: The Challenge To Reclaim Feminism*, Pluto Press, London, 1993
A. Auster. *How the War Was Remembered: Hollywood and Vietnam*, Praeger, New York, NY, 1988
R. Baker & T. Russell. *The Essential Guide To Hong Kong Movies*, Eastern Heroes, London, 1994
—. *The Essential Guide To the Best of Eastern Heroes*, Eastern Heroes, London, 1995
—. *The Essential Guide To Deadly China Dolls*, Eastern Heroes, London, 1996
M. Barker, ed. *The Video Nasties: Freedom and Censorship In the Media*, Pluto Press, London, 1984
—. & J. Petley, eds. *Ill Effects: The Media/ Violence Debate*, Routledge, London, 1997
L. Bawden, ed. *The Oxford Companion To Film*, Oxford University Press, Oxford, 1976
J. Baxter. *George Lucas*, HarperCollins, London, 1999

J. Beck, ed. *Animation Art*, Flame Tree Publishing, London, 2004
M. Beja. *Film and Literature: An Introduction,* Longman, London, 1979
R. Bergan & R. Karney. *Bloomsbury Foreign Film Guide*, Bloomsbury, London, 1988
I. Bergman. *Talking With Ingmar Bergman*, Dallas, TX, 1983
—. *Bergman on Bergman, Interviews with Ingmar Bergman*, eds. S. Björkman, *et al,* tr. P. B. Austin, Touchstone, New York, NY, 1986
—. *The Magic Lantern: An Autobiography*, London, 1988
C. Berry. *Perspectives On Chinese Cinema*, B.F.I., London, 1991
P. Biskind. *Easy Riders, Raging Bulls: How the Sex 'n' Drugs 'n' Rock 'n' Roll Generation Saved Hollywood*, Bloomsbury, London, 1998
—. *Down and Dirty Pictures: Miramax, Sundance and the Rise of Independent Film*, Bloomsbury, London, 2004
M. Bliss. *Between the Bullets: The Spiritual Cinema of John Woo*, Scarecrow Press, Lanham, MD, 2002
A. Block & L. Wilson, eds. *George Lucas's Blockbusting*, HarperCollins, New York, 2010
D. Bordwell & K. Thompson. *Film Art: An Introduction*, McGraw-Hill Publishing Company, New York, NY, 1979
—. *et al. The Classical Hollywood Cinema: Film Style and Mode of Production To 1960*, Routledge, London, 1985
—. *Narration In the Fiction Film*, Routledge, London, 1988
—. *Making Meaning*, Harvard University Press, Cambridge, MA, 1989
—. & N. Caroll, eds. *Post-Theory: Reconstructing Film Studies*, University of Wisconsin Press, Madison, WI, 1996
—. *Planet Hong Kong: Popular Cinema and the Art of Entertainment*, Harvard University Press, 2000
—. "Aesthetics in Action: *Kungfu*, Gunplay and Cinematic Expressivity", in E. Yau, 2001
—. *The Way Hollywood Tells It*, University of California Press, Berkeley, CA, 2006
J. Bower, ed. *The Cinema of Japan and Korea*, Wallflower Press, London, 2004
D. Breskin. *Inner Voices: Filmmakers In Conversation*, Da Capo, New York, 1997
A. Britton *et al. American Nightmare: Essays On the Horror Film*, Toronto, 1979
A. Brown. *Directing Hong Kong: The Political Cinema of John Woo and Wong Kar-Wai*, Routledge/ Curzon, 2001
R. Brown. *Overtones and Undertones: Reading Film Music*, University of California Press, Berkeley, CA, 1994
N. Browne *et al*, eds. *New Chinese Cinema*, Cambridge University Press, 1994
S. Bukatman. *Terminal Identity: The Virtual Subject In Postmodern Science Fiction*, Duke University Press, Durham, NC, 1993
G. Burt. *The Art of Film Music*, Northeastern University Press, 1994
B. Camp & J. Davis. *Anime Classics*, Stone Bridge Press, CA, 2007
J. Campbell. *The Power of Myth,* with B. Moyers, ed. B.S. Flowers, Doubleday, New York, NY, 1988
J. Chan. *I Am Jackie Chan*, with Jeff Yang, Pan Books, 1998
—. *Never Grow Up*, Simon & Schuster, London, 2018
J. Charles. *The Hong Kong Filmography: 1977-1997*, McFarland, 2000
D. Chou. "*Once Upon a Time In China and America*", S.M.R. Home Theatre, Nov. 1998.
R. Chu. "*Swordman II* and *The East Is Red*', Bright Lights, 13, 1994
C. Chun-shu & Shelley Hsueh-lun Chang. *Redefining History: Ghosts, Spirits, and Human Society in Pu Sung-ling's World, 1640–1715*, University of Michigan Press, Ann Arbor, 1998
D. Chute & Cheng-Sim Lim, eds. *Heroic Grace: The Chinese Martial Arts Film*, University of California, Los Angeles, Film and Television Archive, 2003
P. Clark. *Chinese Cinema: Culture and Politics Since 1949,* Cambridge University Press, 1987
J. Clements & H. McCarthy, eds. *The Anime Encyclopedia*, Stone Bridge Press, Berkeley, CA, 2001/ 2007/ 2015
S. Cohan & I.R. Hark, eds. *Screening the Male: Exploring Masculinities In Hollywood Cinema*, Routledge, London, 1993
J. Collins *et al*, eds. *Film Theory Goes To the Movies*, Routledge, New York, NY, 1993
D.A. Cook. *A History of Narrative Film*, W.W. Norton, New York, NY, 1981, 1990, 1996
P. Cook, ed. *The Cinema Book*, British Film Institute, London, 1985/ 1999
S. Cornelius & I. Smith. *New Chinese Cinema*, Wallflower Press, London, 2002
J. Crist, ed. *Take 22: Moviemakers On Moviemaking*, Continuum, New York, NY, 1991
F. Dannen & B. Long. *Hong Kong Babylon*, Faber, London, 1997
G. Deleuze & F. Guattari. *Cinema 1: The Movement Image*, Athlone Press, London, 1989
—. *Cinema 2: The Time Image*, Athlone Press, London, 1989
C. Desjardins. *Outlaw Masters of Japanese Film*, I.B. Tauris, London, 2005
D. Desser. *Eros Plus Massacre: An Introduction to the Japanese New Wave Cinema*, Indiana University Press, Bloomington, IN, 1988
L. Dittmar & G. Michael. *From Hanoi To Hollywood*, Rutgers University Press, NJ, 1991
J. Donald, ed. *Fantasy and the Cinema*, British Film Institute, London, 1989

K.J. Donnelly, ed. *Film Music*, Edinburgh University Press, Edinburgh, 2001
C. Ducker & Stuart Cutler. *The H.K.S. Guide To Jet Li*, Hong Kong Superstars, London, 2000
M. Eagleton, ed. *Feminist Literary Theory: A Reader*, Blackwell, Oxford, 1986
—. ed. *Feminist Literary Criticism*, Longman, London, 1991
A. Easthope, ed. *Contemporary Film Theory*, Longman, London, 1993
P. Ettedgui. *Production Design & Art Direction*, RotoVision, 1999
D. Fairservice. *Film Editing*, Manchester University Press, Manchester, 2001
K. Fang. *John Woo's A Better Tomorrow, The New Hong Kong Cinema*, Hong Kong University Press, Hong Kong, 2004
C. Finch. *Special Effects*, Abbeville, 1984
J. Finler. *The Movie Director's Story*, Octopus Books, London, 1985
—. *The Hollywood Story*, Wallflower Press, London, 2003
C. Fleming. *High Concept: Don Simpson and the Hollywood Culture of Excess*, Bloomsbury, London, 1998
J. Fletcher & A. Benjamin, eds. *Abjection, Melancholia and Love: The Work of Julia Kristeva*, Routledge, London, 1990
K. Fowkes. *Giving Up the Ghost: Spirits, Ghosts and Angels In Mainstream Comedy Films*, Wayne State University Press, Detroit, MI, 1998
A. Frank. *Horror Films*, Hamlyn, London, 1977
—. *The Horror Film Handbook*, Barnes & Noble, 1982
K. French, ed. *Screen Violence*, Bloomsbury, London, 1996
P. Fu & D. Desser, eds. *The Cinema of Hong Kong*, Cambridge University Press, Cambridge, 2002
Lisa Funnell. *Warrior Women: Gender, Race, and the Transnational Chinese Action Star*, State University of New York Press, 2014
M. Gallagher. "Masculinity In Translation: Jackie Chan", *Velvet Light Trap*, 39, 1997
—. *Tony Leung Chiu-wai*, British Film Instititute, 2018
L. Gamman & M. Marshment, eds. *The Female Gaze: Women as Viewers of Popular Culture*, Women's Press, London, 1988
J. Geiger & R. Rutsky, eds. *Film Analysis*, Norton & Company, New York, NY, 2005
K. Gelder & S. Thornton, eds. *The Subcultures Reader*, Routledge, London, 1997
—. ed. *The Horror Reader*, Routledge, London, 2000
J. Gelmis. *The Film Director as Superstar*, Penguin, London, 1974
C. Gentry. *Jackie Chan*, Taylor, Dallas, TX, 1997
Jean-Luc Godard. *Godard On Godard*, eds. J. Narobi & T. Milne, Da Capo, New York, NY, 1986
—. *Interviews*, ed. D. Sterritt, University of Mississippi Press, Jackson, 1998
L. Goldberg et al, eds. *Science Fiction Filmmaking In the 1980s*, McFarland, Jefferson, 1995
M. Goodwin & N. Wise. *On the Edge: The Life and Times of Francis Coppola*, William Morrow, New York, NY, 1989
B.K. Grant, ed. *Film Genre*, Scarecrow Press, Metuchen, NJ, 1977
—. ed. *Planks of Reason: Essays On the Horror Film*, Scarecrow Press, Metuchen, NJ, 1984
—. *Film Genre Reader II*, University of Texas Press, Austin, TX, 1995
—. ed. *The Dread of Difference: Gender and the Horror Film*, University of Texas Press, Austin, TX, 1996
E. Grosz. *Sexual Subversions*, Allen & Unwin, London, 1989
—. *Jacques Lacan: A Feminist Introduction*, Routledge, London, 1990
—. *Volatile Bodies*, Indiana University Press, Bloomington, IN, 1994
—. *Space, Time and Perversion*, Routledge, London, 1995
K. Hall. *John Woo: The Films*, McFarland & Co., Jefferson, N.C., 1999
L. Halliwell. *Halliwell's Filmgoer's Companion*, 7th edition, Granada, London, 1980
D. Hamamoto & S. Liu, eds. *Countervision: Asian-American Film Criticism*, Temple University Press, Philadelphia, PA, 2000
S. Hammond. *Hollywood East*, Contemporary Books, Lincoln, IL, 2000
P. Hardy, ed. *The Aurum Encyclopedia of Science Fiction*, Aurum, London, 1991
C. Heard. *Ten Thousand Bullets: The Cinematic Journey of John Woo*, Lone Eagle Publishing Co., L.A., 2000
S. & N. Hibbin. *The Official James Bond Movie Book*, Hamlyn, London, 1989
G. Hickenlooper. *Reel Conversations: Candid Interviews With Film's Foremost Directors and Critics*, Citadel, New York, NY, 1991
J. Hillier. *The New Hollywood*, Studio Vista, London, 1992
—. *American Independent Cinema: A Sight & Sound Reader*, British Film Institute, London, 2001
L.C. Hillstrom, ed. *International Dictionary of Films and Filmmakers: Directors*, St James Press, London, 1997
Sam Ho, ed. *The Swordsman and His Juang Hu: Tsui Hark and Hong Kong Film*, Hong Kong University Press, Hong Kong, 2002
Hong Kong Film Archive. *The Making of Martial Arts Films*, Hong Kong Provisional Urban Council, 1999
Hong Kong International Film Festival. *Hong Kong Panorama*, Leisure and Cultural Services

Department
Hong Kong International Film Festival. *Hong Kong New Wave: Twenty Years After*, Provisional Urban Council of Hong Kong, 1999
Hong Kong International Film Festival. *Hong Kong Cinema '79-'89*, Leisure and Cultural Services Department, 2000
D. Hudson. *Draculas, Vampires, and Other Undead Forms*, Rowman & Littlefield, 2009
D. Hughes. *Comic Book Movies*, Virgin, London, 2003
L. Hughes. *The Rough Guide To Gangster Movies*, Penguin, 2005
L. Hunt. "Once Upon a Time In China: Kung Fu From Bruce Lee To Jet Li", *Framework*, 40, 1999
—. *Kung-fu Cult Masters: From Bruce Lee To 'Crouching Tiger'*, Wallflower Press, London, 2003
J. Hunter. *Eros In Hell: Sex, Blood and Madness In Japanese Cinema*, Creation Books, London, 1998
J. Inverne. *Musicals*, Faber, London, 2009
L. Irigiaray. *The Irigaray Reader*, ed. M. Whitford, Blackwell, Oxford, 1991
S. Jackson & J. Jones, eds. *Contemporary Feminist Theories*, Edinburgh University Press, Edinburgh, 1998
S. Jaworzyn, ed. *Shock: The Essential Guide To Exploitation Cinema*, Titan Books, London, 1996
S. Jeffords. *Hard Bodies: Hollywood Masculinity In the Reagan Era*, Rutgers University Press, New Brunswick, NJ, 1994
E. Jeffreys & L. Edwards, eds. *Celebrity In China*, Hong Kong University Press, Hong Kong, 2010
K. Kalinak. *Settling the Score: Music and the Classical Hollywood Film*, University of Wisconsin Press, Madison, WI, 1992
B.F. Kawin. *Mindscreen: Bergman, Godard and First-Person Film*, Princeton University Press, Princeton, NJ, 1978
—. *How Movies Work*, Macmillan, New York, NY, 1987
P. Keough, ed. *Flesh and Blood: The National Society of Film Critics on Sex, Violence, and Censorship*, Mercury House, San Francisco, CA, 1995
M. Kinder. *Playing With Power In Movies*, University of California Press, Berkeley, CA, 1991
P. Kolker. *The Altering Eye: Contemporary International Cinema*, Oxford University Press, New York, NY, 1983
—. *A Cinema of Loneliness: Penn, Stone, Kubrick, Scorsese, Spielberg, Altman*, Oxford University Press, New York, NY, 2000
P. Kramer. *The Big Picture: Hollywood Cinema From Star Wars To Titanic*, British Film Institute, London, 2001
—. *The New Hollywood*, Wallflower Press, London, 2005
J. Kristeva. *About Chinese Women*, tr. A. Barrows, Marion Boyars, London, 1977
—. *Desire In Language: A Semiotic Approach To Literature and Art*, ed. L.S. Roudiez, tr. T. Gora *et al*, Blackwell 1982
—. *Powers of Horror: An Essay on Abjection*, tr. L.S. Roudiez, Columbia University Press, New York, NY, 1982
—. *Revolution In Poetic Language*, tr. M. Walker, Columbia University Press, New York, NY, 1984
—. *The Kristeva Reader*, ed. T. Moi, Blackwell, Oxford, 1986
—. *Tales of Love*, tr. L.S. Roudiez, Columbia University Press, New York, NY, 1987
—. *Black Sun: Depression and Melancholy*, tr. L.S. Roudiez, Columbia University Press, New York, NY, 1989
—. *Strangers To Ourselves*, tr. L.S. Roudiez, Harvester Wheatsheaf 1991
J. Kwok Wah Lau. "Imploding Genre, Gender and History: Peking Opera Blues", in J. Geiger, 2005
M. Lanning. *Vietnam At the Movies*, Fawcett Columbine, New York, NY, 1994
R. Lapsley & M. Westlake, eds. *Film Theory: An Introduction*, Manchester University Press, Manchester, 1988
Shing-hou Lau, ed. *A Study of the Hong Kong Martial Arts Film*, Hong Kong International Film Festival, 1980
—. *A Study of the Hong Kong Swordplay Film, 1945-80*, Hong Kong International Film Festival, 1981
Law Kar, ed. *Fifty Years of Elecric Shadows*, Hong Kong International Film Festival, 1997
M. Lee. "*Once Upon a Time In China*", Criterion, 2021
J. Lent. *The Asian Film Industry*, Austin, TX, 1990
T. Leung Siu-hung. "Mastering Action", Hong Kong Cinemagic, March, 2006
E. Levy. *Cinema of Outsiders: The Rise of American Independent Film*, New York University Press, New York, NY, 1999
J. Lewis. *The Road To Romance and Ruin: Teen Films and Youth Culture*, Routledge, London, 1992
—. *Whom God Wishes To Destroy: Francis Coppola and the New Hollywood*, Duke

University Press, Durham, NC, 1995
—. ed. *New American Cinema*, Duke University Press, Durham, NC, 1998
—. *Hollywood v. Hard Core: How the Struggle Over Censorship Created the Modern Film Industry*, New York University Press, New York, NY, 2000
J. Leyda. ed. *Film Makers Speak: Voices of Film Experience*, Da Capo, New York, NY, 1977
V. LoBrutto. *Sound-On-Film*, Praeger, New York, NY, 1994
B. Logan. *Hong Kong Action Cinema*, Titan, London, 1995
S. Lu, ed. *Transnational Chinese Cinemas*, University of Hawaii Press, Honolulu, 1997
H. Ludi. *Movie Worlds: Production Design In Film*, Mengers, Stuttgart, 2000
B. McCabe. *The Rough Guide To Comedy Movies*, Rough Guides, London, 2005
R. Maltby. *Harmless Entertainment: Hollywood and the Ideology of Consensus*, Scarecrow Press, Metuchen, NJ, 1983
—. & I. Craven. *Hollywood Cinema: An Introduction*, Blackwell, Oxford, 1995
—. *Hollywood Cinema*, 2nd ed., Blackwell, Oxford, 2003
E. Marks & I. de Courtivron, eds. *New French Feminisms: an anthology*, Harvester Wheatsheaf, Hemel Hempstead, 1981
G. Mast *et al*, eds. *Film Theory and Criticism: Introductory Readings*, Oxford University Press, New York, NY, 1992a
—. & B Kawin. *A Short History of the Movies*, Macmillan, New York, NY, 1992b
C. Marx. *Jet Li*, Martial Arts Masters, Rosen Publishing Group, 2002
T.D. Matthews. *Censored*, Chatto & Windus, London, 1994
F. McConnell. *Storytelling and Mythmaking*, Oxford University Press, New York, NY, 1979
S.Y. McDougal. *Made Into Movies: From Literature To Film*, Holt, Rinehart and Winston, New York, NY, 1985
M. Medved. *Hollywood vs. America*, HarperCollins, London, 1992
R. Meyers. *Martial Arts Movies*, Citadel Press, NJ, 1985
—. *Great Martial Arts Movies*, Citadel Press, NJ, 2001
D. Millar. *Cinema Secrets: Special Effects*, Apple Press, 1990
T. Miller *et al*, eds. *Global Hollywood*, British Film Institute, London, 2001
T. Moi. *Sexual/ Textual Politics: Feminist Literary Theory*, Methuen, London, 1983
J. Monaco. *The New Wave: Truffaut, Godard, Chabrol, Rohmer, Rivette*, Oxford University Press, New York, NY, 1977
—. *American Film Now*, New American Library, London, 1979
—. *How To Read a Film*, Oxford University Press, Oxford, 1981
R. Murray. *Images In the Dark: An Encyclopedia of Gay and Lesbian Film and Video*, Titan Books, London, 1998
S. Neale. *Cinema and Technology*, Macmillan, London, 1985
—. & M. Smith, eds. *Contemporary Hollywood Cinema*, Routledge, London, 1998
—. *Genre and Contemporary Hollywood*, Routledge, London, 2002
J. Nelmes, ed. *An Introduction To Film Studies*, Routledge, London, 1996
D. Neumann, ed. *Film Architecture: From Metropolis To Blade Runner*, Prestel-Verlag, New York, NY, 1996
K. Newman. *Nightmare Movies*, Harmony, New York, NY, 1988
—. *Millennium Movies*, Titan Books, London, 1999
G. Nowell-Smith, ed. *The Oxford History of World Cinema*, Oxford University Press, Oxford, 1996
D. O'Brien. *Spooky Encounters: A Gwailo's Guide To Hong Kong Horror*, Headpress, 2004
T. Ohanian & M. Phillips. *Digital Filmmaking*, 2nd ed., Focal Press, Boston, MA, 2000
J. Orr. *Contemporary Cinema*, Edinburgh University Press, Edinburgh, 1998
B. Palmer *et al*. *The Encyclopedia of Martial Arts Movies*, Scarecrow Press, NJ, 1995
A. Paludan. *Chronicle of the Chinese Emperors*, Thames & Hudson, 1998
L. Pang. *Masculinities and Hong Kong Cinema*, Kent State University Press, 2005
D. Parkinson. *The Rough Guide To Film Musicals*, Penguin, London, 2007
J. Parish. *Jet Li: A Biography*, Thunder's Mouth Press, New York, 2002
F. Patten. *Watching Anime, Reading Manga*, Stone Bridge Press, CA, 2004
D. Peary & G. Peary, eds. *The American Animated Cartoon*, Dutton, New York, NY, 1980
—. *Cult Movies 2*, Vermilion, London, 1984
—. *Cult Movies 3*, Sigwick & Jackson, London, 1989
C. Penley, ed. *Feminism and Film Theory*, Routledge, London, 1988
D. Petrie. *Screening Europe: Image and Identity In Contemporary European Cinema*, British Film Institute, London, 1992
P. Phillips. *Understanding Film Texts*, British Film Institute, London, 2000
M. Pierson. *Special Effects*, Columbia University Press, New York, NY, 2002
L. Pietropaolo & A. Testaferri, eds. *Feminisms In the Cinema*, Indiana University Press, Bloomington, IN, 1995
D. Pollock. *Skywalking: The Life and Films of George Lucas*, Crown, New York, NY, 1983, 1990, 2000
M. Polly. *Bruce Lee*, Simon & Schuster, New York, 2018
S. Prince, ed. *Screening Violence*, Athlone Press, London, 2000
D. Prindle. *Risky Business: The Political Economy of Hollywood*, Westview, Boulder, CO,

1993
N. Proferes. *Film Directing Fundamentals*, Focal Press, Boston, MA, 2001
M. Pye & Lynda Myles. *The Movie Brats: How the Film Generation Took Over Hollywood*, Faber, London, 1979
T. Reeves. *The Worldwide Guide To Movie Locations*, Titan Books, London, 2003
P. Rice & P. Waugh, eds. *Modern Literary Theory: A Reader*, Arnold, London, 1992
D. Richie. *The Films of Akira Kurosawa*, University of California Press, Berkeley, CA, 1965
R. Rickitt. *Special Effects*, Aurum, London, 2006
B. Robb. *Screams and Nightmares*, Titan Books, London, 1998
J. Robertson. *The British Board of Film Censors*, Croom Helm, 1985
D. Robinson. *World Cinema*, Methuen, London, 1981
W.H. Rockett. *Devouring Whirlwind: Terror and Transcendence In the Cinema of Cruelty*, Greenwood Press, New York, NY, 1988
S. Rohdie. *The Passion of Pier Paolo Pasolini*, British Film Institute, London, 1995
J. Romney & A. Wootton, eds. *Celluloid Jukebox: Popular Music and the Movies Since the 50s*, British Film Institute, London, 1995
P. Rosen, ed. *Narrative, Apparatus, Ideology: A Film Theory Reader*, Columbia University Press, New York, NY, 1986
J. Rosenbaum. *Placing Movies*, University of California Press, Berkeley, CA, 1995
R. Rosenblum & R. Karen. *When the Shooting Stops... The Cutting Begins: A Film Editor's Story*, Da Capo Press, New York, NY, 1979
J. Ross. *The Incredibly Strange Film Book: An Alternative History of Cinema*, Simon and Schuster, 1993
The Rough Guide To China, Penguin, 2017
R. Roud. *Jean-Luc Godard*, Thames & Hudson, London, 1970
J. Rovin & K. Tracy. *The Essential Jackie Chan Sourcebook*, Pocket Books, New York, 1997
M. Rubin. *Thrillers*, Cambridge University Press, Cambridge, 1999
K. Russell. *A British Picture: An Autobiography*, Heinemann, London, 1989
V. Russo. *The Celluloid Closet: Homosexuality In the Movies*, Harper & Row, New York, NY, 1981
K. Sandler. *Reading the Rabbit: Explorations In Warner Bros. Animation*, Rutgers University Press, Brunswick, NJ, 1998
A. Sarris. *The American Cinema*, Dutton, New York, NY, 1968
T. Sato. *Currents In Japanese Cinema*, Kodansha, New York, 1982
D. Schaefer & L. Salvato, eds. *Masters of Light*, University of California Press, Berkeley, CA, 1984
T. Schatz. *Hollywood Genres*, Random House, New York, NY, 1981
—. *Old Hollywood/ New Hollywood*, UMI Research Press, Ann Arbor, MI, 1983
—. *The Genius of the System: Hollywood Filmmaking In the Studio Era*, Pantheon, New York, NY 1988
F. Schodt. *Inside the Robot Kingdom: Japan, Mechatronics and the Coming Robotopia*, Kodansha, Tokyo, 1988
—. *Manga! Manga! The World of Japanese Magazines*, Kodansha International, London, 1997
—. *Dreamland Japan: Writings On Modern Manga*, Stone Bridge Press, Berkeley, CA, 2002
P. Schrader. *Transcendental Style In Film: Ozu, Bresson, Dreyer*, Da Capo Press, 1972
A. Schroeder. *Tsui Hark's Zu: Warriors From the Magic Mountain*, Hong Kong University Press, Hong Kong, 2004
R. Schubart. *Super Bitches and Action Babes: The Female Hero In Popular Cinema, 1970-2006*, McFarland, 2007
M. Schumacher. *Francis Ford Coppola*, Bloomsbury, London, 2000
M. Scorsese. *Scorsese On Scorsese*, ed. D. Thompson & I. Christie, Faber, London, 1989, 1995
Screen Reader I: Cinema/ Ideology/ Politics, Society for Education in Film & TV, 1977
Screen Reader II: Cinema and Semiotics, British Film Institute, London, 1982
C. Sharrett, ed. *Crisis Cinema*, Maisonneuve Press, Washington, DC, 1993
—. *Mythologies of Violence In Postmodern Media*, Wayne State University Press, 1999
M. Shiel & T. Fitzmaurice, eds. *Screenng the City*, Verso, London, 2003
D. Shipman. *The Story of Cinema*, Hodder & Stoughton, London, 1984
T. Shone. *Blockbuster: How the Jaws and Jedi Generation Turned Hollywood Into a Boom-Town*, Scribner, London, 2005
E. Showalter, ed. *The New Feminist Criticism*, Virago, London, 1986
E. Siciliano. *Pasolini: A Biography*, Bloomsbury, London, 1987
L. Sider et al, eds. *Soundscapes: The School of Sound Lectures 1998-2001*, Wallflower Press, London, 2003
M. Singer. *A History of the American Avant-Garde Cinema*, American Federation of the Arts, New York, NY, 1976
P. Adams Sitney, ed. *The Film Culture Reader*, Praeger, New York, NY, 1970
—. ed. *The Avant-Garde Film: A Reader of Theory and Criticism*, New York University Press,

New York, NY, 1978
—. *Visionary Film: The American Avant-Garde, 1943-1978*, 2nd ed., Oxford University Press, New York, NY, 1979
G. Smith. *Epic Films*, McFarland, Jefferson, NC, 1991
J. Smith. *Looking Away: Hollywood and Vietnam*, Scribner's, New York, NY, 1975
T.G. Smith. *Industrial Light and Magic: The Art of Special Effects*, Columbus Books, 1986
E. Smoodin. *Animating Culture: Hollywood Cartoons From the Sound Era*, Roundhouse, 1993
—. ed. *Disney Discourse: Producing the Magic Kingdom*, Routledge, London, 1994
V. Sobchack. *The Limits of Infinity: The American Science Fiction Film*, A.S. Barnes, New York, NY, 1980
—. *Screening Space: The American Science Fiction Film*, Ungar, New York, NY, 1987/ 1993
J. Squire, ed. *The Movie Business Book*, Fireside, New York, NY, 1992
J. Staiger. *Interpreting Films*, Princeton University Press, Princeton, NJ, 1992
—. *Perverse Spectators: The Practices of Film Reception*, New York University Press, New York, NY, 2000
N. Stair. *Michelle Yeoh,* Rosen Publishing Group, 2001
B. Steene. *Ingmar Bergman*, Twayne, Boston, MA, 1968
L. Stern. *The Scorsese Connection*, British Film Institute, London, 1995
D. Sterritt. *The Films of Jean-Luc Godard*, Cambridge University Press, Cambridge, 1999
G. Stewart. *Between Film and Screen: Modernism's Photo Synthesis*, University of Chicago Press, Chicago, IL, 1999
M. Stokes & R. Maltby, eds. *Identifying Hollywood Audiences*, British Film Institute, London, 1999
J. Storey, ed. *Cultural Theory and Popular Culture*, Harvester Wheatsheaf, Hemel Hempstead, 1994
J.M. Straczynski. *The Complete Book of Scriptwriting*, Titan Books, London, 1997
J. Stringer. "Problems With the Treatment of Hong Kong Cinema As Camp", *Asian Cinema*, 8, 2, 1996
—. ed. *Movie Blockbusters*, Routledge, London, 2003
C. Sylvester, ed. *The Penguin Book of Hollywood*, Penguin, London, 1999
K. Tam & W. Dissanayake. *New Chinese Cinema*, Oxford University Press, Hong Kong, 1998
A. Tarkovsky. *Sculpting In Time: Reflections On the Cinema*, tr. K. Hunter-Blair, Faber, London, 1989
C. Tashiro. *Pretty Pictures: Production Design and the History Film*, University of Texas Press, 1998
Y. Tasker. *Spectacular Bodies: Gender, Genre and the Action Cinema*, Routledge, London, 1993
R. Taylor et al, eds. *The B.F.I. Companion To Eastern European and Russian Cinema*, British Film Institute, London, 2000
S. Teo. *Hong Kong Cinema*, British Film Institute, London, 1997
—. "Tsui Hark", in C. Yau, 1998
B. Thomas. *Video Hound's Dragon: Asian Action and Cult Flicks*, Visible Ink Press, 2003
K. Thompson & D. Bordwell. *Film History: An Introduction*, McGraw-Hill, New York, NY, 1994/ 2010
—. *Storytelling In the New Hollywood*, Harvard University Press, Cambridge, MA, 1999
D. Thomson. *A Biographical Dictionary of Film,* Deutsch, London, 1995
S. Thrower, ed. *Eyeball: Compendium: Sex and Horror, Art and Exploitation*, F.A.B. Press, Godalming, Surrey, 2003
C. Tohill & P. Tombs. *Immoral Tales: Sex and Horror Cinema In Europe 1956-1984*, Titan Books, London, 1995
J. Trevelyan. *What the Censor Saw*, Michael Joseph, London, 1973
A.D. Vacche. *Cinema and Painting*, Athlone Press, London, 1996
K. Van Gunden. *Fantasy Films*, McFarland, Jefferson, NC 1989
—. *Postmodern Auteurs: Coppola, Lucas, De Palma, Spielberg and Scorsese*, McFarland, Jefferson, NC 1991
M.C. Vaz. *From Star Wars To Indiana Jones*, Chronicle, San Francisco, CA, 1994
—. & P.R. Duignan. *Industrial Light & Magic*, Virgin, London, 1996
G. Vincendeau, ed. *Encyclopedia of European Cinema*, British Film Institute, London, 1995
—. ed. *Film/ Literature/ Heritage: A Sight & Sound Reader*, British Film Institute, London, 2001
P. Virillio. *War and Cinema*, Verso, London, 1992
D. Vivier & T. Podvin. "Through the Lens of Arthur Wong", Hong Kong Cinemagic, Jan 2005
H. Vogel. *Entertainment Industry Economics*, Cambridge University Press, Cambridge, 1995
C. Vogler. *The Writer's Journey: Mythic Structure For Storytellers and Screenwriters*, Pan, London, 1998
J. Wasko. *Movies and Money*, Ablex, NJ, 1982
—. *Hollywood In the Information Age*, Polity Press, Cambridge, 1994
E. Weiss. & J. Belton, eds. *Film Sound: Theory and Practice*, Columbia University Press,

New York, NY, 1989
T. Weisser. *Asian Cult Cinema*, Boulveard Books, New York, NY, 1997
O. Welles. *This is Orson Welles*, HarperCollins, London, 1992
P. Wells. *Understanding Animation*, Routledge, London, 1998
D. West. *Chasing Dragons: An Introduction To the Martial Arts Film*, I.B. Tauris, London, 2006
L. Williams, ed. *Viewing Positions: Ways of Seeing Film*, Rutgers University Press, New Brunswick, NJ, 1995
T. Williams. "To Live and Die In Hong Kong", *Cineaction*, 36, 1995
—. "Kwan Tak-hing and the New Generation", *Asian Cinema*, 10, 1, 1998
—. "Space, Place and Spectacle: the Crisis Cinema of John Woo", in P. Fu, 2002
R. Witterstaetter. *Dying For Action: The Life and Times of Jackie Chan*, Warner Books, New York, 1997
M. Wolf. *The Entertainment Economy*, Penguin, London, 1999
P. Wollen: *Signs and Meaning In the Cinema*, Secker & Warburg, London, 1972
J. Woo. Interview, in J. Arroyo, 2000
—. *Interviews; Conversations With Filmmakers Series*, ed. R. Elder, University Press of Mississippi, 2005
M. Wood. *Cine East: Hong Kong Cinema Through the Looking Glass*, F.A.B. Press, 1998
R. Wood. *Hollywood From Vietnam To Reagan... and Beyond*, Columbia University Press, New York, NY, 2003
T. Woods. *Beginning Postmodernism,* Manchester University Press, Manchester, 1999
J. Wyatt. *High Concept: Movies and Marketing In Hollywood*, University of Texas Press, Austin, TX, 1994
J. Yang et al. *Eastern Standard Time: A Guide To Asian Influence On American Culture*, Houghton Mifflin, Boston, MA, 1997
—. *Once Upon a Time In China*, Atria Books, New York, NY, 2003
E.C.M. Yau, ed. *At Full Speed: Hong Kong Cinema In a Borderless World,* University of Minnesota Press, Minneapolis, MN, 1998
Z. Yimou. *Zhang Yimou: Interviews, Conversations With Filmmakers Series*, ed. F. Gateward, University Press of Mississippi, 2001
Judith T. Zeitlin. *Historian of the Strange: Pu Songling and the Chinese Classical Tale*, Stanford University Press, Stanford, CA, 1993
Y. Zhang & X. Zhiwei, eds. *Encyclopedia of Chinese Film*, Routledge, 1998
J. Zipes. *The Enchanted Screen: The Unknown History of Fairy-tale Films*, Routledge, New York, NY, 2011
S. Zizek. *Enjoy Your Symptom Jacques Lacan In Hollywood and Out*, Routledge, New York, NY, 1992
—. *The Fright of Real Tears: The Uses and Misuses of Lacan In Film Theory*, British Film Institute, London, 1999

JEREMY ROBINSON has published poetry, fiction, and studies of J.R.R. Tolkien, Samuel Beckett, Thomas Hardy, André Gide and D.H. Lawrence. Robinson has edited poetry books by Novalis, Ursula Le Guin, Friedrich Hölderlin, Francesco Petrarch, Dante Alighieri, Arseny Tarkovsky, and Rainer Maria Rilke.

Books on film and animation include: *The Akira Book* • *The Art of Katsuhiro Otomo* • *The Art of Masamune Shirow* • *The Ghost In the Shell Book* • *Fullmetal Alchemist* • *Cowboy Bebop: The Anime and Movie* • *The Cinema of Hayao Miyazaki* • *Hayao Miyazaki: Pocket Guide* • *Princess Mononoke: Pocket Movie Guide* • *Spirited Away: Pocket Movie Guide* • *Blade Runner and the Cinema of Philip K. Dick* • *Blade Runner: Pocket Movie Guide* • *The Cinema of Donald Cammell* • *Performance: Donald Cammell: Nic Roeg: Pocket Movie Guide* • *Pasolini: Il Cinema di Poesia/The Cinema of Poetry* • *Salo: Pocket Movie Guide* • *The Trilogy of Life Movies: Pocket Movie Guide* • *The Gospel According To Matthew: Pocket Movie Guide* • *The Ecstatic Cinema of Tony Ching Siu-tung* • *Tsui Hark: The Dragon Master of Chinese Cinema* • *The Swordsman: Pocket Movie Guide* • *A Chinese Ghost Story: Pocket Movie Guide* • *Ken Russell: England's Great Visionary Film Director and Music Lover* • *Tommy: Ken Russell: The Who: Pocket Movie Guide* • *Women In Love: Ken Russell: D.H. Lawrence: Pocket Movie Guide* • *The Devils: Ken Russell: Pocket Movie Guide* • *Walerian Borowczyk: Cinema of Erotic Dreams* • *The Beast: Pocket Movie Guide* • *The Lord of the Rings Movies* • *The Fellowship of the Ring: Pocket Movie Guide* • *The Two Towers: Pocket Movie Guide* • *The Return of the King: Pocket Movie Guide* • *Jean-Luc Godard: The Passion of Cinema* • *The Sacred Cinema of Andrei Tarkovsky* • *Andrei Tarkovsky: Pocket Guide.*

'It's amazing for me to see my work treated with such passion and respect. There is nothing resembling it in the U.S. in relation to my work.'
(Andrea Dworkin)

'This model monograph – it is an exemplary job, and I'm very proud that he has accorded me a couple of mentions… The subject matter of his book is beautifully organised and dead on beam.'
(Lawrence Durrell, on *The Light Eternal: A Study of J.M.W. Turner*)

'Jeremy Robinson's poetry is certainly jammed with ideas, and I find it very interesting for that reason. It's certainly a strong imprint of his personality.'
(Colin Wilson)

'*Sex-Magic-Poetry-Cornwall* is a very rich essay… It is a very good piece… vastly stimulating and insightful.'
(Peter Redgrove)

CRESCENT MOON PUBLISHING

web: www.crmoon.com e-mail: cresmopub@yahoo.co.uk

ARTS, PAINTING, SCULPTURE

The Art of Andy Goldsworthy
Andy Goldsworthy: Touching Nature
Andy Goldsworthy in Close-Up
Andy Goldsworthy: Pocket Guide
Andy Goldsworthy In America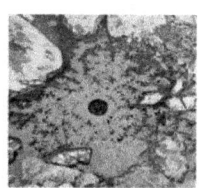
Land Art: A Complete Guide
The Art of Richard Long
Richard Long: Pocket Guide
Land Art In the UK
Land Art in Close-Up
Land Art In the U.S.A.
Land Art: Pocket Guide
Installation Art in Close-Up
Minimal Art and Artists In the 1960s and After
Colourfield Painting
Land Art DVD, TV documentary
Andy Goldsworthy DVD, TV documentary
The Erotic Object: Sexuality in Sculpture From Prehistory to the Present Day
Sex in Art: Pornography and Pleasure in Painting and Sculpture
Postwar Art
Sacred Gardens: The Garden in Myth, Religion and Art
Glorification: Religious Abstraction in Renaissance and 20th Century Art
Early Netherlandish Painting
Leonardo da Vinci
Piero della Francesca
Giovanni Bellini
Fra Angelico: Art and Religion in the Renaissance
Mark Rothko: The Art of Transcendence
Frank Stella: American Abstract Artist
Jasper Johns
Brice Marden
Alison Wilding: The Embrace of Sculpture
Vincent van Gogh: Visionary Landscapes
Eric Gill: Nuptials of God
Constantin Brancusi: Sculpting the Essence of Things
Max Beckmann
Caravaggio
Gustave Moreau
Egon Schiele: Sex and Death In Purple Stockings
Delizioso Fotografico Fervore: Works In Process 1
Sacro Cuore: Works In Process 2
The Light Eternal: J.M.W. Turner
The Madonna Glorified: Karen Arthurs

LITERATURE

J.R.R. Tolkien: The Books, The Films, The Whole Cultural Phenomenon
J.R.R. Tolkien: Pocket Guide
Tolkien's Heroic Quest
The *Earthsea* Books of Ursula Le Guin
Beauties, Beasts and Enchantment: Classic French Fairy Tales
German Popular Stories by the Brothers Grimm
Philip Pullman and *His Dark Materials*
Sexing Hardy: Thomas Hardy and Feminism
Thomas Hardy's *Tess of the d'Urbervilles*
Thomas Hardy's *Jude the Obscure*
Thomas Hardy: The Tragic Novels
Love and Tragedy: Thomas Hardy
The Poetry of Landscape in Hardy
Wessex Revisited: Thomas Hardy and John Cowper Powys
Wolfgang Iser: Essays and Interviews
Petrarch, Dante and the Troubadours
Maurice Sendak and the Art of Children's Book Illustration
Andrea Dworkin
Cixous, Irigaray, Kristeva: The *Jouissance* of French Feminism
Julia Kristeva: Art, Love, Melancholy, Philosophy, Semiotics and Psychoanalysis
Hélène Cixous I Love You: The *Jouissance* of Writing
Luce Irigaray: Lips, Kissing, and the Politics of Sexual Difference
Peter Redgrove: Here Comes the Flood
Peter Redgrove: Sex-Magic-Poetry-Cornwall
Lawrence Durrell: Between Love and Death, East and West
Love, Culture & Poetry: Lawrence Durrell
Cavafy: Anatomy of a Soul
German Romantic Poetry: Goethe, Novalis, Heine, Hölderlin
Feminism and Shakespeare
Shakespeare: Love, Poetry & Magic
The Passion of D.H. Lawrence
D.H. Lawrence: Symbolic Landscapes
D.H. Lawrence: Infinite Sensual Violence
Rimbaud: Arthur Rimbaud and the Magic of Poetry
The Ecstasies of John Cowper Powys
Sensualism and Mythology: The Wessex Novels of John Cowper Powys
Amorous Life: John Cowper Powys and the Manifestation of Affectivity (H.W. Fawkner)
Postmodern Powys: New Essays on John Cowper Powys (Joe Boulter)
Rethinking Powys: Critical Essays on John Cowper Powys
Paul Bowles & Bernardo Bertolucci
Rainer Maria Rilke
Joseph Conrad: *Heart of Darkness*
In the Dim Void: Samuel Beckett
Samuel Beckett Goes into the Silence
André Gide: Fiction and Fervour
Jackie Collins and the Blockbuster Novel
Blinded By Her Light: The Love-Poetry of Robert Graves
The Passion of Colours: Travels In Mediterranean Lands
Poetic Forms

MEDIA, CINEMA, FEMINISM and CULTURAL STUDIES

J.R.R. Tolkien: The Books, The Films, The Whole Cultural Phenomenon
J.R.R. Tolkien: Pocket Guide
The *Lord of the Rings* Movies: Pocket Guide
The Cinema of Hayao Miyazaki
Hayao Miyazaki: *Princess Mononoke*: Pocket Movie Guide
Hayao Miyazaki: *Spirited Away*: Pocket Movie Guide
Tim Burton : Hallowe'en For Hollywood
Ken Russell
Ken Russell: *Tommy*: Pocket Movie Guide
The Ghost Dance: The Origins of Religion
The Peyote Cult
Cixous, Irigaray, Kristeva: The *Jouissance* of French Feminism
Julia Kristeva: Art, Love, Melancholy, Philosophy, Semiotics and Psychoanalysis
Luce Irigaray: Lips, Kissing, and the Politics of Sexual Difference
Hélene Cixous I Love You: The *Jouissance* of Writing
Andrea Dworkin
'Cosmo Woman': The World of Women's Magazines
Women in Pop Music
HomeGround: The Kate Bush Anthology
Discovering the Goddess (Geoffrey Ashe)
The Poetry of Cinema
The Sacred Cinema of Andrei Tarkovsky
Andrei Tarkovsky: Pocket Guide
Andrei Tarkovsky: *Mirror*: Pocket Movie Guide
Andrei Tarkovsky: *The Sacrifice*: Pocket Movie Guide
Walerian Borowczyk: Cinema of Erotic Dreams
Jean-Luc Godard: The Passion of Cinema
Jean-Luc Godard: *Hail Mary*: Pocket Movie Guide
Jean-Luc Godard: *Contempt*: Pocket Movie Guide
Jean-Luc Godard: *Pierrot le Fou*: Pocket Movie Guide
John Hughes and Eighties Cinema
Ferris Bueller's Day Off: Pocket Movie Guide
Jean-Luc Godard: Pocket Guide
The Cinema of Richard Linklater
Liv Tyler: Star In Ascendance
Blade Runner and the Films of Philip K. Dick
Paul Bowles and Bernardo Bertolucci
Media Hell: Radio, TV and the Press
An Open Letter to the BBC
Detonation Britain: Nuclear War in the UK
Feminism and Shakespeare
Wild Zones: Pornography, Art and Feminism
Sex in Art: Pornography and Pleasure in Painting and Sculpture
Sexing Hardy: Thomas Hardy and Feminism

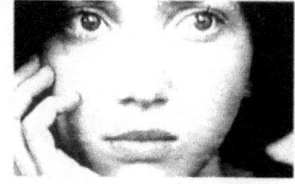

The Light Eternal is a model monograph, an exemplary job. The subject matter of the book is beautifully organised and dead on beam. (Lawrence Durrell)
It is amazing for me to see my work treated with such passion and respect. (Andrea Dworkin)

CRESCENT MOON PUBLISHING
P.O. Box 1312, Maidstone, Kent, ME14 5XU, Great Britain. www.crmoon.com

cresmopub@yahoo.co.uk   www.crescentmoon.org.uk

www.ingramcontent.com/pod-product-compliance
Lightning Source LLC
Chambersburg PA
CBHW071314150426
43191CB00007B/620